Ben

Intergenerational Cycles
of Trauma and Violence

A NORTON PROFESSIONAL BOOK

INTERGENERATIONAL CYCLES OF TRAUMA AND VIOLENCE

An Attachment and Family Systems Perspective

PAMELA C. ALEXANDER

W. W. Norton & Company
New York • London

For information about permission to reproduce selections from this book, write to
Permissions, W. W. Norton & Company, Inc., 500 Fifth Avenue, New York, NY 10110

For information about special discounts for bulk purchases, please contact
W. W. Norton Special Sales at specialsales@wwnorton.com or 800-233-4830

Manufacturing by Courier Westford
Production manager: Leeann Graham

Library of Congress Cataloging-in-Publication Data
Alexander, Pamela C.
Intergenerational cycles of trauma and violence : an attachment
and family systems perspective / Pamela C. Alexander.
pages cm. — (A Norton professional book)
Includes bibliographical references and index.
ISBN 978-0-393-70718-2 (hardcover)
1. Attachment behavior. 2. Parent and child. 3. Child abuse.
4. Intergenerational relations. I. Title.
BF575.A86A44 2015
155.9'24—dc23
2014021532

ISBN: 978-0-393-70718-2

W. W. Norton & Company, Inc., 500 Fifth Avenue, New York, N.Y. 10110
www.wwnorton.com
W. W. Norton & Company Ltd., Castle House, 75/76 Wells Street, London W1T 3QT

1 2 3 4 5 6 7 8 9 0

Contents

Acknowledgments

I would like to dedicate this volume to my secure base—my husband Elmore who encouraged me, prodded me and showed unflinching confidence in my ability to make a contribution to the field. His interest in what I was reading and writing fostered my own curiosity in the connections between seemingly disparate ideas and areas of research. Our son Eric taught me what attachment really is. I also want to acknowledge the patience and support of my friends Lynne and John who were willing to tolerate my equivocal presence on several trips this past year when our jaunts during the day were interrupted with my constant typing of references on the back porch in the evening. (For Mary Beth and Ernie, it was their front sunroom.) Dale Kelman is a long-time friend and wonderful clinician who diligently read the whole book and challenged me with her questions throughout. Joe Rollo helped me apply my insights on past trauma and current stressors to police officers.

I especially want to acknowledge Deborah Malmud at Norton Publishing (as well as Chris Courtois who introduced me to her). Deborah not only helped me organize the outline of the book but also extended me a very kind version of tough love in meeting deadlines—it's what I needed and I can't thank Deborah enough. I also want to thank my advisees-turned-colleagues-turned friends who have worked with me over the years on how family relationships and attachment are important bases for understanding trauma—among them, Victoria Follette, Cathy Anderson,

Bethany Brand, Cindy Schaeffer, Mary Loos, and Lisa Kretz. I know that I have learned more from them than they from me and I have always valued their insights. Finally, I want to thank the many survivors of trauma whom I have interviewed and worked with during my career. Their overall level of functioning in the face of painful, often horrific circumstances provides the best illustration of resilience and interruption of cycles of violence and trauma.

Preface

My interest in the intergenerational transmission of violence developed out of my focus on family history as an important window into a person's identity. Working in community mental health in rural Tennessee in the late 1970's, I counseled many women who presented with depression and anxiety. When I routinely asked them about their family, many told me of an experience of incest. Little was written about incest at that time; even a nationally-known clinic's responses to my inquiries led me to initially conclude that, stereotypically, this was an occurrence more common among the rural poor. I subsequently received funding from NIMH to conduct the first randomized clinical trial of group therapy for adult female incest survivors and learned how rampant the problem of incest was. I also quickly learned the fallacy of focusing on one type of family violence without attention to other types. The overlap of different types of maltreatment is so great as to equate the study of singular forms of family violence using exclusion criteria as comparable to studying unicorns—they just don't exist.

However, another bias in the research of family violence has seemed to remain. Namely, the necessary spotlight on the struggles of women in abusive relationships has sometimes inadvertently resulted in an attempt to separate violence and maltreatment from the context of the family. Notions of patriarchy have often closed off and pre-empted important discussions even though it is not unusual for women in individual and group therapy to express even more anger at their mothers than at their fathers. While the suggestion is frequently made that these women have internalized society's derogation of mothers, there is a danger of dismissing their stated experiences as reflective only of a sociological construct.

Similarly, many outpatient treatment facilities and shelters for survivors of partner violence still explicitly refuse to ask women about a history of childhood trauma for fear of seeming to blame the victim. However, in conducting hundreds of family interviews with women in violent relationships, I have heard many women express appreciation for my broaching a topic perceived as either taboo or irrelevant by the agency. Similarly, in a large randomized clinical trial of men court-ordered to batterer group therapy (Alexander, Morris, Tracy, & Frye, 2010), virtually all participants wanted to present their family genogram and to actively explore and understand their own behavior within the context of their family of origin. In other words, women and men, victims and perpetrators all seem to recognize the importance and relevance of their family histories with regard to their own vulnerabilities and their own behavior. Instead of trying to convince them otherwise, it seems inherently more respectful to follow their lead and to be as curious about our clients' families as they are themselves.

Therefore, this book is focused on the parent-child attachment and family contexts of violence and trauma, not the least of which because this is what our clients tell us again and again is important in their lives. I have included only a few of their accounts and, in order to protect their privacy, have presented composites of their experiences. Clients also remind us repeatedly that their families are complex and complicated and that only by hearing their stories can we understand them better and help them make sense of what happened. Thus, maltreatment cannot be simply categorized in terms of identifiable instances of violence or even characteristics of the abuse, but is much more pertinent to the nature of the relationship in which it occurred or to the reactions of important people in the individual's life. In fact, trauma may not even involve any identifiable occurrence of abuse. Therefore, in order to decipher what actually constitutes maltreatment or trauma and what instead fits into the heading of negative life experiences with little lasting impact, it is essential to listen to our clients as they seek to understand themselves, their parents, their families, their neighborhoods and their culture. Even the research on the neurobiology of trauma and the role of genetics highlights the critical importance of these contexts in the development of the brain and the risk for ongoing violence.

Just as survivors' stories need to inform research, rigorous research needs to serve as the basis for the development of evidence-based practices that can assist survivors in addressing their unresolved trauma and preventing intergenerational cycles of abuse. Therefore, this book also aims to explore and summarize the most current studies on those factors that either exacerbate or mitigate the intergenerational transmission of violence. The many research studies referred to in this volume can thus enhance but not substitute for the richness of our clients' stories, the depth of their understanding and their ultimate resilience in attempting to comprehend and counteract their own experiences of abuse and trauma. Hearing their stories and making use of the research are the best ways to help us help them interrupt the cycles of trauma and violence.

Intergenerational Cycles
of Trauma and Violence

CHAPTER 1

Introduction

A notion that is generally accepted in most societies, including our own, is that experiences from childhood affect our behavior in adulthood, especially how we treat our children and our intimate partners. Indeed, theories of intergenerational transmission of violence assume that if we ourselves have been abused and neglected as children, we will be abusive and neglectful to others close to us, thus extending the cycle across generations. However, many individuals who were maltreated as children do not replicate this cycle. Similarly, we have made little sense of the individual raised in a "good family" who is violent either as a child or as an adult. These discontinuities of cycles of violence and trauma have baffled professionals and nonprofessionals alike. However, broadening our vision and attending to new areas of research can help to illuminate this conundrum and to consider new avenues of intervention. This book aims to do just that.

In this chapter, a justification for the study of intergenerational cycles of trauma and violence is followed by a review of related research. Limitations of existing research include questions regarding self-reports of maltreatment, shortcomings of longitudinal studies, and an excessively narrow definition of what constitutes trauma. It is also suggested that a focus on the discontinuities of the cycle of violence may ultimately be more useful in terms of identifying protective factors and the basis for resilience, moderators of this cycle, and the need to broaden our focus. The choice of a conceptual model also affects the emphasis of research and suggested interventions. It is the premise of this book that attachment theory and family systems theory within the broader context of a developmental evolutionary-based perspective provide the most comprehensive basis for understanding when and why trauma and violence experienced in one generation affects subsequent generations.

WHY STUDY CYCLES OF TRAUMA AND VIOLENCE?

Why study intergenerational cycles? First, we need to study them in order to guide the development of interventions that can ultimately provide hope for individuals and families impacted by violence. If we understand the pathways that lead to the replication of patterns of violence as well as those that interrupt these patterns, it will be possible to intervene earlier to disrupt the cycle. Furthermore, attending to the functionality of "dysfunctional" behavior can help us understand how environments themselves (families, neighborhoods, and other subcultures) may need to change in order to foster more broadly adaptive behavior. Even in working with adult trauma survivors, an appreciation of intergenerational cycles should remind the clinician to inquire about a survivor's parenting and relationship with an intimate partner.

Second, attending to the discontinuities of this cycle is just as essential. Understanding discontinuities from the perspective of individuals who have escaped the cycle may suggest innovative intervention approaches for children at risk. For example, to the extent that relationships can alleviate the negative effects of even the most severe trauma, then identifying and fostering such relationships in the life of a child, adolescent, or adult survivor can have an important impact. Interventions with a current partner of a trauma survivor can address the secondary traumatization that partners of trauma victims frequently experience and help reverse the effects of past trauma. Furthermore, making sense of one's past and rewriting one's own narrative of past experiences may interrupt the cycle.

Finally, understanding discontinuities from the perspective of individuals without an overt history of abuse but who become abusive themselves can help us define, detect, and address some of the essential outcomes of trauma. A focus on this type of discontinuity can provide direction for intervening with abusive individuals without a history of maltreatment. By using a broader definition of trauma, we can see that an absence of overt abuse does not necessarily mean an absence of trauma. Therefore, becoming attuned to the subtle but powerful effects of neglect and unresolved trauma will help professionals respond to the needs of clients and their families.

It is the premise of this book that an increased risk for abusive behavior or revictimization as a function of one's own experiences of abuse or trauma in childhood can best be understood through the complementary lenses of attachment theory (focusing on the relationship between the child and the caregiver) and family systems theory (focusing on the larger context of this relationship). That is, what a child acquires from his or her relationship with the caregiver is not simply a reflection of what the child has learned from experiencing or witnessing abuse but, more importantly, from the child's experience of the relationship itself, on an implicit, emotional, physical, and neurobiological level. Just as the child's experience of an abusive relationship can contribute to subsequent aggression toward others, the child's relational experience with a caregiver or some other important individual can overcome seemingly insurmountable adverse effects, thereby interrupting the cycle of violence and trauma. Moreover, the parent-child relationship itself will necessarily be modified and best understood within the larger context of the family and the broader social system. Thus, both the parent-child attachment relationship and the family context can either counteract and lessen the effects of trauma or, alternatively, amplify its effects. These attachment and family relationships will also be modified themselves and will themselves modify the neurobiological and genetic substrate of the individual child. Therefore, any examination of the concordance between abusive behavior in the first generation and abusive behavior (or revictimization) in the second generation without attention to these relationships and these individual differences will necessarily fail.

RESEARCH ON INTERGENERATIONAL CYCLES

Research literature generally supports the assumption of intergenerational cycles. Although rates may differ between studies, retrospective research finds that abusive parents are significantly more likely to report a history of abuse or neglect themselves (Collin-Vezina & Cyr, 2003; Kim, 2009; Putallaz, Costanzo, Grimes, & Sherman, 1998). Similarly, a history of child maltreatment or witnessing abusive behavior greatly increases the risks of perpetrating and of being the victim of intimate partner violence (IPV), both for men and women (Fang & Corso, 2007; Heyman & Slep, 2002; Kernsmith, 2006). For example, in a telephone survey of 1,249 adults, all forms of family-of-origin violence were found to predict all forms of current relationship violence (Kwong, Bartholomew, Henderson, & Trinke, 2003). Furthermore, the effects appeared to be specific to intimate relationships and not to antisocial or criminal behavior outside the home (Kernsmith, 2006; Murrell, Christoff, & Henning, 2007).

Even prospective studies in which children with documented histories of maltreatment are followed longitudinally over time find that individuals who were abused in childhood are significantly more likely to later be described by their children as abusive themselves (Pears & Capaldi, 2001). In one of the earliest prospective studies of parenting in an at-risk sample, 70% of mothers who were abused as children exhibited abusive or borderline care by the time their children were 2 years of age (Egeland, Jacobvitz, & Papatola, 1987). Similar evidence has emerged with regard to the prediction of IPV. In Cathy Widom's longitudinal study of individuals with substantiated cases of child physical abuse, child sexual abuse, or neglect, along with matched controls, a history of child abuse or neglect was predictive of the perpetration of IPV in both males and females (White & Widom, 2003), violent and aggressive behavior (Widom, Schuck, & White, 2006), and revictimization (McIntyre & Widom, 2011; Widom, Czaja, & Dutton, 2008). In another study, adolescents who witnessed verbal or physical aggression between their parents were significantly more likely to later engage in verbal or physical aggression against their romantic partners (Cui, Durtschi, Donnellan, Lorenz, & Conger, 2010). Finally, in a prospective study of 543 children followed over 20 years (Ehrensaft et al., 2003), child maltreatment, the witnessing of IPV, and power-assertive punishment were all predictive of injuring one's partner. Witnessing IPV predicted subsequent victimization by a partner. Therefore, retrospective and prospective studies with both males and females have found indisputable evidence of the effects of child maltreatment and trauma on abusive behavior toward one's child or partner as well as an increased risk for revictimization. However, this observed relationship is far from perfect, as the following review attempts to show.

UNANSWERED QUESTIONS

In spite of exposure to violence, many maltreated children do not become abusive or neglectful. Furthermore, some children become abusive even without a history of maltreatment. For example, Kaufman and Zigler (1987) noted that while the rate of abusive parenting among individuals who have themselves been abused as children is six times higher than in the general population, the percentage of individuals with a history of abuse who are abusive themselves is approximately 30%. In his review of the research, Oliver (1993) noted that approximately one-third of child victims maltreat (abuse or neglect) as parents, one-third do not, and one-third are vulnerable to social stress in whether they become abusive. In their longitudinal study, Pears and Capaldi (2001) found only a 23% rate of intergenerational transmission—that is, significant but low. A meta-analysis of the intergenerational transmission of IPV came to a similar conclusion, depending upon the type of sample (Stith et al., 2000).

Why then is the evidence on cycles of violence so flawed? Much of the reason can be attributed to methodological weaknesses reviewed below. Beyond this, however, is a failure to fully consider the parent-child relationship and the broader family context in which maltreatment may or may not occur. Attending to these contexts can help to illuminate the intergenerational pathways to violence as well as the factors that interrupt these cycles.

Self-Reports of Maltreatment

In the late 19th century, both Sigmund Freud and Pierre Janet proposed that the chronic physical symptoms exhibited by many of their female patients resulted from trauma rather than somatic causes. Janet referred to this cutting off of traumatic memories from consciousness as *dissociation*; Freud called it *double consciousness*. Both men agreed that it was necessary to bring these traumatic memories and associated emotions to awareness in order to resolve the symptoms of hysteria. Because most of these female patients reported a history of child sexual abuse, Freud (1905/1953) developed his *seduction theory*. However, Victorian Europe was not willing to entertain the possibility of sexual perversion of men toward their daughters. Therefore, Freud discarded his seduction theory and instead proposed that women's reports of sexual advances by their fathers actually reflected women's fantasies of a sexual relationship with their father. Thus was born one of the most influential ideas of recent Western civilization—the Oedipal complex. The unwillingness of society and mental health professionals to question the validity of this theory in the many decades since its formulation, even in the presence of numerous reports by clients to the contrary and at times incontrovertible physical evidence, speaks to the extreme threat posed to society by the possibility of child sexual abuse.

The questioning of self-reports of abuse resurfaced again in the 1990s when the American Psychological Association charged the Working Group on Investigation of Memories of Childhood Abuse to review the research on the recovery of child abuse–related memories. A major point of contention was whether adults who reported having had periods of amnesia for a history of child sexual abuse either had not been abused at all and were responding to the suggestion of their therapists or had simply earlier failed to report the abuse (Alpert, Brown, & Courtois, 1998; Ornstein, Ceci, & Loftus, 1998).

However, the preponderance of rigorous research makes clear that self-reported maltreatment history does not tend to be associated with false positives (claiming a history of abuse when none occurred). Instead, longitudinal studies of children with substantiated cases of maltreatment are associated with either a relative accuracy of adult recollections of child physical abuse and child sexual abuse or instead a prevalence of false negatives (denying a history of abuse that has actually occurred). For example, in Widom's prospective study of maltreated individuals (in which the abuse had been substantiated in childhood), 40% of adults underreported a history of physical abuse (Widom & Shepard, 1996). Moreover, 84% of male victims of child sexual abuse and 36% of female victims denied having been abused (Widom & Morris, 1997). Similarly, 38% of a separate sample of female child sexual abuse survivors followed over time subsequently failed to recall their abuse, with those who were younger at the time of the abuse or who had been abused by someone they knew less likely to recall the abuse (Williams, 1994). Thus, to the extent that there is a discrepancy of self-report with fact, the bias is almost always in the direction of underreporting a history of abuse.

This tendency toward false negatives is exacerbated by two other shortcomings that frequently occur in longitudinal studies. First, many prospective studies are characterized by insufficient follow-up times to assess whether abuse has occurred (Putallaz et al., 1998). Therefore, researchers may prematurely conclude that a cycle of violence has been averted. Second, there is frequently inadequate documentation of maltreatment among comparison subjects presumed to be free of a maltreatment history, leading to fewer observed differences between index and comparison cases (Widom, 1989). The result is undoubtedly an underestimation of the prevalence of intergenerational transmission (Belsky, 1993).

A Narrow Definition of Maltreatment

Another methodological weakness in research on this topic arises from inadequate definitions of maltreatment as well as inattention to other kinds of trauma. For example, longitudinal research frequently relies upon child protective service substantiation as the gold standard for deciding whether or not abuse has occurred (cf. Widom, 1989). However, given the extensive ambiguity and variability within and between jurisdictions as to the definition of abuse as well as the inconsistent influence of clinical judgment and social norms, the resulting classification of "caseness" is anything but standard (Newcomb & Locke, 2001). Moreover, specific characteristics of the abuse, such as severity, frequency, age of onset, and relationship with the perpetrator, may be even more definitive than caseness as to how the abuse is experienced. Polyvictimization, or the experience of multiple types of maltreatment, has an even more insidious effect on outcomes and yet may be ignored in the determination of whether abuse has occurred (Cort, Toth, Cerulli, & Rogosch, 2011; Heyman & Slep, 2002; Pears & Capaldi, 2001; Robboy & Anderson, 2011). Research thus frequently fails to fully describe the abuse experience—let alone the context of the abusive relationship or the meaning of the abuse to the victim.

Second, many studies limit their definition of maltreatment to histories of physical or sexual abuse or witnessing violence. However, histories of neglect and emotional abuse (constructs frequently ignored by both prospective and retrospective studies) are even more damaging and more likely to contribute to problems with parenting and intimate relationships (Hildyard & Wolfe, 2002; Newcomb & Locke, 2001; Weeks & Widom, 1998; Widom, 1989; Yates & Wekerle, 2009). Similarly, few inquiries are typically made about abuse by siblings or about witnessing abuse of siblings, both of which are highly predictive of delinquency, aggression, and other symptoms (Button & Gealt, 2010; Simonelli, Mullis, Elliott, & Pierce, 2002; Teicher & Vitaliano, 2011). Third, only some researchers regard witnessing IPV as inherently traumatic. Moreover, other sources of trauma, such as traumatic loss or the unavailability of a parent, are routinely ignored, even though their long-term impacts may explain aggression even more than a history of abuse (Corvo, 2006). Finally, researchers often fail to explore the predictors of revictimization—one consequence of being abused, neglected, or otherwise maltreated as a child is an increased risk of being abused by others unrelated to the initial abuser—including peers and partners. While research on the intergenerational transmission of IPV typically assesses victimization by a partner, research on cycles of child abuse may or may not, even though revictimization itself may contribute to the continuation of the cycle.

DISCONTINUITIES OF CYCLES OF VIOLENCE

A more fruitful way of understanding the essence of maltreatment is through a focus on the discontinuities of the cycle. In other words, what characterizes individuals with a history of maltreatment who do not become violent themselves? Conversely, what characterizes the background of individuals without an overt history of abuse who do abuse others? A review of protective factors, other potential moderators of the abuse experience, and a consideration of what constitutes trauma will address these questions.

Protective Factors and Resilience

Nonrepeaters of the cycle of violence can be understood in part by considering resilience. Defining resilience as "the lack of perpetration of child maltreatment . . . in the context of risk" (Easterbrooks, Chaudhuri, Bartlett, & Coperman, 2011, p. 42), parents who break the cycle of violence are more likely to have had at least one of several important experiences. One characteristic of an individual who breaks the cycle is having an emotionally supportive relationship with a parent or other adult during childhood (Egeland et al., 1988; Kaufman & Zigler, 1987). The family of origin thus serves as an important context in modifying the effects of the initial abusive relationship. Other pathways to this resilience include positive current relationships such as emotional support from a partner or from a psychotherapist (DuMont, Widom, & Czaja, 2007; Egeland et al., 1988; Lackey & Williams, 1995; Langeland & Dijkstra, 1995; Oliver, 1993).

While a positive relationship with a psychotherapist reflects an experience of emotional support, it also may facilitate a second important attribute of nonrepeaters—namely, an understanding and awareness of the details, emotional context, and effects of the abuse one has experienced. Individuals who interrupt the cycle of abuse with their own children are less likely to idealize their parents and more likely to remember specific instances of abuse as well as their emotional reaction to the abuse (Egeland et al., 1988). This coherent narrative of one's history thus appears to allow parents to "face the reality of past and present personal relationships" (Oliver, 1993, p. 1322) and to make conscious choices about how to raise their own children.

The lack of protection from the effects of maltreatment would thus appear to be due in large part to the absence of an emotionally supportive relationship and to a distorted view of one's past. These two factors can be considered to be moderators of the cycle of violence—that is, external factors that influence the degree to which childhood trauma has a deleterious effect on subsequent behavior. Of course, the question of causality always arises with regard to resilience—is there something distinctive about individuals who are able to elicit the support of others or who are able to make sense of an abusive past? This question should lead us to consider a third newly recognized contributor to resilience—that is, an individual's genetic substrate. Although this genetic substrate may itself be altered by environmental stress through the process of epigenesis, genes may partly determine whether a child is either more or less impacted by exposure to violence or maternal insensitivity, and also the degree to which a child may benefit from an especially supportive relationship.

Other Moderators

Among the many other potential moderators of the impact on a child of a history of abuse is the gender of the parent. Interestingly, maltreatment by one's mother is the most predictive of both the perpetration and receipt of physical and psychological aggression (Kwong et al., 2003). Other researchers have similarly noted the importance of mother-to-child aggression in predicting both IPV perpetration and victimization (Fritz, Slep, & O'Leary, 2012; Hendy et al., 2003; Langhinrichsen-Rohling, Neidig, & Thorn, 1995). Instead of viewing these statistics as a basis for mother blaming, it is important to acknowledge the differentially large role that mothers, relative to fathers, typically have in raising children in our society. The effect of this disproportionate influence of mothers compared to fathers can also be seen in higher rates of disorganized behavior and somatoform dissociative disorders among the children of abusive or disruptive mothers as opposed to abusive or disruptive fathers (Abrams, Rifkin, & Hesse, 2006; Roelofs, Keijers, Hoogduin, Naring, & Moene, 2002). Similarly, intergenerational traumatic effects on Holocaust off-spring are more pronounced in reaction to maternal than paternal PTSD (Yehuda, Bell, Bierer, & Schmeidler, 2008). As I argue in Chapter 2, these differences do not reflect something inherent about mothers as much as the relative importance of primary caregivers over nonprimary caregivers, regardless of their gender.

This is not to minimize the role of the father as a source either of stress and abuse or support both to his children and to his partner (Langeland & Dijkstra, 1995). For example, a man's conflict with his wife (including IPV) as well as his absence directly impacts his children's adjustment (El-Sheikh & Whitson, 2006; Koss et al., 2011; Marshall, English, & Stewart, 2001). In fact, Egeland (1988) has described paternal deprivation as an insidious form of maltreatment. Furthermore, a man's aggression toward his wife can indirectly affect his children through its impact on his wife's parenting (Casanueva & Martin, 2007; Lee & Guterman, 2010). Even if the father is himself not abusive to the child or mother, his relationship with his wife can greatly affect her ability to overcome the negative effects of her abuse history on her parenting (Cohn, Silver, Cowan, Cowan, & Pearson, 1992).

Other moderators include the gender of the child, although the effects of child gender vary within the larger context of neighborhood and culture (Munson, McMahon, & Spieker, 2001). Furthermore, cultural differences in child-rearing practices will greatly affect the meaning attributed by children to the punishment they have received (Deater-Deckard, Dodge, & Sorbring, 2005). These contextual factors therefore are important in determining the impact of maltreatment. Hence, many discontinuities in the cycle of violence and trauma may not be discontinuities at all, but may merely reflect an incomplete consideration of the important factors in play.

Broadening the Focus of Intergenerational Transmission

The other manifestation of discontinuity is the presence of violent or aggressive behavior in an individual without a history of abuse—an occurrence that has always led puzzled observers to question, "How is this possible?" Broadening the focus of maltreatment or trauma may help make sense of this type of discontinuity. For instance, intergenerational transmission could be reflected in the failure of a traumatized parent to protect a child from another perpetrator. Furthermore, maltreatment may skip a generation but still reflect the impact of a parent's maltreatment history on the tendency to engage in hostile or helpless parenting (Lyons-Ruth, Yellin, Melnick, & Atwood, 2003, 2005), as described in Chapter 2. In fact, "strong alternating intergenerational sequences" of abuse are quite common (Oliver, 1993). For example, sexual abuse perpetrated by the parent might lead to depression in the child, but not necessarily sexual abuse, which might lead to aggression in the grandchild, but not necessarily sexual abuse (Alexander & Warner, 2003). Even nonabusive parenting associated with that parent's history of trauma may impact the young child's or adult child's vulnerability to abuse by someone else or to the adult child's increased risk for abusive behavior. Furthermore, the relatively new field of epigenetics suggests that trauma experienced by a woman who is pregnant or even prior to the conception of her child may turn genes on or off within the fetus, increasing that child's risk for aggression, and may even be transmitted genetically to that adult child's offspring. Therefore, a much more comprehensive approach is needed to understand the essence of what constitutes maltreatment and trauma.

Figure 1.1 reflects many, but probably not all, of the possible pathways through which intergenerational transmission may occur as well as exit pathways that interrupt the cycle. That is, any of the conditions observed in the first generation (G1) potentially lead, in interaction with moderators, to any of the outcomes in the second generation (G2), and so on into the third generation (G3).

MODELS OF INTERGENERATIONAL TRANSMISSION

A broader conceptualization of these cycles of violence and trauma would seek to answer the following four questions: First, how does the experience of trauma increase one's risk for abusing or traumatizing others? Second, how does the experience of trauma increase one's risk for further abuse or traumatization by others (i.e., for revictimization)? Third, even if a child is not maltreated and does not witness abuse, how does being raised by a parent with a trauma history increase the child's risk for abus-

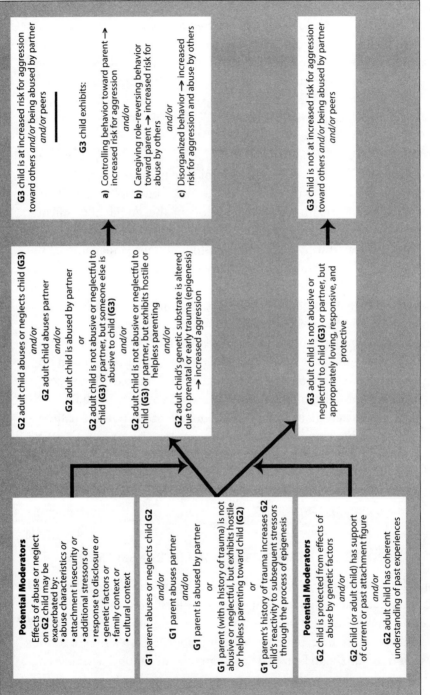

Figure 1.1 Cycles of Trauma and Violence

ing others or abuse by others? Finally, and perhaps most importantly, how does an individual with a history of maltreatment and trauma escape this cycle to become a loving parent and partner? These four questions are answered very differently based on one's conceptual model of what it means to be raised by a parent with a trauma history. In the following section, several of the most prominent models of the intergenerational transmission of violence are briefly described.

Social Learning Theory

Originally proposed by Bandura (1973, 1977), social learning theory suggests that children learn to be aggressive through modeling specific behaviors, especially from adults with whom they closely identify, and through reinforcement of those behaviors. Generalized modeling would be expected for overall levels of aggression within a family and is particularly relevant to cycles of parent-child aggression (Kalmuss, 1984). Type-specific modeling refers to role-specific (i.e., victim versus perpetrator) and gender-specific modeling and is proposed to be more consistent with cycles of IPV.

In addition to behaviors, social learning theory suggests that children acquire certain attitudes and beliefs that lead them to accept violence as normative and effective for resolving conflict—attitudes and beliefs that may contribute to subsequent abusive behavior toward a child or partner. More specifically, Kenneth Dodge and his colleagues have observed that abused children tend to exhibit certain social information processing patterns that would explain their aggressive behavior, including a hostile attributional bias regarding the intentions of others, a hypervigilance to hostile cues, and ready access to aggressive responses from memory (Dodge, Pettit, Bates, & Valente, 1995). Interestingly, these characteristics have also been observed among partner-abusive men (Holtzworth-Munroe, 1992; Holtzworth-Munroe & Hutchinson, 1993).

However, critiques of social learning theory have also surfaced. Few studies have examined whether the proposed conditions in the family of origin (i.e., identification with the perpetrator, reinforcement for aggressive behavior) actually occur (Delsol & Margolin, 2004). Furthermore, why does violence affect some kids and not others and why are the patterns of transmission so diverse (Feldman, 1997)? What about affect, internalizing problems (such as depression, jealousy, rage) and personality problems (such as borderline personality disorder)? Social learning theory also fails to address the very significant role of neglect in predicting violent outcomes. Although an early meta-analysis suggested a stronger effect of family violence history on men as perpetrators than on women as victims (Stith et al., 2000), a more recent study found no evidence of either role or gender specificity (Kwong et al., 2003). Namely, all types of family violence predicted both the perpetration and receipt of IPV for both males and females. When gender specificity does emerge, it is in a counterintuitive way—according to Rosenbaum and Leisring (2003), male batterers tend to receive less love and more aggression from mothers and neglect from fathers (obviating the gender-specific role of fathers with regard either to aggressive behavior or to the reinforcement of the child's use of aggression). Therefore, social learning theory fails to capture the complexity of what mediates between childhood trauma and subsequent aggressive behavior.

Attachment Theory

Attachment theory proposes that there is a biologically based bond that ensures the child's proximity to the caregiver, especially under conditions of stress (Bowlby, 1969/1982). Because human infants cannot survive without access to a caregiver, children will engage in all sorts of distortions of cognition and affect in order to maintain connection with a caregiver. Attachment theory also explains the development of affect and cognition within the child. By monitoring the infant's facial cues and by regulating the child's autonomic nervous system, the parent provides the basis for the development of the infant brain, social bonds, and the hypothalamic-pituitary axis, setting the stage for the child's lifelong capacity to self-soothe and regulate his or her own affect when stressed (Schore, 2010). Moreover, through the parent's patterns of interaction with the child, the child comes to experience the parent as responsive and trustworthy (and himself or herself as worthy of this care) or as unresponsive, rejecting, unreliable, or even frightening (and himself or herself as unworthy and even unlovable). As a consequence of these interactions, children develop cognitive schemas or internal working models of the parent-child relationship and of themselves.

These interactional patterns were first identified in a separation and reunion laboratory paradigm called the Strange Situation (Ainsworth,

Blehar, Waters, & Wall, 1978), which was validated by extensive observations of the parent-child dyad in the home. Organized strategies adopted by the child to maintain access to the parent consist of a secure pattern of interaction and two insecure patterns (see Chapter 2). However, it became apparent that children with a history of maltreatment tend to exhibit rather bizarre approach-avoidant behaviors in the presence of the parent (Carlson, Cicchetti, Barnett, & Braunwald, 1989). These behaviors are also observed in the children of parents with a history of unresolved trauma or loss (Ainsworth & Eichberg, 1991; Hughes, Turton, McGauley, & Fonagy, 2006). Therefore, a new category, disorganized attachment behavior, was described to reflect the interactions of parents and children suffering from trauma (Main & Solomon, 1986, 1990).

These four categories of attachment behavior not only differentiate children on the basis of their adjustment, affect regulation, social interactions, and cognition, but are also remarkably predictive of similar behavior patterns and outcomes in adulthood (Fraley, 2002). Given that the disorganized attachment category is most pertinent to trauma, it is especially germane to intergenerational cycles of child abuse (Solomon & George, 2006) and IPV (Holtzworth-Munroe, Stuart, & Hutchinson, 1997). However, the organized attachment categories refine the presentation of symptoms exhibited by parents, children, and partners with a history of trauma or who are currently experiencing trauma.

Attachment theory is notably relevant to the concept of complex trauma, which takes issue with the very narrow diagnostic criteria for post-traumatic stress disorder (PTSD). Unlike the identifiable threat of death or violation of bodily integrity required in the *DSM's* Criterion A1 of the PTSD diagnosis, complex psychological traumatic stressors "(1) are repetitive or prolonged; (2) involve direct harm and/or neglect and abandonment by caregivers or ostensibly responsible adults; (3) occur at developmentally vulnerable times in the victim's life, such as early childhood; and (4) have great potential to compromise severely a child's development" (Courtois & Ford, 2009, p. 1). Given that family violence necessarily occurs within the context of an ongoing attachment relationship, the traditional PTSD diagnosis fails to capture the sequelae of emotion dysregulation, dissociation, somatization, and distortions of information processing that lead to a child's increased risk for aggression or revictimization. Therefore, attachment theory is uniquely suited to the study of cycles of violence and trauma.

However, attachment theory has its own limitations. Although Bowlby emphasized the importance of attending to the family context (Marvin & Stewart, 1990), attachment researchers have generally failed to do so—instead focusing on dyadic relationships (between parents and children and between romantic partners). Attachment theory also frequently fails to adequately consider the larger contexts of neighborhood and culture.

Family Systems Theory

A perspective that does focus on the family context of individual behavior and dyads is family systems theory. With regard to family violence, it highlights both the direct and indirect effects of living in a home characterized by violence. Direct effects can be seen in children's emotional and behavioral symptoms. Indirect effects refer to maternal stress and the emotional or physiological effects of family violence on the mother and her ability to parent, resulting in reduced attention to her children and reduced monitoring of their behavior. Indirect effects of family violence also include housing instability, reduced family income, the consequences of living in a dangerous neighborhood, and parental substance abuse. While acknowledging the role of modeling, this perspective also examines the effects of family disruption on attachment relationships and on children's internalizing and externalizing problems—in other words, their inability to regulate their affect (Cyr, Euser, Bakermans-Kranenburg, & van IJzendoorn, 2010).

Attachment theory and family systems theory share many of the same assumptions, such as viewing distress in functional terms and focusing on patterns of dyadic or family interactions, rather than on the individual. Also, both approaches emphasize the reciprocal nature of behavior—between partners and between the parent and the child. Family systems theory expands this focus to examine the reciprocal nature of behavior between subsystems—how interparental conflict directly impacts parent-child conflict and attachment insecurity, how parent-child conflict can create stress in the marital system, and how stress experienced by a family member from an outside source (e.g., unemployment of a parent, bullying of a child at school) can affect the whole family. The curative impact of one family subsystem on another subsystem can also be observed. Adolescents' sense of security with each of their parents is directly linked to their parents' sense of security with each other (Woodhouse, Dykas, &

Cassidy, 2009). Similarly, current couple relationships can overcome the effects of past trauma on one or both parents. In fact, the limitation of most models of intergenerational transmission is a failure to consider the current relationship (Kwong et al., 2003)—family systems theory does this.

Family systems theory also adds a broader dimension than simply the impact of one dyad on another dyad by studying more complex dynamics such as triangulation and competing loyalties within a family as well as the functioning of the whole family system as a secure base for each of the individual members (Byng-Hall, 1999). In other words, family systems theory directs attention to the context of attachment relationships and the larger family unit. It emphasizes what attachment theory has always acknowledged to be important, but what attachment researchers have generally tended to ignore.

Finally, family systems theory calls attention to the even broader context of culture, which impacts the individual, intimate partners, the parent-child dyad, and the family. For example, the neighborhood and society have indisputable roles in contributing to the experience of trauma and even in defining what constitutes trauma. Moreover, the legacies of groups such as Native Americans and victims of the Holocaust who have experienced genocide, displacement, and other types of persecution highlight the importance of historical trauma. Fortunately, for members of all of these groups, attachment relationships, the family, and the process of meaning making can offer the opportunity to ameliorate the impact of this trauma in the next generation.

Life History Theory

A perspective that complements attachment theory and family systems theory and that is also relevant to intergenerational cycles of violence (if not trauma) is life history theory (Belsky, Steinberg, & Draper, 1991). It focuses on the evolutionary adaptiveness of behavior that maximizes an individual's reproductive fitness. Stressful environments direct the allocation of resources toward strategies that are adaptive under those conditions even if they might be less functional under safer conditions or for society as a whole (Belsky, Schlomer, & Ellis, 2012). So called "slower" life strategies associated with safer environments lead to more committed and stable sexual relationships, later reproduction, fewer children, and greater investment of time and resources in those children. By comparison, "faster" life strategies associated with harsher, more dangerous, and less predictable environments lead to less committed and stable sexual relationships, earlier reproduction, more children, less investment in each of those children, less delay of gratification, and more aggressive and risky behavior. If one's prospective life span is short, it makes evolutionary sense to reproduce as quickly as possible. This perspective is particularly applicable to one frequently observed outcome of a history of child sexual abuse—namely, teenage pregnancy with its increased risk for young women's revictimization by a partner and abusive parenting toward a child (see Chapter 6).

However, life history theory is also more broadly applicable to intergenerational cycles of violence. It emphasizes the functionality of behavior and its fit with a particular set of life circumstances. It suggests that parenting occurs within a context that implicitly informs a child of the nature of that environment and the types of stressors that the child will encounter (Belsky et al., 2012). For example, even the neurobiological or epigenetic effects of prenatal anxiety may prepare a developing fetus for the likely stressors that will be experienced. Research grounded in life history theory has demonstrated the importance of unpredictable parenting experienced early in life as contributing to a faster life history strategy with risky sexual behavior, aggressive and delinquent behaviors, and more criminal activity (Simpson, Griskevicius, Kuo, Sung, & Collins, 2012). Given that unpredictable parenting and harsh family environments also characterize the most vulnerable attachment relationships and the greatest risk for intergenerational cycles of violence, life history theory complements a developmental perspective focusing on attachment and families.

In conclusion, the relationship between the child and the caregiver is integral to what is experienced by the child as abusive, neglectful, frightening, or traumatic. This felt experience of the child is what determines its impact on the child and the likely continuity of the maltreatment or trauma into the future. The larger family system either fosters the supportiveness of this relationship and protects the child from stress or, alternately, increases the harmful effects of that relationship on the child. Therefore, by providing the most comprehensive explanation for the intergenerational transmission of violence and trauma, the perspectives of attachment theory and family systems theory also suggest ways to interrupt this cycle.

In deriving suggestions for interrupting this cycle of violence, this book first describes in Chapter 2 the relevance of attachment theory to the study of trauma. Chapter 3 explores how the family context of the parent-child relationship from the formation of the couple relationship even prior to the birth of the child sets the stage for the parents' interactions with each other and the child. Although couples' mutual support can overcome the impact of each partner's history of trauma, problematic interactions may dissolve normal intergenerational boundaries and increase the child's risk for maltreatment. Of course, even when relationships within the family are supportive and appropriate, the family system as a whole is nevertheless subject to external stressors. Chapter 4 describes the impact of trauma on the neurobiology of the developing child as well as the variety of ways in which genes may correlate with, interact with, or be altered by the environmental contexts of the attachment relationship and the family system. Chapter 5 focuses on an important set of outcomes of a history of maltreatment—namely, peer victimization observed among young children, dating violence, and intimate partner violence. Chapter 6 looks exclusively at child sexual abuse—its family context, its effects, and the trajectories of risky behaviors, partner violence, parenting problems, sexual revictimization, and sexual offending. This chapter also explores the many pathways to resilience and the interruption of this intergenerational cycle. Chapter 7 delves into sources of violence and trauma that are external to the family but that may interact with prior trauma experiences to increase the risk for subsequent family violence. These include political terrorism, combat exposure, critical incident exposure among law enforcement personnel, foster care and adoption, and the incarceration of parents. Finally, Chapter 8 reflects upon other factors that may influence the intergenerational transmission of violence and trauma, including cultural views of family violence and attachment relationships, the gender of the child, and the type of maltreatment experienced. The book concludes with yet another consideration of resilience—its definition dependent upon the nature of the environment. Contributors to resilience can be found at many levels of analysis—the neurobiological, the individual, the relationship, and the larger social context. Examining what we know about naturally occurring sources of resilience allows us to develop the most effective interventions for interrupting cycles of trauma and violence.

CHAPTER 2

The Parent-Child Attachment Relationship

The premise of this chapter, and indeed of the whole book, is that the intergenerational transmission of violence and trauma does not depend solely upon a child being overtly maltreated by a parent who was also maltreated. This certainly occurs much too frequently, but is not absolutely required in order for a child to experience the parent's (usually mother's) trauma and to then become more vulnerable to victimization by others or to victimizing others. What is central to intergenerational transmission is the child's connection to the parent. Building upon and/ or resolving this relationship is also central to interrupting a potential cycle of violence and trauma. Attachment theory offers a window into this powerful bond.

OVERVIEW OF ATTACHMENT THEORY

The attachment system is one of several systems that control specific aspects of human behavior. For example, the reptilian brain controls body homeostasis; the limbic system controls caregiving, care seeking, dominance-submission, sexual mating, and cooperation; and the neocortex controls the construction of meaning. Bowlby (1969/1982) postulated that attachment, associated with the limbic system, is a biologically based bond that ensures proximity of the human child to the caregiver and therefore is essential for the survival of the child, especially during periods of danger or peril. When the child's attachment needs are met in the moment, the attachment behavior or proximity-seeking ceases and the child resumes exploration of the environment. The child thus uses the parent both as a *secure base* from which to explore the environment and as a *safe haven* to whom to retreat when stressed or fearful.

From an evolutionary perspective, human children cannot fail to be attached because they cannot survive without a caregiver's responsiveness. Abandonment or even the careless inattention of a caregiver can lead to a child's realistic sense of terror—perhaps that is why parental neglect often has more deleterious effects than abuse (Hildyard & Wolfe, 2002; Sleed & Fonagy, 2010). Therefore, a child will do whatever is necessary to monitor the parent's presence and to maintain a connection with the parent, especially under conditions of danger or threat.

As stated previously, attachment theory is both a model of affect and a model of cognition. With regard to affect, the mother's initial role is to accurately read the infant's facial cues in order to infer his or her internal states and then to mirror the child's emotional cues via her own facial cues, tone of voice, and language. In so doing, the mother labels and validates the child's cues and basically teaches the child what he or she is feeling. Importantly, the mother then displays a different set of emotions in order to calm and soothe the child. Through this process (known as *reflective functioning*; Fonagy, 1999; Fonagy, Target, & Gergely, 2000), the child not only comes to understand and to learn to regulate affect but also to recognize that his or her affect is distinct from that of the mother. The ability of the mother to accurately interpret and respond contingently to the infant's emotional cues is integral to the development of the right hemisphere of the brain (see Chapter 4) as well as to the child's acquisition of identity. As an indicator of the mother's capacity to derive meaning from her own and her child's affective states, reflective functioning is closely related to her own capacity for affect regulation (Jurist & Meehan, 2009). It also predicts infants' attachment security (Meins et al., 2012). Therefore, the mother's lack of awareness of her own internal states or her preoccupation with her own unresolved experience of trauma has the potential to seriously compromise the child's sense of self, lifelong ability to regulate emotions, and even neural substrate.

Attachment theory's role as a model of cognition is derived from its function of encoding these initial parent-child interactions into unconscious internal working models (IWMs) of relationships. Thus, the child may come to view the parent as responsive and trustworthy (and the self as worthy of attention), or the parent as rejecting (and the self as undeserving of care), or the parent as inconsistent and changeable (and the

self as confused and unstable), or even the parent as inherently dangerous (and the self as damaged, flawed, and destructive). These internal
working models form the basis for the child's strategy to maintain the
attachment relationship with the parent. Since attachment is based on a
particular relationship, a child's attachment with one parent is relatively
independent of that to the other parent (Bridges, Connell, & Belsky,
1988) and tends to be relatively independent of temperament (Seifer,
Schiller, Sameroff, Resnick, & Riordan, 1996). (Interesting exceptions to
this generalization are explored in terms of genetic moderators of the
relationship between trauma and attachment in Chapter 4.)

In a classic article on attachment, Sroufe and Fleeson (1986) proposed that IWMs of whole relationships reside within individuals, which
are then carried forward into new relationships. In other words, the
child internalizes both sides of the attachment relationship, leading to
the proclivity to both model the original attachment figure and to elicit
from others reactions similar to that of the attachment figure. That is
why the victimization of others and revictimization by others are so
intertwined.

Although subject to change as a function of intervening life circumstances, IWMs are fairly stable, as illustrated by a meta-analysis of longitudinal studies showing a moderate correspondence between the infant's
attachment classification and that of the adult (Fraley, 2002). Thus,
describing the child's IWM regarding attachment (as inferred from the
child's behavior) can serve as a basis for explaining the long-term effects
of parent-child attachment. Reciprocally, the parent's state of mind
regarding attachment can serve to explain the basis for her interaction
with her child as contributing to the child's developing IWM. Therefore,
the following discussion of attachment categories in children and adults
also briefly describes the adult's parenting behavior with the child.

ASSESSMENT OF ATTACHMENT IN CHILDREN AND ADULTS

The Strange Situation

In order to document the different sets of strategies that children use to
maintain their connection with the parent, Mary Ainsworth and her colleagues (1978) developed a playroom laboratory paradigm called the
Strange Situation, which consists of a series of separations and reunions

between the parent and the child, performed when the child is 12–18 months of age. How the child reacts to the entry of a stranger, to the mother's departure from the room, and then to the mother's reentry is the basis for the classification of the nature of the child's attachment to the parent. The paradigm was validated by Ainsworth's extensive observations of mothers and children in their homes, albeit in a low-risk middle-class sample. Ainsworth identified three primary sets of behavioral strategies (secure, avoidant, and anxious/ambivalent) through which the child maintains connection with the mother during the Strange Situation. These strategies are referred to as organized in that they are consistently used by the child with that parent and are ultimately successful, although with certain costs for the two insecure (avoidant and anxious/ambivalent) strategies. An additional classification (disorganized attachment) was added when it became apparent that the three organized classifications did not adequately capture the behavior of some children in the Strange Situation.

Adult Attachment Interview

The adult counterparts of the child's organized attachment classifications are assessed with the Adult Attachment Interview (AAI; Main & Goldwyn, 1998) and reflect the adult's current state of mind regarding attachment. The AAI inquires about the respondent's earliest memories of each parent, adjectives and supporting examples to describe each parent, memories of rejection, loss or trauma, and general attitudes toward attachment relationships. It is not scored on the basis of the content of respondents' stories, but instead with the use of discourse analysis to assess how respondents tell their story. The scoring of *coherence* (the most important quality of secure attachment) is based on Grice's (1975) cooperative principles of communication: namely, (1) *quality* ("be truthful and have evidence for what you say"), (2) *quantity* ("be succinct, yet complete"), (3) *relation* ("be relevant"), and (4) *manner* ("be clear and orderly"). There are three categories of organized states of mind regarding attachment (secure/autonomous, dismissing, and preoccupied) and one category of a disorganized or unresolved state of mind. Before describing these categories in more detail, it is necessary to contrast the two different research traditions that have relied upon attachment theory to explain intimate interpersonal relationships.

AAI Versus Self-Report Measures of Attachment

The two bodies of research that have assessed attachment in intimate relationships are based on developmental psychology with its use of the Strange Situation and the AAI and personality/social psychology with its use of self-report measures of attachment. Importantly, they are not equivalent (Bernier, Larose, & Boivin, 2007; Bouthillier, Julien, Dube, Belanger, & Hamelin, 2002; Crowell, Treboux, & Waters, 1999; Mayseless & Scharf, 2007; Riggs et al., 2007; Roisman, Holland, et al., 2007). By way of explanation for this divergence, Shaver, Belsky, and Brennan (2000) argued that the AAI was validated by its prediction of child attachment in the Strange Situation whereas self-report measures were validated by their prediction of features of romantic relationships. However, this distinction between parent-child attachment and partner attachment does not necessarily reflect the differences between the two lines of research; self-report measures of childhood attachment are not equivalent to the AAI while the Current Relationship Interview, derived from the AAI (CRI; Treboux, Crowell, & Waters, 2004), is similar to attachment states of mind as assessed with the AAI (Bouthillier et al., 2002). Furthermore, married couples' attachment classifications on the AAI were associated with their individual-level observed communication and perspective-taking skills and their interactional synchrony at a dyadic level of analysis; self-report measures predicted neither (Bouthillier et al., 2002). Similarly, the AAI predicted maternal sensitivity and child attachment security, while self-reported attachment styles did not (Bernier & Matte-Gagne, 2011). On the other hand, attachment styles predicted self-reported marital satisfaction while attachment state of mind did not.

Another relevant distinction between the two methodological approaches is that the AAI assesses unconscious mental processes while self-report measures assess conscious processes. Namely, coding of the AAI is based on the degree of coherence and types of distortions between semantic (verbal) mental representations of attachment and episodic representations (as reflected in the supporting examples of the adjectives used to describe each parent). Self-report measures, on the other hand, rely solely upon semantic descriptions of attachment relationships. Although neither of these approaches assesses nonverbal or procedural aspects of attachment representations (Crittenden, 2006), the IWMs reflected in the AAI capture more of the unconscious general state of mind regarding attachment than do self-report measures.

This difference becomes especially important when the population of interest is clinical or characterized by a greater probability of insecure attachment, as is the case among individuals with a history of violence or trauma. Thus, by relying upon discourse analysis, the AAI reveals the systematic distortions of memory and emotion that potentially confound most self-report questionnaires of attachment. For these reasons, this book focuses primarily on research grounded in the developmental psychology paradigms of the Strange Situation and the AAI.

Secure Attachment

Secure Attachment in Children

The attachment category of secure attachment is associated with the mother's warmth, responsiveness, and emotional availability when interacting with the child at home. In the Strange Situation, the securely attached child typically plays with the toys, may react to the separation with some distress, but then reconnects with the mother either physically or visually upon her reentry into the room; the child is then soothed by the mother and rapidly returns to play. The child's use of the mother as a secure base from which to explore the environment as well as a safe haven from whom to receive comfort and reassurance is not only effective but is internalized by the child in the ability to self-soothe and in the development of positive expectations of self and others. Securely attached children are socially competent, positive, and popular and expect that others will be available to them (Bohlin, Hagekull, & Rydell, 2000; Ziv, Oppenheim & Sagi-Schwartz, 2004).

Secure/Autonomous Attachment in Adults

Approximately 58% of mothers in North American nonclinical samples are classified as secure/autonomous on the AAI (Bakermans-Kranenburg & van IJzendoorn, 2009). As can be seen by responses on the AAI, the secure adult may or may not have had a happy childhood and may even exhibit awareness of relationship problems by describing himself or herself as avoidant on self-report measures (Jacobvitz, Curran, & Moller, 2002). Nonetheless, the adult clearly values attachment relationships, responds to the questions coherently, has access to both positive and negative memories without being overwhelmed by them, and engages the interviewer in a collaborative way. Being securely attached does not of course preclude the possibility of abusive or traumatic experiences. However, an individual who is securely attached as a child or gradually becomes securely attached as an adult will respond to the trauma experience in a substantively different way, as revealed in the following case study.

> Ellen described a long history of rejection by both of her parents. She was sent to a children's home for 1½ years by her biological father after her mother left following numerous experiences of intimate partner violence. At Christmas, Ellen was the only child left in the orphanage, although her father was supposed to pick her up. She reported being frequently physically abused by her father and sleeping with a knife under her pillow. She recounted being locked in her bedroom except for meals and bathroom breaks the whole summer after eighth grade because she had friends over without permission. Her mother (with whom she later resided) would go for months without speaking to her or acknowledging her. Her experience of sexual abuse by an uncle with whom she lived during the summer began when she was 8 years old. Nevertheless, she acknowledged that in many ways it was preferable to what was going on at home in that she received more love and respect from her aunt and uncle than at home. She stated that, as a teen and young adult, she had a long history of unsuccessful relationships, drug abuse, and prostitution. But she was able to hold on to and acknowledge contradictory feelings simultaneously, describing her mother as annoying and understandable. Moreover, her valuing of attachment relationships was prominent in her responses on the AAI—she clearly valued her relationship with her daughter and was forgiving of her mother. She noted that she had always had good friendships with women and attributed her increased security and more positive self-concept to meeting her husband several years earlier—their relationship had developed slowly and in a healthy way. She would probably be an example of earned security—that is, an individual who experienced negative parenting in childhood but was able to rely on alternative support figures and thus to form a secure attachment with her infant (Saunders, Jacobvitz, Zaccagnino, Beverung, & Hazen, 2011).

Parenting by Secure/Autonomous Adults

A meta-analysis of studies exploring the relationship between parents' attachment representations (as measured by the AAI) and their children's attachment (as assessed in the Strange Situation) determined that a mother's secure/autonomous attachment is highly predictive of her children's security of attachment (van IJzendoorn, 1995). To a lesser but still significant degree, a mother's security of attachment is also predictive of her ability to read her infant's attachment signals, suggesting that she not only perceived her child's emotional cues but also responded to them more promptly and adequately than did parents of insecure children. Furthermore, secure/autonomous attachment in a parent is associated with openness and flexibility in acknowledging emotions in herself and her children (DeOliveira, Moran, & Pederson, 2005). Other longitudinal research on mothers who were assessed on the AAI prenatally and in interaction with their children at 14 months of age similarly found that secure/autonomous mothers were more sensitive and responsive and that their children were more cooperative (Flykt, Kanninen, Sinkkonen, & Punamaki, 2010; Kennedy, 2008). Secure mothers also exhibited more delight and encouragement of their child's exploration behavior (Britner, Marvin, & Pianta, 2005). In fact, Belsky (1997) has characterized secure/autonomous parenting as "high-investment parenting" in evolutionary terms. It should be noted, however, that even though a mother's state of mind regarding attachment on the AAI is predictive of her child's attachment behavior in the Strange Situation and even her child's IQ, there remains a gap in this transmission that does not appear to be explained by maternal sensitivity, at least in low-risk middle-class samples (Bailey, Moran, Pederson, & Bento, 2007; Busch & Lieberman, 2010; Jacobvitz, Leon, & Hazen, 2006; Raval et al., 2001; van IJzendoorn, Schuengel, & Bakermans-Kranenburg, 1999; Ward & Carlson, 1995).

With regard to any potential transmission of trauma, it can be assumed that secure/autonomous parents would be more able to regulate their own affect during frustrating interactions with their child (thereby warding off their own impulsive punitive reactions), to monitor and assess potential sources of danger to their child (thus protecting their child from abuse by others), and to detect and respond to their child's nonverbal or verbal expressions of discomfort or fear in the company of others (thus interrupting any ongoing abuse or maltreatment of the child by others).

Secure/autonomous adults are clearly the most equipped to support and protect their children from maltreatment. In addition, the securely attached child's positive expectations of self and others will facilitate help seeking from others in situations of threat.

Avoidant Attachment

Avoidant Attachment in Children

Avoidant attachment is associated with the parent's insensitivity and rejection of the child precisely when the child is distressed or needy. The parent may even exhibit an actual aversion to physical contact with the child. Therefore, the child learns that the best way to maintain connection with this parent is through deactivating the attachment needs that appear to drive the parent away (Izard & Kobak, 1991). Consequently, in the Strange Situation, the avoidant child will actively avoid or rebuff the mother upon her return to the room, instead focusing on the toys. The apparent function of this behavior is to emphasize nonverbally to the mother that the child is not making any demands upon her for reassurance. While successful in maintaining a connection with the parent, the compulsively self-reliant child unfortunately does not learn how to recognize and modulate negative affect (Spangler & Grossmann, 1993). In conversations with their mothers, such children minimize emotions (Dubois-Comtois, Cyr, & Moss 2011), and interactions with teachers are often negative (O'Connor & McCartney, 2006). In their interactions with peers, avoidant children tend to exhibit more instrumental aggression and are more vulnerable to the effects of contextual risk (Belsky & Fearon, 2002; McElwain, Cox, Burchinal, & Macfie, 2003). Therefore, they are at risk for physical aggression toward others and perhaps for physical aggression by others.

Dismissing Attachment in Adults

In this attachment category, comprising approximately 23% of North American low-risk samples (Bakermans-Kranenburg & van IJzendoorn, 2009), the adult responds to the AAI by either idealizing or denigrating the parents without supporting examples. Dismissing adults minimize the importance of attachment relationships and self-report little overt distress, presenting as "more normal than normal," thus often displaying the bias of seeing themselves as secure on self-report measures of attachment (Crittenden, Partridge, & Claussen, 1991; Jacobvitz et al., 2002; Spangler & Grossmann, 1993). At the same time, they exhibit marked physiological arousal when distressed (Dozier & Kobak, 1992; Mikulincer, 1998). The following case study demonstrates this attempt to deactivate attachment needs.

> Kathleen was sexually abused by her father from ages 8 to 12, but described it as more of a teaching relationship; he completely withdrew when she confronted him. She reported much rejection, stating, "I always felt like an intruder in my own house." She was told by her parents that she was selfish, would never be a good mother and looked like a whore. She recounted that her coping strategies at the time included rebellion, blocking of memories, and self-reliance. ("I never sought physical comfort. I licked my own wounds.") Kathleen left home at age 15, living with an older boyfriend until she graduated from high school. She currently denied any effect of her relationships with her parents on her. ("There's no way to please these people. At this point, my parents have no influence on me.") Her description of herself was glowing. ("I'm a wonderful mother— I have very good parenting skills. I do so much better than other women who've been abused.") Most jarringly, she noted that the reason for her participation in this interview study of incest survivors was to demonstrate how trivial the experience of incest was in her life. Thus, like the avoidant child who has learned to deactivate her attachment needs and consequently is unaware of her own emotions and feelings, the dismissing adult similarly works hard to minimize the importance of attachment relationships.

Parenting by Dismissing Adults

Not only is a dismissing parent more likely to have a child who is characterized as avoidant in the Strange Situation (van IJzendoorn, 1995), but observations of the mother's interactions with the child suggest that she is more likely to minimize her child's emotions as well as her own, is less warm, sensitive, and responsive than are secure mothers, and can be characterized in evolutionary terms as engaging in "low-investment parenting" (Adam, Gunnar, & Tanaka, 2004; Belsky, 1997; Chen, Lin, & Li, 2012; DeOliveira et al., 2005; Flykt et al., 2010; Kennedy, 2008; Pederson, Gleason, Moran, & Bento, 1998). Similarly, a dimensional scoring of the AAI found that dismissing attachment was negatively correlated with maternal sensitivity, while unrelated to a dimension of maternal autonomy support (Whipple, Bernier, & Mageau, 2011).

Dismissing attachment has several implications for the intergenerational transmission of trauma or violence. A dismissing parent's lack of self-awareness, inability to regulate negative emotional states, and underlying physiological arousal in situations of stress combine to greatly increase her potential to actually physically abuse her children. Furthermore, idealization of her own parents, especially if they were abusive, may preclude the dismissing mother from consciously deciding to respond differently to her own child. In other words, the dismissing parent's inability to empathize with her own feelings of hurt and rejection will inevitably interfere with her ability to empathize with similar feelings in her child. Even if a dismissing parent is not herself abusive to her child, her general insensitivity to her child, especially when the child is distressed, may interfere with her ability to protect her child from others. Finally, to the extent that an avoidant child feels unloved and unwanted, he or she may be more vulnerable to abuse by others inside and outside the home. Therefore, dismissing attachment in a parent can significantly increase the vulnerability of her child to maltreatment either by her or someone else.

Anxious Attachment

Anxious/Ambivalent Attachment in Children

This attachment category is associated with the parent's inconsistency, ranging from neglect, on one hand, to overprotectiveness or intrusiveness in the child's play (Cassidy & Berlin, 1994). In the Strange Situation, the anxious/ambivalent child displays difficulty attending to the toys and instead seems preoccupied with the mother. In order to gain the attention of this inattentive parent, the child heightens the display of negative affect. When the parent becomes annoyed by the child's fussy, angry, and demanding behaviors, the child shifts to a clingy, coy, guilt-inducing demeanor, leading to a vicious cycle between the parent and the child

(Crittenden, 1997). Although effective in eliciting the parent's attention, the child is never fully able to be soothed by the parent or to use the parent as a secure base. Anxious/ambivalent children are more likely to exaggerate emotions in conversations with their mothers, to exhibit dependent and fussy behavior with others, and to display less self-assertion with friends, less pretend play, and less confidence in the availability of others (Cassidy & Berlin, 1994; Dubois-Comtois et al., 2011; McElwain et al., 2003; Ziv et al., 2004). They are often babied but disliked by teachers (Main, 2000). Anxious/ambivalent attachment has also been associated in adolescents with withdrawal, internalization, and introversion (Nakashi-Eisikovits, Dutra, & Westen, 2002).

Preoccupied Attachment in Adults

Comprising approximately 19% of mothers in North American nonclinical samples (Bakermans-Kranenburg & van IJzendoorn, 2009), on the AAI, the preoccupied adult seems to be unable to move beyond past experiences with her own parent, leading to a rambling narrative and long, drawn-out, confusing stories. Thus, she displays low coherence because of the superfluous, confused, and irrelevant information throughout the interview. Preoccupation may take a variety of forms, including passivity, angry or conflicted narratives, or fearful preoccupation with the attachment figure, often observed in connection with an experience of trauma. The preoccupied individual does not typically have the self-awareness that would be required to accurately self-report on written measures of attachment (Jacobvitz et al., 2002). Other research suggests that the preoccupied adult tends to be dependent but dissatisfied in intimate relationships, seeking but unable to make use of others' support, displaying intense and volatile emotions, including affective disorders, and tending to view conflict and expressions of anger as indications of intimacy and closeness (Main & Goldwyn, 1998; Mikulincer, 1998; Pietromonaco & Barrett, 1997, 2000; Ward, Lee, & Polan, 2006). The following case study highlights some of these characteristics.

> Susan was sexually abused by her father, with whom there was not much connection. In contrast, in a long and meandering interview, she focused greatly on her mother in the AAI, with very mixed ambivalent feelings. She referred to her mother's "sweet lovely dis-

position" but was inconsistent with specific details about her mother —for example, her mother was nonsupportive when the abuse was disclosed, telling her to stay away from her father when he was drinking. Most tellingly, Susan recounted a combination of neglect and overinvolvement by her mother. For example, her mother left her with a babysitter full time (with few intervening visits) from the time Susan was 6 months to 2 years of age because it was more convenient for her mother than having to take a subway to drop her off and pick her up. At the same time, Susan described her mother as "extremely protective" of her emotionally, with her mother going into elaborate detail about sex when Susan was 4 years old and then inspecting her vagina when she was 13 to see if she was still a virgin. Susan also revealed excessive attentiveness to her mother. ("I wanted my mother to be happy. I didn't want to be prettier than she was. I made excuses for her.") The result of Susan's upbringing could be seen in her current relationships. For example, she exhibited behavior similar to what she condemned in her mother—she mentioned leaving her own son with her mother for 3 years because her mother wanted him, while describing herself as overprotective with her child. She also exhibited the low self-esteem and emotional dependency common among preoccupied individuals ("My boyfriend has been out of my life for 7 years—in and out—mostly out, but mostly in my head, too. It's been going on more in my head than it's real.") This case study emphasizes the impact of an adult's preoccupation with her own parent and her partner to the detriment of her caregiving for her own child.

Parenting by Preoccupied Adults

Parents who are preoccupied by and dependent upon their own attachment figure (whether it be a parent or a partner) will necessarily have difficulty effectively engaging in caregiving toward their child (Mayseless, 1998). Consequently, they are more likely to mistrust their own ability to sufficiently protect their child and are more apt to perceive the environment as dangerous (Mayseless, 1998). One could certainly see how a history of trauma as well as the current experience of living in a dangerous household or neighborhood could contribute to these beliefs in any parent. Unfortunately, as a consequence of these beliefs, a preoccupied parent is more likely to closely monitor and overprotect her child and to foster dependency to the point of being intrusive (Adam et al., 2004; Cassidy & Berlin, 1994). In fact, preoccupied attachment in a parent was negatively correlated with the mother's support of the child's autonomy while unrelated to her sensitivity (Whipple et al., 2011). Given the inherent impossibility, however, of monitoring a child fully ("one cannot be alert, involved, and available *all* the time," Mayseless, 1998, p. 29), the preoccupied parent will inevitably become overwhelmed with the parenting task and will vacillate between frustration and anger toward the child and neglect. Indeed, mothers of ambivalent children were observed to show less positive affect in play while reporting more separation anxiety (Harel & Scher, 2003). Even so, they failed to respond effectively to their child's bid for attention after a stressful separation. This parenting stance combined with the anxious/ambivalent child's hyperactivation of attachment needs in order to elicit the attention of the inconsistent parent leads to a frustrating interaction for both.

There are several ways in which this parenting style could contribute to a child's risk for maltreatment. The preoccupied parent's negative affectivity and problems with emotion regulation could lead to reactive aggression against the child. Alternatively, the parent's continuing preoccupation with her own parent or partner could interfere with her protectiveness if that parent or partner happens to be abusive. Moreover, the parent's inconsistency and intermittent neglect of her child could prevent her from recognizing the child's distress due to other sources of abuse. The anxious/ambivalent child's coy behavior could be misinterpreted as a confusing sexualized message, increasing the child's vulnerability to abuse inside and outside the home. Finally, the generally inconsistent and annoying behavior of the anxious/ambivalent child may impede caregivers (including teachers and other adults) from attending to the child's needs. Therefore, this parent-child dyad may be at particular risk for the intergenerational transmission of violence and trauma.

Disorganized Attachment

Disorganized Attachment in Children

It eventually became apparent to attachment researchers that the three-category classification of children described above did not seem to capture the behavior in the Strange Situation of children with a known history of trauma (Carlson et al., 1989). Main and Solomon (1986, 1990) noted the following characteristics of these children's disorganized or disoriented behavior: odd contradictory approach-avoidant behaviors with the attachment figure, such as approaching the parent upon reunion with the gaze averted; freezing or exhibiting trance-like dazed expressions at the parent's approach; asking to be picked up and then heaving themselves out of their parents' arms. In other words, these children seemed to lack a systematic strategy for seeking reassurance and comfort from the mother or even gaining access to her. The behavior of these children in the Strange Situation suggests several pathways to disorganized attachment—either from direct abuse of the child or from the mother's unresolved trauma (DeOliveira, Bailey, Moran, & Pederson, 2004). Children who are categorized as disorganized (D) are also given one of the organized attachment classifications as evidence of an underlying strategy. Disorganized attachment is specific to a particular relationship, not to the child; that is, a child is usually disorganized with only one parent (Lyons-Ruth & Jacobvitz, 1999). Therefore, it appears to be unrelated to temperament, constitutional variables, emotionality ratings at 12, 18, or 24 months, or gender (Lyons-Ruth & Jacobvitz, 1999; van IJzendoorn et al., 1999). Genetic factors may interact with an experience of trauma to predict its occurrence (see Chapter 4). Given the pertinence of this attachment category to the experience of trauma, the behavior of latency-age disorganized children is described below.

Unresolved Attachment in Adults

The adult counterpart of the disorganized child is the unresolved (U) category, denoting 18% of North American nonclinical mothers as an additional code (Bakermans-Kranenburg & van IJzendoorn, 2009), although including many more in clinical samples. They are so classified on the basis of apparent lapses in reasoning or dissociated ideas or memories when responding to questions on the AAI about childhood experiences of loss or trauma. As such, both adults with a history of trauma and those with a history of disorganized attachment are more likely to be classified as unresolved on the AAI (Subic-Wrana, Beetz, Wiltink, & Beutel, 2011; Weinfield, Whaley, & Egeland, 2004). A parent's unresolved loss may similarly lead to disorganized attachment in children (Hughes, Turton,

Hopper, McGauley, & Fonagy, 2001; Jacobvitz et al., 2006). Furthermore, an experience of loss can trigger the emotions associated with a previous experience of childhood trauma (Hughes, Turton, Hopper, McGauley & Fonagy, 2004). What is important to reiterate is that it is not the trauma or loss per se, but instead its lack of resolution that is important for its effects on the unresolved adult and on that adult's parenting (Ainsworth & Eichberg, 1991; Schuengel, Bakermans-Kranenburg, & van IJzendoorn, 1999).

In addition to the unresolved category, the Cannot Classify (CC) category is used to designate a collapse of an attachment strategy in the AAI at a global level. Both U and CC individuals are typically characterized by severe affect dysregulation, as evidenced by increased rates of PTSD, borderline personality disorders, substance abuse, dissociation, and other internalizing disorders (Agrawal, Gunderson, Holmes, & Lyons-Ruth, 2004; Alexander et al., 1998; Bailey, Moran, & Pederson, 2007; Bakermans-Kranenburg & van IJzendoorn, 2009; Borelli, Goshin, Joestl, Clark, & Byrne, 2010; Buchheim, George, Liebl, Moser, & Benecke, 2007; Madigan, Vaillancourt, McKibbon, & Benoit, 2012; Riggs et al., 2007; Stovall-McClough & Cloitre, 2006; van IJzendoorn & Bakermans-Kranenburg, 2008). Like children with disorganized attachment, unresolved adults are given an additional secure or insecure classification as indication of an underlying strategy. The following case study illustrates some of the implications of these experiences.

Frances was vaginally and anally raped by her father at age 5. She described her father as highly unpredictable, engaging in random acts of physical violence against her for his apparent amusement. She compared him to Ted Bundy. At the same time, she recounted major neglect by her mother, noting that although her father traveled frequently, her mother would occasionally leave her at home for up to a week at a time to care for her younger brother when she was no more than 9 years old. She described her mother as bizarre and probably mentally ill, making the children eat rotting food from the refrigerator and beating a pet to death with a mallet as punishment for Frances's misbehavior. On another occasion, her mother attempted to drown her in the bathtub. In spite of the severe abuse by her father, she described herself as closer to him than to her mother, saying that she was always glad for him to return home as a

break from her mother. Frances had been diagnosed with dissociative identity disorder, and an alter personality emerged during the
course of the interview. Frances was married with two young daughters, but was in the process of separating from her husband because
of his expectation of sexual intimacy. She reported being unable to
sit at the dinner table with her family because of flashbacks of her
father's temper outbursts during meals. Moreover, while there was
no evidence of her husband's sexual abuse of their children, her
frequent withdrawal from her children and her insistence that her
husband bathe them because of her own negative associations with
bathtubs could clearly have increased their risk for abuse. Thus, the
impact of her symptoms on the family context could potentially contribute to an intergenerational cycle of abuse, especially in interaction with her husband's history of trauma.

PATHWAYS TO DISORGANIZED ATTACHMENT

There appear to be a number of different pathways to disorganized attachment and, by extension, to cycles of violence and trauma. Maltreatment
by a parent may be the most obvious pathway. However, different groups
of researchers have discovered that certain parenting behaviors, even in
the absence of overt abuse or neglect by the parent, are associated with
disorganized attachment behaviors in the child. Further research suggests that social-environmental risks (including family context and low
socioeconomic status) may also contribute to disorganized attachment,
with similar outcomes. Finally, the underlying attachment security of the
parent or the child is associated with different patterns of interactions
seen in parent-child dyads, even if the parent is unresolved and the child
is disorganized. The following sections describe these various pathways.

Frightened or Frightening Behavior

On the most concrete level, the unresolved parent engages in frightened
or frightening (FR) behavior toward the child, reacting either to the child
or to some unseen stimulus in the environment as a source of threat
(Main & Hesse, 1990). For example, the parent may threaten the child
for no particular reason, engaging in seemingly predatory types of behavior such as stalking the child while crawling on hands and knees or plac-

ing her hands around the child's throat from behind. The parent may dissociate, signaling to the child that the parent is not present. Because of unresolved fears triggered by the child, the parent may appear to be frightened by the child and may physically retreat from the child (Hesse & Main, 1999). The parent may engage in sexualized behavior toward the child—a pattern of behavior first described by Sroufe and Ward (1980), in which, for example, a mother was observed to ask her young son for a kiss, grabbing his buttock when he turned away and then pulling him toward her to kiss him on the lips. In all of these instances, the child is put into the paradoxical position of needing to turn to the same attachment figure for comfort who is causing the child's fear—Hesse and Main (1999) have referred to this conundrum as "fright without solution." Hesse and Main (1999) also made clear that FR behaviors do not result from the parent's fear of something external but observable to the child, especially if the parent quickly reassures the child, or to harsh or angry parental behavior toward the child that is remedied by the child's compliance.

When subtypes of FR behavior were examined, Hesse and Main (2006) concluded that there are three primary forms of FR behavior—frightened, threatening, and dissociative—and that they parallel the classic mammalian reactions to fright: flight, attack, and freezing behavior. Interestingly, the dissociative-FR subscale has been found to be the only subscale related to unresolved attachment and the best predictor of disorganized attachment (Abrams et al., 2006).

Parental Atypical Behaviors and Hostile or Helpless Parenting

FR behaviors do not seem to completely explain the development of disorganized attachment. Therefore, Lyons-Ruth and her colleagues coded Strange Situation videotapes for five maternal atypical behaviors—affective communication errors, role confusion, intrusiveness/negativity, disorientation, and the mother's withdrawal from the child (Lyons-Ruth, Bronfman, & Parsons, 1999). On the basis of this AMBIANCE coding system, they concluded that affective communication errors, consisting of contradictory communications, inappropriate responses, or a mother's failure to respond to the child's clear communication, were most predictive of disorganized attachment. Researchers disagree as to whether these atypical parental behaviors explain the relationship between unresolved

states of mind and disorganized attachment or whether they are independent and additive predictors of disorganization (Goldberg, Benoit,
Blokland, & Madigan, 2003; Madigan, Bakermans-Kranenburg, et al.,
2006; Madigan, Moran, & Pederson, 2006). In any case, they appear to
remain relatively stable over time and therefore may be a useful focus for
parent-child interventions (Madigan, Voci, & Benoit, 2011).

All mothers of disorganized children exhibit affective communication
errors. However, subsequent analyses of these observed parental behaviors determined that negative-intrusive and role-confused behaviors were
highly correlated even though they represented an apparently contradictory mix of rejecting and attention-seeking behaviors toward the infant.
These parental behaviors were labeled "hostile" or self-referential (Lyons-
Ruth, Melnick, Bronfman, Sherry, & Llanas, 2004). In contrast, mothers
exhibiting the parenting behaviors characterized by fearfulness, withdrawal, and inhibition were labeled as "helpless-fearful" regarding attachment. Their children would approach the mothers, express distress, and
seek some physical contact, while also exhibiting behaviors such as freezing, apprehension, and avoidance in interactions with the mother (Lyons-
Ruth et al., 2004).

In order to explore the respective histories of mothers displaying either
hostile or helpless-fearful behaviors toward their children, Lyons-Ruth
and her colleagues developed a new coding system for the AAI that more
thoroughly reflected an adult's experience of trauma. They noted several
limitations of the AAI's coding of unresolved attachment (Lyons-Ruth et
al., 2003). For example, only that portion of the AAI that specifically
inquires about trauma or loss is coded for U and then only if the respondent actually acknowledges a history of trauma or loss (a self-report that
may be less likely among severely traumatized or dissociative individuals).
Furthermore, the AAI was originally developed on a middle-class low-risk
sample as opposed to a clinical population experiencing chronic trauma.

Therefore, Lyons-Ruth and her colleagues relied upon discourse patterns throughout the whole AAI while also asking more explicitly about
respondents' experience of maltreatment (which they termed "pervasively
unintegrated states of mind"). They then derived the following codes of
hostile/helpless (H/H) states of mind: global devaluation of a caregiver
often combined with identification with a hostile caregiver (reflecting
contradictory and unintegrated preoccupations with a caregiver), recurrent references to fearful affect (that may lack an unidentified source),

the sense of self as bad, laughter at recollections of pain (suggesting affective numbing), and ruptured attachments with family members in adulthood (indicative of intense, unstable relationships). Not only did this coding system not overlap with the U or CC categories, but it was a much better predictor of disorganized-insecure behavior in children of these parents (Lyons-Ruth et al., 2003, 2005). H/H states of mind were associated with mothers' histories of emotional abuse, sexual abuse, and physical neglect, with their role confusion, and with their risk for maltreating or neglecting their infants, thus demonstrating their role in intergenerational cycles of trauma and violence (Frigerio, Costantino, Ceppi, & Barone, 2013; Milot et al., 2014; Vulliez-Coady, Obsuth, Torreiro-Casal, Ellertsdottir, & Lyons-Ruth, 2013).

Parents' Abdication of Caregiving

Another perspective on the parenting behavior of the unresolved adult was offered by Solomon and George (1999b), who proposed that the essence of disorganized attachment was the parent's activation of the child's attachment system (for example, by frightening the child with strong parental rejection or threats to abandon or send the child away), followed by a failure to resolve the child's need for attachment. Consistent with Hesse and Main's (1999) description of parental behaviors that are not associated with disorganized attachment, Solomon and George noted the importance of the secure mother's reparative behavior in reassuring a child who has been accidentally frightened by the parent. In contrast, the unresolved parent may become punitive and enraged, may withdraw from the child, even locking herself in a room, or may engage in the role-reversing behavior noted by Hesse and Main (1999) and by Lyons-Ruth, Bronfman, and Parsons (1999). In any case, by seeing herself as helpless with regard to her child and in failing to terminate the child's attachment behavior, the unresolved parent is abdicating her role as a parent and also passively placing her child at risk for abuse by others. This pattern of parenting stems in large part from the mother's own experience of a "rage pattern" in her family of origin, characterized by physical or verbal abuse, unpredictable rage, or substance abuse. In fact, 87% of mothers of disorganized children, even in a middle-class sample, described experiencing this rage parenting, as opposed to only 20% who experienced lack of resolution due to loss or trauma (Solomon & George,

2006). Therefore, when asked directly, mothers of disorganized children frequently acknowledge mental representations of threat and helplessness that could explain their abdication of parenting.

Disorganized Attachment as a Dissociative Process

A mother's dissociative behavior was found to be the only mediator between a mother's unresolved trauma and her child's disorganized attachment (Abrams et al., 2006). Disoriented behavior is one of the atypical parental behaviors assessed by the AMBIANCE system (Lyons-Ruth, Bronfman, & Parsons, 1999) and could also be reflected in Solomon and George's (1999b) notion of parents' abdication of caregiving. Furthermore, the dissociation may be accompanied by role confusion and self-referential behavior, referenced by all three of the previous perspectives on parenting behavior described above.

So why would dissociation and role reversal contribute to disorganized attachment? Liotti (1992) attempted to provide an answer. He stated that the child's very presence may elicit reminders of the parent's own history of abuse, leading the parent to attempt to reverse roles with the child and to rely upon the child to control the parent's anxiety. Unfortunately, the parent's frightening abandonment of the caregiving role creates a dilemma for the child—even though the parent is the source of the problem, the child will necessarily look to the source of the fear (the attachment figure) to allay this fear. The child's only solution is to develop multiple incompatible models of the parent and the self, resulting in the development of dissociation in the child.

Support for this notion can be found from several sources. First, in a longitudinal study, disorganized attachment in infancy predicted dissociation at age 19 years, even when controlling for intervening trauma (Ogawa, Sroufe, Weinfield, Carlson, & Egeland, 1997). Similarly, in a sample of 112 incest survivors, the subsample characterized by dissociative identity disorder (including Frances in the previous case study) portrayed themselves as distant from their mothers and described their fathers as their primary attachment figures—even though the abuse perpetrated by these men had been especially severe (Anderson & Alexander, 1996). In some cases, the father actively interfered with the mother-child relationship; in other families, the mother's mental illness disrupted her capacity for parenting. For whatever reason, the child had to turn for comfort to the only attachment figure perceived to be available, requiring the child to separate her view of the father as the source of the solution from her view of him as the source of the problem. Thus, for this child, fear became associated with soothing (cf. Liotti, 2011). This finding also emphasized the danger of viewing attachment relationships only in dyadic terms—the family context explains a great deal about the dyad (see Chapter 3).

Another consequence of this compartmentalized IWM of relationships is the development of the "drama triangle" (Karpman, 1968, cited in Liotti, 2008), in which the attachment figure is seen as the persecutor (engaging in frightening behavior) but also positively as the rescuer and possibly as the victim (of either unseen dangers or even of the child to the degree that the parent seems frightened of the child). The self is viewed as the victim of the parent, as the role-reversing rescuer of the parent, and frequently as an evil persecutor of the parent by seemingly causing the parent to be afraid. The last role was demonstrated in a study in which dissociation was directly correlated with the degree to which subjects described themselves as bad or evil (Loos & Alexander, 2001). Given that dissociation is strongly predictive of both violent behavior (Daisy & Hien, 2014; Narang & Contreras, 2000; Simoneti, Scott, & Murphy, 2000) and vulnerability to victimization by others (Hulette, Kaehler, & Freyd, 2011), this dynamic is particularly relevant to cycles of violence.

Multiple Risk Environments

Another pathway to disorganized attachment, other than a parent's maltreatment of a child or the parent's history of unresolved trauma or loss, is through the parent's experience of multiple risk environments. In a meta-analysis of 59 nonmaltreated high-risk samples and 10 maltreated samples of children, the cumulative effects of five socioeconomic risk factors (low income, substance abuse, young maternal age at child birth, low level of education, and single parenthood) contributed as much to disorganization as did child maltreatment, albeit with less underlying attachment insecurity than among maltreated children (Cyr et al., 2010). In fact, as opposed to the previously described absence of an effect of maternal sensitivity in explaining the transmission of attachment security, a meta-analysis found that, in low socioeconomic status groups, maternal insensitivity (rather than pathological or atypical parenting) did lead to disorganized attachment (van IJzendoorn et al., 1999). Similarly, in a sample of adolescent mothers, insensitive parenting explained the link between a mother's unresolved state of mind and her child's disorganized attachment (Bailey, Moran, Pederson, & Bento, 2007). Furthermore, disorganized attachment in children is substantially more common in families characterized by violence, affect dysregulation, substance abuse, and rage and frightening behavior on the part of family members (Solomon & George, 2011b; Zeanah et al., 1999).

The ramifications of these multiple risk environments are many and complicated. A parent's history of trauma or unresolved attachment could either be correlated with or could lead to an increased exposure to these risk environments. For example, substance abuse stemming from a parent's history of trauma will necessarily cause other environmental and perhaps even biological ill effects upon a child. Furthermore, these environmental risks could affect parenting behavior and the child's vulnerability to problematic parenting and to abuse by others (Bernier & Meins, 2008). The direct and interactive effects of these socioenvironmental risks with the child's genetic and neurobiological substrate add yet other layers of complexity. At this point, it is sufficient to note that stresses outside of the mother-child dyad are just as important as the mother's history of trauma and even overt experiences of maltreatment in undermining a child's security of attachment and in setting the stage for a cycle of violence.

Disorganized Attachment as a Response to Danger and Unpredictability

Crittenden (2001) has argued that the behavior of many maltreated children is by no means "disorganized." In fact, according to Crittenden, "secure" behavior only makes sense within the context of safe, protective, and nondeceptive parenting. Instead of thinking of the set goal of attachment as maintaining proximity with the caregiver (i.e., a species-level response of humans to potentially dangerous situations; Main, 1977), Crittenden has proposed that adaptation should be conceptualized as behavior that is functional for the individual to ensure the availability of the caregiver (Landa & Duschinsky, 2013). From an evolutionary perspective, "flexibility and variability, far more than security and its mental or behavioral correlates, are what enable humans to survive so many unpleasant and dangerous conditions" (Crittenden, 2001, p. 594). Furthermore, preconscious self-protective behavior based on an immediate reaction to fear may be much more adaptive in a dangerous situation than more time-consuming behavior that requires conscious thought (Crittenden, 2001). Thus, given the prevalence of abusive and neglectful parenting, it is essential that children's awareness of danger and threat is just as relevant to many children's survival as is awareness of comfort and safety.

Frankenhuis and Del Giudice (2012) similarly noted that hypersensitivity to danger among children living in a harsh or hostile family serves an important evolutionary function. When a parent is unreliable and unpredictable, more plastic or variable behavior on the part of the child may more realistically match the need for sampling the parent's ever-changing behavioral cues. There are certainly definite costs to the child of not displaying the more "mature" and specialized behavior that is characteristic of a child growing up in a safer, more predictable family. However, the miscalibration resulting from failing to display a variety of behaviors with a changeable parent can be deadly. Thus, "disorganized" behavior may actually represent the most adaptive and functional behavior to ensure an unpredictable parent's availability to a child. Similarly, consistent with a life history perspective, the aggressive and risky externalizing behaviors often associated with disorganized attachment may actually be highly adaptive to life within a harsh, hostile, or unpredictable family environment. Therefore, the disorganized child's behavior must be evaluated for its adaptiveness to the attachment relationship in which it developed. Unfortunately, of course, behavior that was adaptive to this relationship may no longer be adaptive in other settings such as school or other less dangerous environments.

Underlying Attachment Security

As described previously, the coding of disorganized attachment in the Strange Situation and the coding of unresolved attachment on the AAI are accompanied by a secondary categorization of the child and adult as either secure or insecure. The implications for this distinction can be seen in comparisons between parents of disorganized-insecure (D-insecure) and disorganized-secure (D-secure) infants and between unresolved-insecure and unresolved-secure adults. Mothers of D-insecure children are more likely to have themselves grown up in chaotic and abusive homes, to have experienced severe psychosocial problems (reflecting the risk environments discussed above), and to exhibit hostile-intrusive behavior, role boundary confusion, and more atypical behaviors overall in their interactions with their children (Lyons-Ruth, Repacholi, McLeod, & Silva, 1991; Lyons-Ruth, Bronfman, & Parsons, 1999). These mothers thus exhibit the hostile parenting behaviors and self-reported hostile IWMs of relationships described earlier. They are also more likely to be unpredictable in their parenting behavior.

In contrast, mothers of D-secure children are more likely to have experienced loss, such as parental death in childhood or parental divorce, are more likely to withdraw from their infants at home without actively rejecting them, and are more likely to exhibit frightened-inhibited behavior with no evidence of frightening behavior (Lyons-Ruth et al., 1991; Lyons-Ruth, Bronfman, & Parsons, 1999). Their display of FR behaviors is at significantly lower levels than among the mothers of disorganized-insecure children (Jacobvitz et al., 2006). Moreover, although hesitant and fearful with their child, mothers of D-secure children ultimately tend to comply with their infants' bids for attention (Lyons-Ruth, Bronfman, & Atwood, 1999). These mothers fit the description of helpless-fearful parenting described earlier. Therefore, a disorganized child's underlying attachment security appears to be associated with less intrusive and hostile behaviors on the part of the parent. However, D-secure infants have negative outcomes equal to those of D-insecure children, including elevated cortisol in reaction to minor stressors (Spangler & Grossmann, 1993) and distress during their interactions with their respective parents at home (Lyons-Ruth, Bronfman, & Parsons, 1999). For example, an infant's experience of maternal withdrawal (more often seen with the mothers of D-secure children) predicted that child's borderline symptoms and suicidality or self-injury in late adolescence (Lyons-Ruth, Bureau, Holmes, Easterbrooks, & Brooks, 2013).

Similar comparisons have been made between U-insecure parents and U-secure parents. Only U-insecure mothers display significant FR behaviors and they are more likely either to have experienced loss at a younger or to have lost an attachment figure than unresolved mothers who do not engage in FR behaviors (Jacobvitz, Hazen, & Riggs, 1997). In contrast, U-secure mothers display even fewer FR behaviors in their interactions with their children than do secure mothers (Schuengel et al., 1999).

Moreover, their underlying security appears to be associated with these women's decreased risk of psychopathology (Ward et al., 2006). However, while comparisons between dyads of unresolved mothers and disorganized children may suggest the benefit of underlying attachment security, most of this research fails to consider the family context of these dyads. This family context may help explain why even disorganized-secure children and the offspring of unresolved-secure mothers have many of the same outcomes as dyads with underlying insecurity.

OUTCOMES OF DISORGANIZED ATTACHMENT

By the age of 6 years, most D-secure and D-insecure children exhibit controlling behavior toward their parent (Main & Cassidy, 1988; Main, Kaplan, & Cassidy, 1985). The reason for this is clear. As the child's cognitive ability increases with age, he or she attempts to reduce the mother's (and the child's own) apparent anxiety and stress by taking charge of the situation. In fact, the child's increase in controlling behavior is correlated with the mother's decreased anxiety and depression (Moss, Thibaudeau, Cyr, & Rousseau, 2001). Unfortunately, even though the child's behavior may appear more organized, his or her mental representations (as shown in stories and doll play) continue to reveal fearful and chaotic mental images (Hesse & Main, 1999; Solomon & George, 2011a; Teti, 1999). There are two main types of controlling behavior (controlling-punitive and controlling-caregiving) as well as a third category (behaviorally disorganized) that is used to describe children who seem to lack the skills or the opportunity to become controlling (Hennighausen, Bureau, David, Holmes, & Lyons-Ruth, 2011). It should be noted that both of the controlling strategies reflect role reversal with the parent, although differing in form.

Controlling-Punitive Children

Associated with D-insecure attachment in infants (Lyons-Ruth, Bronfman, & Parsons, 1999), the controlling-punitive child exhibits harsh commands, verbal threats, and even physical aggression toward the mother, almost as if the child is baiting the mother in a competition for power (George & Solomon, 2011; Moss, Bureau, St-Laurent, & Tarabulsy, 2011). The mother for her part appears intimidated, helpless, withdrawn, and stressed by her child, describing the child as increasingly moody, hyperactive, and out of control, and resenting the role-reversing behavior (Jacobvitz & Hazen, 1999; Moss, Cyr, & Dubois-Comtois, 2004; Moss, Bureau, et al., 2011). Although both the mother and the teacher emphasize the child's externalizing behavior problems, the themes of danger and chaos that emerge in the child's doll play suggest that he or she is highly unsettled in part by the mother's disrupted communication, unresolved fearful experiences, and intermittent dissociation (Moss et al., 2004; Moss, Bureau, et al., 2011; Solomon, George, & DeJong, 1995).

Controlling-Caregiving Children

Like the controlling-punitive child, the controlling-caregiving child looks organized in behavior but not in mental representations (Teti, 1999). However, this child is more likely to display inhibition and anxiety (Hennighausen et al., 2011; Solomon et al., 1995). Associated with D-secure attachment in infants (Lyons-Ruth, Bronfman, & Parsons, 1999), the controlling-caregiving child is cheery, polite, and shows few signs of distress in the mother's presence, while attempting to structure the interaction with the mother in a helpful, protective way (Hennighausen et al., 2011; Moss, Bureau, et al., 2011). The mother appears to respond positively to this role-reversing behavior, praising and almost eulogizing the child for his or her precociousness (Moss et al., 2004; Solomon & George, 2011b). At the same time, the mother seems passive, disengaged, and disinvested, so the child's needs for reassurance, protection, and safety remain unmet (Moss et al., 2004; Moss, Bureau, et al., 2011).

This style of interaction is typically associated with the mother's withdrawn, dazed, or absent behavior, often due in part to the mother's experience of complicated loss (Bureau, Easterbrooks, & Lyons-Ruth, 2009a; Hennighausen et al., 2011; Moss et al., 2004; Moss, Bureau, et al., 2011; Solomon & George, 2011b). Indeed, the mother's history of loss seems to interfere with attending to her child's expression of distress (Moss, Bureau, et al., 2011). While the mother's behavior has also been described as hostile, domineering, or constricted in anger and aggression (Hazen, Jacobvitz, Higgins, Allen, & Jin, 2011; Jacobvitz & Hazen, 1999), different types of behavior seem to elicit controlling-caregiving from boys and girls. Namely, girls tend to become caregivers when their mother is hostile, while both boys and girls become watchful, vigilant, and caregiving when their mother appears withdrawn, helpless, or dissociative (Hazen et al., 2011). Although frequently receiving attention from teachers because they are not aggressive (Moss, Bureau, et al., 2011), the controlling-caregiving child is rated high on scales of internalizing behaviors (Hazen et al., 2011; Hennighausen et al., 2011).

Behaviorally Disorganized Children

Displaying behavior that is often worse than that of controlling children (Teti, 1999), behaviorally disorganized children are more likely to have experienced abuse (Cicchetti & Barnett, 1991). Even in middle childhood, their behavior resembles that of disorganized infants, characterized by verbal and nonverbal disorganization and abrupt changes of state (Moss, Bureau, et al., 2011). They exhibit confusion and apprehension at the approach of the attachment figure (Moss, Bureau, et al., 2011) and their actions resemble the behavioral collapse of the disorganized infant (George & Solomon, 2011). Their parents' very deficient caregiving, current ongoing stress, marital problems, hospitalizations due to serious illness or accident, shifting alliances, and perhaps the child's developmental limitations all conspire to impede the behaviorally disorganized child from developing a strategy to control the parent's anxiety and fearfulness (George & Solomon, 2011; Moss et al., 2004; Moss, Bureau, et al., 2011; Teti, 1999). In other words, this group of children frequently displays the effects of multiple family and environmental risks—the quintessentially unpredictable family environment. Consequently, this child exhibits both externalizing and internalizing behavior problems, but with either outcome is unlikely to receive teacher support (Moss, Bureau, et al., 2011; O'Connor, Collins, & Supplee, 2012). Similarly, the odd disconnected behaviors exhibited with peers may keep this child socially isolated (Jacobvitz & Hazen, 1999).

Longer-Term Consequences of Controlling and Disorganized Behavior

Research is only beginning to explore the longer-term effects of controlling and disorganized behavior in children with a history of disorganized attachment. For example, the controlling-punitive stance of middle childhood is characterized by either unilateral or reciprocal punitive behavior in adolescence, while controlling-caregiving behavior is associated with either caregiving, containing, or mixed caregiving and punitive behavior (Hennighausen et al., 2011). Furthermore, retrospective reports of having engaged in controlling behavior in childhood or adolescence were common among women with borderline personality disorder, who also were more likely to have a history of hostile or helpless parenting (Lyons-Ruth, Melnick, Patrick, & Hobson, 2007). Similarly, in a longitudinal study, children who were characterized as disorganized and controlling at age 8 were more likely to exhibit borderline traits in late adolescence (Lyons-Ruth et al., 2013).

A factor analysis of the dyadic interactions of parents and late adolescents (some of whom had been followed since infancy) revealed three disorganized constructs—punitive, caregiving, and disoriented (Obsuth, Hennighausen, Brumariu, & Lyons-Ruth, 2014). Adolescents' punitive interactions with their parents were unrelated to disorganized attachment in infancy but were associated with H/H representations on the AAI as well as parents' reports of helplessness in the parenting role, adolescents' dissociative symptoms and adolescents' self-reported abuse toward and by their romantic partners. Adolescents' caregiving/role-confused interactions with parents were similarly unrelated to a history of disorganized attachment but were associated with dissociative symptoms and abuse toward romantic partners. Finally, disoriented adolescent behavior (marked by odd, out-of-context behavior) was significantly associated with disorganized behavior in infancy, with unresolved loss or trauma on their AAIs, with parents' role confusion and lack of investment, and with adolescents' dissociative symptoms. While this type of interaction was associated with poor quality of romantic relationships, it was not predictive of partner abuse.

The lack of a clear-cut transition in disorganized attachment from infancy to childhood to adolescence to adulthood suggests that there undoubtedly are entry and exit points to these trajectories and that other factors such as family context, environmental stressors, and neurobiology may also play a role. However, the apparently different pathways to these disorganized behaviors (including disorganized attachment in infancy, H/H representations of parenting, current unresolved states of mind, and parental role confusion) overlap and are related in many other samples to parents' experiences of loss or trauma, to the development of disorganized attachment in children, to a history of abuse, and to the prediction of relationship violence. Therefore, given that these dyadic interactions potentially mediate between a mother's history of unresolved trauma, role confusion and abdication of parenting (whether or not accompanied by abusive parenting) and an adolescent's or adult's vulnerability to victimization or violent behavior, these parent-child interaction patterns are rightfully the focus of many therapies.

IMPLICATIONS FOR INTERVENTIONS

There are a number of approaches for intervening with children with a history of trauma. In working with the parent-child dyad, it is important to distinguish between the mother's caregiving and her own attachment (Webster & Hackett, 2011). It is also important to assess and address the family context of the parent or the parent-child dyad (Chapter 3).

The Parent-Child Dyad

The goals of interventions focusing on the mother's caregiving are to serve as a secure base for the mother and thus to help her help the child feel safe (Bowlby, 1988; Cassidy & Mohr, 2001). To this end, the results of several meta-analyses have concluded that brief, behavioral dyadic parent-child interventions focusing explicitly on increasing the mother's sensitivity to the child are most effective (Bakermans-Kranenburg, van IJzendoorn, & Juffer, 2003, 2005). Particularly useful are video feedback interventions that provide the mother with feedback on both positive caregiver behaviors as well as insensitive or disruptive behaviors that emerge during her free play sessions with the child (Madigan, Hawkins, Goldberg, & Benoit, 2006; Van Zeijl et al., 2006). One home visitation program combined video feedback sessions with discussions of attachment and emotion regulation (Moss, Dubois-Comtois, et al., 2011). Ultimately, the mother helps her child feel safe by learning to understand the child's fears (including perhaps her own frightening behavior), learning to empathize with her child without feeling overwhelmed by his or her fears, and learning to protect the child from himself or herself and others by setting clear limits (Cassidy & Mohr, 2001).

The Mother

Unfortunately, interventions addressing the mother's caregiving behaviors are not as effective for mothers with a history of unresolved trauma (Moran, Bailey, Gleason, DeOliveira, & Pederson, 2008; Moran, Pederson, & Krupka, 2005). Attachment-related parent-child interventions may inadvertently trigger parents' unresolved attachment anxieties and lead to emotion dysregulation and poor reflective functioning (Foroughe & Muller, 2011; Gardner, Loya, & Hyman, 2014). In such a case, the therapist will need to address the mother's own experience of childhood trauma or hostile/helpless parenting and then to explicitly relate her childhood experiences of attachment to her current caregiving (Hughes et al., 2006; Koren-Karie, Oppenheim, & Getzler-Yosef, 2008; Lyons-Ruth & Spielman, 2004; Velderman, Bakermans-Kranenburg, Juffer, & van IJzendoorn, 2006). Only then will the mother be able to respond with sensitivity to her child's emotional needs.

Several interventions focus specifically on the mother's reflective functioning (Slade, Sadler, & Mayes, 2005). One treatment that uses individual therapy to titrate anxiety more carefully is the Mothers and Toddlers Program (MTP), which is a 12-session, attachment-based therapy for substance-abusing mothers of young children (Suchman et al., 2010; Suchman, DeCoste, Rosenberger, & McMahon, 2012). The therapist helps build the mother's capacity to reflect on her own strong emotions and their impact on the child as well as her capacity to reflect on her child's emotions and their impact on her. A randomized clinical trial found that, in comparison to a parent education intervention, MTP mothers exhibited better reflective functioning that was associated with improved caregiving behavior. In interventions such as these, the overriding concern with the mother is, as with the child, one of safety—developing an egalitarian collaborative therapeutic alliance with the mother to facilitate her use of the therapist as a secure base, helping her to feel physically safe and to mourn her lack of safety in the past and even assessing how her fears of her child may interfere with her feelings of safety with her child (Cassidy & Mohr, 2001; Liotti, 2011).

The Child

The role of the child should not be underestimated in this process, especially given that the essence of disorganized attachment is a breakdown of the child's ability to make use of the caregiver. There is some evidence that the video feedback interventions described above are particularly successful with children who have certain genetic polymorphisms (see Chapter 4) that make them differentially responsive to a supportive environment (Bakermans-Kranenburg, van IJzendoorn, Mesman, Alink, & Juffer, 2008; Bakermans-Kranenburg, van IJzendoorn, Pijlman, Mesman, & Juffer, 2008). Furthermore, the controlling strategies seen in the child or adolescent with a history of disorganized attachment developed as a form of self-regulation, suggesting that an initial focus on attachment issues may be too threatening. Therefore, Hilburn-Cobb (2004) encouraged a shift to a more cognitive and instrumental therapy with such a child until the therapeutic alliance has been firmly established. Moreover, not only their controlling or disorganized behavior, but also their miscues in general make interventions with this population of children challenging for therapists, parents, and even foster or adoptive parents (Marvin & Whelan, 2003).

The Therapist

In therapeutic interactions with parents and adolescents, the challenge of dealing with their most primal fears and distorted expectations of intimate relationships demands that the therapist be aware of the possible presentations of these clients and of the therapist's own possible countertransferential reactions (Alexander & Anderson, 1994). The secure client's perspective taking, affect regulation, and adeptness at using interpersonal supports will probably not elicit any complicated countertransference from the therapist. In contrast, the dismissing client's interpersonal distancing, devaluing, and entitlement may elicit a therapist's competitiveness, feelings of incompetence, mutual avoidance, and anger. Therefore, the therapist working with the client who is dismissing (either as the primary presentation or as the underlying attachment strategy) will need to practice remaining centered and curious, with some confidence that, if successfully engaged, this client is likely to show improvements in outcome (Fonagy et al., 1996).

The preoccupied client's helpless and dependent presentation, combined with intense affect and a vacillation between dependent coy behavior and demanding angry behavior, is particularly likely to elicit a strong countertransference. As a result, the therapist working with the preoccupied client will often feel overwhelmed, suffocated, and perhaps overprotective in reaction to the client's frequent risky behavior. The unremitting quantity of crises may feel exhausting and frustrating. Consequently, the therapist will need to be clear about his or her own boundaries and power, including the realization that while the therapist can and should warn the client about the consequences of certain actions, the therapist does not have the ability to control or rescue the client. Instead, the emphases of therapy with the preoccupied client need to include safety issues (Herman, 1992) and helping the client modulate affect.

Finally, the unresolved client may be the most challenging of all, presenting with major emotion dysregulation (including dissociation) with little awareness of this affect, both seeing herself as too invisible and ineffectual to influence others while feeling vulnerable and attacked by others, including the therapist. The overwhelming quality of this client's crises is certain to elicit the therapist's feelings of exhaustion, helplessness, excessive responsibility, and a sense of being manipulated. Furthermore, any countertransference reactions of fear by the therapist will re-create the relational atmosphere of disorganized attachment (Liotti, 2011). The therapist is indeed faced with a dilemma—exploring attachment-related issues could elicit disorganized IWMs while adopting a too-distant stance could be perceived as indifferent or neglectful (Liotti, 2011). Therefore, the therapist working with the unresolved client will need to work very slowly and respectfully, initially focusing on "there and then" as opposed to "here and now." The therapist may need to avoid feedback on his or her own reactions, while instead helping clients to anticipate their responses to anxiety. The therapist may also decide to frequently use informed consent to remind clients of their choice to remember and not remember. This stance helps clients prepare for affective flooding and gives them an anchor of predictability. Finally, the therapist may need to normalize clients' inevitable mistrust of the therapist and others.

In conclusion, if trauma necessarily develops from a failure of an attachment relationship, then the only way to resolve it is through another attachment relationship—between the parent and the child, the parent and the therapist, the child and the therapist, or the parent and the partner.

CHAPTER 3

Family Context of Attachment Relationships

Attachment relationships between parents and children or between partners do not develop outside of a context. Instead, all attachment relationships exist within families, which provide the context for the formation and maintenance of the new attachment relationship. Even the notion of the single-parent family is a misnomer given the impact of separation or divorce upon a parent's functioning; at the very least, the internalized attachment relationships with one's own parents serve as an influential family context for a parent's relationship with his or her own children or for an individual's relationship with his or her partner.

Although Bowlby always emphasized the role of the family (Marvin & Stewart, 1990), attachment researchers have tended to ignore it. Therefore, the goal of this chapter is to identify some of the many ways that the family may determine, explain, magnify, or counteract the effect of a history of trauma on parenting and on a child's vulnerability for maltreatment or aggressive behavior.

The similarities between attachment theory and family systems theory are numerous and suggest a common bond. Like attachment relationships, families are divided into subsystems, based on their functions, which define the organizational structure of the family. These typically include the couple (or marital) subsystem, the parental subsystem, the sibling subsystem, and other more idiosyncratic subsystems, based in part on the age and gender of children. Families also have a hierarchical organization, with the unidirectional parent-child caregiving attachment distinct from the mutual care-seeking and caregiving roles of the couple's attachment relationship (Clulow, 2007). Most importantly, both perspectives see the relationship as the basic unit of analysis. Thus, both models think of human behavior in systemic terms, see distress as functional (i.e., as serving some relational purpose), and focus on patterns of dyadic and family functioning (Crittenden & Dallos, 2009). Both models also see relationships as evolving over time with historical transgenerational influences and typical developmental stages. Consistent with a systems perspective, dynamism and change are viewed as essential—neither a family nor an attachment relationship can thrive without adapting to new developmental challenges, new relationships, and new external stressors. Resistance to change is a characteristic of a troubled family system; similarly, insecure attachment is more likely to be associated with the carryover of one's childhood attachment representation into the attachment representation with one's partner (Cohin & Miljkovitch, 2007). In other words, rigidity and defensive exclusion of new information can interfere with the necessary updating of internal working models (IWMs) in both an attachment relationship and a family system.

Structurally, Marvin and Stewart (1990) noted the similarities between the three organized attachment categories of secure, dismissing, and preoccupied attachment and the three family organizational patterns of adaptive, disengaged, and enmeshed structures described by Minuchin (1974). Furthermore, just as one subsystem within a family (e.g., the children) can affect another (e.g., the marital subsystem), so also one attachment relationship can affect another. For example, individuals may avoid emotional attachments in their families of creation because of attachment experiences in their families of origin (Byng-Hall, 1990). Similarly, a parent may make inappropriate use of an attachment figure (such as role reversal with a child) to compensate for the absence of a satisfying attachment relationship with a partner. In fact, Crittenden and Dallos (2009) have argued that the triangle represents a bridge between family systems and attachment theory in that the child functions in dyadic relationships with both parents as well as with the parent's dyad.

Just as families are meaning-making systems that derive their own social constructions of reality, so too are individuals within attachment relationships. The ability to develop a meaningful, coherent narrative of one's experience is the essence of secure attachment, diminishing the effect of childhood adversity on later relationship outcomes (Crowell, Warner, Davis, Marraccini, & Dearing, 2010). Reflective functioning within an attachment relationship (that is, acknowledging one's own and the other person's distinct thoughts, feelings, and intentions) has as its counterpart interactional awareness within a family (Byng-Hall, 2008).

Like a parent's provision of a secure base and safe haven for a child and a couple's provision of a secure base and safe haven for each other, a primary goal of a family is to provide a secure base and safe haven for all its members. The absence of these functions inevitably proves problematic for a child and for partners (Byng-Hall, 1995). Finally, analogous to the role of the secure base in the family and attachment relationship, the therapist provides a secure base from which individuals, couples, and families can explore new working models of relationships and new modes of interacting (Byng-Hall, 1995).

Therefore, with attention to both development and structure, this chapter focuses on how the family context of attachment relationships is integral to understanding the intergenerational transmission of violence and trauma. Family systems theory also compensates for a frequent limitation of attachment research—that is, focusing so exclusively upon the mother-child relationship that it fails to consider the role of the father. This chapter follows the development of the couple's relationship, the parenting relationship, whole family relationships, and external stressors affecting the whole family.

FORMATION OF COUPLE RELATIONSHIP

Choice of a Partner

There is good evidence that, to some extent, individuals choose their partners on the basis of their family history and their preexisting state of mind with regard to attachment. Evidence of assortative mating exists with regard to insecure attachment and unresolved attachment (Nauha & Silven, 2000; van IJzendoorn & Bakermans-Kranenburg, 1996). Couples have also been found to be similar in their recollections of parenting, with the degree of concordance being independent of socioeconomic status or current psychiatric symptoms (Lustenberger et al., 2008). Since the concordance does not increase with age, it is not attributable to convergence over the course of the marriage. Other research has found concordance on characteristics often associated with a history of trauma, such as substance abuse and antisocial personality disorder (Galbaud du Fort, Boothroyd, Bland, Newman, & Kakuma, 2002; Low, Cui, & Merikangas,

2007; Schuckit, Smith, Eng, & Kunovac, 2002). Finally, several studies have found concordance (again controlling for convergence over time) on the basis of actual history of trauma (Chen & Carolan, 2010; Whisman, 2014). In one study, for example, women with a history of psychological abuse were more likely to prefer men with traits associated with abusiveness, such as possessiveness (Zayas & Shoda, 2007). Reciprocally, men who self-reported engaging in psychological aggression were more likely to prefer women with attachment anxiety.

The reasons for this assortative mating may vary. As described by Rhule-Louie and McMahon (2007), *social homogamy* posits that similarity with regard to demographic background or past experiences may influence or limit one's potential pool of partners, resulting in similarities on other traits. Thus, to the extent that trauma history affects peer academic achievement and peer relationships (see Chapter 5) or reproductive strategy (see Chapter 6), it could also affect the type of individual with whom one may eventually partner.

An alternative explanation, *phenotypic preference*, suggests that partners are chosen explicitly for traits that are similar to one's own. A variation on this perspective is derived from self-verification theory, which states that individuals prefer self-confirming feedback, even if the feedback is unfavorable (Swann, Hixon, Stein-Seroussi, & Gilbert, 1990). Research has found that psychological distress predicted Latina teenagers' choice of a partner who had negative relationships with women in one study (Goodyear, Newcomb, & Locke, 2002) and negative feedback seeking in a sample of heterosexual dating couples, above and beyond the effects of self-esteem (Weinstock & Whisman, 2004). Furthermore, the notion of phenotypic preference is consistent with the idea of IWMs and the choice of a partner on the basis of one's expectations about relationships, whether they be similar or complementary.

These different perspectives on assortative mating are not mutually exclusive, and they all may play a role in varying degrees. Whatever the cause, the choice of a partner has important implications for intergenerational risk, both with regard to a genetic basis for violence (via antisocial behavior, substance abuse, dysthymia, or impulsivity) and to problematic parenting. Thus, assortative mating on the basis of factors related to trauma or violence could potentially increase a child's exposure to violence. For example, in a large diverse sample of men court ordered to batterer treatment, dual-trauma couples in which both partners had a history of childhood trauma were characterized by especially severe violence (Alexander, 2014). Moreover, their female partners were less likely to seek help and more likely to downplay the men's aggression, portending the continuance of this volatile relationship. Thus, both these women and their children remained at a substantially greater risk for maltreatment. Similarly, the conflict management interactions of couples who were both unresolved in their attachment were significantly more negative, sometimes to a frighteningly intense degree (see Chapter 5; Creasey, 2002, 2014). In fact, many of their behaviors resembled those of highly controlling children with a history of disorganized attachment.

Transition to Marriage

Whether or not an individual has a history of trauma, attachment relationships in one's family of origin may influence adult intimate relationships. In fact, 78% of a sample of 157 couples assessed 3 months prior to their marriage and 18 months following the marriage were given the same primary AAI classification (secure, dismissing, preoccupied) both times (Crowell, Treboux, & Waters, 2002). Two-thirds of those individuals who changed became more secure, suggesting that the new relationship represented an opportunity for revision of a past insecure IWM. Findings indicated that a change from insecure to secure attachment was associated with a higher education, living away from one's parents, and/or living with one's partner prior to marriage, suggesting the importance of openness to new experiences as a way of breaking out of more rigid mental representations or family patterns. Of particular interest in this study was the finding that more than half of those individuals who had initially been classified as unresolved remained so 21 months later. While most of the individuals who became resolved had a history of loss rather than abuse, those who were stable unresolved were more likely to be experiencing stressful life events or aggression in their relationships, highlighting the argument that the choice of a partner has important ramifications for either triggering or maintaining unresolved experiences of abuse.

Another study by the same authors examined the concordance of attachment representations within couples as assessed prior to their marriage on the AAI and following their marriage on the Current Relationship Interview (CRI; Treboux et al., 2004). Thus, individuals were classified as $Secure_{AAI}/Secure_{CRI}$, $Secure_{AAI}/Insecure_{CRI}$, $Insecure_{AAI}/Secu$-

re$_{CRI}$, or Insecure$_{AAI}$/Insecure$_{CRI}$. Different patterns of marital interactions characterized each group, with individuals who were secure at both time points exhibiting the most overall satisfaction with their relationships. While the Insecure$_{AAI}$/Insecure$_{CRI}$ individuals reported the most conflict, they were not necessarily the most distressed. Their new relationship appeared to meet their expectations or IWMs based on past relationships; this finding points to the frequent stability of problematic relationships. While the Insecure$_{AAI}$/Secure$_{CRI}$ individuals appeared to be functioning well, they were more likely to report a drop in positive feelings about the relationship when stressed; the authors described them as the "proverbial house built on sand." Finally, the Secure$_{AAI}$/Insecure$_{CRI}$ individuals expressed the most distress of all, even though their AAI attachment seemed to protect them from some of the conflict experienced by the Insecure$_{AAI}$/Insecure$_{CRI}$ group. They were the most likely to separate or divorce, especially when their CRI attachment was preoccupied rather than dismissing; thus, they appeared to be less likely to tolerate an unsatisfying relationship.

These findings have several implications for the intergenerational cycle of violence. On one hand, the choice of a partner who reinforces one's negative expectations of relationships can lead to a stable but distressed and potentially dangerous relationship, increasing a child's risk for abuse or trauma in part because change is less likely. On the other hand, individuals can change their mental representations of relationships, becoming more secure and more resolved regarding experiences of loss or abuse. This change might be tentative in the face of stressful life events and it appears to be associated less with the attachment security of the partner and more with an individual's own willingness to explore a new secure-base way of interacting with a partner (Crowell et al., 2002). However, this change represents resilience and the interruption of a violence cycle.

PARENTING RELATIONSHIP

As demonstrated in the previous section, individuals' IWMs and life experiences affect their choice of a partner. Namely, someone who has developed a secure state of mind from having received sensitive, supportive, and responsive parenting is more likely (although not guaranteed) to seek out and remain with a partner who is similarly inclined. Alternatively, having been maltreated, rejected, or expected to meet the emotional needs of one's parents at the expense of one's own needs will foster the development of IWMs consistent with these experiences. Thus, adult attachment as well as experiences of trauma will influence the choice of a partner and interactions with that partner. Reciprocally, those couple interactions may either reinforce initial adult attachment or greatly modify it, thus potentially breaking intergenerational patterns (Cowan & Cowan, 2005). In either case, couple relationships will have a strong impact on child outcomes.

Transition to Parenthood

The act of becoming a parent is a major developmental challenge. While it is marked by a drop in marital satisfaction for secure and insecure individuals alike, it is particularly problematic for insecure individuals (Castellano, Velotti, Crowell, & Zavattini, 2013; Velotti, Castellano, & Zavattini, 2011). Dismissing individuals are less likely to engage in behaviors to maintain closeness to their partner even before the birth of a child, and preoccupied individuals experience a precipitous drop in closeness with the birth of a child (Curran, Hazen, Jacobvitz, & Feldman, 2005). On the other hand, securely attached mothers describe sadness, anxiety, and low-level anger postpartum that resolve quickly (Behringer, Reiner, & Spangler, 2011). In other words, they freely express and then shake off negative feelings.

This transition to parenthood is not only important in predicting future interactions but also in predicting father absence (and single parenthood for the mother) and the father's degree of involvement in the parenting relationship. In a discussion of relational trauma, Baradon (2010, p. 130) posed these questions: "What roles may a father who is present in the family play when the trauma lies in the mother-infant relationship? Does trauma in the father-infant relationship differ from trauma in the mother-infant relationship? Does the absence of the father constitute a trauma?" The following section attempts to address the role of the father, including the effect of his absence versus presence and the degree of his involvement; his role as an abuser of his children; his ability to interrupt cycles of violence by buffering the effect of a mother's history of trauma on her parenting; the impact of marital conflict on his parenting, his partner's parenting, and the adjustment of the child; and finally, his role as a coparent with his partner. What is essential to emphasize is that the mother's partner (typically, but not necessarily the father) matters.

Father Absence or Presence and Degree of Involvement

Egeland (1988) noted that "paternal deprivation" is an especially insidious form of maltreatment. This statement is true for several reasons. First, on a very concrete level, a father's absence is associated with the family's economic deprivation, contributing to increased rates of child physical abuse and neglect (Dubowitz, 2006; Dufour, Lavergne, Larrivee, & Trocme, 2008). Thus, single parenthood carries its own set of stressors and may be especially pertinent to the intergenerational transmission of trauma.

Second, a biological father's absence is associated with the presence of a nonbiological surrogate parent, increasing a child's risk for neglect and abuse (Berger, Paxson, & Waldfogel, 2009; Coohey & Zhang, 2006; Dixon, Browne, Hamilton-Giachritsis, & Ostapuik, 2010; Dixon, Hamilton-Giachritsis, Browne, & Ostapuik, 2007; Lee, Lightfoot, & Edleson, 2008). For example, the entry of a father surrogate into a home was found to double a child's risk for maltreatment as compared to either a home with no father figure or a home with a biological father (Radhakrishna, Bou-Saada, Hunter, Catellier, & Kotch, 2001). Furthermore, a study in Brazil found that biological mothers were more than twice as likely to physically abuse their children given the presence of a stepfather as opposed to the presence of the biological father of the children (Alexandre, Nadanovsky, Moraes, & Reichenheim, 2010).

Third, in a study of separated or divorced families, infants with regular overnight visits with their father were less likely to be secure and more likely to be disorganized in their attachment to their mothers than were infants from a comparison group (Solomon & George, 1999a). Infants were also more likely to be disorganized with their father, regardless of visitation arrangements. Parental conflict contributed to the child's disorganized attachment, a finding also reported in another study of fathers not residing with the mother (Finger, Hans, Bernstein, & Cox, 2009). Finger et al. (2009) noted several possible explanations—in couples not living together, their conflict could be more frightening when it is sudden and unexpected; the child may only see the father in conflictual situations; and to the extent that the conflict is related to custody or visitation issues, the child may see himself or herself as the source of the parent's frightened or frightening behavior. In any case, the child's experience of a lack of protection associated with conflicts regarding visitation leads to disorganized attachment, with all its implications for cycles of violence or trauma.

As opposed to the negative effects of father absence, father presence and involvement has salutary effects on children, including better cognitive development, greater social competence, and lower levels of aggression and depression (Dubowitz et al., 2001; Marshall et al., 2001). A father's positive involvement with his child is predictive of the child's attachment security and lowers the mother's risk for abusive parenting (Caldera, 2004; Guterman, Lee, Lee, Waldfogel, & Rathouz, 2009; Newland, Coyl, & Freeman, 2008). Even in a high-risk sample of homeless and runaway adolescents, positive paternal relationships were associated with less substance use and less criminal behavior among teens, leading the authors to conclude that attachments to fathers were especially protective against negative outcomes (Stein, Milburn, Zane, & Rotheram-Borus, 2009). Therefore, the presence and positive involvement of fathers has a direct impact on the attachment security and well-being of a child.

Fathers as Abusive to Their Children

As opposed to the positive effects of a father's presence and involvement with his child, fathers may certainly be as abusive to their children as are mothers. Locke and Newcomb (2004) emphasized that it is vital to attend to both parents' history of child maltreatment, a failing of research in attachment and child abuse in general. In the very few comparisons of abusive mothers and fathers that have been conducted, the latter were noted to have more rigid expectations of their children, and less cohesive, expressive, and organized families than abusive mothers (Pittman & Buckley, 2006; Schaeffer, Alexander, Bethke, & Kretz, 2005). While mothers' history of child maltreatment was associated more generally with poor parenting, fathers' history of emotional neglect was associated with lack of parental warmth, and their history of child sexual abuse (CSA) was associated with a rejecting style of parenting (Locke & Newcomb, 2004). In one study comparing abusive mothers and fathers, the men were significantly more violent and antisocial, exhibiting fewer mental health problems and fewer feelings of isolation than their female counterparts (Dixon et al., 2007). In contrast, mothers who abused their children (and were not themselves victims of intimate partner violence, IPV) were more likely to have histories of child maltreatment, mental health problems, and other parenting risk factors than fathers who abused only their children (and not their partners). This research, therefore, highlights the role of trauma history in predicting abusive mothers' parenting as compared to the parenting of abusive fathers, an observation that has also emerged in the literature on dating violence and IPV (Chapter 5). This research also suggests that much more needs to be known about the direct effects of fathers' maltreatment history in the intergenerational transmission of violence.

Impact of Couple Interactions on Parenting and Child Adjustment

Fathers as Buffering the Impact of Mothers' Trauma History

In addition to exacerbating the effects of trauma history on parenting, couple relationships are instrumental in interrupting intergenerational cycles of violence and trauma (Cowan & Cowan, 2005). As mentioned in Chapter 1, a mother's supportive relationship with her partner will buffer the effects of her trauma history on her parenting (Egeland et al., 1988; Kaufman & Zigler, 1987; Langeland & Dijkstra, 1995; Leerkes & Crockenberg, 2006). A man's attachment security also appears to override the effect of his wife's insecurity on their toddler's compliance or their observed marital interactions (Cohn et al., 1992; Volling, Blandon, & Kolak, 2006). Interestingly, the effect was not observed in the opposite direction. Namely, couples in which the wife was secure and the husband insecure were observed to have even more conflict than couples in which both partners were insecure (Cowan, Bradburn, & Cowan, 2005). While not all studies have found an effect of one partner's secure attachment on buffering interparental conflict (Wampler, Shi, Nelson, & Kimball, 2003), Finger et al. (2009) found that the association between interparental conflict and a child's disorganized attachment with the mother was completely absent when the parents were coresiding. Therefore, a father's attachment security and support of his wife (or even his mere presence) may protect children from risks associated with her history of trauma and from interparental conflict.

Effects of Interparental Conflict on Parenting

The effects of buffering aside, research suggests that relational conflict may have more impact on parenting than relational support (Finger et al., 2009). Interparental conflict is not only an obvious risk factor for IPV, but it has a major impact on the parenting of mothers and fathers and on the adjustment of their children. Since couple conflict may result in part from each partner's respective history of attachment and trauma, it is an important mediator in the cycles of violence and trauma. The distinction between couple conflict and IPV is often just a matter of degree, with similar effects on child adjustment. This chapter focuses on the more proximal effects on children and adolescents of interparental conflict, while a discussion of IPV in Chapter 5 considers children's exposure to IPV as a determinant of their own eventual violence or vulnerability to victimization.

The spillover model of interparental conflict (Margolin, Christensen, & John, 1996) proposes that tensions from one family subsystem (typically, the couple) may impact other family subsystems (typically, the parent-child relationship, although perhaps also the sibling subsystem). Two different meta-analyses concluded that the evidence for a spillover effect is quite strong, with a moderate effect size (Erel & Burman, 1995; Krishnakumar & Buehler, 2000). That is, couple conflict leads to family instability, parenting problems, and emotional insecurity in a child, resulting in the child's inability to regulate affect and in negative behavioral outcomes (Davies & Cummings, 1994; Davies, Harold, Goeke-Morey, & Cummings, 2002). The emotional dysregulation may also impact the amount and quality of a child's sleep, thus compromising academic achievement (El-Sheikh, Buckhalt, Keller, Cummings, & Acebo, 2007). As might be expected, overt interparental conflict is associated more with externalizing behavior problems in a child and covert conflict with internalizing behavior problems (Bradford, Vaughn, & Barber, 2008). Moreover, overt conflict tends to be mediated by parent-child conflict and harsh discipline in the prediction of externalizing problems, while covert conflict is mediated by psychological intrusiveness and low parental acceptance in the prediction of internalizing problems (Benson, Buehler, & Gerard, 2008; Bradford & Barber, 2005; Buehler & Gerard, 2002; Gerard, Krishnakumar, & Buehler, 2006).

Couple conflict appears to have differential effects on mothers and fathers. Mothers appear to be more reactive to their partner's withdrawal than to conflict per se, leading to their increased intrusiveness and criticism toward their children (Cox, Paley, Payne, & Burchinal, 1999; Katz & Gottman, 1996). For example, a longitudinal study found that partner withdrawal led to increases in adrenocortical reactivity in mothers, but not in fathers, resulting in mothers' psychologically controlling behavior and inconsistent discipline with their children (Sturge-Apple, Davies, Cicchetti, & Cummings, 2009). In fact, even spillover from the workday is more likely to lead to withdrawal in men, perhaps helping to account for women's angry marital behavior (Schulz, Cowan, Cowan, & Brennan, 2004). Interparental conflict does appear to be associated with a child's decreased responsiveness to the mother (Stroud, Durbin, Wilson, & Mendelsohn, 2011). However, aside from increasing a mother's relationship insecurity with her partner, it does not necessarily affect her parenting (Davies, Sturge-Apple, Woitach, & Cummings, 2009).

In contrast, fathers' parenting appears to be much more affected by interparental conflict than is mothers' parenting, leading to their high intrusiveness, psychological control, and insensitivity in reaction to a child's distress (Davies, Sturge-Apple, Woitach, et al., 2009; Katz & Gottman, 1996). For example, partner conflict experienced before the birth of a child in fathers with insecure attachment predicted less positive and more negative family interactions 2 years later (Paley et al., 2005). Couple conflict also has the effect of decreasing a father's involvement with his child, thus seriously weakening the father-child relationship (Coiro & Emery, 1998; Katz & Gottman, 1996; Stroud et al., 2011). The impact of partner conflict on fathers' parenting behavior is clearly related to relationship insecurity with the partner, with low levels of partner affection increasing the impact of interparental conflict on a father's affection for his child (Davies, Sturge-Apple, Woitach, et al., 2009; Fauchier & Margolin, 2004).

Davies, Sturge-Apple, Woitach, et al. (2009) speculated why there would be a greater impact of spillover on fathers' behavior than mothers' behavior. First, mothers may be better able to compartmentalize their spousal and parenting roles. Second, mothers who are unhappy with their interactions with their partner may interfere with his caregiving role with their child. Finally, from an evolutionary perspective, paternal uncertainty associated with partner conflict could affect the caregiving and involvement of the father with the child, while this would be an irrelevant impact on the mother, given her certainty that the child was indeed hers.

While research has confirmed that interparental conflict is associated with insecure mother-child and father-child attachment (Frosch, Mangelsdorf, & McHale, 2000; Schermerhorn, Cummings, & Davies, 2008), the specific effects appear to vary by the gender of the parent (Ross & Fuertes, 2010). Although the effects of this conflict on children may be partially mediated by parenting, as reviewed above (Frosch et al., 2000), there also appears to be a direct unmediated effect of couple conflict on children (Cummings, Keller, & Davies, 2005). In other words, chronic partner conflict by itself can lead to a child's experience of the parents as frightened or frightening, thus contributing directly to disorganized attachment (Finger et al., 2009; Owen & Cox, 1997). On the other hand, secure parent-child attachment may moderate the impact of this conflict on child outcomes such as self-blame and peer interactions (DeBoard-Lucas, Fosco, Raynor, & Grych, 2010; Lindsey, Caldera, & Tankersley, 2009). In fact, parenting may be more likely to moderate the impact of marital conflict on children than mediate it (Frosch & Mangelsdorf, 2001).

Coparenting

A more direct manifestation of the effect of partner interactions on parenting is through the construct of coparenting, referring to how parents function together with regard to their children. It is distinct from the secure base role of spouses to each other and instead refers to mutual support regarding parenting issues (Woodhouse et al., 2009). When functioning effectively, it "communicates to children solidarity between the parenting figures, a consistent and predictable set of rules and standards (regardless of whether the child lives in a single household or in multiple ones), and a safe and secure home base" (McHale, 2007, p. 374). A meta-analysis found that coparenting had a small but significant effect on child adjustment, even beyond the effects of marital quality and individual parenting (Teubert & Pinquart, 2010). Supportive coparenting is associated with greater infant-father attachment security, but not infant-mother security, especially with boys (Brown, Schoppe-Sullivan, Mangelsdorf, & Neff, 2010). Conversely, undermining parenting and low levels of sup-

portive coparenting result in behavior problems and poor peer relationships in preschoolers and in risky behavior in adolescents (Baril, Crouter,
& McHale, 2007; Katz & Low, 2004; McHale, 1995; Schoppe, Mangelsdorf, & Frosch, 2001). Moreover, competitive coparenting has been associated with both parents' perception (on the Attachment Q-Sort) of less
secure parent-child attachment (Caldera & Lindsey, 2006).

Coparenting is also related to parents' attachment security, but in an
interesting way. Namely, coparental conflict was predicted both by maternal insecure attachment and paternal secure attachment (Talbot, Baker,
& McHale, 2009). The authors speculated that the reason for the latter
finding might be societal expectations that women be primarily responsible for child rearing. Therefore, the default position for most insecure
men would be to avoid coparenting, with its attachment-related demands,
with most mothers willing to tolerate their partner's lack of involvement.
In support of this notion, an observational study found that fathers' withdrawal during coparenting interactions was associated with less engagement and warmth and with fathers' perceptions of mothers' disrespect of
their parenting (Elliston, McHale, Talbot, Parmley, & Kuersten-Hogan,
2008). However, a securely attached father might be likely to initiate a
more active role in coparenting, leading to clashes with his partner, especially if she is insecure in her attachment. Obviously, this conflict might
be temporary, representing a period of adjustment. Even if not, however,
the coparenting may be beneficial for the child in the long run in terms
of reaping the benefits of positive father involvement.

Coparenting may be beneficial for the couple as well. While most
assume that a strong couple relationship will lead to coparenting and
positive parenting practices, research has indicated that an alternate
model also fits the data (Morrill, Hines, Mahmood, & Cordova, 2010).
That is, a coparenting alliance contributes to both a strong couple relationship and to positive parenting practices. Thus, interventions that
encourage the involvement of fathers in parenting and coparenting may
also serve to strengthen the partners' relationship, enhancing the adjustment and security of the child and, in the long run, reducing the stress of
parenting on the mother.

Interestingly, infants are active partners in the triad with parents in
their own microlevel behaviors that either help or hinder the triadic
interactions (McHale, 2007). Much of the research on these triadic
interactions has been conducted using the Lausanne Trilogue Play (LTP)

situation (Fivaz-Depeursinge & Corboz-Warnery, 1999), in which the parents alternate playing together with the infant, and then the parents talk to each other with the infant as the bystander. Video cameras film the parents together and the infant, with the two videotapes then synchronized. Infants as young as 3 months engage in simultaneous and reciprocal interactions with their parents. The infants' capacity to engage in these triangular interactions (operationalized as the frequency of the infant's rapid multishift gaze between the parents) is associated with coparental adjustment, assessed in multiple ways including a narrative assessment of coparental coordination (McHale, Fivaz-Depeursinge, Dickstein, Robertson, & Daley, 2008). The authors concluded that the influences between the parents and the infant were mutual, with infants reacting to the coparental alliance but also helping to recruit and sustain coparental engagement. Furthermore, infants who do not need to defensively disengage from parents who are competitive and conflictual will develop enhanced triangular capacity that will undoubtedly contribute to the child's sociability, reflective functioning, and a more complicated understanding of relationships (McHale et al., 2008). Thus, this body of research is especially important in highlighting the danger of focusing only on parent-child dyads without attention to the triad.

BOUNDARY DISSOLUTION

As described in Chapter 2, problematic parenting and disorganized attachment are associated with different versions of boundary dissolution between a parent and child, including intrusiveness and, most notably, role reversal (Lyons-Ruth et al., 2004). Boundary dissolution has been defined in a number of different ways. Attachment theory focuses on a child's use of control in order to gain attention from a distracted or confused parent. Developmental psychopathology focuses on the parent's attempt to recruit the child to meet the parent's needs for comfort, parenting, intimacy, or play (Macfie, McElwain, Houts, & Cox, 2005). Family systems theory focuses on the triad instead of the dyad. It proposes that the boundaries around family subsystems define what kinds of interactions are appropriate across subsystems (e.g., parents nurturing their children) and inappropriate across subsystems (e.g., parent-child sexual intimacy). Therefore, it suggests that role reversal can best be understood as an intergenerational boundary disturbance between the parental and child subsystems (Fivaz-Depeursinge, Frascarolo, Lopes, Dimitrova, & Favez, 2007). Although these various conceptualizations of boundary disturbances overlap, several different forms have been identified, consisting of intrusiveness, spousification, parentification, and coalitions.

Intrusiveness

Sometimes also referred to as enmeshment, intrusiveness refers to a parent's coercive control in an attempt to control the child's inner life through guilt induction, the withdrawal of love, and invalidation (Kerig, 2005; Mayseless & Scharf, 2009). It may also involve possessiveness and overprotectiveness, leading to the infantilization of a child. Intrusive control serves to inhibit the child's development by a parent who needs to be needed (Garber, 2011). It is distinct from closeness and caregiving, which responds to the needs of the child (Green & Werner, 1996). Instead, it is empirically associated with a parent's memories of overprotection and high entanglement with her or his own parent, resulting in anxious/ambivalent attachment in the child (Green & Werner, 1996; Kretchmar & Jacobvitz, 2002; Mayseless, Bartholomew, Henderson, & Trinke, 2004). As such, it frequently leads to internalizing disorders, poor coping, and a lack of individuation (Jacobvitz, Hazen, Curran, & Hitchens, 2004; Kerig, 2005; Mayseless & Scharf, 2009).

Spousification

As one of the first forms of boundary dissolution to be studied with observational research, a set of parental behaviors was observed during a cleanup task in a small but interesting subset of lower socioeconomic status mothers with their 2-year-old children (Sroufe & Ward, 1980). These mothers exhibited sensual physical contact (e.g., rubbing the child's buttocks or stomach), sensual teasing, and maternal requests for affection. This behavior was distinct from normal affection in that it interrupted the child's activity instead of responding to the child. The mother's behavior was directed almost exclusively to male children, was associated with physical punishment and threats of punishment, and was unrelated to cooperation, encouragement, or emotional support. It was also associated with the mother's history of CSA or spousification. The authors described the dynamic as a combination of overstimulation of the child, punishment for his being undercontrolled, and modeling undercontrol by physically abusing him. This seductiveness at 24 months of age was significantly correlated with continued seductive behavior and with role reversal or peer-like behavior at 42 months of age. It was also associated with the absence of the mother's stable partner relationship and was correlated with the mother's derision and derogation of her daughters (Shaffer & Sroufe, 2005; Sroufe, Jacobvitz, Mangelsdorf, DeAngelo, & Ward, 1985). Furthermore, the boundary dissolution at 42 months of age predicted the child's hyperactivity at age 6, teachers' reports of inattention and impulsivity at age 13, and behavior problems at age 16, unrelated to overall family functioning (Shaffer & Sroufe, 2005). In another sample, overly familiar behavior (including spousification) at age 13 was associated with violence perpetration and victimization in early adulthood (Linder & Collins, 2005). The authors concluded that, even when not directly linked to a history of CSA, this quasi-seductive role reversal could lead either to a young adult overrelying on partners to meet emotional needs or to an individual's tolerance of exploitative relationships—hence, an increased risk of victimization in a subsequent relationship.

Parentification

Parentification is the prototypical role reversal in which the parent relies on the child for nurturance and assistance (Kerig, 2005). Much of parentification is determined intergenerationally. For example, mothers who described role reversal with their own mothers on the AAI were subsequently observed to engage in role reversal with their daughters (Macfie, McElwain, et al., 2005). For fathers who described role reversal with their mothers on the AAI, their wives were observed to engage in role reversal with their sons, suggesting that the fathers had internalized and then recreated the whole family system (as opposed to modeling a specific role, as would be predicted by social learning theory). The effects of this experience of parentification on children are significant, both because it diverts children's attention and energy from age-appropriate developmental tasks and because the parental abdication of caregiving deprives the child of necessary support in coping with developmental challenges (Shaffer & Sroufe, 2005). Therefore, it leads to externalizing problems, a core sense of shame and self-blame, social problems, and excessive reassurance seeking (Byng-Hall, 2002; Katz, Petracca, & Rabinowitz, 2004;

Kerig, 2005; Macfie, Houts, McElwain, & Cox, 2005; Nuttall, Valentino, & Borkowski, 2012; Wells & Jones, 2000). It is also associated with physical abusiveness by the parent and by disorganized attachment, with the controlling behavior described in Chapter 2 (Byng-Hall, 2002; Kerig, 2005). Long-term effects have also been observed in a sample of women who had been abused by their partners (Alexander, 2009). Namely, a report of role reversal with both mothers and fathers on the AAI (as well as a history of CSA) were significantly associated with abuse by multiple partners in adulthood. As noted in Chapter 2, role reversal could reflect both excessive caregiving and tolerance of others' demands, but also the affect dysregulation stemming from disorganized attachment, with which it is also correlated. Therefore, a number of different pathways could lead from parentification to subsequent victimization.

Parentification varies as a function of gender. Girls are more likely to experience role reversal than boys and mothers are more likely to engage in role reversal with their children than are fathers (Alexander, 2003; Herer & Mayseless, 2000; Mayseless et al., 2004; Peris & Emery, 2005). Furthermore, the form that the boundary dissolution takes differs by the gender of both parent and child. For example, in one sample, mothers' conflictual behavior toward their partners was associated with the fathers' role reversal with the child. Conversely, fathers' conflictual behavior toward the mothers was associated with the fathers' withdrawal and with the mothers' role reversal with the child (Macfie, Houts, Pressel, & Cox, 2008). Boundary dissolution of girls with their mothers tends to take the form of parentification and is predicted by marital conflict, parental divorce, neglect, rejection, and the daughter's history of CSA (Alexander, 2003; Shaffer & Sroufe, 2005; Mayseless et al., 2004). Boundary dissolution of girls with their fathers is less common but, when it occurs, tends to take the form of spousification and is predicted by the father's mental illness and the daughter's history of CSA (Alexander, 2003; Mayseless et al., 2004; Shaffer & Sroufe, 2005). Boundary dissolution of sons with their fathers is marginally associated with the father's alcohol abuse, reflecting in part the son's identification with the father's alcoholism (Alexander, 2003).

Finally, in any discussion of parentification, it is essential to distinguish adaptive from destructive parentification. The former is not necessarily role reversal when it refers to instrumental versus emotional caretaking (such as seen in children from immigrant families, large families, or other families facing socioeconomic stressors), when it is transient and the child is not overly burdened by the role, and when the child is supported by both parents and treated fairly (Burton, 2007; Byng-Hall, 2002; Kerig, 2005; McMahon & Luthar, 2007). As such, it is associated not with psychopathology, but rather with better coping with stress (McMahon & Luthar, 2007; Walsh, Shulman, Bar-On, & Tsur, 2006). In addition to being context dependent, boundary dissolution is also age dependent as roles between parents and children gradually become more equalized with the age of the child (Shaffer & Sroufe, 2005), with adult children caring for aging and infirm parents being another example of adaptive parentification.

Family Coalitions

None of the different types of boundary dissolution described above develop spontaneously within a parent-child dyadic relationship. Although an intergenerational influence is indisputable, boundary dissolution is invariably associated in part with the current family context. Frequent couple conflict and the child's involvement in the couple conflict are associated with different forms of role reversal and with the child's externalizing problems resulting from the experience (Ablow, Measelle, Cowan, & Cowan, 2009; Koss et al., 2011; Leon & Rudy, 2005). For example, in a sample of mothers, only those mothers with a history of CSA who were also dissatisfied in their marriage reported engaging in parentification with their child (Alexander, Teti, & Anderson, 2000). In another sample, children who were both physically abused and who witnessed violence between their parents were more overresponsive and overinvolving toward their parents, exhibiting the type of caregiving controlling behavior typically seen in children with disorganized attachment (Timmer, Thompson, Culver, Urquiza, & Altenhofen, 2012).

In fact, when boundary dissolution, as described above, is looked at more broadly, it can often be viewed in terms of the parental subsystem and child triad. As described previously, infants as young as 3 months old have the capacity to share attention and emotions with both parents simultaneously. However, with couple conflict, these triangular bids for attention are either ignored or distorted, leading to a coalition of two against one (Fivaz-Depeursinge et al., 2007). According to Minuchin (1974), chronic boundary problems result when one subsystem (typically, the couple or parental subsystem) uses the same nonmember to diffuse their conflict. These coalitions control tension between the parents and take one of the following three forms.

Detouring allows the parents to agree and avoid conflict by reinforcing the child's behavior and then uniting in either attacking the child through scapegoating or protecting the child by attributing a victim and infantilizing role to him or her. For example, a child's disruptive behavior may unfortunately function quite effectively to divert attention from parental conflict or may be expressed as child-centered coparenting (Fivaz-Depeursinge, Lopes, Python, & Favez, 2009; Fosco & Grych, 2008).

In a *stable cross-generational coalition* (or binding), the child is allied with one parent against the other. This pattern is often combined with role reversal (either parentification or spousification); it has been associated in the LTP paradigm with one parent being so physically close to the child as to exclude the other parent, who either accepts the situation or competes for the child's attention (Fivaz-Depeursinge, 2008). Even when the child does interact with the second parent, the child orients toward the first parent. This dynamic is especially common in families with girls, given that fathers in this situation are more likely to disengage from the family, allowing the mother to bind with the daughter (McHale & Fivaz-Depeursinge, 1999). This type of coalition is also more common following a separation or divorce and during custody disputes when the child aligns with one parent and rejects the other (Cheng & Kuo, 2008; Gagne, Drapeau, Melancon, Saint-Jacques, & Lepine, 2007; Johnston, Walters, & Olesen, 2005; Peris & Emery, 2005). Like the parentification described earlier, this type of stable coalition observed when the child was 2 years old predicted significant internalizing problems 5 years later, especially among girls, who were presumably more often recruited into this type of family dynamic (Jacobvitz et al., 2004).

Finally, *triangulation* refers to a configuration of shifting alliances in which each parent demands the child's allegiance against the other parent. It can even be observed with infants in the LTP paradigm, in which parents simultaneously play different games with the child, resulting in the infant oscillating between protesting both parents' behavior and trying to protect himself or herself from the interactions (Fivaz-Depeursinge, 2008). Needless to say, triangulation is observed when parental conflict is more frequent, hostile, and poorly resolved (Fosco & Grych, 2008; Gagne et al., 2007). It is also observed when coparenting is competitive, especially in families with boys in which both parents remain involved in parenting (Fivaz-Depeursinge et al., 2009; McHale, 1995). As noted in Chapter 2, triangulation may be more common in seriously dysfunctional families, such as those with behaviorally disorganized children who cannot accommodate to the shifting alliances enough to engage in a stable coalition with either parent. Triangulation has also been observed in families with a drug-dependent adolescent, most notably in families with a preoccupied mother, a dismissing father, and an unresolved adolescent (Schindler, Thomasius, Sack, Gemeinhardt, & Kustner, 2007).

This triangulation takes a heavy toll on the child, leading to both internalizing and externalizing problems, perceptions of peer rejection, and increased self-blame (Buehler, Franck, & Cook, 2009; Buehler & Welsh, 2009; Fosco & Grych, 2008, 2010; Franck & Buehler, 2007; Schwarz, 2009). It also leads to poor peer interactions, including girls' social and physical aggression with peers (Peris, Goeke-Morey, Cummings, & Emery, 2008; Underwood, Beron, Gentsch, Galperin, & Risser, 2008).

Implications of Boundary Dissolution for Cycles of Violence

The implications of these different patterns of boundary dissolution for the intergenerational transmission of violence can best be illustrated through reference to a study in which parents were assessed prenatally on the AAI and again in triadic interactions when their child was 8 months old and 24 months old (Hazen, Jacobvitz, & McFarland, 2005). The authors noted that potential sources of the intergenerational transmission of boundary problems (and the internalizing and externalizing problems associated with these boundary problems) included the following: (1) parents may have experienced role reversal in childhood, contributing to a similar interaction with their own children; (2) parents may be preoccupied or unresolved/insecure in their attachment, leading to the intrusive or role-reversing behavior that contributes to disorganized attachment (see Chapter 2); (3) parents may choose partners who are similarly unresolved in their attachment, increasing the risk for conflict and violence in the couple dyad or parent-child relationship due to the complications associated with dual-trauma couples; and (4) parents may re-create patterns of cross-generational alliances, detouring, or triangulation in their family of creation.

Evidence of these potential influences emerged, albeit differently for fathers and mothers. Namely, fathers' history of role reversal with their own mothers and their hostile and role-reversed caregiving were predictive of both parents engaging in enmeshed, guilt-inducing, coy, or helpless behavior with their child. This dynamic could obviously increase the parents' risk of violence toward each other (with its associated risk of abuse to the child) and increase the child's risk of engaging in disorganized controlling behavior toward one or both parents. For their part, mothers who were preoccupied or unresolved/insecure in their attachment were more likely to engage in criticism and control of their husbands' parenting. Perhaps partly as a result, their partner engaged in role-reversed and hostile caregiving toward their child. This dynamic is particularly pertinent to the intergenerational transmission of CSA (see Chapter 6), in which a mother's history of sexual abuse (with its increased likelihood of preoccupied and/or unresolved attachment) is associated with her daughter's increased risk of sexual abuse by her role-reversing and hostile caregiving father. These findings also highlight how essential it is to consider the intergenerational influence of both parents individually and in interaction with each other—not just the influence of the parent with a history of trauma. As noted by the authors, the wives were the primary caregivers, but it was the husbands' history of role reversal that was most predictive of the enmeshed interactions of both parents.

WHOLE FAMILY FUNCTIONING

Research on attachment and research on family violence have gradually broadened the focus of consideration from the dyad (either parent-child or couple) to the triad consisting of the parents and the child. However, families often consist of more members than just the triad. Furthermore, the family as a whole may be affected by external stressors and may respond to internal and external stressors with dynamics pertinent to the experience of trauma. For example, whole family functioning is even more predictive of a child's behavior than is a history of parent-child attachment; similarly, the functioning of the whole family predicts children's externalizing behavior above and beyond the effects of the couple interaction and parenting style (Dubois-Comtois & Moss, 2008; Johnson, Cowan, & Cowan, 1999). Of course, research on larger family systems becomes more challenging with the addition of every new member. However, with these limitations in mind, the following section focuses more broadly on the family as a whole, including sibling relationships and the concept of cumulative risk, reflecting the interaction of the family with external stressors.

Sibling Relationships

Whether siblings actually function as attachment figures for each other is an unsettled question. Berlin, Cassidy, and Appleyard (2008) contended that sibs may experience a common affectional bond, but not attachment in that they do not typically derive security from each other. On the other hand, the latter statement might be modified by the relative ages of the siblings as well as the presence or absence of support from parents. Others have maintained that siblings can contribute to a secure attachment environment, that twins in particular are more likely to use each other as a secure base, and, in a very concrete sense, that closeness between siblings can significantly ameliorate the risk of certain problematic outcomes such as substance abuse (Samek & Rueter, 2011; Tancredy & Fraley, 2006; Whelan, 2003). Siblings are significantly concordant with regard to the security of their attachment to parents, although not concordant with regard to subcategories of insecure attachment (van IJzendoorn et al., 2000). Furthermore, the attachment of one child to a parent may be affected by the relationship of a sibling to that parent—hence, the experience of jealousy (Fearon, Bakermans-Kranenburg, & van IJzendoorn, 2010).

Siblings may differ in their experience of maltreatment, exposure to intimate partner violence, perceived threat, or self-blame within a family (Piotrowski, 2011; Richmond & Stocker, 2009; Skopp, McDonald, Manke, & Jouriles, 2005). While there is a high correlation between siblings with regard to parental neglect (Hines, Kantor, & Holt, 2006), a study of siblings of "index" children referred to child protective services found variability in the experience of abuse (Hamilton-Giachritsis & Browne, 2005). That is, in 44% of the families, the index child was scapegoated; in 37% of the families, all the children experienced nonspecific maltreatment; and in 20% of the families, maltreatment was specific to some but not all of the siblings.

The impact of the abuse of one sibling on the experience of the others has also been studied. Clinicians have noted that the nonabused sibs of victims of CSA tend to be ignored, even though they typically experience reactions such as blaming the victim, guilt, anger, anxiety, depression, and risk of abuse (Nally, 2003). Moreover, the impact of CSA on the nonabused sibling is especially significant when the abuser is the boy's father and/or the abused child is male (Hill, 2003). Finally, in a large sample of young adults, the damaging effect of witnessing the physical abuse of a sibling was much more substantial on all of the outcome measures than even the effects of witnessing violence between one's parents (Teicher & Vitaliano, 2011). Therefore, both the differential and common experiences of trauma within a family should be considered in any assessment of maltreatment.

Siblings are also important as potential sources of trauma. While the determinants and impacts of sibling incest are reviewed in Chapter 6, this section explores the determinants and effects of sibling aggression. Not surprisingly, parental hostility, marital conflict, and parents' maltreatment of children and each other all contribute to the risk of sibling aggression (Hoffman, Kiecolt, & Edwards, 2005; Sims, Dodd, & Tejeda, 2008; Williams, Conger, & Blozis, 2007). General family stress and economic pressure may also contribute to its occurrence, with rates higher among boys with brothers and among the children of mothers with lower levels of education (Ensor, Marks, Jacobs, & Hughes, 2010; Hardy, 2001; Hoffman et al., 2005; Williams et al., 2007). Most importantly, the effects of sibling aggression may be severe, leading to bullying and the refusal to share or interact with unfamiliar peers, trauma symptoms, and the perpetration of dating violence by both males and females (Finkelhor, Turner, & Ormrod, 2006; Noland, Liller, McDermott, Coulter, & Seraphine, 2004; Simonelli et al., 2002; Sims et al., 2008). Given that sibling aggression is more frequent than other sources of child abuse and given that it is predictive of substance abuse, delinquency, and aggression even controlling for other forms of family violence (Button & Gealt, 2010), it is a source of trauma that is too frequently ignored but must be included in any consideration of cycles of violence.

Family Chaos and Cumulative Risk

In Chapter 2, the behaviorally disorganized child was described as experiencing significantly more negative outcomes with regard to both internalizing and externalizing disorders. Among the predictors of behavioral disorganization, in addition to child maltreatment, are chaos and instability within the home. Although family chaos and the cumulative risk of multiple family problems do not always lead to disorganized attachment, they do contribute to a child's poor inhibitory control, lower IQ, behavior problems, aggressive behavior, polyvictimization, and poor sibling relationships (Bendersky, Bennett, & Lewis, 2006; Deater-Deckard et al., 2009; Finkelhor, Ormrod, Turner, & Holt, 2009; Hardaway, Wilson, Shaw, & Dishion, 2012; Kretschmer & Pike, 2009). Family chaos also reduces a child's resilience in the face of physical maltreatment (Jaffee, Caspi, Moffitt, Polo-Tomas, & Taylor, 2007). Therefore, it is relevant to the study of cycles of violence.

Any definition of family chaos has two important aspects: (1) chaos in the physical setting, including noise, crowding and disorganization, confusion, and unpredictability of routines within the home; and (2) psychosocial instability, including parent maladjustment (as reflected in incarceration, substance abuse, mental illness, or long-term hospitalizations), changes in parents' intimate partners, changes in children's schools, residential instability, separations from primary caregivers, unstable foster care arrangements, unstable employment, and changes in family incomes (Ackerman & Brown, 2010). Obviously, many of these indicators of psychosocial instability may also be associated with the occurrence of family violence. Cumulative risk of these different factors is a family-level variable, overlapping with but distinct from poverty, and best reflected as an aggregate measure (Evans, Li, & Sepanski Whipple, 2013). While physical chaos is most predictive of reduced cognitive development, psychosocial instability predicts socioemotional processes and psychological distress, mediated through factors such as caregiver mood, maternal responsiveness, and interparental conflict (Ackerman & Brown, 2010; Doan, Fuller-Rowell, & Evans, 2012). Family instability is associated not only with externalizing and internalizing behaviors, but also with teacher reports of reduced frustration tolerance, poorer social skills and task orientation, lower academic achievement, and disruptions in school (Marcynyszyn, Evans, & Eckenrode, 2008).

The cumulative risk of living in a chaotic or multiproblem household affects children in a number of ways—through the disruption of their ability to self-regulate and to cope with stress, through physiological responses, and through motivational processes, such as attentional control and capacity to tolerate frustration (Ackerman & Brown, 2010; Evans & Kim, 2013). The effects of a chaotic environment are also moderated by other variables such as family and peer support, protective parenting, planful self-regulation, the child's age (with a greater negative impact on younger children), and by genetic factors that confer greater sensitivity to stress (see Chapter 4; Appleyard, Egeland, van Dulmen, & Sroufe, 2005; Brody et al., 2013a, 2013b).

A cumulative risk model, consisting of the family chaos and instability indicators described above, is much more powerful in the prediction of child maltreatment and the severity of its effects than either individual risk factors or conceptual risk domains (Begle, Dumas, & Hanson, 2010; MacKenzie, Kotch, & Lee, 2011; Turner et al., 2012). For example, children with the highest levels of cumulative risk are 10 times more likely to be placed in foster care (Kohl, Edleson, English, & Barth, 2005). Moreover, having only two or three risk factors increases their risk for externalizing behavior problems 19-fold (Gabalda, Thompson, & Kaslow, 2010). In fact, the cumulative risk typically experienced by demographically similar, nonexposed controls compared to children with prenatal cocaine exposure overshadows any effect of the cocaine exposure on children's outcomes (Tronick & Beeghly, 1999).

This review of cumulative risk should not be used to minimize the impact of resilience in multiproblem poor families. Factors such as strong family ties and the resource of friends and neighbors greatly ameliorate the problems associated with family chaos and external stressors (Sousa, 2005). Furthermore, in a study of at-risk boys from multiproblem families, a child's individual characteristics such as intelligence, emotionality, sociability, and teacher-reported likability constituted a cumulative measure of protective factors that was even a better predictor of outcomes than cumulative risk measures (Owens, Shaw, Giovannelli, Garcia, & Yaggi, 1999). Therefore, whether considering risk or resilience, it is misleading to speculate on the intergenerational effects of child maltreatment without reference to the contexts of family functioning and family stressors—yet another reason for considering the broader family context.

IMPLICATIONS FOR TREATMENT

Given that the experience of trauma necessarily affects and is affected by current attachment relationships, it is often most appropriate to intervene with traumatized clients in conjunction with members of their current family of creation. Even when intervening with individuals, it is important to keep in mind the influence of the family of creation, as a potential source of either support or further trauma—in either case, it is integral to interrupting intergenerational cycles of violence. Therefore, this section reviews several interventions that incorporate both attachment theory and family systems perspectives in addressing the experience of trauma. In addition to interventions with fathers (the often ignored member of the family), couple approaches and family therapy approaches are described.

Supporting Father Involvement

As reviewed above, there is extensive research on the effects of positive father involvement and the negative effects of father absence and couple conflict on children's risk for maltreatment, disorganized attachment, and other deleterious outcomes. Yet few clinicians and researchers have taken the next step to suggest modes of intervention for achieving the father's involvement and for preventing family distress. Philip and Carolyn Cowan are the foremost exception—they proposed preventive strategies to help couples transition to marriage, parenthood, a child's entry into school, and the decision to divorce (Cowan & Cowan, 2012). Furthermore, a randomized clinical trial demonstrated the effectiveness of a 24-week couples group in preventing a decline in couple satisfaction from pre- to postpartum (Schulz, Cowan, & Cowan, 2006).

The Cowans also developed a curriculum for a group-based intervention for low-income Mexican American and European American parents to increase fathers' positive involvement with their preschoolers. The curriculum is based on a five-domain risk protective model focusing on: (1) parents' individual adaptation; (2) couple relationship quality; (3) relationship quality in each parent's family of origin; (4) quality of the parent-child relationship; and (5) balance between life stressors and social supports. A randomized clinical trial was conducted comparing 16-week groups for couples that included either an emphasis on relationship issues or parenting issues with a low-dose comparison group. Both couples group conditions were more effective than the comparison group in improving fathers' positive involvement with their children, mothers' interactions with their children, and the child's behavior, based on teacher reports (Cowan, Cowan, Pruett, & Pruett, 2007; Cowan, Cowan, Pruett, Pruett, & Wong, 2009). Moreover, the groups that focused on the couple relationships were even more effective than the parent-focused groups in reducing parent conflict, improving the parenting behavior of both parents, enhancing children's performance on achievement tests in school, and reducing levels of teacher-reported externalizing behavior. Designed for couples who were married, cohabiting, or living separately but raising a child together, the couples group condition that focused on the couple relationship significantly maintained couple satisfaction and decreased children's hyperactivity and aggression 10 years later (Cowan, Cowan, & Barry, 2011). Therefore, intervening directly with the couple (including non-coresiding couples in high-risk environments; Finger et al., 2009) appears to be a feasible and effective way to maintain fathers' involvement in the parenting process and to reduce a child's risk for negative outcomes.

Couples Therapy

Emotionally Focused Therapy

Based on the work of Sue Johnson (2004), emotionally focused therapy explicitly addresses couples' attachment concerns and the impact of emotion on the quality of close relationships. The three stages of treatment include (1) ensuring safety through identifying and de-escalating negative cycles, by helping couples frame the negative cycles and not each other as the "enemy"; (2) creating new interactions to restructure the relationship into a more secure bond, by reengaging withdrawn partners and softening the behavior of more critical, blaming partners; and (3) helping couples consolidate and integrate the changes they have made (Johnson, 2002; Johnson & Courtois, 2009). Additional considerations for working with couples with histories of trauma include coordinating with an individual therapist who is working with the specific trauma victim; assessing the risk of physical aggression (which would rule out or delay the use of emotionally focused therapy); addressing posttraumatic reactions with the use of an educational component about traumatic stress; moving more slowly with potentially a longer regimen of treatment; and emphasizing the therapist's alliance with the couple to an even greater degree than is necessary for couples without trauma histories (Johnson & Courtois, 2009). Techniques may include tracking and reflecting emotional experiences; validating partners' reactions to each other; heightening emotional reactions through questions, repetition, images, metaphors, or enactments; using empathic conjecture and interpretation; and reframing or shifting the meaning of trauma and attachment processes.

Reflective Functioning in Couples Therapy

Couples therapy may also incorporate the notion of reflective functioning or mentalization described in Chapter 2. Namely, one important goal of the therapist is to help couples view themselves and each other as distinct from each other and as seeing, thinking, feeling individuals (Clulow, 2007). The therapist focuses on identifying instances in which clients equate their inner states with outer realities, helping them to understand that having a thought does not necessarily mean that it is true. Clulow (2007) noted that validating thoughts and feelings is especially relevant to individuals or couples who are dismissing in their attachment, while establishing boundaries of thoughts and feelings through the exploration of transference and countertransference is especially important to individuals or couples who are preoccupied or unresolved in their attachment.

The reflective functioning and attachment status of the therapist are also important, given the need for accurate mirroring of emotions in working with couples with histories of trauma. Studies in which therapists were administered the AAI demonstrated that therapists who were secure or earned-secure in their attachment were more likely to establish a good working alliance and to better manage the feelings evoked by difficult or challenging clients (Rizq & Target, 2010b; Schauenburg et al., 2010). On the other hand, therapists with preoccupied attachment had more difficulty in maintaining a therapeutic alliance with their clients (Dinger, Strack, Sachsse, & Schauenburg, 2009). Therapists with lower levels of reflective functioning were either more likely to distance themselves from strong feelings or to become overwhelmed by them (Rizq & Target, 2010a). Given the greater than normal need for a strong therapeutic alliance and well-defined interpersonal boundaries when working with trauma survivors, the therapist's attachment status and capacity to engage in reflective functioning have important repercussions for the success of therapy.

Family Therapy Approaches

Many of the evidence-based family therapy approaches for addressing trauma actually focus on the parent-child dyad (see Chapter 2). Other family-level interventions may be most appropriate when the source of the trauma was either extrafamilial, perpetrated by someone who is no longer in the home, or merely witnessed by someone in the family. For example, the Family Systems Trauma Affect Regulation: Guide for Education and Therapy (Ford & Saltzman, 2009) is a psychoeducational approach to teach family members about the biology of traumatic stress and to give the family a set of skills for supporting individual and family self-regulation through the development of rules, boundaries, communication, and decision-making processes. Another approach, Families Overcoming and Coping Under Stress (Ford & Saltzman, 2009) integrates psychoeducational, narrative, and cognitive-behavioral approaches. Its use of individual and family trauma narrative timelines is especially pertinent to an attachment and family systems approach, with the goals of helping family members make meaning of their experience as well as highlighting differences in their perceptions of the trauma.

Attachment-based family therapy (Diamond, Siqueland, & Diamond, 2003) was developed specifically for families with depressed adolescents but has also been empirically validated with adolescents who were suicidal, including those with a history of sexual trauma (Diamond et al., 2010; Diamond, Creed, Gillham, Gallop, & Hamilton, 2012). It consists of five interrelated treatment tasks: (1) the relational reframe, focusing on the need to repair the parent-adolescent schism instead of pathologizing the adolescent; (2) alliance building with the adolescent, typically meeting alone with him or her to identify treatment goals; (3) alliance building with the parents, meeting alone with them to explore intergenerational themes and parental conflict; (4) reattachment, meeting jointly with the family and encouraging the adolescent to begin the dialogue with the parents by voicing specific complaints; and (5) promoting competency in the adolescent (Diamond et al., 2003).

The biggest challenge for family therapists is addressing trauma that has arisen within the family unit. Given the potential for ongoing abuse and other ramifications for individual family members who disclose abuse or other family secrets within a family session, family therapy is typically used much later in the process when the safety of family members can be ensured. Individual or group therapy might sidestep concerns about safety by allowing the client to deal with the family of origin or family of creation in absentia—exploring the role of attachment and family relationships, perhaps with the use of a family tree to detect and underscore multigenerational patterns and influences. Furthermore, individuals may decide that it is advisable to cut off relationships that have little hope of reconciliation (Kretchmar & Jacobvitz, 2002). However, if family members choose to remain in a relationship, it is usually necessary to follow individual or group sessions with couples therapy or family therapy (see Chapter 5). Even if clients are in treatment to address trauma experienced in their family of origin, both the trauma itself and its resolution in therapy will impact current attachment relationships; failing to attend to current attachment-related anxieties that will arise in therapy could undermine the success of that therapy and harm the current relationship (Follette, Alexander, & Follette, 1991).

In conclusion, the family is the crucible for our most important experiences and our most important relationships. It affects our physiology and shapes our views of ourselves and our world. It also provides an opportunity for change. Therefore, researchers and clinicians ignore the family environment of abuse survivors at their own peril. Interrupting cycles of violence and trauma requires understanding and intervening within this important context.

CHAPTER 4

Neurobiology and Genetics

With the development of more sophisticated, less expensive, and less invasive research techniques, it has become more feasible to explore how parent-child relationships and family contexts affect brain development and children's physiological responses to stress. It has also become more possible to assess whether and how parent-child similarities in aggressive behavior are due to genetic similarities and to identify genetic anomalies that predispose children to the negative effects of a stressful environment and the positive effects of a supportive environment. Finally, advances in the field of epigenetics suggest how even the expression of DNA is affected by environmental stressors. Therefore, as opposed to the notion of nature superseding nurture in intergenerational cycles, research findings have increasingly concluded that neurobiology and genetics interact with parenting and family context and are also themselves influenced by the environment. The following review explores some of the ways in which both biology and psychology shape cycles of violence and trauma.

NEUROBIOLOGY OF ATTACHMENT AND
THE EXPERIENCE OF TRAUMA

The development of the human brain is integrally tied to the mother-infant attachment relationship. In fact, the stage is set for the interaction between attachment and infant brain development even before the child is born and continues to unfold in the first few years of life. Thus, even aside from any direct maltreatment experiences, the child is either more vulnerable to or more protected from trauma. These early influences are critically important in determining the child's own emotion regulation and response to subsequent stressors.

Influences on the Mother-Child Attachment Relationship

Prenatal Stress

Animal models indicate that stress and glucocorticoid exposure experienced prenatally by the fetus may program the offspring's subsequent response to stress (O'Connor, Bergman, Sarkar, & Glover, 2013). In humans, the impact of a mother's history of trauma on the infant's developing brain and eventual attachment security is felt through her experience of prenatal anxiety. Prenatal stress has been found to predict cognitive ability, observed fearfulness, sleep problems, and negative temperament in toddlers and young children (Bergman, Sarkar, O'Connor, Modi, & Glover, 2007; Blair, Glynn, Sandman, & Davis, 2011; Buss, Davis, Hobel, & Sandman, 2011; O'Connor et al., 2007). The effects of prenatal stress on children also include ADHD, conduct disorder, aggression, and anxiety (Glover, 2011), with an evolutionary explanation suggesting that preprogrammed anxiety may be more pertinent to the preparation of a child for its environment than is exposure to maternal depression, which does not typically show these effects. As argued below, the effects of prenatal stress on the developing fetus may be explained in part through the process of epigenesis, in which the DNA expression of the fetus's genes is altered by environmental stressors including the milieu within the womb.

As with other physiological effects, the impact of a mother's prenatal stress on her child is moderated by mother-infant attachment, with effects on cognitive ability only observed in children with an insecure attachment and effects on fearfulness only observed in children with anxious/ambivalent attachment (Bergman, Sarkar, Glover, & O'Connor, 2008, 2010). Marital conflict contributes to prenatal stress and the relationship with the partner moderates the impact of a mother's stress on her infant (Talge, Neal, & Glover, 2007). Therefore, the impact of prenatal stress on the developing fetus is not independent of attachment and the family context.

Mother's Response to the Infant

A mother's attachment security also affects her initial response to her infant. For example, an adult's insecure attachment was associated with greater electrodermal reactivity and reduced feelings of love when listening to a recording of an infant crying (Groh & Roisman, 2009). Similarly, insecure mothers showed a decreased response to face stimuli and a more pronounced negativity in the face-sensitive component of event-related potentials (Fraedrich, Lakatos, & Spangler, 2010). Psychophysiological studies also demonstrate the mutual nature of the mother-child relationship, with the crying of high-risk infants eliciting parental psychophysiological responses reflecting aversiveness and a disposition to aggression (Fox & Hanes, 2008).

Oxytocin

The attachment relationship between mother and child is both dependent upon the effects of the neuropeptide oxytocin on the mother and reciprocally leads to the release of oxytocin in the child. Oxytocin is especially associated with maternal-child attachment, given that its effects are modulated by estrogen (Campbell, 2008). For example, on functional MRI scans, mothers with secure attachment showed activation of the dopaminergic reward centers, including the oxytocin-associated hypothalamic-pituitary-adrenal (HPA) axis, in response to viewing their own infant's smiling or crying faces (Strathearn, Fonagy, Amico, & Montague, 2009). Similarly, mothers exhibited an increase in their levels of plasma salivary oxytocin following high levels of mother-infant affectionate contact (Feldman, Gordon, Schneiderman, Weisman, & Zagoory-Sharon, 2010). Conversely, mothers with insecure-dismissing attachment exhibited reduced activation of the dopaminergic reward system in response to their infant's facial cues and decreased peripheral oxytocin in response to contact with their infant (Strathearn, 2011). Consistent with the effects of family context on attachment and parenting (Chapter 3), oxytocin's effects are moderated by the parent's current social context, memories of attachment, and attachment relationships throughout life (Bartz et al., 2010; Feldman, Gordon, & Zagoory-Sharon, 2011; Gordon, Zagoory-Sharon, Leckman, & Feldman, 2010; Olff et al., 2013).

Moreover, oxytocin facilitates the linkage between environmental stimuli and the infant's memory of the mother (Marazziti et al., 2008). Ironically, the infant's initial attachment to the mother is enabled in part by the immaturity of the infant's nervous system. For example, rat pups develop a rapid, robust preference for the caregiver, even when the presence of the caregiver is paired with electric shock. This behavior appears to be due to the hypofunctional amygdala, which prevents the pup from developing an aversion to an abusive caregiver (Moriceau & Sullivan, 2005). The immature amygdala is not yet capable of associating aversive behavior with alarm or avoidance and instead labels all stimuli as merely "familiar," an association that is unconditionally reinforcing (Coan, 2008). Thus, this filial bonding of an infant with its parent occurs rapidly and unconditionally.

Attachment and the Developing Brain

Through the process of mutual gaze and the monitoring of the child's facial cues, the mother's and infant's autonomic nervous systems are synchronized. In fact, mothers and their children exhibit parallel sympathetic cardiac acceleration and then parasympathetic cardiac deceleration in response to the smile of the other (Schore, 2002). The primary site for this synchronization between mother and child is the orbitofrontal (ventromedial) cortex of the right hemisphere. Schore (2002) referred to this as "the thinking part of the emotional brain" in that it serves as the executive control center for the entire right brain. One of the most important functions of the right orbitofrontal cortex is to modulate the response of the amygdala by either reducing the sense of threat or amplifying it. Namely, fear learning is mediated by two pathways to the amygdala, which is itself regulated by the right orbitofrontal cortex (Coan, 2008). Highly specific sensory information from the thalamus as well as slower and more complex information from the visual cortex may both activate the amygdala and be conditioned by aversive stimuli (e.g., a loud noise, pain). The amygdala is highly sensitive to facial cues and, along with the hippocampus, consolidates both positive and negative long-term memories (Coan, 2008). Thus, through its impact on "automatic" forms of emotion regulation including conditioning and extinction learning and "effortful" forms of regulation requiring attention, working memory, and cognitive reappraisals, the orbitofrontal cortex is connected both with attachment and with emotion regulation.

The amygdala, prefrontal cortex, and hippocampus send information to the hypothalamus, which links the central nervous system to the endocrine system, via the release of cortisol in the HPA axis. In other words, in response to a perceived threat, the hypothalamus releases corticotropin-releasing hormone, which stimulates the release of adrenocorticotropic hormone in the pituitary gland, thus increasing the production of cortisol and catecholamines in the adrenal cortex and preparing the body for optimal functioning under conditions of stress. The cortisol that circulates in the brain then activates glucocorticoid receptors in the hippocampus, leading to a feedback loop to inhibit HPA axis activity (Coan, 2008). Importantly, the hypothalamus is responsive to the effects of social soothing to downregulate HPA axis activity. Thus, the "good-enough" parent regulates her own and her child's autonomic nervous system and in this way modulates the child's excessively high and excessively low levels of arousal (Schore, 2010). In the case of maltreatment or relational trauma, the parent either actively overstimulates the child through abuse and frightening behavior, or alternatively, understimulates the child through neglect. In either case, the parent fails to protect the child from other sources of stress and danger, and through her inaccessibility, fails to regulate the child's over- or underarousal (Schore, 2010). The infant's reaction to this interpersonal stress is felt through the body's two primary stress response systems—the autonomic nervous system and the HPA axis.

Stress and the Autonomic Nervous System

The autonomic nervous system (ANS) consists of the sympathetic nervous system (SNS) which, when activated, prepares the body for the classic fight-or-flight reaction, and the parasympathetic nervous system (PNS), which acts as the brake on the ANS to conserve and restore energy. In the initial stage of threat, the infant reacts with alarm, activating the SNS and leading to the increased secretion of the corticotropin-releasing stress hormone. The activation of the SNS also triggers increased amounts of the neuropeptide vasopressin, associated with perceived lack of safety. This explains the infant's behavioral symptoms of "fear-terror" and is consistent with Bowlby's notion of protest.

If the child's intense interactions with the external environment fail to elicit a response, there is a sudden shift to a state of hypoarousal or dissociation, with corresponding attention to the internal world (Schore, 2002). This is reflected in the activation of the PNS and is characterized by metabolic shutdown and cardiac deceleration. Ideally, as stated previously, the PNS promotes rest, repair, and restoration. However, situations experienced by the infant as hopeless lead to extreme inhibition and passivity in which survival is dependent upon the conservation of energy and the feigning of death in order to remain unnoticed—in essence, a last-resort strategy (Porges, 1997; Schore, 2003). During this state, activation of the more primitive dorsal vagal complex in the brain stem medulla decreases blood pressure, metabolic activity, and heart rate. Moreover, endogenous opioids are released to facilitate the blunting of pain and distress (Schore, 2002).

SNS activity is typically measured in two different ways. Skin conductance level (SCL) baseline and reactivity to lab challenges are reflections of sweat glands innervated by the SNS. Salivary alpha-amylase is another marker of SNS activity. Both high resting SNS levels and heightened SNS reactivity have been associated with hypersensitivity to the environment and aggressive responses (Diamond, Fagundes, & Cribbet, 2012; Murray-Close, Holland, & Roisman, 2012). However, hyporeactive SNS activity has also been associated with aggression, suggesting that physiological underarousal can result in either fearlessness or a need for stimulation (Murray-Close et al., 2012). PNS activity is measured by respiratory sinus arrhythmia (RSA) baseline and reactivity, reflecting rhythmic fluctuations in the heart rate associated with spontaneous breathing. RSA is a manifestation of vagal tone (or the PNS at rest) and reactivity, referring to changes in cardiac output via vagal pathways that facilitate physiological regulation and response to stressors. Generally, a high basal RSA reflects positive emotionality (Diamond & Cribbet, 2013; El-Sheikh, Hinnant, & Erath, 2011) and a decrease in RSA reactivity to stress (vagal suppression) indicates active coping with the environment (Porges, 2007). However, high RSA has also been associated with aggression (Diamond, Fagundes, et al., 2012; Murray-Close et al., 2012), suggesting that an optimal level of functioning is most protective against aggression.

Maltreatment, Family Stress, and the ANS

Early life adversity, including exposure to family conflict, has been associated with both SNS and PNS functioning, explained in part by the type of emotion generated by the exposure (Ali & Pruessner, 2012; Davies, Sturge-Apple, Cicchetti, Manning, & Zale, 2009; Lovallo, 2013). Patterns of both hyperreactivity and hyporeactivity of the ANS appear to mediate between histories of maltreatment and subsequent aggression. For example, SNS hyperreactivity to the high-pitched sounds of crying infants has been found to predict harsh parenting in adults (Joosen, Mesman, Bakermans-Kranenburg, & van IJzendoorn, 2013; Out, Bakermans-Kranenburg, van Pelt, & van IJzendoorn, 2012), while a blunted RSA withdrawal (i.e., a sustained RSA reactivity to stress) was associated with externalizing behaviors in a clinical sample of young children (Fortunato, Gatzke-Kopp, & Ram, 2013). Moreover, El-Sheikh and her colleagues have suggested that individual differences in children's patterns of arousal and regulation, as reflected in the ANS, may explain differential responding to environmental stressors such as marital conflict. In a series of three studies with children and their parents (using multiple reports of marital conflict and children's externalizing behaviors), children's aggression in the face of marital conflict was predicted both by coactivation of the SNS and PNS (high SCL baseline or reactivity combined with high RSA baseline or reactivity) and by coinhibition of the two systems (El-Sheikh et al., 2009). Thus, in either case, physiological vulnerabilities may interfere with engaged and controlled reactions to stress and may increase the risk for aggressive behavior among children exposed to marital conflict.

ANS Reactivity and Gender

The impact of ANS reactivity as the link between maltreatment history and subsequent aggression appears to be moderated by gender. In general, aggression by females is more likely to be associated with hyperreactivity and hypersensitivity to the environment as characterized by the activation of intense emotions. For example, high SCL levels and less RSA suppression (in interaction with a stressful environment) were correlated with externalizing behaviors in girls and relational aggression in women (Diamond, Fagundes, et al., 2012; Murray-Close et al., 2012). Similarly, RSA hyperreactivity while viewing threatening slides predicted antisocial features in women (Sylvers, Brennan, Lilienfeld, & Alden, 2010). More puzzlingly, a combination of either low baseline RSA and SCL reactivity or high baseline RSA and SCL reactivity increased the likelihood that girls with a history of child abuse would engage in aggression as adolescents (Gordis et al., 2010). In contrast, aggression by males tends to be more associated with ANS hyporeactivity or atypical emotion regulation. Namely, more RSA suppression interacted with living in a single-parent home to predict externalizing behaviors in boys (Diamond, Fagundes, et al., 2012). Similarly, an excessively high resting level of RSA predicted relational aggression in men (Murray-Close et al., 2012). Finally, electrodermal hyporeactivity in men was associated with antisocial features (Sylvers et al., 2010). Thus, different patterns of anomalous ANS functioning predict aggressive behavior in males and females, albeit in interaction with the nature of the stressor. For example, the ANS risk for relational aggression is especially severe within the context of a low-quality relationship (Murray-Close et al., 2012).

Stress and the HPA Axis

As opposed to the ANS, the HPA axis engages in a slower and more protracted response to stress (McCrory, De Brito, & Viding, 2010). The cortisol produced by this system makes available stored glucose and lipids in order to meet the energy demands of an individual's need for vigilance to threat and subsequent action. Feedback loops help prevent chronic activation of the HPA axis. The HPA axis has a diurnal pattern with higher levels of cortisol shortly after awakening and a gradual decrease over the course of the day. Therefore, results from studies that measure cortisol levels at only one time during the day are often misleading.

The HPA axis is particularly relevant for attachment-related stress. For example, severely disrupted maternal communication is associated with an increased divergence between mothers' and infants' cortisol levels (Crockett, Holmes, Granger, & Lyons-Ruth, 2013). Moreover, in a study of healthy mother-toddler dyads, cortisol levels in the children were affected more by their participation in the Strange Situation, suggesting more of a response to attachment-related threat, while SNS levels were affected more by a cleanup task, suggesting more of a response to control (Laurent, Ablow, & Measelle, 2012). Studies with rodents and nonhuman primates have highlighted the importance of maternal care in fostering stress resilience in offspring and maternal stress in affecting offspring's cortisol levels and increasing their fearful behaviors (McCrory et al., 2010). For example, infants' exposure to higher levels of amniotic fluid cortisol (resulting from their mothers' prenatal anxiety) resulted in higher prestress cortisol levels and blunted response to stress exposure (O'Connor et al., 2013). Furthermore, the effects of prenatal anxiety on children's cortisol levels persist into adolescence (O'Donnell et al., 2013).

Maltreatment, Family Stress, and the HPA Axis

Maltreatment frequently contributes to dysregulation of the HPA axis. In a meta-analysis, a history of CSA was found to lead to hyperactivation of the HPA axis, including hyperfunctioning of the amygdala and decreased activity of the hippocampus, resulting in a compromised glucocorticoid-negative feedback loop (Nunes, Watanabe, Morimoto, Moriya, & Reiche, 2010). However, this dysregulation may be manifested as either excessive or insufficient cortisol, moderated in part by gender, type of maltreatment, and severity of stress, as the following review shows.

Two general patterns have been observed in samples of maltreated individuals. First, a blunted pattern is characterized by a lower morning level and a more attenuated decrease over time (hypocortisolism). It has been seen in samples of foster children with histories of severe neglect (Carpenter, Shattuck, Tyrka, Geracioti, & Price, 2011; MacMillan et al., 2009; van der Vegt, van der Ende, Kirschbaum, Verhulst, & Tiemeier, 2009). For example, 92% of a sample of toddlers in foster care exhibited atypically low morning cortisol (Nelson & Spieker, 2013). This pattern is also more common among children with internalizing symptoms who have experienced an earlier onset of abuse (Cicchetti, Rogosch, Gunnar, & Toth, 2010). In adults with a history of maltreatment, the effects appear to be amplified with age, suggesting a cumulative response to stress (Carpenter et al., 2009, 2011; Power, Thomas, Li, & Hertzman, 2012).

The second anomalous pattern is characterized by hyperreactivity or higher than normal morning levels of cortisol and a much steeper decline over the course of the day. Although generally seen in milder cases of depression and maltreatment (Harkness, Stewart, & Wynne-Edwards, 2011; van der Vegt et al., 2009), it has also been observed among women with severe abuse, neglected children, and foster children (Graham, Yockelson, et al., 2012; Nicolson, Davis, Kruszewski, & Zautra, 2010; Sullivan, Bennett, & Lewis, 2013), obviating any easy conclusions.

In comparisons of men and women, more pervasive maltreatment is more likely to be associated with the blunted cortisol pattern among females and the steeper decline among males (Doom, Cicchetti, Rogosch,

& Dackis, 2013; Hackman, Betancourt, Brodsky, Hurt, & Farah, 2012; Power et al., 2012). Given that differences in patterns have also been associated with different types of maltreatment (Blair, Berry, Mills-Koonce, & Granger, 2013; Bruce, Fisher, Pears, & Levine, 2009), there are many sources of variance in comparing these two patterns.

Aggression and the HPA Axis

Both chronic hyper- and hypoarousal of the HPA axis are associated with high rates of aggression (Veenema, 2009). The blunted pattern has been particularly associated with aggressiveness, as evidenced by more risk-taking, reactive aggression (especially in males), behavior problems, persistent aggression, psychopathy, and children's aggression mediated by low self-control (Bohnke, Bertsch, Kruk, & Naumann, 2010; Cima, Smeets, & Jelicic, 2008; Daughters, Gorka, Malusiewicz, & Anderson, 2013; Lopez-Duran, Olson, Hajal, Felt, & Vazquez, 2009; Oosterlaan, Geurts, Knol, & Sergeant, 2005; Platje et al., 2013; Poustka et al., 2010; Shoal, Giancola, & Kirillova, 2003; Van De Wiel, van Goozen, Matthys, Snoek, & Van Engeland, 2004). As with hyporeactive SNS activity, low basal cortisol may lead to aggression through its impact on either fearlessness or a need for stimulation (Murray-Close, Han, Cicchetti, Crick, & Rogosch, 2008). An interaction between a low level of cortisol and a high level of testosterone predicted both aggression and functional MRI activation to angry versus happy faces in the amygdala and hypothalamus — subcortical areas related to reactive aggression (Hermans, Ramsey, & van Honk, 2008; Popma et al., 2007).

The pattern of higher baseline cortisol and a steeper decline has also been associated with aggression, namely dysregulated behavior in psychiatric inpatients (Luebbe, Elledge, Kiel, & Stoppelbein, 2012) and in interaction with high levels of testosterone, reactive aggression in women (Denson, Mehta, & Ho Tan, 2013). Interestingly, a longitudinal study suggested that instead of causing aggression or withdrawn behavior, lower morning cortisol may result from higher levels of aggression and a higher afternoon level may result from withdrawn behavior, both of which are associated with a history of maltreatment (Alink, Cicchetti, Kim, & Rogosch, 2012). Therefore, the connection between HPA axis activity and aggression may be iterative, explaining why effects accumulate with age.

ANS and HPA Axis Activity

While research has begun to explore how interactions of the HPA axis with the ANS explain the impact of a history of maltreatment on aggressive behavior (Gordis, Granger, Susman, & Trickett, 2006), it is not yet clear how they affect each other. Early life adversity and internalizing problems frequently lead to elevated SNS reactivity, low RSA levels, and a blunted cortisol response (Ali & Pruessner, 2012; El-Sheikh, Arsiwalla, Hinnant, & Erath, 2011; Lovallo, 2013). However, especially in the case of maltreated or delinquent youth, there are no significant links between the two systems and no apparent interactions (de Vries-Bouw et al., 2012; Gordis, Granger, Susman, & Trickett, 2008). It is possible that the different stress systems not only respond to different types of stressors, but are also mediated by different types of emotions. For example, among toddlers who were exposed to IPV, angry responses were associated with cortisol levels and PNS functioning; in contrast, fearful responses were associated with SNS functioning (Davies, Sturge-Apple, Cicchetti, et al., 2009). Undoubtedly, differences such as these are attributable to as-yet-unspecified interactions between the dynamics of the stressor (be it marital conflict, maltreatment, or some other stressor), preexisting individual differences in the child, gender, developmental stage, and comorbid disorders, such as depression, PTSD, or psychopathy (Gowin et al., 2013; van Goozen, Fairchild, Snoek, & Harold, 2007). Furthermore, within aggressive interactions, such as in IPV, both partners' physiological functioning may play a role in increasing the risk for violent behavior (Feinberg, Jones, Granger, & Bontempo, 2011).

Adaptive Calibration Model

One attempt to integrate findings regarding individual differences in stress responsivity as reflected in ANS and HPA axis activity was proposed by Del Giudice, Ellis, and Shirtcliff (2011) with the adaptive calibration model. It states that an individual's stress responsivity represents a functional match to environmental conditions. Moreover, four prototypical patterns are associated with combinations of physiological characteristics of the SNS, PNS, and the HPA axis (Del Giudice, Hinnant, Ellis, & El-Sheikh, 2012). These patterns are adaptive to the respective environmental conditions faced by the individual in terms of maximizing the chance for survival and reproduction. Significantly, in one test of the model, the patterns of stress response were predicted by the quality of family relationships and not by ecological stressors, such as low socioeconomic status, low income, maternal depression, and alcohol use (Del Giudice et al., 2012).

The *sensitive* profile is characterized by high PNS basal and responsivity levels, moderate to high SNS basal and responsivity levels, and moderate HPA basal activity with high responsivity. It is associated with functioning within a safe, low-stress environment, such as would be expected with secure attachment in a supportive family environment. The moderate basal levels and high levels of responsivity contribute to openness, flexible and engaged attention to the environment, and sensitivity to social feedback, all of which contribute to cooperation and learning.

The *buffered* profile is characterized by moderate PNS basal and responsivity levels, low to moderate SNS basal and responsivity levels, and moderate HPA basal and responsivity levels. It is associated with living in a moderately stressful environment in which the individual's responsivity is not as great as in the sensitive profile but is accompanied by less anxiety, aggression, and risk proneness than in the other two profiles. (It could hypothetically be more prevalent among individuals with dismissing attachment who have more physiological indicators of stress than do secure individuals, but generally function more adequately than either preoccupied or unresolved individuals.)

The *vigilant* profile is characterized by hyperreactivity—in other words, a low PNS basal level, low to moderate responsivity, high SNS basal and responsivity levels, and high to moderate HPA basal and high responsivity levels. This pattern is associated with life in a dangerous, unpredictable environment. It is marked by high trait anxiety and mixtures of aggression/externalizing and withdrawn/internalizing behaviors. The authors hypothesized that this pattern would look different in males and females, with males exhibiting more risk taking, impulsivity, and reactive aggression. Females were hypothesized to exhibit more social anxiety, less impulsivity, and more fearful or withdrawn behavior. A third subtype of the vigilant profile was hypothesized to exhibit elements of both the agonistic and withdrawn behaviors. It has similarities to preoccupied or unresolved attachment.

Finally, the *unemotional* profile is characterized by hyporeactivity—

that is, low PNS basal and responsivity levels, low SNS basal and responsivity levels, and low HPA axis basal and responsivity levels. It is associated with low stress responsivity as an adaptation to an environment marked by severe and traumatic stress, although its prevalence may also be associated with genetic predisposition irrespective of environmental stress. While this pattern was hypothesized to be marked by low empathy and high impulsivity, risk taking, and antisocial behavior in males, it is not yet clear that this male bias exists (Del Giudice et al., 2012).

Much more work is required to test the validity of this model as well as its association with attachment states of mind, different types of maltreatment, and different family contexts. The model does, however, represent an effort to integrate a plethora of research findings on the two stress systems according to an evolutionary approach that assumes the basic functionality of physiological responses to a variety of environments.

Long-Term Effects of Trauma on the Brain

Structural Brain Differences

A variety of effects of trauma have been identified in studies of the brains of children, adolescents, and adults, as reviewed by Teicher and Samson (2013). These effects include alterations in the corpus callosum in both children and adults (McCrory et al., 2010) and reduced volume of the hippocampus in adults—significant in that the hippocampus is the most stress-sensitive structure in the brain. There is also evidence of attenuated development of the neocortex, including the orbitofrontal cortex, the dorsolateral prefrontal cortex, and the visual and auditory cortex. Not surprisingly, enhanced amygdala reactivity to sad or negative faces is a consistent finding. In a study of the cortical networks of adults with and without a history of maltreatment in childhood, a decreased number of neural connections were observed in the brain regions associated with emotion regulation, attention, and social cognition (Teicher, Anderson, Ohashi, & Polcari, 2013). In contrast, enhanced neural connections were observed in regions associated with self-awareness; these results were interpreted as explaining the heightened experience of cravings and greater self-centered mental imagery and cognition frequently observed in survivors of trauma (Teicher et al., 2013).

Abuse Characteristics

Different types of abuse may impact the brain differently, with verbal abuse affecting Wernicke's and Broca's areas and the gray matter volume in auditory cortex (Teicher & Samson, 2013). In contrast, witnessing domestic violence has been associated with reduced gray matter volume in the visual cortex. Furthermore, the impact of maltreatment on the developing brain varies by timing with abuse occurring during sensitive periods associated with specific effects. For example, the hippocampus appears to be particularly susceptible to abuse experienced between the ages of 3 and 5, the corpus callosum to maltreatment between the ages of 9 and 10, and the prefrontal cortex to maltreatment experienced between 14 and 16 years of age (Teicher & Samson, 2013). Studies of adolescents' cortisol stress response to a social stress test also indicated the importance of the timing of the abuse (Bosch et al., 2012). Pre- and postnatal adversity was associated with increased cortisol reactivity, adversity experienced during ages 6–11 years was associated with a high cortisol level (especially in conjunction with pre- and postnatal adversity), and adversity experienced during ages 12–13 and 14–15 were associated with a low cortisol level. Finally, some effects of maltreatment may be delayed, with the impact of early stress on the hippocampus first seen between puberty and adulthood (Teicher & Samson, 2013). Therefore, consistent with a developmental psychopathology perspective, different effects of abuse may emerge at different points in development.

Psychiatric Disorders

The effects of maltreatment on increased risk for psychiatric disorders (such as major depression, substance abuse, anxiety disorders, and PTSD) have been well documented. However, Teicher and Samson (2013) argued that a history of maltreatment greatly exacerbates the effect of these disorders by causing them to emerge earlier, and with greater severity, more comorbidity, a less favorable response to treatment, and brain abnormalities. Thus, individuals who have been maltreated comprise a distinct subtype across these psychiatric disorders.

   In conclusion, neurobiological and psychophysiological research provides another explanation for the observed relationships between a parent's history of trauma and the child's neural development and susceptibility to violence. These intergenerational connections have also been explored from the perspective of genetics, although never independent from the effects of parenting and the environment, as the following review shows.

GENETICS

This book so far has focused on how parenting and other environmental influences either increase or decrease the likelihood that a child will engage in violent behavior or be subject to victimization by others. However, not all children raised in the same household (who experience a shared environment) are affected in the same ways by either sensitive or abusive parenting. Part of these differences can be attributed to their non-shared environments. In other words, children are raised differently as a function of their gender, birth order, personality characteristics, and the family context at the time of their birth and childhood. In fact, even identical twins have some degree of nonshared environment. Furthermore, it is possible that children of abusive parents become aggressive because they share the same genes as their parents. Similarly, it is possible that children of traumatized parents become disorganized in their attachment because they share the same genetic vulnerabilities that contributed to their parents' response to the trauma.

Unlike the impact of parenting and other environmental influences, research suggests that genes have few direct effects on behaviors such as delinquency and crime (Simons & Lei, 2013). Instead, the role of genetics is far more complicated and far more interesting. The rest of this chapter explores the variety of ways in which genes correlate with, interact with, or are even themselves affected by the environment in order to then contribute to the intergenerational transmission of violence.

Gene-Environment Correlations

Passive Gene-Environment Correlation

The most obvious alternative to an environmental explanation for the effects of maltreatment on children's externalizing problems is that parents and children share the same genes for aggressive behavior. Behavior genetic designs can be used to assess or rule out this possibility—comparing the correlations between parents' and children's behavior in monozygotic (MZ) and dizygotic (DZ) twins, siblings, unrelated adopted siblings, and children of twins. Most of these studies have ruled out the role of passive gene-environment correlation (rGE) in accounting for cycles of violence. In other words, the impact of interparental conflict, divorce, harsh parenting, and parental negativity on children's externalizing behavior is not primarily due to sharing the same genotype with one's parents (Burt, Barnes, McGue, & Iacono, 2008; Deater-Deckard, Ivy, & Petrill, 2006; D'Onofrio et al., 2005; Glover, Mullineaux, Deater-Deckard, & Petrill, 2010; Harold et al., 2013).

Moreover, mother-child mutuality or coregulation of the child's emotional and behavior is child specific within families and not due to passive rGE (Deater-Deckard & Petrill, 2004). Given the role of early childbearing on offspring's antisocial behavior (one pathway of intergenerational transmission described in Chapter 6), a comparison of children of siblings and children of twins in Sweden allowed an assessment of the degree to which children's antisocial behavior could be attributed to underlying genetic similarity between mothers and children rather than to the impact of parenting (Coyne, Langstrom, Rickert, Lichtenstein, & D'Onofrio, 2013). As hypothesized, the children of mothers who were younger at the age of their first birth were more likely to be convicted of a crime; there was little evidence for a passive rGE as an explanation for the findings. Even a sibling study of childhood trauma's effect on adult psychosis found that the discordance between siblings was due to differential dosage of trauma exposure and not due to reporting bias or passive rGE (Heins et al., 2011).

On the other hand, evidence for a passive rGE between a chaotic home environment and children exhibiting low effortful control (a characteristic that could contribute to a trajectory of academic problems and association with negative peer groups) did emerge in a longitudinal study of twin pairs (Lemery-Chalfant, Kao, Swann, & Goldsmith, 2013). Furthermore, effortful control was more heritable in chaotic homes, and negative affectivity was more heritable in crowded or unsafe homes, suggesting that the importance of the broader family context (Chapter 3) is due not only to its effects on parenting and family interactions but also to its effects on heritability of certain traits.

Evocative Gene-Environment Correlation

Evocative rGE stems from individuals inadvertently eliciting certain environmental experiences consistent with their genotypes (Klahr & Burt, 2013). Thus, children possessing genetic propensities toward conduct disorders, for example, may elicit maltreatment from their parents. A study of twin families found indeed that certain genetic characteristics of the child evoked maternal control, although did not affect maternal warmth (Klahr, Thomas, Hopwood, Klump, & Burt, 2013). Similarly, evocative rGE explained how a boy's self-control (determined in part by a serotonergic polymorphism) elicited positive parenting from his mother (Pener-Tessler et al., 2013) and how parent-child dyadic mutuality resulted from positive affect, responsiveness, and cooperation evoked from parents by their children (Deater-Deckard & O'Connor, 2000).

Several studies looked more explicitly at the relationship between negative parenting and aggressive behaviors in children. In a longitudinal study of twin pairs, child aggression measured at ages 13–14 was found to evoke negative parenting, which then affected adolescent antisocial behavior measured at ages 16–17 (Narusyte, Andershed, Neiderhiser, & Lichsteinstein, 2007). A study of adoptive parents and their children (a portion of whom were at genetic risk for antisocial behavior) found evidence of a significant but minor role for the observed relationship between negative parenting and externalizing behaviors in children (O'Connor, Deater-Deckard, Fulker, Rutter, & Plomin, 1998). A large longitudinal study of twin and sibling pairs also concluded that parental maltreatment occurred in response to a child's conduct problems and not the other way around, although the observed effects were small (Schulz-Heik et al., 2010). Furthermore, the results of a large study of same-sex twin or sibling pairs from intact families and stepfamilies suggested that the impact of child-based genetic traits on the parent-child relationship increased as marital adjustment decreased (Ulbricht et al., 2013). That is, a child with a more difficult temperament (characterized by impulsivity, negativity, or aggression) evoked more negative parenting within the context of marital discord than did a sibling with an easier temperament. This interaction between marital stress and evocative rGE was particularly pronounced among mothers, suggesting that they were even more attuned and reactive to their child's temperamental traits than were fathers when they were distressed in the marriage.

However, evocative effects are not always apparent. A longitudinal study of adoptive families found that parent-child conflict led to conduct problems in children and not the other way around, thus ruling out the role of evocative rGE in cycles of violence (Klahr, McGue, Iacono, & Burt, 2011). Therefore, research on children's ability to evoke either positive or negative reactions from their parents is inconclusive, although its potential interaction with the family context warrants more attention.

Active Gene-Environment Correlation

In addition to inadvertently eliciting reactions from parents that then reinforce the child's behaviors, children and adults may actively seek out environmental influences on their behavior. Much of the research in this area has used comparisons of MZ and DZ twins to look at the genetic determinants of substance abuse, a behavior clearly related to both victimization and the perpetration of violence (Cleveland, Wiebe, & Rowe, 2005; Hicks et al., 2013; Loehlin, 2010). While all three of these studies found evidence of genetic influences on actively seeking out a substance-abusing peer group, the results of Loehlin (2010) were small and limited to females, and Hicks et al.'s (2013) results also found evidence of direct genetic effects of substance abuse.

Finally, Harden (2014) made the argument that the topic of adolescent sexuality and early pregnancy (a frequent outcome of a history of CSA; see Chapter 6) should include consideration of a genetic component. She proposed that well-designed studies should be able to differentiate shared environments (e.g., effects of parenting) from passive rGE (e.g., early sexuality and pregnancy due to sharing genes with an equally risk-taking parent) from evocative rGE (e.g., the occurrence of parent-child conflict stemming from a girl's early physical maturation and then leading to her early sexual behavior) and from active rGE (e.g., an adolescent with dopaminergic sensation-seeking genes foregoing the use of condoms). Interestingly, she also referred to a study in which genetic effects on early consensual sexual behavior among CSA survivors were negligible (Waldron et al., 2008), suggesting instead the primacy of trauma and family context in contributing to adolescent pregnancy among CSA survivors. Epigenetics, however, may play a role in the early sexuality of these young women, as described below.

Gene × Environment Interactions

Candidate Genes

A variety of candidate genes have been identified as potentially related to attachment security, disorganized attachment, and aggression, and therefore as pertinent to the study of intergenerational cycles of violence. For example, given dopamine's role in attentional, motivational, and reward mechanisms (Robbins & Everitt, 1999), studies have examined the effects of the minor allele of the DRD4-7 repeat polymorphism. Second, the gene for catechol-O-methyltransferase (COMT) has received attention because it is involved in the inactivation of the catecholamine neurotransmitters, including dopamine. Its most-studied polymorphism is Val 158Met, which decreases the function of the enzyme, leading to higher synaptic dopamine levels, affecting the interaction between the prefrontal cortex and the limbic system (and thus emotional processing).

Third, seretonin's involvement in affect and emotion has focused attention on the 5HTTLPR polymorphism of the serotonin transporter gene, with the short allele (either *ss* or *sl*) frequently associated with problematic outcomes. Seretonin is also related to sensitive responsiveness toward infants (Bakermans-Kranenburg & van IJzendoorn, 2008). Finally, as described previously, oxytocin is closely related to social bonding and parenting behaviors; therefore, polymorphisms in the oxytocin receptor gene (OXTR) are of particular interest. While many other genes and their polymorphisms are also potentially related to the intergenerational transmission of violence, these are the ones that will be the primary (although not exclusive) focus of a review of gene × environment (G × E) interactions.

Differential Susceptibility

The *diathesis-stress model* suggests that some individuals are especially vulnerable to the effects of negative environmental influences as a function of their underlying genetic makeup. In contrast, the *differential-susceptibility model* proposes that these individuals are more sensitive to the effects of the environment as a function of their genes (Belsky & Pluess, 2009). That is, not only do these plasticity genes render carriers of these genetic variants more vulnerable to the effects of harsh parenting and other environmental hardships but when environmental conditions are supportive, these genetic variants lead to outcomes that are more positive than those experienced by individuals lacking these polymorphisms. Thus, there is an evolutionary advantage of variability among children in their plasticity and susceptibility to environmental influences, including parenting. These gene alleles can affect individuals for worse or for better depending upon the environmental conditions with which they interact. As Belsky and Pluess (2009) have noted, past research has failed to consider that a supportive environment may result not only in an absence of symptoms in children possessing these genotypes, but actually superior functioning relative to children who do not carry these particular alleles. Research has repeatedly validated this notion, as the following review shows. Given that common plasticity markers include negative emotionality, impulsivity, and anger proneness (Belsky & Pluess, 2009), the implications for understanding and interrupting cycles of violence are exciting and dramatic.

G × E and Parenting

The stage is initially set for gene-environment interactions to contribute to cycles of violence and trauma through their impact on parents. For example, individuals who carried the short allele (either *ss* or *sl*) of the 5HTTLPR gene were significantly more likely to respond with depression to negative life events or to a history of unsupportive parenting (Caspi et al., 2003; Taylor et al., 2006). At the same time, these individuals exhibited the fewest symptoms of depression when their early environment and recent life events had been positive. Similarly, individuals with either the short 5-HTTLPR allele or the DRD4-7 repeat allele were more likely to be unresolved in their attachment in reaction to problems experienced during childhood, suggesting the influence of the serotonergic and dopaminergic systems on the lack of resolution regarding experiences of loss or trauma (Bakermans-Kranenburg, van IJzendoorn, Caspers, & Philibert, 2011; Caspers et al., 2009). In contrast, individuals with the DRD4-7 repeat allele had the lowest scores for unresolved loss or trauma when they did not report a history of harsh parenting (Bakermans-Kranenburg et al., 2011). It should also be noted that a study of German adults who were administered the AAI found no impact on attachment of the 5-HTTLPR polymorphism and a protective effect of the DRD4-7 repeat allele (Reiner & Spangler, 2010). Therefore, interpretations of findings warrant caution.

Genetic polymorphisms also directly affect maternal behaviors. For example, as compared to mothers not possessing the allele, mothers possessing the short (or functionally similar L_G) 5-HTTLPR allele were more sensitive to their children and more likely to exhibit a higher relationship quality with their infant if they had experienced positive caregiving themselves as children (Mileva-Seitz et al., 2011). On the other hand, mothers who lacked this allele were more likely to orient away from their babies if they also had a history of negative parenting, perhaps protecting their children from the impact of their own negative history of parenting (or affecting their children in a different way). Another study found a cumulative impact of plasticity genes on parenting, with the presence of more of these alleles (including the DRD4-7 repeat and the short allele of 5HTTLPR) associated with more differential susceptibility to the parent's own history of maternal parenting in adolescence (Beaver & Belsky, 2012). That is, parents with these alleles experienced more parental stress than noncarriers of these alleles when they reported a history of negative mother-child interactions in adolescence and less parental stress than comparison parents when their experience in adolescence had been positive. Dopaminergic receptor and transporter genes were also found to affect levels of maternal negativity, paternal negativity, and child maltreatment for Caucasian males (Beaver, Shutt, Vaughn, DeLisi, & Wright, 2012).

Finally, the impact of these genetic variants on parenting can be seen through their effects on the relationship context of parents. For example, a polymorphism of the GABRA2 gene appeared to interact with a history of harsh parenting to predict greater hostility toward romantic partners (Simons et al., 2013), pertinent to this discussion because of its relevance both to IPV and to the impact of partner conflict on parenting. In contrast, a supportive history of parenting led to less partner aggression as compared to individuals with other genotypes. Furthermore, mothers with the GG genotype of the oxytocin receptor (OXTR) gene were much more negatively affected by spillover from interpartner conflict, leading to their harsh and punitive caregiving behaviors toward their children (Sturge-Apple, Cicchetti, Davies, & Suor, 2012). However, they displayed greater sensitivity toward their children than parents with other genotypes at low levels of interparental conflict. Therefore, consistent with the notion of differential susceptibility, certain genetic variants interact with childhood history and current circumstances to contribute to either especially harsh parenting or especially sensitive parenting.

G × E Effects on Children

Just as the presence of certain alleles increases the susceptibility of parents to both positive and negative effects of the environment on their caregiving behaviors, genetic polymorphisms affect how a child responds to either abusive or sensitive parenting. For example, negative parenting interacted with the DRD4-7 repeat allele to predict lower levels of effortful control and more inattention problems, with lower levels of inattention observed in response to highly sensitive care (Berry, Deater-Deckard, McCartney, Wang, & Petrill, 2013; Smith, Sheikh, et al., 2012). Furthermore, children carrying either serotonergic or dopaminergic risk alleles were more susceptible to the effects of insecure attachment and to the effects of high maternal negativity in the prediction of their levels of negative emotionality and fear as infants and their proclivities to poor levels of self-regulation and stress reactivity as children and youth (Gilissen, Bakermans-Kranenburg, van IJzendoorn, & Linting, 2008; Kochanska, Philibert, & Barry, 2009; Pauli-Pott, Friedel, Hinncy, & Hebebrand, 2009; Wright, Schnupp, Beaver, Delisi, & Vaughn, 2012). As with other research, secure attachment and low levels of maternal negativity interacted with these genes to predict exceptionally good self-regulation. Belsky and Beaver (2011) found a similar cumulative impact of multiple plasticity alleles on both greater and lesser degrees of self-regulation in male adolescents, as a function of supportive versus unsupportive experiences of parenting. Other studies found that children's compliance with their mothers' direction was affected by the interaction of the quality of mothers' parenting with the COMT genotype and polymorphisms of the serotonin transporter gene in a manner consistent with differential susceptibility (Kok et al., 2013; Sulik et al., 2012).

As emphasized in Chapter 2, not just maternal negativity but also maternal withdrawal can lead to disorganized attachment in a child. Consistent with this observation, maternal disengagement interacted with genetic effects in the development of aggressive behaviors in children (Boutwell, Beaver, Barnes, & Vaske, 2012). Maternal anxiety assessed prenatally and postnatally also interacted with the child's short 5HTTLPR allele to predict the child's emotional problems at age 5 (Tiemeier et al., 2012). To complicate matters further, a G × G × E interaction was found in a sample of rural African American youths (Brody et al., 2013b). Namely, carrying both the short 5HTTLPR allele and the DRD4-7 repeat allele interacted with the supportiveness of the family environment at ages 11–13 to predict physical health consequences at age 19. Therefore, it is likely that even more complex interactions contribute to outcomes.

Gene-environment interactions also predict insecure and disorganized attachment in a child. Early research found that the DRD4-7 repeat allele interacted with other alleles to predict disorganized attachment and more anxiety and resistance in the Strange Situation (Lakatos et al., 2002, 2003). While Bakermans-Kranenburg and van IJzendoorn (2004) did not replicate this finding, they did subsequently find that the child's DRD4-7 repeat allele interacted with the mother's history of unresolved loss or trauma to predict the child's disorganized attachment and externalizing behaviors to a highly significant degree—18.8-fold (van IJzendoorn & Bakermans-Kranenburg, 2006). On the other hand, Gervai et al. (2007) found that the presence of the DRD4-7 repeat allele was unrelated to the association between maternal affective communication and disorganized attachment.

More recent research has found that mothers' low responsiveness was associated with their child's insecure and disorganized attachment only in children with the short 5HTTLPR alleles (Barry, Kochanska, & Philibert, 2008; Spangler, Johann, Ronai, & Zimmermann, 2009). Similarly, while maternal responsiveness uniquely predicted children's attachment security, the presence of the short 5HTTLPR allele in the child predicted the child's emotional reactivity as evidenced by attachment classifications characterized by higher emotional distress (i.e., disorganized attachment and anxious/ambivalent attachment; Raby et al., 2012). Therefore, a mother's sensitivity and responsiveness were especially important for highly reactive children.

The interactive effects of the 5HTTLPR polymorphism with insecure attachment have also been observed in adolescents with regard to aggressive behavior, depression among boys, ruminative anxiety, and substance abuse (Olsson et al., 2005; Starr, Hammen, Brennan, & Naiman, 2013; Zimmerman, Mohr, & Spangler, 2009). It is noteworthy that in all three of these studies, the short 5HTTLPR allele was associated with significantly less risk among adolescents who were securely attached. Similarly, certain dopaminergic genes (DRD4 and COMT) were found to moderate the impact of parents' divorce on adolescents' self-reported externalizing behaviors (Nederhof, Belsky, Ormel, & Oldehinkel, 2012).

Gene-environment interactions are also relevant to the experience of children in orphanages and foster care. The Val66Met polymorphism of the brain-derived neurotrophic factor gene was found to interact with the length of time in orphanages among youth from Southeast Asia, Russia/ Europe, and the Caribbean/South America in predicting attention problems (Gunnar et al., 2012). Namely, youth with at least one copy of the Met allele (*Val/Met* or *Met/Met* genotypes) were positively affected by early adoption and negatively affected by adoption occurring at an older age relative to youth with the *Val/Val* genotype. The Val66Met polymorphism and the short 5HTTLPR allele also interacted with the quality of caregiving to predict levels of indiscriminate social behavior among children from orphanages in Bucharest (Drury et al., 2012). That is, children with both of these alleles displayed the most signs of indiscriminate social behavior at age 54 months if they had been previously randomly assigned to care as usual and the least signs of indiscriminate social behavior if they had received high-quality foster care. The type of intervention had no impact on children who had neither of these alleles.

Other G × E Effects

Although parenting and family functioning are generally the most important environmental determinants of child behavior, other environmental effects become increasingly important as children become adolescents. Adolescents with polymorphisms of the plasticity genes described above exhibit greater sensitivity (to good or bad effect) to these other environmental influences. For example, G × E effects have been noted for sensitivity to peer influences on substance abuse, mediated in part by dopamine's effects on social bonding with alcohol- and drug-using peers (Brody et al., 2012; Creswell et al., 2012; Daw et al., 2013).

The neighborhood in which a family resides is yet another important contextual factor. As discussed in Chapter 3 with regard to the broader context of the family, living in a stressful and dangerous community can impact children through its effects on their parents and, as they age, through its more direct effects on their personal safety, autonomy, peers, aspirations, and school experience. Genetic variability has been found to interact with adverse family contexts to predict lower academic attainment and competencies in adolescence (Wickrama & O'Neal, 2013). Furthermore, with dopamine's influence on impulsive decision making, individuals carrying the DRD4-7 repeat genotype who were raised in lower socioeconomic status neighborhoods were significantly more likely to prefer immediate, smaller rewards over larger but delayed rewards than were individuals without this genotype (Sweitzer et al., 2013). Consistent with a differential susceptibility model, they were also more likely than individuals without this genotype to delay gratification if they had not experienced early childhood socioeconomic disadvantage.

Lower academic achievement and poor delay of gratification are certainly not synonymous with aggressive behavior. However, they may contribute to cycles of violence through their associations with negative peer group influences. Other research has examined more directly the interaction of genetic variants with neighborhood disadvantage in the prediction of aggressive behavior. For example, dopaminergic genetic variants have been found to predict violent behavior when combined with exposure to neighborhood disadvantage and higher violent crime rates (Barnes & Jacobs, 2013). Furthermore, an MAOA polymorphism interacted with perceived prejudice to increase the probability of arrest for males (Schwartz & Beaver, 2011). The plasticity of variants of dopamine receptor genes, the serotonin transporter gene (5HTTLPR), and MAOA was observed in a longitudinal study of African Americans (Simons et al., 2011, 2012). Under adverse social conditions, carriers of these genotypes were more likely to exhibit aggression and adopt the street code. Under favorable conditions, they exhibited less aggression than others without these genotypes.

Thus, much of this research indicates that genes may interact with environmental circumstances to influence life history trajectories. In a more explicit test of this assumption, Gibbons et al. (2012) examined the effects of environmental risk and poverty, low levels of parental monitoring, and perceived racial discrimination. In this sample, African American adolescents who carried the short 5HTTLPR allele and the DRD4-7 repeat allele were significantly more likely to engage in faster (and more risky) life history strategy behaviors if they had experienced more racial discrimination and less likely than adolescents without these alleles if they had experienced less discrimination. Given the relevance of risky life history strategies to sexual revictimization, involvement in an abusive romantic relationship, and abusive parenting, a study such as this has important implications for intergenerational cycles of violence and trauma.

In conclusion, research on sensitivity to negative parenting and to contextual influences in the family, peer group, and neighborhood suggest that these G × E effects may all contribute to the intergenerational transmission of violence. On the other hand, the strong evidence of differential susceptibility suggests that individuals who are the most vulnerable to adverse parenting and environmental conditions are also the same individuals most likely to benefit from support (Simons et al., 2011).

Epigenesis

Methylation

This field of research proposes that stress experienced (primarily) by the mother can lead to stable changes in the offspring's DNA expression without actually altering the DNA sequence. While there are several ways in which this change in the expression of the gene can occur, the most commonly studied mechanism is methylation. Namely, the gene consists of four bases (guanine, cytosine, adenine, and thymine) whose unique sequence determines protein synthesis within the cell. When a methyl group attaches to a cytosine nucleotide, the gene is effectively silenced through the inhibition of the transcription of DNA to RNA. This process occurs primarily within the regulatory regions of the gene in close proximity to the transcription site. Commonly studied sites associated with DNA methylation include the serotonergic promoter region (5HTTLPR), the glucocorticoid receptor, arginine vasopressin, and brain-derived neurotrophic factor (Beach et al., 2013; Ventura-Junca & Herrera, 2012). Methylation of a gene can occur at any time within its life cycle and can either silence, diminish, or augment gene expression depending upon the direction of the gene's effect (Yehuda & Bierer, 2009). Furthermore, because the bond between the methyl group and the cytosine nucleotide is very strong, the change in gene expression, while potentially reversible, is often long lasting (Champagne & Curley, 2009). In fact, methylated genes (and altered gene expression) can be transmitted across generations through the process of mitosis and, in some cases, during meiosis (Pretorius, 2010). Therefore, epigenesis is not limited to the impact on the child of stress that was experienced by the parent but even on genetic expression within the grandchild. More recent research has been conducted on humans through the measurement of the fraction of cytosine molecules in a sample that are methylated at a specific location (Beach et al., 2013). This research suggests that different sources of stress can lead to methylated genes with behavioral consequences.

Prenatal Stress

Much of the research on epigenesis is based on animal models, including the impact of prenatal stress on methylation. Prenatal stress not only changes the hormonal milieu of the developing fetus but may also change gene expression through the process of methylation. For example, fetal alcohol-exposed rats evidenced methylation and decreased functioning of peptides associated with stress functions, and these deficits persisted for two generations of male offspring (Govorko, Bekdash, Zhang, & Sarkar, 2012). Furthermore, even prenatal "by-stander" stress stemming from stress to a cage mate led to increased DNA methylation in the frontal cortex and hippocampus of rat offspring (Mychasiuk et al., 2011).

Pregnancy-related anxiety has been correlated with methylation of the human glucocorticoid receptor gene (Hompes et al., 2013). Thus, many of the observed associations between prenatal stress and infant neurodevelopment are explained by epigenesis. On the other hand, postnatal experiences may moderate these early epigenetic effects (Monk, Spicer, & Champagne, 2012).

Maltreatment and Childhood Adversity

Just as postnatal experiences can diminish the effects of prenatal stress on methylation, postnatal experiences can themselves have epigenetic effects. Notably, child maltreatment (and other types of childhood adversity such as parental loss and inadequate nurturing) is associated with methylation of glucocorticoid receptors leading to attenuated cortisol responses, an indicator of poor subsequent reactions to stress (Tyrka, Price, Marsit, Walters, & Carpenter, 2012). Significantly higher levels of methylation observed in samples of adolescents and adults who were maltreated in childhood have been associated with later health problems, suicide, impulsivity, and aggression (Pregeli & Videtic, 2010; Rylands et al., 2012; Wang et al., 2012; Yang et al., 2013).

Different types of adversity in childhood lead to different patterns of methylation. For example, early parental death, associated with hyper-methylation of the glucocorticoid receptor that was mediated by the MAOA-L allele, has been found to increase the risk of conduct disorders in males who experienced childhood adversity (Melas et al., 2013). Thus, there may be an epigenetic × genetic basis to the prevalence of childhood loss observed by Corvo (2006) in his study of partner-abusing males. The effects of methylation are not limited to childhood; therefore, poverty, combat exposure, PTSD, alcohol use, and even work stress and burnout have been associated with methylation, increasing an individual's vulner-ability to subsequently experienced stress and perhaps to one's offspring's reaction to stress (Alasaari et al., 2012; Rusiecki et al., 2013; Talley, 2009; Uddin et al., 2010; Zahs et al., 2012).

Paternal Effects of Epigenesis

Even though most studies have assumed the primacy of maternal effects on the process of epigenesis in children, more recent research is begin-ning to explore the role of the father in the methylation of the child's genes. Research on mice has noted that the exposure of male mice to chronic stress before breeding changed sperm content, leading to signifi-cantly reduced HPA stress axis responsivity and to measures of depression- and anxiety-like behaviors in their offspring (Dietz et al., 2011; Rodgers, Morgan, Bronson, Revello, & Bale, 2013). Other research on mice sug-gested that enriched environmental influences on the fathers not only contributed to increased growth of offspring but also to increased mater-nal reproductive investment in the offspring (Mashoodh, Franks, Curley, & Champagne, 2012). Finally, in perhaps the only study to date to exam-ine paternal effects on epigenesis in humans, maternal stressors in infancy and paternal stressors during preschool predicted differential methylation in a sample of adolescents (Essex et al., 2013). Clearly, more research is needed to examine the differential and interactive effects of mothers and fathers on methylation and the change in gene expression in their off-spring.

Epigenesis and Gene-Environment Interactions

The story becomes even more interesting when considering the relation-ship between epigenesis and gene-environment interactions. For example, in a sample of women who had been adopted shortly after birth, a subsequent history of CSA was associated with higher levels of methylation and antisocial features, even controlling for genetic risk for psychopathology in their biological parents (Beach et al., 2013). In addition, a genetic risk for psychopathology interacted with the experience of CSA to increase the likelihood of epigenetic changes—thus, there was a $G \times E$ effect on the process of epigenesis.

Reciprocally, epigenesis may play a role in the expression of genes associated with plasticity (i.e., sensitivity to the effects of the environment). Labonte et al. (2012) found that the most significantly methylated genes in individuals with a history of severe abuse (as compared to controls) were those involved in cellular and neuronal plasticity. Similarly, an interaction between methylation, the usually protective long 5HTTLPR allele, and the experience of loss or trauma resulted in a lack of resolution regarding attachment, as assessed with the AAI (van IJzendoorn, Caspers, Bakermans-Kranenburg, Beach, & Philibert, 2010). The short variant of the 5HTTLPR allele only predicted unresolved loss or trauma in the relative absence of methylation, whereas the short variant interacted with more methylation to predict less unresolved loss or trauma, thus reversing the typical interactive effects of this genetic allele. Therefore, while a gene-environment interaction can alter the subsequent expression of genetic traits, environmental factors such as maltreatment can change the likelihood of genetic expression in those alleles that are most susceptible to environmental influences—it can make them more plastic or even reverse the normal direction of their plasticity. Thus, a simple comparison between nature and nurture is meaningless—instead, nature and nurture interact and affect each other in countless ways.

IMPLICATIONS FOR TREATMENT

Ironically, a significant conclusion from research on genetics is that interventions with the environment (most notably parenting) can interrupt intergenerational cycles of violence and trauma. For example, the theory of differential susceptibility argues for the power of therapeutic interventions with children at risk (i.e., carriers of plasticity genes as indicated by markers such as difficult temperament, impulsivity, and anger proneness; Belsky & Pluess, 2009). Several studies have indeed provided evidence of differential response to treatment as a function of genetic polymorphisms, although this remains a relatively unstudied phenomenon. The VIPP-SD parenting intervention referred to in Chapter 2 was effective in lowering cortisol production, stress reactivity, and externalizing behaviors in children with the DRD4-7 repeat allele but not in children without this plasticity allele (Bakermans-Kranenburg, van IJzendoorn, Mesman, et al., 2008; Bakermans-Kranenburg, van IJzendoorn, Pijlman, et al., 2008). In a study of behavioral parent training for children with ADHD (van den Hoofdakker et al., 2012), differential effects of treatment were attributable to the presence of a dopamine transporter genotype (the DAT1-10-repeat allele). The findings were interpreted as reflecting the aberrant sensitivity to reinforcement via dopamine of children with ADHD carrying this polymorphism. More broadly, these studies suggest the potential for interventions pertinent to the specific dynamics of a particular disorder.

The notion of differential susceptibility also adds to our understanding of resilience. On one hand, by virtue of the absence of genetic polymorphisms described above, some children are less likely to be adversely affected by harsh parenting and less likely to exhibit intergenerational transmission of violence. On the other hand, those children who do possess more of the plasticity genes reviewed above may be more responsive to early and positive interventions. Resilience may thus be a bimodal description of individuals who are more impervious to difficult circumstances and individuals who are especially responsive to positive surroundings. Bonanno (2004) has proposed that human resilience in reaction to loss and trauma is actually much more common than often believed. Resilience also encompasses a variety of different pathways, suggesting the occasional utility of counterintuitive approaches, such as the encouragement of self-enhancement rather than realistic assessments of the self and one's current situation. Exploration of those strategies spontaneously used by individuals who have survived and even thrived in the face of loss and trauma might increase our therapeutic repertoire.

The discovery of epigenetic effects of maltreatment calls for the use of early parenting interventions—preferably, even prior to the birth of the child. Resolution of pregnancy-specific prenatal anxiety is essential to prevent abusive parenting, the inadvertent misattunement of a mother to her child, and even the hormonal and epigenetic effects of prenatal anxiety that may contribute to the child's lifelong susceptibility to stress. As Harwood (2006, p. 5) has said, "Head Start is too late." Research on paternal epigenetic effects, although currently based primarily on animal models, suggests an urgent need and a promising new direction for intervening with high-risk fathers. Finally, as with research reviewed in Chapter 3 on the family context of attachment relationships, research on oxytocin, gene-environment interactions, and the modification of epigenetic effects by environmental influences reminds us that social bonding and current attachment relationships can overcome the effects of neurobiology and genetics. Thus, nurture is supplemented by but not superseded by nature.

CHAPTER 5

Peer Victimization and Partner Violence

The consequences of disorganized attachment include controlling behavior, which, along with insecure attachment, has definite implications for the perpetration of and vulnerability to partner violence in adolescents and adults (Chapter 2). However, the effects of maltreatment, trauma, and insecure or disorganized attachment can be observed even earlier in the form of peer victimization.

PEER VICTIMIZATION

Bullies, Victims, and Bully-Victims

Peer victimization is quite common, even among young children. For example, 10% of a sample of third to sixth grade boys and girls were classified as extremely physically and verbally victimized by their peers (Perry, Kusel, & Perry, 1988). Another large sample of middle school students found that 41% were either bullies or victims (Lovegrove, Henry, & Slater, 2012). School bullying overlaps significantly with cyberbullying (Kessel Schneider, O'Donnell, Stueve, & Coulter, 2012). Moreover, there appears to be a stable propensity to be victimized, as assessed across time (Perry et al., 1988; Sweeting, Young, West, & Der, 2006). Furthermore, both the bully and the victim are typically rejected by the larger peer group, increasing the likelihood that they will be interacting with each other by default (Perry et al., 1988).

Bullying may take the form of either physical or relational aggression, with the latter consisting of emotional abuse and the hurtful manipulation of friends and peers (Crick & Bigbee, 1998). While boys are more likely to be physically or overtly victimized, girls are more likely to engage in and be subject to relational victimization (Casas et al., 2006; Storch, Brassard, & Masia-Warner, 2003). While bullies engaging in relational aggression have fewer behavior problems, they are also the least likely to be prosocial, exhibiting cool manipulation (Wolke, Woods, Bloomfield, & Karstadt, 2000). Both physical and relational aggression have a negative impact on the perpetrator and the victim alike, with effects including behavior problems, hyperactivity, lower prosocial behavior, a fear of negative evaluation, physiological symptoms, anxiety, depression, social avoidance, loneliness, and even suicidal ideation and self-injurious behavior (Crick & Bigbee, 1998; Gladstone, Parker, & Malhi, 2006; Hilt, Cha, & Nolen-Hoeksema, 2008; Peter, Roberts, & Buzdugan, 2008; Storch et al., 2003; Sweeting et al., 2006; Wolke et al., 2000).

While there are neurobiological correlates to bullying, it is unclear whether they precede or follow from the bullying. For example, in a sample of high-risk children, physically aggressive behavior was associated with the pattern of high morning cortisol levels followed by a steep decline (described in Chapter 4), whereas relational aggression was associated with the blunted pattern (Murray-Close et al., 2008). Furthermore, cortisol dysregulation was correlated with both physical and relational aggression in both genders. The relationship between these patterns of dysregulation and aggression were even more pronounced among non-maltreated children than those with a history of maltreatment. Thus, the HPA axis in some children may be dysregulated even independent of a history of maltreatment. However, this sample's high-risk status did not rule out the possibility of prenatal, familial, or other environmental stressors.

Furthermore, many of these effects are long-lasting, as indicated by the reports of current symptoms of shame, anxiety, depression, loneliness, and relationship problems among adults who were bullied as children (Carlisle & Rofes, 2007; Faith, Storch, Roberti, & Ledley, 2008; Ireland & Power, 2004). Bullying often continues into adolescence and adulthood, leading to an increased risk for later dating violence and intimate partner violence (IPV; Corvo & deLara, 2010; Goldstein, Chesir-Teran, & McFaul, 2008; Haapasalo, 2000; Herrenkohl, Catalano, Hemphill, & Toumbourou, 2009).

Victimization tends to be uncorrelated with aggression, suggesting that some portion of victims are not just passive but also provocative (Olweus, 1978). Thus, in addition to pure bullies and pure victims, there is a small but significant group of children who are both anxious as bullies and provocative as victims (Woods & White, 2005). These "bully-victims" are similar to pure bullies in terms of their anger toward others and their tendency to sensation seeking, but also similar to pure victims in terms of their experience of lower levels of social inclusion (Lovegrove et al., 2012). They are even more likely than other groups to exhibit deficits in reflective functioning, to have the highest levels of arousal, emotional loneliness, severe behavior problems, and psychiatric symptoms years later, and to be rejected by their peers (Ireland & Power, 2004; Kochenderfer-Ladd, 2003; Kumpulainen & Rasanen, 2000; Shakoor et al., 2012; Wolke et al., 2000; Woods & White, 2005). Research on parent-child attachment helps to explain the experiences of these bully-victims as well as bullies and victims more generally.

Attachment and Peer Victimization

A seminal study that explored the impact of parent-child attachment on peer victimization was conducted by Troy and Sroufe (1987). Three blind independent judges observed the interactions of 38 4- to 5-year old children whose attachment status had been assessed in the Strange Situation when they were toddlers. The children were assigned to same-gender play pairs for a total of 19 dyads, and their behavior was coded for both physical and relational aggression. Five of seven dyads with at least one child with avoidant attachment showed victimization, whereas no victimization was observed in any of the seven dyads that did not include a child with avoidant attachment. Thus, all victimizers were avoidant and all victims were insecurely attached (either avoidant or anxious/ambivalent). In contrast, securely attached children were never in a victimizing relationship, whether or not the play partner was avoidant. That is, secure children simply did not allow themselves to be vulnerable, either making the interaction as positive as possible, choosing not to relate to their aggressive partner at all, or, in rare instances, countering their play partner's aggression with just enough force to dissuade their partner from continuing to be aggressive. Thus, positive internal working models formed in their secure relationships with their parents prevented them from seeing themselves as either a victim or a victimizer.

On the other hand, children who were anxious/ambivalent appeared motivated to make contact with the other child no matter the cost, while also exhibiting relatively incompetent social skills. For example, one victim within a dyad made 119 attempts to initiate an interaction with the avoidant play partner even though all but 19 of those attempts were met with rejection. For their part, avoidant children either adopted the role of the victimizer or of the victim, and in one dyad, two girls who were both avoidant appeared to alternate the roles of victim and victimizer. Finally, it should be noted that this study was conducted prior to the identification of the disorganized attachment category. Therefore, it is likely that at least some of the insecure children could be more accurately characterized as disorganized in attachment, with their interactions reflecting either controlling or behaviorally disorganized behavior (Chapter 2).

Avoidant Attachment and Peer Victimization

Other research has also examined the relationship between attachment categories and children's peer victimization. For example, avoidant attachment assessed at 15 and 36 months predicted children's instrumental aggression during play with a same-gender friend at 36 months of age (McElwain et al., 2003). While other researchers have similarly found more externalizing behavior among children with avoidant attachment (Booth-LaForce et al., 2006), Dykas, Ziv, and Cassidy (2008) administered the AAI to adolescents and found that dismissing adolescents were perceived as aggressive and shy-withdrawn and were victimized and less socially accepted by peers. Dismissing girls were more likely to be neglected. Thus, in this study, dismissing adolescents were both aggressive and victimized.

Anxious/Ambivalent Attachment and Peer Victimization

Other research confirms the connection between anxious/ambivalent attachment and an increased vulnerability to victimization by peers. In their interactions at age 36 months with a same-gender friend (as opposed to an unrelated peer, as in the study by Troy & Sroufe, 1987), anxious/ambivalent children exhibited less self-assertion and control as well as less attention and pretend play (McElwain et al., 2003). This deficit in social skills may have reflected their ongoing preoccupation with the attachment figure. Anxious/ambivalent children tend both to see themselves as victims in social interactions and to accept that role in their interactions with peers (Cassidy & Berlin, 1994; Wright, Binney, & Smith, 1995). They also exhibit less competent social information processing and, as in their experience with their mothers, do not expect peers to be available to them (Ziv et al., 2004).

Disorganized Attachment and Peer Victimization

Just like bully-victims who share characteristics both with pure bullies and pure victims, disorganized children share characteristics with both avoidant and anxious/ambivalent children. For example, they exhibit more controlling behavior than children from all other attachment categories, but in a low-risk sample, only with friends (McElwain et al., 2003), highlighting that their need for control is a mechanism for dealing with the anxiety stemming from emotional closeness. Study after study has concluded that children with disorganized attachment exhibit the highest levels of externalizing behavior problems and aggressive behavior (Bureau & Moss, 2010; Goodman, Bartlett, & Stroh, 2013; Granot & Mayseless, 2012; Green, Stanley, & Peters, 2007; Lyons-Ruth, 1996; Lyons-Ruth, Easterbrooks, & Cibelli, 1997; Moss et al., 2006; O'Connor, Bureau, McCartney, & Lyons-Ruth, 2011; Fearon & Belsky, 2011; Shaw, Owens, Vondra, & Keenan, 1996). In fact, a meta-analysis of 42 independent samples (N = 4,614) found that disorganized attachment was much more strongly associated with externalizing symptoms than was avoidant attachment (Groh, Roisman, van IJzendoorn, Bakermans-Kranenburg, & Fearon, 2012). Moreover, a longitudinal study found that, independent of childhood abuse, both maternal withdrawal in infancy and disorganized attachment behavior in middle childhood predicted antisocial features 20 years later (Shi, Bureau, Easterbrooks, Zhao, & Lyons-Ruth, 2012).

Children with disorganized attachment also exhibit the highest levels of internalizing behavior problems and distress, with child reports of depression and shyness, and with parent reports of social anxiety, inattention, and thought problems (Borelli, David, Crowley, & Mayes, 2010; Granot & Mayseless, 2012; Moss et al., 2006; O'Connor et al., 2011). However, the distress does not appear to be secondary to the peer rejection associated with bullying; instead, it appears to follow from the child's disrupted attachment relationships, as seen even in infancy (Lyons-Ruth, 1996). Furthermore, the behaviorally disorganized and controlling punitive subtypes of disorganized children show the most internalizing and externalizing behavior problems of all (O'Connor et al., 2011). Other research has found that elementary school–aged children with the highest levels of both internalizing and externalizing symptoms are at greatest risk for victimization by peers, while young adolescents with these symptoms are most vulnerable to sexual victimization (Turner, Finkelhor, & Ormrod, 2010). Therefore, even in middle childhood, a history of disorganized attachment sets the stage for lifelong experiences of aggressive behavior toward others and victimization by others.

Maltreatment, Parenting and Peer Victimization

Both bullying and victimization have been associated with a history of maltreatment and exposure to family violence. For example, in a study of maltreated and nonmaltreated boys and girls who were assessed in three ways (by self-report ratings, peer nominations, and counselor reports of aggression), a history of maltreatment was associated with physical aggression in boys and relational aggression in girls (Cullerton-Sen et al., 2008). In differentiating types of abuse, a history of physical abuse was associated with physical aggression, sexual abuse with relational aggression in girls only, and neglect with social withdrawal, social rejection, and feelings of incompetence—all typical characteristics of victims (Finzi, Ram, Har-Even, Schnit, & Weizman, 2001; Cullerton-Sen et al., 2008). Furthermore, while both bullies and victims were more likely to have a history of maltreatment, bullying was more likely among children who had experienced acts of abuse (physical or sexual abuse), while bully-victims had the highest rate of maltreatment overall (Holt, Finkelhor, & Kantor, 2007; Shields & Cicchetti, 2001; Teisl, Rogosch, Oshri, & Cicchetti, 2012).

Potential mediators between a history of maltreatment and involvement in bullying include emotion dysregulation, depression, anger, and social skills deficits while moderators include parent-child relationships, peer relationships, and teacher relationships (Hong, Espelage, Grogan-Kaylor, & Allen-Meares, 2012; Shields & Cicchetti, 2001; Shields, Ryan, & Cicchetti, 2001). Maltreated children's representations of self and others are also associated with specific types of maltreatment, suggesting a potential explanation for differences in bullying and victimization based on the type of maltreatment. For example, on a storytelling task, physically abused and neglected children saw themselves as angry and opposing others, neglected children saw others as hurt, sad, or anxious, and sexually abused children saw others as liking them and, compared to physically abused children, expressed a more frequent desire to be close to others (Waldinger, Toth, & Gerber, 2001).

In addition to maltreatment, research has been conducted more generally on parenting characteristics associated with children's bullying and victimization. One oft-noted correlate of victimization, especially in boys, is parental overprotectiveness (Bibou-Nakou, Tsiantis, Assimopoulos, & Chatzilambou, 2013; Figula, Margitics, Pauwlik, & Xzarmari, 2011; Finnegan, Hodges, & Perry, 1998; Ladd & Ladd, 1998). The intensely close parent-child relationship described in these studies is reminiscent of the dynamics observed in anxious/ambivalent attachment (cf. Mayseless, 1998) as well as the spousification observed by Sroufe and Ward (1980). Vulnerability to victimization is also associated, especially for girls, with maternal rejection and intrusive, critical, controlling, and demanding parenting (Finnegan et al., 1998; Holt, Kantor, & Finkelhor, 2009; Ladd & Ladd, 1998). While the child's submissive, conflict-avoidant stance may be useful in dealing with an overbearing parent (and in cases of disorganized attachment, may resemble a controlling-caregiving stance), this behavior is much less adaptive in interactions with peers (Ladd & Ladd, 1998). Furthermore, Finnegan et al. (1998) made the argument that hindering the development of gender-related competencies (autonomy in boys and sociability in girls) may increase both boys' and girls' risk for victimization.

Not surprisingly, a conflictual family environment is associated with an increased risk of bullying and bully-victim behavior in both boys and girls (Bibou-Nakou et al., 2013; Figula et al., 2011). Consistent with the literature on disorganized attachment in Chapter 2 and the family context in Chapter 3, children from multiproblem families are at the greatest risk for both bullying and victimization (Bowes et al., 2009; Holt et al., 2009; Turner, Finkelhor, Hamby, & Shattuck, 2013).

Finally, it is important to note the role of the father in the development of either prosocial or aggressive behavior. On one hand, paternal support and father-child attachment security are associated with higher levels of self-efficacy in a child, lower rates of aggression, and a decreased likelihood to be rejected or victimized by peers (Booth-LaForce et al., 2006; Rubin et al., 2004). On the other hand, fathers' substance abuse is associated with boys' bullying behavior (Eiden et al., 2010). Similarly, fathers' authoritarian parenting leads to relational aggression in both sons and daughters (Casas et al., 2006). Therefore, with peer victimization as with other types of aggressive behavior, it is ill advised to focus only on the mother-child relationship.

Callous-Unemotional Traits as Precursors to Psychopathy

Callous-Unemotional Traits and Bullying

Some children and adolescents who exhibit aggressive behavior are also characterized by callous-unemotional (CU) traits—namely, a lack of empathy and concern about the feelings of others (American Psychiatric Association, 2013). Seen as a precursor to adult psychopathy, CU traits are clearly implicated, either alone or in combination with conduct problems, in the perpetration of severe proactive and reactive aggression in both boys and girls (Fanti, 2013; Pardini, Stepp, Hipwell, Stouthamer-Loeber, & Loeber, 2012; Thornton, Frick, Crepanzano, & Terranova, 2013). Consistent with other research on gender differences in aggression, CU traits are especially predictive of physical bullying in boys and relational aggression in girls (Crapanzano, Frick, & Terranova, 2010; Viding, Simmonds, Petrides, & Frederickson, 2009). CU traits predict cyberbullying and the behavior of adolescent sex offenders, including the degree of their violence toward victims and the amount of planning of the sexual offense (Fanti, Demetriou, & Hawa, 2012; Lawing, Frick, & Cruise, 2010). CU traits are also associated with the roles of assisting and encouraging other bullies to hurt victims (Crapanzano, Frick, Childs, & Terranova, 2011). An example of an individual presumably high in CU traits who engaged in these latter bullying roles is Charles Manson, who was only 7 years old when he was observed encouraging young girls to physically aggress against a boy he did not like and then denied responsibility for his behavior (Guinn, 2013).

Etiology of CU Traits

There are several different perspectives on the etiology of CU traits. First, there is strong evidence for a genetic vulnerability to aggression in some portion of the population scoring high on CU traits (and by extension, psychopathy). For example, the heritability estimates for children are high for those with CU traits, irrespective of whether or not they also display conduct problems (Forsman, Lichtenstein, Andershed, & Larsson, 2008; Larsson, Andershed, & Lichtenstein, 2006; Larsson, Viding, & Plomin, 2008; Viding, Blair, Moffitt, & Plomin, 2005; Viding, Frick, & Plomin, 2007; Viding & Jones, 2008; Viding, Jones, Frick, Moffitt, & Plomin, 2008). Furthermore, results of a twin study suggested highest heritability for boys with a stable and high trajectory of CU traits, with an almost exclusive role of shared environment among girls with a stable and high trajectory of CU traits (Fontaine, Rijsdijk, McCrory, & Viding, 2010). Consistent with this notion, many studies conclude that the physiological substrate of CU traits is unrelated to maltreatment, parenting, and environmental experiences. For example, CU traits were uniquely associated with impairments in fear recognition, while a history of maltreatment was associated with superior fear and sadness recognition (Leist & Dadds, 2009). Furthermore, negative parental discipline was predictive of conduct problems, but not of CU traits, with positive parenting behavior similarly unrelated to CU traits (Falk & Lee, 2012; Viding, Fontaine, Oliver, & Plomin, 2009).

In contrast, other research has found evidence of a history of maltreatment or negative parenting in the development of CU and psychopathic traits (Graham, Kimonis, Wasserman, & Kline, 2012; Lemitre, 2008). For example, an observed significant association between maternal and child CU traits was fully mediated by parental hostility and parenting dysfunction (Loney, Huntenburg, Counts-Allan, & Schmeelk, 2007). Other studies have similarly found evidence of negative and harsh parenting in some adolescents with CU traits, although the effects were modest (Waller, Gardner, & Hyde, 2013; Waller et al., 2012). For other children with CU traits, there appears to be a definite interaction between genetic vulnerability and environmental stress (including maltreatment). Namely, individuals who were homozygous for the long allele of the serotonin transporter (5-HTTLPR) genotype showed increased CU traits to the degree that they had experienced a socioeconomic disadvantage (Sadeh et al., 2010). Other research has similarly suggested that some children may have an underlying physiological vulnerability that may increase their risk for aggressive behavior when they are exposed to marital conflict (El-Sheikh & Erath, 2011; El-Sheikh, Keller, & Erath, 2007; El-Sheikh et al., 2009).

An attachment perspective has noted that CU traits are correlated with disorganized attachment (Bohlin, Eninger, Brocki, & Thorell, 2012; Pasalich, Dadds, Hawes, & Brennan, 2012). However, as noted in Chapter 2, other parental behaviors such as maternal withdrawal and role reversal may lead to the development of disorganized attachment even in the absence of overt maltreatment. Consistent with this notion, a number of studies have found that low levels of maternal care, nurturance, warmth, and involvement are predictive of CU traits, even controlling for abuse and neglect (Fanti & Munoz Centifanti, 2013; Kimonis, Cross, Howard, & Donoghue, 2013; Kroneman, Hipwell, Loeber, Koot, & Pardini, 2011; MacDonald, 2012; Pasalich, Dadds, Hawes, & Brennan, 2011). Maternal prenatal risks have also been associated with CU traits, suggesting a possible epigenetic effect (Barker, Oliver, Viding, Salekin, & Maughan, 2011). Epigenesis might also play a role in the underlying physiological vulnerability to exposure to marital conflict described by El-Sheikh and her colleagues above. Therefore, studies finding a lack of correlation between maltreatment and CU traits may have been defining their construct of negative parenting too narrowly.

Alternatively, consistent with the notion of an evocative gene-environment correlation, some children with CU traits may elicit negative parenting, suggesting that the observed effects of lack of maternal warmth and involvement might result from the child's CU traits rather than causing them. For example, longitudinal studies of changes in CU traits and parenting behavior have found that parents become more punishing, inconsistent with their discipline, less involved over time, and reduce their monitoring of their child's behavior (Hawes, Dadds, Frost, & Hasking, 2011; Munoz, Pakalniskiene, & Frick, 2011). Thus, there may be reciprocal effects of CU traits and parenting behaviors, obviating any easy conclusions about the effects of parenting, implicating a more complex relationship between parenting and CU traits. Moreover, a recent study found that an interaction between disorganized attachment and CU traits in 3-year-old children predicted aggressive behavior in middle childhood (Willoughby, Mills-Koonce, Gottfredson, & Wagner, 2014).

Finally, a perspective that attempts to reconcile these divergent findings suggests that there are different pathways of etiology to CU traits, with some children manifesting no environmental basis and other children reacting at least in part to a history of maltreatment or problematic parenting. Namely, among adolescents with high levels of CU traits, those who exhibited little anxiety in response to emotionally distressing pictures were less likely than adolescents who exhibited high anxiety to have experienced abuse (Kimonis, Frick, Cauffman, Goldweber, & Skeem, 2012; Kimonis, Frick, Munoz, & Aucoin, 2008). The authors concluded that the former group may possess a deficit in the processing of emotional cues that is unrelated to a history of maltreatment. Thus, the research on CU traits in children and adolescents is important not only because it predicts psychopathy and violent behavior in adults, but also because it is a microcosm of the many etiological pathways to the intergenerational transmission of violence.

DATING VIOLENCE

Dating violence is ubiquitous. Based on a sample of 13,601 university students in 32 nations, Straus (2008) determined that almost one-third of both males and females reported that they had physically assaulted a dating partner in the previous 12 months. Moreover, the reports of both males and females have confirmed either no gender differences in the base rates of dating violence perpetration and victimization or a preponderance of bidirectional violence (Bossarte, Simon, & Swahn, 2008; Eaton, Davis, Barrios, Brener, & Noonan, 2007; Wolfe, Scott, Wekerle, & Pittman, 2001). In the study by Straus (2008), the bidirectional pattern was the most common, characterizing two-thirds of all cases, followed by female-only violence, which was twice as common as male-only violence and encompassed severe as well as minor violence. Other studies have found significantly more perpetration of dating violence by girls than by boys— again, on the basis of both girls' and boys' reports (Chase, Treboux, O'Leary, & Strassberg, 1998; Malik, Sorenson, & Aneshensel, 1997; Rivera-Rivera, Allen-Leigh, Rodriguez-Ortega, Chavez-Ayala, & Lazcano-Ponce, 2007; Sharpe & Taylor, 1999; Valois, Oeltmann, Wallter, & Hussey, 1999).

Even when violence is mutual, it is by no means less damaging. Researchers in many studies have concluded that mutual dating violence relationships are significantly more injurious than one-sided violence and they are truly reciprocal, in that the average amount of violence perpetrated was no different from the average amount of violence received (Gray & Foshee, 1997; Marcus, 2012; Sharpe & Taylor, 1999). Mutual dating violence is also associated with the greatest acceptance of dating violence, suggesting that the partners supported both their own and their partners' use of violence, pointing to its continuation (Gray & Foshee, 1997). However, no matter who initiates the abuse, researchers have concluded that the repercussions of dating violence are significantly more negative for girls than for boys. Girls who engage in violence frequently are more likely to be the recipients of severe abuse and to be traumatized by the experience, describing themselves as feeling more afraid and threatened (Arriaga & Foshee, 2004; Capaldi, Kim, & Shortt, 2004; Harned, 2001; Molidor & Tolman, 1998; O'Keefe, 2005; Scott, Wolfe, & Wekerle, 2003). Therefore, gender effects are found in the consequences of dating violence even if not in the rates of perpetration.

Determinants of Dating Violence

Proximal determinants of the perpetration of violence and victimization within dating relationships for both males and females include substance abuse (especially alcohol use), association with antisocial peers, academic problems, low parental monitoring, and high dating frequency (Bandyopadhyay, Deokar, & Omar, 2010; Banyard, Cross, & Modecki, 2006; Chapple, 2003; Leen et al., 2013; McDonnell, Ott, & Mitchell, 2010; Schnurr & Lohman, 2008, 2013; Shorey, Stuart, & Cornelius, 2011). Furthermore, current conflict—with either family members, peers or even best friends—predicted adolescent violent behavior and attitudes (Narayan, Englund, Carlson, & Egeland, 2014; Quigley, Jaycox, McCaffrey, & Grant, 2006).

These proximal causes may reflect in part the more distal determinants of dating violence that include child maltreatment and exposure to family violence. That is, both males and females who have been exposed to family violence are more likely to be involved in an aggressive dating relationship (Chapple, 2003; Gover, Kaukinen, & Fox, 2008; Karakurt, Keiley, & Posada, 2013; Narayan et al., 2014; Rapoza & Baker, 2008). However, the effect of a history of maltreatment may be especially significant for girls, due to the relative primacy of trauma symptoms and affect dysregulation in predicting their aggression (Dodge, 2004; Scott et al., 2003). Researchers have found that affect dysregulation (anger, depression, anxiety, and PTSD) mediated the effect of child maltreatment history on violent behavior to a much greater degree among girls than among boys (Wekerle et al., 2001; Wolfe et al., 2001; Wolfe, Wekerle, Scott, Straatman, & Grasley, 2004). Furthermore, adolescent girls' vulnerability to involvement in a violent dating relationship is exacerbated by the connections between a history of child sexual abuse (CSA), teen pregnancy, and both aggression and victimization (see Chapter 6). Namely, family violence exposure and childhood aggression are predictive both of teen pregnancy and of the tendency to associate with deviant peers (Kinsfogel & Grych, 2004; Miller-Johnson et al., 1999), increasing females' risk for dating violence victimization and perpetration (Arriaga & Foshee, 2004; Foshee, Benefield, Ennett, Bauman, & Suchindran, 2004; O'Keefe, 1998; Sharpe & Taylor, 1999). One obvious variant of this is assortative mating with an equally violent partner (Capaldi et al., 2004; Zoccolillo, Paquette, Azar, Cote, & Tremblay, 2004), a finding that is consistent with the high rates of bidirectional violence in adolescent samples.

Implications for Prevention

Based on feminist theory or social learning theory, most programs have focused on increasing knowledge about dating violence, changing attitudes, and improving communication and conflict resolution skills. Although a number of these programs have reported attitude change and increased knowledge by the end of treatment (e.g., Avery-Leaf, Cascardi, O'Leary, & Cano, 1997; Jaycox et al., 2006; Jones, 1998; Lavoie, Vezina, Piche, & Boivin, 1995; Weisz & Black, 2001), either changes did not persist at follow-up (e.g., Jaycox et al., 2006) or follow-ups were very short-term (e.g., Lavoie et al., 1995). The predictive validity of attitudes and knowledge as proxies for behavior was also undermined by the finding that most students rated dating violence as completely unacceptable at pretreatment even if they themselves had engaged in violent behavior (Avery-Leaf et al., 1997; Jaycox et al., 2006).

The two most rigorous studies evaluated the Safe Dates Program (Foshee et al., 1998, 2004) and the Youth Relationship Project (Wolfe et al., 2003). The Safe Dates Program consisted of school activities and led to a reduction of physical and sexual dating violence perpetration and victimization at 4 years follow-up. The Youth Relationship Project was developed specifically for 14–16-year-olds with histories of child maltreatment and focused on education about relationships, conflict resolution, communication skills, and social action activities. Although it also resulted in less abusiveness and less distress, the decrease in perpetration of violence was not accompanied by a change in skills. Dodge (2004) has argued that programs relying upon reasoning-based strategies and skills-based emotional control may be appropriate for boys, but do not address the need for emotion resolution in aggressive girls, given the prevalence of trauma histories in this population. Therefore, there remains a need for dating violence prevention programs that incorporate segments on maltreatment history and affect regulation.

INTIMATE PARTNER VIOLENCE

Our society's assumptions about the cycles of IPV have been informed by two perspectives: a feminist view of patriarchal social norms and a social learning theory focus on young men modeling the father-to-mother violence they have observed in their families of origin. However, as I review below, data from many well-designed longitudinal studies do not support the perspectives of patriarchy and social learning theory as the primary explanations for IPV. For example, this perspective is unable to account for the consistent research finding that women engage in aggression against their partners at rates relatively equal to those of men (Desmarais, Reeves, Nicholls, Telford, & Fiebert, 2012). A feminist or social learning theory approach is also at a loss to explain and address partner violence that occurs at an equivalent rate within LGBT relationships (Brown & Pantalone, 2011). Moreover, this approach fails to account for the development of violent behavior and victimization that can be seen in the research on the antecedents of bullying and victimization, dating violence, and IPV in adulthood (Corvo & deLara, 2010; Ehrensaft, 2008). Unfortunately, adherence to these traditional models has led to state-mandated psychoeducational interventions that are ineffective, ignore the complexities of the couple's relationship, and are disrespectful of women's autonomy. Therefore, it is argued that a more useful alternative to the well-intentioned but empirically limited view of power and control is an approach that focuses on the reactions of individuals to intimacy, as reflected in both attachment and family systems theory (Bartholomew & Allison, 2006; Hamel, 2005).

Unidirectional Versus Bidirectional (Mutual) Partner Violence

Michael Johnson (1995, 2006a) proposed that it was important to distinguish between "situational couple violence," characterized by occasional outbursts of violent behavior from both men and women, and "intimate terrorism," characterized by violent and controlling behavior by one partner (primarily the male) over his nonviolent partner. Johnson (2006a) noted that the latter form of violence is best understood, in the case of heterosexual relationships, as a manifestation of patriarchal views of women in our society. He has also made mention, although less consistently, of "violent resistance," referring to an aggressive reaction to a violent and controlling partner; "mutual violent control," referring to both partners being violent and controlling; and "separation-instigated violence" (Johnson 2006b, 2009; Kelly & Johnson, 2008).

In contrast to Johnson's minimization of situational couple violence, Straus (2011) reviewed 200 empirical studies consisting of IPV data on both men and women and found evidence of "gender symmetry" (i.e., approximately equal percentages of physical aggression by men and women). Moreover, gender symmetry was not just reflective of minor aggression, as would be expected in situational couple violence, but was also characterized by severe injury, agency involvement, and attributes of Johnson's description of intimate terrorism (Straus & Gozjolko, 2014). Other literature reviews and meta-analyses have similarly found IPV to be predominantly bidirectional, followed by female-perpetrated unidirectional violence, with the exception of samples relying on police reports (Desmarais et al., 2012; Langhinrichsen-Rohling, Misra, Selwyn, & Rohling, 2012). As is true of dating violence, bilateral aggression is dangerous to both partners, leading to more physical violence and injury than that typically experienced by victims of unilateral violence (Madsen, Stith, Thomsen, & McCollum, 2012). Moreover, both men and women appear to suffer from significant mental health problems as a result of experiencing IPV (Fergusson, Horwood, & Ridder, 2005; Prospero & Kim, 2009).

Straus (2011) suggested that much of the controversy about gender symmetry in IPV arises from conflating evidence on the perpetration of violence with evidence on the effects of violence, with generally greater effects of IPV on women than men (Anderson, 2002; Lawrence, Orengo-Aguayo, Langer, & Brock, 2012). For example, women generally suffer more physical injury, more fear of their partners, and more depression (Kar & O'Leary, 2010). Women are also more likely to suffer from the economic consequences of IPV and other psychosocial outcomes (Alexander, 2011; Lawrence et al., 2012; Williams & Frieze, 2005). Other research has found that the effects of IPV on men and women are equivalent (Amanor-Boadu et al., 2011). Therefore, as with dating violence, the effects of IPV are often (although not always) greater on women than on men, even when the rates of perpetration may be similar.

Precursors of IPV

Research on the intergenerational predictors of IPV perpetration and victimization also highlight the similar experiences of males and females.

History of Maltreatment

The impact of parent-child physical abuse, psychological abuse, and sexual abuse on subsequent involvement in a violent relationship has been investigated in a variety of studies, including multimethod, prospective designs (Dankoski et al., 2006; Edwards, Dixon, Gidycz, & Desai, 2013; Lohman, Neppl, Senia, & Schofield, 2013; Noll, Trickett, Harris, & Putnam, 2009; Whiting, Simmons, Havens, Smith, & Oka, 2009). In a 20-year longitudinal study (Chapter 1), Ehrensaft and her colleagues (2003) found that conduct disorder, witnessing parental violence, and punitive parenting predicted the perpetration of IPV. Witnessing parental violence and conduct disorder independently predicted victimization by an intimate partner. Significantly, there was no evidence of gender differences with regard to perpetration and victimization.

Also referred to previously, Kwong and colleagues (2003) surveyed a large sample of adults with regard to witnessing parental violence (father-to-mother and mother-to-father), abuse by one's father and mother, and current involvement in a physically or psychologically abusive intimate relationship. They found that all forms of family-of-origin violence were predictive of all forms of relationship violence. Moreover, like Ehrensaft et al. (2003), they found no evidence of either gender-specific or role-specific patterns of transmission. Consistent with the notion of Sroufe and Fleeson (1986), they concluded that both men and women seem to have learned and internalized the roles of both perpetrator and victim when witnessing or experiencing abuse in their family of origin. They also found that abuse by mothers was most predictive of both perpetration and receipt of violence in adulthood. Kwong et al. (2003) also noted the prevalence of bidirectional violence within their community sample. In fact, they found that, like Cappell and Heiner (1990), controlling for this bidirectionality eliminated the significant effect of witnessing parental violence on the perpetration but not the receipt of abuse. Finally, Alexander's (2014) sample of dual-trauma couples exhibited the greatest risk for severe, and often bidirectional, partner violence (Chapter 3).

History of Problematic Parenting

Parenting predictors of IPV are not limited to actual abuse. A history of maternal depression predicted the perpetration of severe violence in young women, although not young men (Keenan-Miller, Hammen, & Brennan, 2007). Unskilled parenting (and not exposure to parents' dyadic aggression) predicted sons' antisocial behavior and later aggression toward a partner (Capaldi & Clark, 1998). Paternal substance abuse was as significant as exposure to family violence in predicting men's IPV (Corvo & Carpenter, 2000). Neglect as a child predicted physical aggression against one's partner even more than a history of physical abuse or witnessing parental violence (Bevan & Higgins, 2002). Furthermore, experiences of separation and loss in childhood predicted men's violent behavior as much as or even more than exposure to violence in the family of origin (Corvo, 2006). Therefore, a child's experience with his or her parents is fundamental to later involvement in a violent intimate relationship, even beyond the effects of maltreatment in ways that neither social learning theory nor notions of patriarchy can explain.

Genetic and Physiological Precursors

Heritability of the propensity toward aggression or impulsivity and disinhibition when confronted with stress must be considered, especially for males (Hines & Saudino, 2009). In fact, a study found that 24% of the variance of physical aggression, 54% of the variance of injurious aggression, and 51% of the variance of sexual coercion were explained by genetic factors (Barnes, TenEyck, Boutwell, & Beaver, 2013). Moreover, the effects of marital conflict and IPV appear to be moderated in part by the child's neurological reactivity and temperament (Davies, Sturge-Apple, & Cicchetti, 2011; El-Sheikh, Hinnant, et al., 2011; El-Sheikh & Whitson, 2006; Parade & Leerkes, 2011). Of course, the impact of a mother's prenatal stress stemming from a conflictual relationship may also play a role in the eventual emotional dysregulation of a child.

Attachment and Perpetration of IPV

Attachment theory not only provides an explanation for the intergenerational influence of the parent on the child's aggressive behavior, but also for the dynamics of the abusive partner relationship itself. In a classic article, Holtzworth-Munroe and Stuart (1994) identified the following clusters of male IPV perpetrators: (a) the family-only batterer, characterized by low severity of violence and low generality of violence; (b) the dysphoric/borderline batterer, characterized by borderline personality, fears of abandonment, dependency, jealousy, and high levels of depression; and (c) the generally violent/antisocial batterer, characterized by antisocial personality, high levels of extrafamilial violence, criminal involvement, and high levels of control. Other research has validated this typology (Hamberger, Lohr, Bonge, & Tolin, 1996; Holtzworth-Munroe, Meehan, Herron, Rehman, & Stuart, 2000, 2003), although the borderline and antisocial types overlap (Delsol, Margolin, & John, 2003; Waltz, Babcock, Jacobson, & Gottman, 2000).

In the two studies examining it, this typology partially overlapped with AAI attachment categories, suggesting the underlying attachment dynamics associated with this typology. In comparisons of batterers with nonviolent but distressed men and with nonviolent nondistressed men, abusive men were more likely to be insecure relative to the other two groups (Babcock, Jacobson, Gottman, & Yerington, 2000; Holtzworth-Munroe et al., 1997). However, all four attachment classifications were observed in these two samples. For example, while a small percentage of the violent group was secure in their attachment, these men were more likely to be defensive (a relatively low-level negative behavior) and less likely to be domineering than insecure husbands. It is unclear whether the presence or levels of mutual violence would also have differentiated this group. The AAI's secure attachment toward parental figures is not necessarily the same as secure attachment with one's current romantic partner; however, secure attachment was more prevalent in the family-only batterer, who may have been responding primarily to dyadic factors within the relationship and whose remorse kept the aggression from escalating (Holtzworth-Munroe & Meehan, 2004).

Second, consistent with the discrepancy between the physiological arousal of dismissing individuals and their self-reports of anger and hostile attribution, dismissing batterers in Babcock et al.'s (2000) sample were characterized by stonewalling, contempt, and wives exhibiting defensive-ness, suggesting an instrumental use of violence to coerce their wives' compliance. Not surprisingly, the dismissing batterers in this sample scored significantly higher on a scale of antisocial behavior. Third, preoc-cupied attachment was prevalent in both samples, although the function of aggression was apparently much different than that exhibited by dis-missing individuals. Namely, preoccupied men were more likely to be belligerent toward their wives and were the only ones to respond to their wives' withdrawal with violence, suggesting a parallel to the borderline batterer's use of violence to engage an uninvolved partner.

Finally, an unresolved history of loss or trauma or a more global col-lapse of an attachment strategy (characterizing the Cannot Classify or CC category) was especially associated with severe violent behavior. For example, only 17% of batterers in Babcock et al.'s (2000) community sam-ple were classified as either U or CC, as opposed to 47% of the men in Holtzworth-Munroe et al.'s (1997) sample of men court ordered to treat-ment. Similarly, in an observational study relating couples' AAI scores to their interpersonal behaviors in a conflict situation, unresolved men and women displayed more domineering behavior than either dismissing or preoccupied individuals (Creasey, 2002). In fact, the most controlling behavior was observed when both members of the couple were unre-solved, with some couples exhibiting over 200 instances of negative behavior in 15 minutes. In a partial replication of this study, Creasey (2014) found once again the exacerbation of poor conflict resolution when both members were unresolved regarding loss or trauma. For exam-ple, even though this was not a clinical sample,

> couples consisting of unresolved partners frequently launched into obscenity-laden arguments that occasionally contained frightening or omi-nous overtures. As one example, an unresolved male repeatedly pretended to snap a rubber band at his partner's eyes, and another indicated he could seriously harm his partner at the moment and "nobody can stop me." Another unresolved male suddenly jumped up during the interaction and proceeded to open and stare into a drawer of a laboratory file cabinet—a highly unusual turn of events that hints of disorganization and possible temporary dissociation. (Creasey, 2014, p. 236)

Furthermore, the potentially buffering role of an underlying secure attachment did not seem to be sufficient to overcome the impact of both individuals being unresolved. Therefore, these studies help explain the heightened risk of IPV among dual-trauma couples.

The relevance of unresolved attachment to the psychological dynamics of IPV is suggested by developmental research as well. The controlling punitive and controlling caregiving behaviors of disorganized children (Chapter 2) would certainly seem to parallel the behaviors of IPV offenders as would the intrusiveness and boundary confusion observed in individuals fitting the hostile profile. Furthermore, dissociative symptoms typically seen in adults who were disorganized as children are not only prevalent among both male and female perpetrators of IPV but are highly predictive of the severity of their violence (Daisy & Hien, 2014; Simoneti et al., 2000). Therefore, the phenotypic similarity of behaviors observed in individuals with pervasively unintegrated states of mind and both borderline and antisocial batterers could be presumed to have arisen from a common set of attachment experiences.

Fonagy's (1999) description of reflective functioning is also relevant to the experience of the intimately violent individual. To the extent that the disorganized infant's emotional expression triggers anxiety or rage (i.e., frightening, frightened, or dissociated behavior) in the parent who fails to see the child as possessing an independent mind, the child's internal state is never acknowledged and labeled by the parent. This results in the child's failure to develop an understanding of his own and others' mental states, leading to the child's internalizing the parent's "feeling of rage, hatred or fear and (the parent's) image of the child as frightening or unmanageable" (Fonagy, 1999, p. 18). Moreover, the child comes to view his own attachment needs as leading to his abandonment by the attachment figure. Fonagy (1999) proposed that the controlling behavior subsequently observed in the disorganized child is a reflection of the child's externalizing of negative self-states through projective identification. Thus, the batterer's violent behavior arises when his partner's independent intentions threaten the batterer's control of his externalized self-states.

Mitch was court ordered to a batterer treatment program where he was interviewed about his family history. Mitch was categorized as dismissing in his attachment, with limited collaboration with the interviewer and overall derogation of his parents. Mitch's father was a wealthy lawyer who dominated the household. His father was hostile and abusive to his mother (slapped her, screamed at her, and threw things at her) and to Mitch and his brother. But he was mainly emotionally abusive and shaming. Mitch's mother was passive and reluctant to stand up to her husband and spent most of her time at the country club while Mitch and his brother were raised by a nanny. Other than feeling sorry for his mother and not feeling afraid of her, Mitch reported being no closer to her than to his father— instead, often feeling angry at her and seeing her as "pathetic."

Mitch recounted a significant experience of separation and abandonment by his parents. Namely, at age 10 he was sent to a boarding school and vividly remembers crying hysterically when his mother dropped him off at school, begging her to take him home. He reported feeling rejected and neglected by both of his parents, with neither one of them ever visiting him at boarding school. He also stated that he and his brother were sent to rival boarding schools, which he perceived as his father's attempts to foster sibling rivalry and distance. It was Mitch's perception that his peer relationships were also disrupted by the family's frequent moves, consistent with their rising social status. Mitch reported that he frequently fought with peers at school and was given to tantrums. He also described himself as stoic with regard to physical pain, with a self-described pride in being able to tolerate pain. Mitch did not have children, precluding the opportunity to assess the impact of his behavior on his own progeny. However, his abuse of his partner resembled the behavior of the dismissing batterer described by Babcock et al. (2000). He was both physically and verbally abusive when seeking his partner's compliance and engaged in stonewalling during conflictual interactions until his partner acquiesced to his demands.

In conclusion, Mitch experienced and witnessed low levels of physical abuse, but more importantly, high levels of emotional and verbal abuse and shaming by his father. He also experienced significant emotional neglect and rejection by both parents. A sense of abandonment featured prominently in his history, which could have contributed to his emotion dysregulation, apparent even in childhood. His stoicism, tolerance of pain, and general derogation of others could have been determined in part by genetic similarities to his father, prenatal or postnatal stress experienced by his mother, and his sensitivity to the conflict between his parents.

Attachment and Ongoing Victimization by a Partner

As noted in the research reviewed earlier, a history of maltreatment or insecure attachment increases an individual's initial risk for both aggression and victimization by a partner. Women's continued vulnerability to IPV is often justifiably attributed to characteristics of the abuser (e.g., his physical power, economic power) or to characteristics of society (e.g., women's economic oppression that makes self-sufficiency difficult). While these reasons do explain the situation of many battered women, there are also a significant number of abused women who are vulnerable to ongoing abuse to the extent that they experience multiple abusive relationships in adulthood or they choose to remain with an abusive partner. The following discussion focuses on the attachment dynamics of these women's continued vulnerability to IPV, as evidenced by their experience of abuse by multiple partners and by their stage of change regarding IPV.

Significant numbers of women who are currently in an abusive relationship have experienced abuse by multiple partners, with rates ranging from 27% to 59% in both clinical and community samples (Bogat, Levendosky, Theran, von Eye, & Davidson, 2003; Coolidge & Anderson, 2002; Kemp, Green, Hovanitz, & Rawlings, 1995; McCloskey, 1997; Woffordt, Mihalic, & Menard, 1994). Unfortunately, by not inquiring about a woman's past history of violence, it is impossible for treatment providers to help her address the issues that keep her vulnerable to ongoing abuse. Those issues include her history of trauma and disrupted attachment relationships from childhood.

Alexander (2009) administered the AAI to a sample of women who were abused either in single relationships in adulthood (44% of the sample) or in multiple relationships (56%). Women from multiply abusive relationships were more likely to be classified as unresolved in their attachment and were more likely to describe role reversal with both parents in childhood, a history of CSA, a history of witnessing violence between parents, and a history of multiple forms of childhood trauma. Thus, there appear to be several different pathways to an increased risk for multiple abusive relationships in adulthood. For example, a history of CSA is also associated with role reversal with both mothers and fathers, a dynamic related to excessive caretaking in adulthood, including perhaps tolerating abusive behavior from a partner (Mayseless et al., 2004). A history of witnessing IPV may normalize the experience for many women. While a lack of resolution regarding abuse or loss is not a necessary condition for subsequent multiple victimization, it was a predictor in this study for 9 of the 10 women who were classified as unresolved. Multiple childhood traumas characterized 77% of the women who were in multiple abusive relationships in adulthood, and 51 out of 52 of these women reported at least one type of childhood trauma. Therefore, childhood trauma increases women's risk for victimization not only in a single relationship in adulthood but also for multiple abusive relationships. For example, a history of multiple abusive relationships in adulthood was more prevalent in women in the sample of dual-trauma couples described earlier (Alexander, 2014). The fact that these couples were characterized by higher levels of violence perpetrated by both partners, higher levels of pathology in the men, and less help seeking in the women points to their danger to women.

Women may also remain vulnerable to ongoing abuse as a function of how they view the IPV they are experiencing. A stages of change model suggests that women in an earlier stage of change are more willing to excuse or minimize their partner's behavior than women who worry about the violence but have not yet decided to take action, or women in a later stage of change who take some action to escape the violence, or women who are successful in maintaining their autonomy from violent relationships (Brown, 1998). In a large sample, women's views of the abusive relationship were unrelated to the actual severity of violence they had experienced (Alexander, Tracy, Radek, & Koverola, 2009). On the other hand, women in an earlier stage of change reported that they had engaged in both minor and major physical aggression against their partner, suggesting that mutual violence could contribute to a woman's excuse of her partner's violence. Furthermore, a woman's minimization of the violence she had experienced was significantly related to her emotional dependence on her partner, which was also the predominant reason given by women for returning to their partner after seeking shelter services (Griffing et al., 2002). Finally, a woman's earlier stage of change was correlated with her satisfaction with her current social supports, an indication either of her reluctance to express dissatisfaction with interpersonal relationships more generally, the possible linkage of her social network to her partner, or her social network's disapproval of her leaving her partner.

Thus, both attachment relationships and the larger family and social context influence abused women's decision making and continued vulnerability to IPV.

Jean scored as unresolved on the AAI, with an underlying rating of fearfully preoccupied. Her scores on a stage-of-change measure indicated that she was in an earlier stage of change, in that she minimized and rationalized her current IPV experience. Her family history was extremely chaotic, with severe physical abuse by her mother and neglect by her father. When she was approximately 4 years old, her mother sent her and her 5-year-old brother upstairs to their younger sister's room, where they found her dead. Jean later discovered that the family (including her maternal grandfather and her father) assumed that her mother had smothered the girl. That was when Jean's father left. Although he eventually gained custody of her and her brother 3 years later, Jean was repeatedly terrorized by her mother in the meantime. She recounted her mother holding her by her ankles over the bannister in order to scare her. Her mother tied her up and put her in a closet, pulled the refrigerator from the wall and made her stay behind the refrigerator until bedtime, made her eat dirt on one occasion as punishment, put her head under water threatening to drown her, and beat her with hangers and sticks embedded with nails. Jean stated that abuse and torture by her mother might begin at bedtime and last all night. While Jean described her father as caring and encouraging, he was also an alcoholic, unreliable, and neglectful, sometimes forgetting to feed her and her brother.

Jean associated separation from her mother with safety. She reported feeling close to her maternal aunt, who would sometimes rescue her from her mother's home. However, this relationship was connected in her mind with a traumatic loss. Namely, the aunt was jailed for an unspecified crime. Jean's father bailed her out, and she was subsequently murdered. Jean's maternal grandfather blamed her father for bailing the aunt out from jail, and the funeral was then marred by drinking and fighting over the aunt's death. (Jean's grandparents also both abused substances.)

Jean's husband was physically abusive and controlling. She stated that she lost her job because of him and she was currently seeking shelter services. Jean's teenage daughters continued to live with their father and Jean worried that they would grow up to be like her—nervous and panicky. In describing her life history overall, she stated that she just learned to survive.

In conclusion, Jean's experience of actual torture at the hands of her mother and the absence and subsequent neglect by her father explain both her dissociation (needing to rely on her mother who was also the source of her abuse) as well as her fearful preoccupation with her mother. Her household was so chaotic, her experiences so life threatening, and substance abuse so rampant that there was literally no safe haven with the sporadic exception of her aunt, who was traumatically taken from her. Her mother was certainly mentally ill, probably with a trauma history herself. Consequently, Jean lacked the opportunity to develop an expectation of safety and respect in close relationships and was not yet able to provide that safety for her daughters. She is an important example of someone for whom shelter and outpatient IPV services are woefully inadequate unless a therapist helps her begin to address her history of childhood trauma.

It should be noted that, in contrast to Jean, many of the women who had experienced IPV and were interviewed for the AAI study (Alexander, 2009) were secure in their attachment and had positive and supportive parents with no evidence of childhood trauma. Not surprisingly, they were at a much later stage of change in their view of their generally single IPV relationship. As difficult as their recent or current circumstances were, these women were much more likely to escape the violence and recover with little risk for abuse in the future.

Substance Abuse as a Proximal Precursor to IPV

The connection between IPV and substance abuse has been noted repeatedly. For example, Temple, Weston, Stuart, and Marshall (2008) found that alcohol use was associated with perpetration of violence by men and with increased risk of victimization in women. In general, substance abuse (including same-day substance abuse) is more common among male perpetrators of violence (Bassuk, Dawson, & Huntington, 2006; Boden, Fergusson, & Horwood, 2012; Friend, Langhinrichsen-

Rohling, & Eichold, 2011; Lipsky, Caetano, & Roy-Byrne, 2011; Simmons, Lehmann, & Cobb, 2008; Teten, Schumacher, Bailey, & Kent, 2009). It is also more prevalent in couples with bidirectional violence (Charles, Whitaker, Le, Swahn, & DiClemente, 2011; Kelly, Izienicki, Bimbi, & Parsons, 2011; Lipsky, Caetano, Field, & Larkin, 2005). In particular, the use of alcohol, cocaine, and marijuana appears to increase the risk for violent behavior (Fals-Stewart, Golden, & Schumacher, 2003; Feingold, Kerr, & Capaldi, 2008; Smith, Homish, Leonard, & Cornelius, 2012; Stalans & Ritchie, 2008; Stuart et al., 2008; Walton et al., 2009). While many researchers have found that substance abuse is associated with victimization among women (Devries et al., 2014; Golinelli, Longshore, & Wenzel, 2009; Schumacher & Holt, 2012; Shannon, Logan, Cole, & Walker, 2008; Testa, Livingston, & Leonard, 2003; Tzilos, Greken, Beatty, Chase, & Ondersma, 2010), this conclusion is not unanimous (Cohn, McCrady, Epstein, & Cook, 2010). Furthermore, Sullivan and her colleagues have deduced that substance abuse frequently results from a woman's experience of IPV and its associated PTSD rather than contributing to a woman's risk (Sullivan, Ashare, Jaquier, & Tennen, 2012; Sullivan & Holt, 2008; Sullivan, Cavanaugh, Buckner, & Edmondson, 2009). Other research has noted that, for both men and women, a history of child abuse increases the likelihood of substance abuse and PTSD, which then contribute to the occurrence of IPV (Tyler & Melander, 2012; Whiting et al., 2009). Therefore, although men seem to be particularly susceptible to the disinhibiting effects of alcohol and other substances, women's use of alcohol and drugs as a form of self-medication for abuse experienced either in childhood or adulthood may contribute to their continued vulnerability.

Intergenerational Transmission of IPV

Interparental conflict leads to affect dysregulation and behavior problems in children for several reasons (Chapter 3). It is frightening to children; it disrupts the parenting of fathers in particular; it interferes with secure parent-child attachment; it undermines coparenting; and it fosters boundary dissolution within the family. The effects on children of living in a household with IPV are severe, but not primarily because children model the behavior. Instead, it is damaging to children because it is frightening, because of its association with abusive and problematic parenting, and because of its impact on the parent-child attachment relationship, as reviewed below.

Association of IPV With Abusive Parenting

A history of IPV has many deleterious effects on both parents and children, including parents' PTSD, substance abuse, and low satisfaction with the child, and an increase in the child's aggression and hostile reactivity (Ehrensaft & Cohen, 2012). However, the impact of being raised in a household with partner violence is not necessarily due to the modeling of behavior witnessed at home. Instead, the increased risk of an adult child's own violence against a partner appears to be mediated by the parent's aggression toward the child and by the child's trauma symptoms (Bevan & Higgins, 2002; Cui et al., 2010). In other words, IPV is highly correlated with the parenting behavior of both fathers and mothers (Appel & Holden, 1998). For example, the same paternal alcoholism, depression, and antisocial traits observed in fathers when children were 12 months of age predicted the fathers' violence toward their partners when the children were 36 months old and the fathers' harsh parenting when the children were 5 years old (Finger et al., 2010). Similarly, husband-to-wife IPV has been associated with the father's child abuse potential, hostility toward his child, and decreased levels of empathy toward his child (Margolin & Gordis, 2003; Margolin, Gordis, & Oliver, 2004; Moore & Florsheim, 2008). IPV is also predictive of mothers' parenting, including harsh-intrusive parenting, more permissive parenting, physical maltreatment, and neglect (Casanueva & Martin, 2007; Dixon et al., 2007; Gustafsson, Cox, & Blair, 2012; Kim, Pears, Fisher, Connelly, & Landsverk, 2010; Margolin & Gordis, 2003; Rea & Rossman, 2005; Taylor, Guterman, Lee, & Rathouz, 2009). Therefore, the effects of IPV on children are much more pervasive than just the modeling of the behavior.

Impact of IPV on Parent-Child Attachment

A series of studies has looked at the impact of IPV on the mother-child attachment relationship based on the Working Model of the Child Interview (Zeanah & Benoit, 1995), which assesses women's mental representations about themselves as mothers and about their relationship with their fetus. In this interview, *balanced* mothers are able to give coherent

narratives about their pregnancy and to reflect on both positive and negative feelings about their fetus. Consistent with a dismissing orientation,
disengaged mothers express few thoughts and feelings about their fetus or
about themselves as mothers. As with preoccupied attachment, *distorted*
mothers tend to see their fetus as an extension of themselves or their partner, and engage in tangential narratives that may include intrusive
thoughts about their own experiences as children.

In a longitudinal study, Huth-Bocks, Levendosky, Theran, and Bogat
(2004) started with the assumption that pregnancy is a particularly salient
time for a mother to reflect on her ability as a caregiver to provide protection to her child and her child's role of seeking protection from her. They
found that an experience of IPV shortly before or after the birth of the
child was associated with a mother's negative mental representations of
her infant and of herself as a mother as well as either disengaged or distorted attachment (Huth-Bocks et al., 2004; Sokolowski, Hans, Bernstein,
& Cox, 2007). Furthermore, these negative mental representations predicted mothers' atypical parenting behavior and the child's insecure or
disorganized attachment in the Strange Situation at age 13 months (Huth-
Bocks, Theran, Levendosky, & Bogat, 2011; Schechter et al., 2008). In
essence, "these babies were received into mothers' arms that either
clutched them too tightly (distorted) or threatened to let them fall (disengaged)" (Levendosky, Bogat, & Huth-Bocks, 2011, p. 515). In either case,
the mother was unable to view her child as a separate independent individual with needs for nurturing and protection.

Thus, one impact of IPV was its disruption of the mother's caregiving
system, leading to her emotion dysregulation and abdication of parenting
and interfering with her ability to parent her child sensitively (George &
Solomon, 2008; Levendosky et al., 2011). Furthermore, her infant's distress frequently triggered her posttraumatic reactions and hostile or helpless state of mind (Lyons-Ruth et al., 2005) eliciting either her view of her
child as helpless and vulnerable like herself (projective identification) or
her view of her child as abusive like the perpetrator (projection). IPV may
also lead to the mother's dissociative response—yet another predictor of
disorganized attachment in her child as well as a predictor of her maltreatment of her child (Levendosky et al., 2011; Narang & Contreras,
2000).

Of course, this intergenerational perspective must also consider preexisting risk factors in the mother. As described previously, a woman's his-

tory of child maltreatment predicts the severity of IPV she experiences during pregnancy, and both these traumas predict her PTSD. Furthermore, research found that a woman's history of childhood physical neglect was correlated with her distorted prenatal mental representations, even controlling for her current experience of IPV (Huth-Bocks, Krause, Ahlfs-Dunn, Gallagher, & Scott, 2013; Malone, Levendosky, Dayton, & Bogat, 2010). In particular, mothers' conflict with their own mothers was associated with increased odds of having disengaged representations of their child while mothers' conflict with their partners was associated with distorted mental representations (Sokolowski et al., 2007). These PTSD symptoms and negative mental representations predicted the child's externalizing behavior and mental representations of self and caregiver (Levendosky, Leahy, Bogat, Davidson, & von Eye, 2006; Schechter et al., 2007). Namely, in child story stem narratives, a mother's experience of IPV and the severity of her PTSD symptoms were associated with the child's dysregulated aggression, attentional bias to danger and distress, avoidance of and withdrawal from conflict in the stories, and less coherence (Schechter et al., 2007). Thus, even though women who are abused by their partners struggle to be good mothers (Lapierre, 2010; Peled & Gil, 2011), the experience of IPV as well as any prior experience of maltreatment in childhood frequently interferes with their capacity to provide protection and care to their child. Given other evidence that the effects of IPV on children's behavior and their likelihood of engaging in aggressive behavior themselves are moderated by the security of their attachment to their parents (El-Sheikh et al., 2008; Hare, Miga, & Allen, 2009), this disruption of the attachment caregiving system may ultimately be the most damaging effect of a child's exposure to IPV.

Protective Factors and Implications for Treatment

Among individuals with a history of family violence who are at high risk for abusive behavior, attributes have been identified that differentiate those who engage in partner violence from those who do not. Not surprisingly, secure attachment to at least one adult in childhood, to a sibling, and especially to one's partner is important, as is being held accountable by family and friends (Guille, 2004; Lackey & Williams, 1995; Styron & Janoff-Bulman, 1997). The ability to create some psychological distance from the experience of violence in one's family of origin through an understanding of this experience also serves as a protective factor (Delsol & Margolin, 2004). Finally, the maturity and conventionality that comes from being older, married, and committed to one's work also interrupts the cycle of violence (Franklin & Kercher, 2012; Lackey, 2003).

Attention to these protective factors would presumably be a reasonable place to start in developing the ideal intervention for IPV. What is clear is that state-mandated treatment models based on notions of patriarchy, such as the Duluth model (Pence & Paymar, 1993) combined with cognitive-behavioral therapy, are very limited in their effectiveness (Babcock, Green, & Robie, 2004). Therefore, more of the same neither rehabilitates men nor protects women from abuse. Inattention to women's violence either in mutually violent relationships or unidirectionally violent relationships keeps women vulnerable in the current relationship (as they fail to seek help and minimize their partner's behavior in part because of their own violence) and keeps them at risk for finding themselves again and again in new abusive relationships. Furthermore, to the extent that ensuring the safety of clients is a primary concern, an exclusive focus on men's behavior and failure to address female-to-male violence, when it exists, is fundamentally unethical with regard to both men and women.

First and foremost, it is essential to conceptualize IPV as a dyadic interactional process (Capaldi, Knoble, Shortt, & Kim, 2012). As such, both partners' histories of childhood trauma (including loss and separation from caregivers), parent-child attachment relationships, histories of bullying and victimization in childhood and adolescence, and prior histories of dating violence and IPV should be assessed, even when the intervention is ultimately enacted only with one partner. For each partner (either conjointly or separately), there should be several goals—first, helping clients develop a coherent understanding of past attachment relationships and experiences of family dysfunction (Hamel, 2005; Hare et al., 2009). Family-of-origin genograms facilitate this purpose (Cohen, 2008), as was consistently observed in sessions using genograms in group treatments of male batterers (Alexander, Morris, Tracy, & Frye, 2010). A second reason for focusing on attachment relationships is to foster the regulation of affect in clients with insecure and unresolved attachment (Dankoski et al., 2006). Patterns of controlling-punitive and controlling-caregiving behavior stemming from disorganized attachment in childhood must be identified and reworked. Interventions for reflective functioning are also consistent with this purpose (Worley, Walsh, & Lewis, 2004).

Given the interactional nature of all relationships, including those that are violent, given the preponderance of mutual violence, and given the commitment of many couples to stay together in spite of the violence, the reluctance (and in many states, the prohibition) to use couples therapy for IPV is short-sighted at best. Assessment of danger and of each partner's desire to remain in the relationship should be conducted individually in order to guard the safety of both men and women. However, the failure to eventually move to a couples approach for couples who intend to stay together ensures that any mutual violence (including the use of relational aggression) will not be addressed and women will continue to suffer disproportionately from the ill effects of IPV.

One of the most well-developed and validated treatment approaches for IPV is domestic violence–focused couples therapy, either with multiple couples in a group format or with individual couples (Stith, McCollum, & Rosen, 2011). Stith and her colleagues emphasized that it is appropriate for couples who have experienced mild to moderate violence, wish to remain in the relationship, and are motivated to end the violence. Assessment of all couples for IPV (even those not seeking therapy for it) is paramount and is accompanied by ongoing monitoring through a session check-in process occurring separately for the partners. Phase 1 of the intervention focuses on skills relevant to each partner, such as mindfulness meditation to foster self-soothing and affect regulation, specific negotiated time-out plans for both partners, and assessment of substance abuse conducted separately with each partner. Phase 2 moves to an emphasis on working conjointly with the couple, initially on less-challenging issues before addressing more conflictual issues, and always with attention to the safety of each partner. Research findings demonstrated the success of the multicouple group therapy and single-couple therapy relative to a comparison group even at a 2-year follow-up (Stith et al., 2011; Stith, Rosen, McCollum, & Thomsen, 2004). Moreover, the multicouple group format appeared to be especially successful in altering men's behavior, with the change in women's behavior more equivocal in the two conditions (Stith et al., 2011).

A pilot group intervention that included one to two preparatory individual sessions for mutually violent couples who were mandated to treatment demonstrated a significant reduction in both partners' physically assaultive and injurious behavior, with the lowest 1-year recidivism when both partners competed the treatment (Wray, Hoyt, & Gerstle, 2013). Finally, consistent with a developmental perspective on cycles of violence, Ehrensaft (2012) created a family-based IPV prevention program of early conduct problems among preschoolers. Given that exposure to any IPV is associated with subsequent overt peer victimization and that exposure to severe IPV is associated with relational aggression and overt peer victimization, Ehrensaft and her colleagues have argued convincingly that IPV prevention must be tied to the prevention of bullying and peer victimization in both boys and girls (Knous-Westfall, Ehrensaft, MacDonell, & Cohen, 2012).

In conclusion, violent behavior does not typically appear suddenly and unexpectedly. Similarly, there are often precursors to vulnerability to victimization within an intimate relationship. Assuming that prevention is preferable to relying only upon treatment once violence has occurred, intervening with young children and their parents and with adolescents may be the most effective means to interrupt the cycles of violence that culminate in IPV and child maltreatment.

CHAPTER 6

Child Sexual Abuse

The impact of a history of sexual abuse unfortunately does not always end in childhood. Survivors of child sexual abuse (CSA) are significantly more likely to be revictimized in adolescence and adulthood (Arata, 2002). Another potential outcome, although somewhat less likely, is an increased risk for sexual offending, especially toward children (Seto & Lalumiere, 2010). Finally, the children of CSA survivors are more likely to be physically or sexually abused, either by the parent who was sexually abused or by someone else (Craig & Sprang, 2007; Testa, Hoffman, & Livingston, 2011). In many ways, CSA represents the prototypical case of intergenerational transmission of trauma.

The question is why. What is unique about CSA that leads to these cycles of violence and revictimization? Finkelhor and Browne (1986) hypothesized that the traumagenic dynamics of CSA (traumatic sexualization, betrayal, stigmatization, and powerlessness) represent the core of the psychological injury associated with the abuse; as such, their presence affects outcomes. Noll (2008) considered the unique effects of CSA on development and noted that these traumagenic dynamics, the pairing of violence with intimacy leading to guilt and self-blame, and even the neurobiological effects of CSA all conspire to create a perfect storm of mental health problems that are generally more damaging than child physical abuse and other types of trauma. This chapter reviews some of the most deleterious effects of CSA, but also goes further to propose that the trajectories of risk for revictimization and continued cycles of violence can best be understood within a framework of attachment and associated family dynamics. Attachment and family support (both in the family of origin and the family of creation) can also lead to the resilience often observed among children who are sexually abused. Therefore, correlates of resilience can indicate helpful emphases of intervention.

DYNAMICS OF THE SEXUALLY ABUSIVE EXPERIENCE

Any discussion of intergenerational cycles requires an arbitrary starting point—arbitrary in that a recursive examination of a family history can always find traits or behaviors or experiences in one's parents or grandparents that could help explain the behavior of any given individual. However, the occurrence of sexual abuse within a family has especially damaging effects that are more likely to contribute to the outcomes to be explored in this chapter—parenting that increases a child's risk for maltreatment, sexual revictimization, and sexual offending. In other words, a closer relationship to the perpetrator (typically a father figure) is predictive of poorer outcomes, including more relationship problems in adulthood, than is typical for extrafamilial abuse (Hebert, Collin-Vezina, Daigneault, Parent, & Tremblay, 2006; Ketring & Feinauer, 1999; Watson & Halford, 2010). Abuse by a parent figure is also correlated with longer duration and greater abuse severity (Sadowski et al., 2003), both of which are associated with negative outcomes (Cyr, McDuff, & Wright, 2006; Feerick & Snow, 2005; Steel, Sanna, Hammond, Whipple, & Cross, 2004). Furthermore, children disclosing abuse by a family member are significantly more likely to experience negative reactions such as disbelief than are children disclosing abuse by an acquaintance or stranger (Ullman, 2007). However, even in cases of extrafamilial abuse, a family's response to disclosure can have an important impact on a child's adjustment (Cyr, McDuff, & Hebert, 2013; O'Leary, Coohey, & Easton, 2010). Furthermore, CSA severity and family or attachment variables make independent contributions to the prediction of psychological outcomes (Alexander, 1993; Edwards & Alexander, 1992; Fassler, Amodeo, Griffin, Clay, & Ellis, 2005). Therefore, consistent with the overall rationale of this book, the experience of CSA is considered within the contexts of attachment and family environment.

Characteristics of the Sexually Abusive Family

Family variables may be even more important than aspects of the CSA experience in predicting a child's outcome (Cortes Arboleda, Canton-

Cortes, & Duarte, 2011). For example, the family context makes a unique contribution to the development of externalizing and sexualized behaviors (Estes & Tidwell, 2002; Hebert, Tremblay, Parent, Daignault, & Piche, 2006). In an exploration of this family context, Howes, Cicchetti, Toth, and Rogosch (2000) observed and compared the system-level functioning of families referred to social services for neglect, physical abuse, and sexual abuse with low-income comparison families. The sexually abusive families were differentiated from all other family types on the basis of four characteristics. They displayed anger (also observed by Alaggia & Kirshenbaum, 2005; Faust, Kenny, & Runyon, 1997), high levels of family chaos (also noted by Svedin, Back, & Soderback, 2002), less role clarity (similar to the enmeshment described by Reinemann, Stark, & Swearer, 2003), and significantly less flexibility in managing interactions (consistent with the rigid and authoritarian structures noted by Alaggia & Kirshenbaum, 2005; Faust et al., 1997; Reinemann et al., 2003). Most importantly, these family characteristics could not be attributed to the presence of multiple types of abuse or even to the presence of the perpetrator within the home (Howes et al., 2000). Thus, the family environment of CSA is marked by affect dysregulation, disorganization, role reversal, and rigid relationships.

Sexually abusive families are also differentiated from physically abusive families in their secretiveness and social isolation (Alexander & Anderson, 1997; Svedin et al., 2002). The isolation both reduces disclosure (Alaggia & Kirshenbaum, 2005) and is reinforced by fathers' negative messages about the world (Reinemann et al., 2003). As summarized by Howes et al. (2000, p. 104), "the deception and betrayal inherent in sexual abuse . . . may at the level of the family, be viewed as a more complete and disorganized collapse of family structure, with role reversal and secrecy taking the place of overtly coercive parenting practices." This collapse of family structure gives rise to the following classic outcomes of CSA.

Emotion Dysregulation

The experience of CSA is frequently traumatic enough to lead to the symptoms of emotion dysregulation captured by a diagnosis of PTSD—namely, hyperarousal, numbing, reexperiencing, and avoidance (Hetzel & McCanne, 2005; Myers et al., 2006; Najdowski & Ullman, 2009; Oddone Paolucci, Genuis, & Violato, 2001). However, CSA is often not a one-time occurrence, as would be the case with other events contributing to a diagnosis of PTSD, such as motor vehicle accidents, natural disasters, or even a rape. Instead, as described by Wagner and Linehan (1997), it is the classic example of invalidation: the child's body is invaded; the child is given confusing messages about the abuse; the child is often abused by a trusted person; the child is forced or encouraged to keep the abuse secret; and the abuse is often minimized if and when it is finally disclosed. Thus, experiences of CSA can often be thought of as complex psychological traumatic stressors "that (1) are repetitive or prolonged; (2) involve direct harm and/or neglect and abandonment by caregivers or ostensibly responsible adults; (3) occur at developmentally vulnerable times in the victim's life, such as early childhood; and (4) have great potential to compromise severely a child's development" (Courtois & Ford, 2009, p. 1). A diagnosis of PTSD generally fails to capture this complex context and the sequelae of emotion dysregulation, dissociation, somatization, and distortions of information processing often exhibited by survivors of CSA. The PTSD diagnosis also does not reflect this complex trauma's frequent comorbidity with Axis I disorders (one-third to one-half of cases), Axis II disorders (one-fourth to one-third of cases), and dissociative disorders (Courtois & Ford, 2009). Therefore, PTSD symptoms describe a limited set of the experiences of the CSA survivor.

Borderline Personality Disorder

A more pervasive and extreme example of emotion dysregulation found in some portion of CSA survivors is the diagnosis of borderline personality disorder (BPD), characterized by affective instability, problems of identity, negative relationships, and self-harm. Its connection to CSA is varied and complex. Approximately 40–60% of patients with a diagnosis of BPD have a history of CSA (Zanarini, Dubo, Lewis, & Williams, 1997) and in some ways, it is a good example of the complicated relationship between maltreatment history and any diagnosis. In a collection of essays on the topic of CSA and BPD, perspectives ranged from CSA as an important risk factor for BPD (Jordan, Schlengr, Caddell, & Fairbank, 1997; Wagner & Linehan, 1997; Zanarini et al., 1997) to CSA contributing to certain severe symptoms of BPD (Dubo, Zanarini, Lewis, & Williams, 1997; Silk, Nigg, Westen, & Lohr, 1997) to CSA predicting only a particular subgroup of patients with BPD (Paris & Frank, 1997).

There is undoubtedly a neurobiological component in BPD, with hypotheses including an abnormality of the serotonergic system (related to self-harm and unstable relationships), the dopaminergic system (related to interpersonal sensitivity), the endogenous opioid system (related to anhedonia and frantic attempts to avoid abandonment), and the polyvagal system (Austin, Riniolo, & Porges, 2007; Bandelow, Schmahl, Falkai, & Wedikind, 2010; Gunderson & Lyons-Ruth, 2008). Whatever the source, emotional vulnerability (characterized by high sensitivity, extremely intense reactions interfering with an ability to self-soothe, and a slow return to emotional baseline) interacts with an invalidating environment to lead to the affect dysregulation associated with BPD (Wagner & Linehan, 1997). Furthermore, while evidence exists for a genetic predisposition (Gunderson & Lyons-Ruth, 2008), epigenesis would suggest the possibility that the emotional sensitivity could have resulted in part from alterations of the central nervous system due to disruptions in early caregiving.

The invalidating environment refers to the caregiver's extreme and inappropriate responses to the child's communication of thoughts and feelings (Wagner & Linehan, 1997), a concept similar to a deficit in reflective function. While this invalidation often takes the form of abuse (e.g., in one sample, 91% of patients with BPD had some form of child abuse, with 59% reporting CSA; Zanarini et al., 1997), it is even more likely to include neglect (94% in this same sample). For example, in Lyons-Ruth's (2008) longitudinal study of at-risk families that followed infants into young adulthood, both borderline and antisocial features at age 19 were predicted independently by a genetic predisposition and by the effects of maternal care—more specifically, by the mother's withdrawal and disrupted communication in reaction to attachment cues from the infant. Although intervening abuse added to the model, its effects were independent of maternal caregiving.

Many researchers have also argued for an underlying basis of unresolved attachment with features of preoccupied attachment, representing an individual's simultaneous desire for intimacy combined with an overwhelming fear of rejection (Agrawal et al., 2004). In a sample of college students who were administered the AAI, 9 of the 11 who were classified as preoccupied met five of eight criteria for BPD. These individuals described ongoing turbulent relationships with mothers, dramatic oscillations between love and hate, and intense and unpredictable verbal attacks by their mothers (Salzman, Salzman, & Wolfson, 1997). Other researchers have also noted a pattern of maternal overprotection, consistent with the dynamics of preoccupied attachment (Ghiassi, Dimaggio, & Brune, 2010; Katerndahl, Burge, & Kellogg, 2005).

It is of course important to note that the biological predisposition to oversensitivity could explain some of these individuals' perceptions of their interactions with their mothers. Moreover, the attribution of borderline features to mother-child interactions may fail to consider the larger family context to which the mother is exposed. This is especially true given that this parent-child interaction tends to occur within a general atmosphere of conflict and chaos (as descriptive of the CSA family environment). For example, even within a sample of women who had been incarcerated for felony offenses in which a background of violence was endemic, BPD was predicted by more severe family violence, including substance abuse, criminal activities, and mental disorders (Jordan et al., 1997). Notably, it was not predicted by race, loss, or separation from parents or feeling endangered. In any case, the results of this experience of disorganized-ambivalent attachment include an increased risk for the emergence in childhood of controlling-caregiving or controlling-punitive or even behaviorally disorganized strategies among individuals with BPD (Lyons-Ruth et al., 2007). These attachment strategies then contribute to the trajectories of risk described below, culminating in parenting problems, sexual revictimization, and sexual offending.

Dissociation and Betrayal Trauma

Another outcome associated with the experience of sexual abuse is an increased risk for dissociation. As described in Chapter 2, a child who is frightened by an attachment figure (whether by abuse, role reversal, or the parent's abdication of caregiving) is placed in the untenable position of fright without solution—that is, needing to seek comfort from the source of the fear (Main & Hesse, 1990). To the degree that the child has nowhere else to turn, the child will necessarily develop multiple incompatible internal working models of the self and the other in order to maintain connection to the attachment figure—this is the basis of dissociation (Liotti, 1992). The secretiveness of the CSA family, with its typically hidden violence, contributes to this dissociation in its separation of the private tyranny of the family with the idealized, often conventional public face presented to the outside world (Ayoub, Fischer, & O'Connor, 2003; Cole, Alexander, & Anderson, 1996). In essence, the child's splitting of affect is reinforced by dissociation of the public from the private.

In her development of the notion of betrayal trauma, Jennifer Freyd (1996) stated that the dynamic of CSA forms the basis for simultaneously knowing and not knowing about one's own experiences and, by extension, one's self. She and her colleagues demonstrated that memory failures are more likely among victims of abuse perpetrated by a caregiver than by someone else, even controlling for age and duration of the abuse (Freyd, DePrince, & Zurbriggen, 2001). Furthermore, traumas high in betrayal (those perpetrated by an attachment figure) have even worse outcomes, including dissociation and PTSD, than low-betrayal traumas that are life threatening, such as a car accident or natural disaster (Freyd, Klest, & Allard, 2005; Tang & Freyd, 2012), highlighting the primacy of the relationship to the perpetrator. Interestingly, a child's dissociation also derives from perceptions of betrayal by a nonabusing parental figure (O'Rinn, Lishak, Muller, & Classen, 2012) and from that parent's history of betrayal trauma (Chu & DePrince, 2006). Therefore, consistent with attachment research, betrayal trauma follows from the inadvertent effects of a parent's own trauma history and not just from active abuse by that parent.

Betrayal trauma has many implications for the increased risk of revictimization. As a function of the child's unwillingness to remain aware of abuse by a caregiver, he or she may develop more generalized problems in detecting, avoiding, and withdrawing from relationships characterized by threat. In support of this notion, violations of social contracts and of precautionary safety rules were less likely to be detected by young adults with histories of dissociation and revictimization (DePrince, 2005). In another study, young adults who had experienced high betrayal trauma in childhood were 4.3 times more likely to have been victimized in adolescence and 5.4 times more likely to have been victimized in adulthood (Gobin & Freyd, 2009). Research has not yet explored whether betrayal trauma could also account for the observed connection between dissociation and violence against others.

Shame and Self-Blame

Finkelhor and Browne's (1986) notion of stigmatization is represented by shame and the related concept of self-blame for the abuse. These are important destructive outcomes of an experience of CSA for both males and females. Research on the abuse characteristics that are most predictive of shame and self-blame include a close relationship with the perpetrator, the severity of the abuse, perceptions of the abuse as disgusting, and avoidance coping or pretending that the abuse did not happen (Quas, Goodman, & Jones, 2003). Shame and self-blame often preclude the disclosure of abuse, contributing to its continued occurrence but also leading to more negative outcomes when it finally is disclosed, especially if the abuse occurred at the hands of a relative (Schonbucher, Maier, Mohler-Kuo, Schnyder, & Landolt, 2012; Sorsoli, Kia-Keating, & Grossman, 2008; Ullman, 2007). Shame and self-blame for the abuse have been associated with poorer psychological adjustment, including such negative outcomes as depression, self-injurious behavior, suicidality, PTSD, and delinquent behavior (Canton-Cortes, Cortes, & Canton, 2012; Coffey, Leitenberg, Henning, Turner, & Bennett, 1996; McMillen & Zuravin, 1997; Palesh et al., 2008; Peters & Range, 1996; Ullman, 2007; Wright, Friedrich, Cinq-Mars, Cyr, & McDuff, 2004). Self-blame not only results from revictimization (i.e., abuse in both childhood and adulthood) but also explains its occurrence (Arata, 2000).

The concept of internalized shame is integral to attachment theory; internalized shame is significantly associated with anxious and disorganized attachment and the degree of family dysfunction (Consedine & Magai, 2003; Hadley, Holloway, & Mallinckrodt, 1993). Functionally, shame has the effect of appeasing and attempting to meet the expectations of others (Consedine & Magai, 2003). This would particularly apply to the parent-child attachment relationship, especially in conjunction with disorganized attachment, in which the child has no organized strategy to engage the parent and avoid rejection. Failing in this effort to engage the parent, the disorganized child may potentially appease the abusive attachment figure by taking on the blame for the abuse and the abuser's (or even the nonoffending parent's) disgust about the abusive behavior. Thus, as mentioned earlier, the presence of shame is correlated with abuse by a relative and with the family's disbelief in reaction to disclosures of abuse. Consistent with this rationale, individuals with unresolved attachment are characterized by a sense of self as fundamentally flawed (Main & Hesse, 1990). Furthermore, as mentioned in Chapter 2, the degree to which an individual described the self as bad predicted the degree of dissociation exhibited by that individual (Loos & Alexander, 2001). Therefore, the importance of shame and self-blame is not limited to their association with an individual's negative concept of self and the psychological distress stemming from this. Instead, shame and self-blame are also important because they constitute ongoing attachment strategies. As such, they predict not only revictimization but also other outcomes of CSA such as sexual offending and problematic parenting.

TRAJECTORIES OF RISK

With all of the possible negative outcomes of CSA described above, what are the pathways to cycles of violence? The effects described above do not characterize all victims, nor do they necessarily appear at the same point of time in development. Many "sleeper effects" of trauma (Briere, 1992) occur only later in development when triggered typically by attachment-related occurrences such as the development of an intimate relationship, pregnancy, the birth of a child, or even breast-feeding (Bowman, 2007). Similarly, situations such as the inability to soothe a crying child can bring back memories of not being comforted oneself as a child (Hooper & Koprowska, 2004). Furthermore, early chance events—either negative or exceptionally positive—can contribute to trajectories of development that either exacerbate or buffer the effects of early trauma. Therefore, this following section describes certain developmental pathways that are often, although by no means necessarily, associated with an increased risk for parenting problems leading to a child's risk of maltreatment or revictimization or physical or sexual offending against others.

Early Onset of Puberty

Development is a function of transitions (e.g., puberty), as well as the timing of these transitions, which have their own causes and effects. It has been speculated that CSA not only affects the timing of the onset of puberty, but may also reactivate negative feelings associated with the initial sexual contact (Natsuaki, Leve, & Mendle, 2011). In fact, an early onset of puberty in girls is associated with a history of CSA along with more frequent and longer duration of abuse (Brown, Cohen, Chen, Smailes, & Johnson, 2004; Mendle, Leve, Van Ryzin, Natsuaki, & Ge, 2011; Romans, Martin, Gendall, & Herbison, 2003; Trickett, Noll, & Putnam, 2011; Wise, Palmer, Rothman, & Rosenberg, 2009; Zabin, Emerson, & Rowland, 2005). Although the exact mechanism is not yet understood, early onset of puberty has been attributed to the chronic activation of the hypothalamic-pituitary-adrenal (HPA) axis, which in turn may affect the hypothalamic-pituitary-ovarian axis, leading to changes in gonadotropin levels and ovarian function (Wise et al., 2009).

Attachment and family-related dynamics may similarly contribute to the early onset of puberty. For example, the onset of menarche is also predicted by parental conflict, a poor quality of the mother-daughter relationship, lower parental socioeconomic status (SES), mother's younger age at childbirth, and the absence of a father (Alvergne, Faurie, & Raymond, 2008; Downing & Bellis, 2009; Kim & Smith, 1999; Meckelman, 2008; Romans et al., 2003; Vigil, Geary, & Byrd-Craven, 2005). For boys, earlier onset of puberty is associated with less emotional closeness to mothers during childhood and lower parental SES (Downing & Bellis, 2009; Kim & Smith, 1999).

Risky Behavior

Whatever the cause, early onset of puberty is associated in both boys and girls with early and problematic substance abuse, younger age at first sexual intercourse, and unprotected sex (Bratberg, Nilsen, Holman, & Vatten, 2005, 2007; Downing & Bellis, 2009; Gaudineau et al., 2010; Kim & Smith, 1999; Meckelmann, 2008; Vigil et al., 2005). Research has also found evidence of more relationship aggression and delinquency (Downing & Bellis, 2009; Lynne, Graber, Nichols, Brooks-Gunn, & Botvin, 2007; Mrug et al., 2008). Thus, as a function of a history of CSA for girls, and family conflict and insecure attachment relationships for both boys and girls, the stage is set for risky behavior, especially with regard to sexuality.

Risky Sexual Behavior

Whether mediated by an early onset of puberty or not, a history of CSA in both boys and girls is associated with early and risky sexual behavior (Batten, Follette, & Aban, 2001; Homma, Wang, Saewyc, & Kishor, 2012;

Jones et al., 2010; Noll, Haralson, Butler, & Shenk, 2011). As was also true for the early onset of puberty, a faster life history strategy of engaging in sexual behavior at a younger age is determined as much by family context and parent-child relationships as CSA history (Simpson et al., 2012). As described in Chapter 1, this evolutionary-developmental model of reproductive strategy posits that the timing of pubertal maturation is determined in part by the rearing environment, including parent-child attachment, family dynamics, and broader ecological factors (Belsky et al., 1991). Namely, reproductive success in adverse family environments will be more likely to result from accelerated physical maturation and sexual behavior that will increase the probability of having at least some surviving offspring. In contrast, individuals who are raised in a more favorable environment will maximize their reproductive strategy by delaying pregnancy in order to acquire the skills and resources necessary to ensure successful competition for mates and high-quality parental investment in offspring.

Consistent with this model, harsh maternal control at 54 months of age was predictive of earlier menarche in daughters and increased frequency of sexual activity (Belsky, Steinberg, Houts, Halpern-Felsher, & NICHD Early Child Care Research Network, 2010). Family stress (a composite variable consisting of mothers' reports of family positivity and negativity, behavioral observation of a parent-child conflict resolution task, and assessment of maternal positive and negative expressed emotion) and ecological stress (father absence, maternal depression, and low SES) were found to predict earlier age at first intercourse and more sexual risk taking for both boys and girls (James, Ellis, Schlomer, & Garber, 2012). This effect was partially mediated by early onset of puberty for girls, but not boys. Moreover, father absence (as a proxy for low paternal investment) played a significant role on outcomes for girls but not boys. Using a different set of longitudinal data, Simpson et al. (2012) found that an unpredictable family environment (parental changes in employment status, residence, and cohabitation status) occurring early in children's development (0–5 years of age) was associated with more sexual partners, aggression, delinquency, and criminal activity in young adults. This effect was mediated by maternal depression and decreased maternal sensitivity. This research thus demonstrates the additional influence of multiple risk environments experienced during a developmentally sensitive period on trajectories of risk for the continuation of the cycle of violence and trauma. Simpson et al. (2012) went on to argue that the microenvironment of unpredictability within the home (or within the parent-child relationship) has an even greater effect on children's development than the macroenvironment of unpredictability outside the home. Therefore, both from a neurobiological stress-related perspective and from an evolutionary perspective, CSA along with ancillary insecure attachment and family dysfunction leads to risky behaviors, often mediated for girls by early onset of puberty.

Substance Abuse

Risky behavior as a consequence of CSA is not limited to sexuality. CSA is a significant predictor of substance abuse (Maniglio, 2011a), with CSA involving intercourse increasing the risk of substance abuse or dependence 5.7- to 6.6-fold (Fergusson, Horwood, & Lynskey, 1996; Kendler et al., 2000). Furthermore, CSA increases the risk for heavy polysubstance use in girls, even after controlling for age, race/ethnicity, parental substance use, and other forms of child maltreatment (Shin, Hong, & Hazen, 2010). In an aptly titled article that could apply to many types of risk behaviors, "Desperately Driven and No Brakes," Andersen and Teicher (2009) made the case that the timing of CSA is important for the development of substance abuse. They reviewed the evidence that exposure to abuse during a sensitive developmental period (typically 3–5 years of age) predisposes the brain to substance abuse vulnerability through its effects on HPA reactivity (priming enhanced stress responses), hippocampal volume loss (affecting sensitization to drugs), the dopamine reward system (elevating basal states of anhedonia, which are then normalized through use of substances), and decreased gray matter in the prefrontal cortex (associated with drug seeking once the drug-related cues have been established). Therefore, CSA that occurs at an earlier age (typically correlated with abuse by a family member) has a more profound impact on a teen's eventual vulnerability to serious substance abuse. This early onset of substance abuse contributes to the trajectories of behaviors leading to problematic parenting, revictimization, and sexual offending.

Teen Pregnancy

Another not so uncommon outcome of CSA, risky behaviors, and often of revictimization is teen pregnancy. CSA by itself is associated with an increased probability of having a child as a teen (Born, 2012; Roberts, O'Connor, Dunn, & Golding, 2004; Young, Deardorff, Ozer, & Lahiff, 2011). One estimate is that 4.5 out of 10 pregnant adolescents may have a prior history of CSA (Noll et al., 2009). There are many potential pathways to this increased risk, including the onset of sexual activity at a younger age and with older men (Born, 2012), substance abuse (Francisco et al., 2008), dissociation (Madigan et al., 2012), and self-blame (Erdmans & Black, 2008). Associated family and attachment dynamics such as a nontraditional family constellation, parent-child conflict, and mother disengagement also increase the risk for teen pregnancy (Francisco et al., 2008). Revictimization similarly plays a role. For example, teens in a violent relationship are four to six times more likely to become pregnant (Saewyc, Pettingell, & Magee, 2003). Another study found that, while the experience of sexual abuse only in childhood or only in adolescence increased the risk for teen pregnancy by 20% and 30% respectively, girls who were sexually abused in childhood and then sexually revictimized in adolescence faced an 80% greater hazard of pregnancy (Young et al., 2011). Not surprisingly, the correlation between CSA history and teen pregnancy is often accompanied by lower satisfaction and investment in intimate relationships (Friesen, Woodward, Horwood, & Fergusson, 2010).

Partner Relationships

Whether or not associated with teen pregnancy, the partner relationships of CSA survivors are frequently characterized by dissatisfaction (Alexander & Warner, 2003; Liang, Williams, & Siegel, 2006; Whisman, 2006). Couples in which one or both partners report a history of CSA are also more likely to experience contempt and defensiveness, negative attitudes about marriage, less sexual satisfaction, and decreased emotional closeness (Dimitrova et al., 2010; Katz & Tirone, 2008; Larson & Lamont, 2005; Walker, Sheffield, Larson, & Holman, 2011). Both men and women with a sexual abuse history have anxiety about abandonment and psychological distress, with little evidence of gender differences (Godbout, Lussier, & Sabourin, 2006; Godbout, Sabourin, & Lussier, 2007; Lamoureux, Palmieri, Jackson, & Hobfoll, 2012).

It is of particular importance that a CSA history increases the risk of partner violence (Babcock & DePrince, 2013; Cyr et al., 2006; Iverson, Mercado, Carpenter, & Street, 2013). This increased risk for the perpetration of violence and bilateral violence has been observed in both men and women and in men having sex with men (Daigneault, Hebert, & McDuff, 2009; DiLillo, Giuffre, Tremblay, & Peterson, 2001; Renner & Whitney, 2012; Welles, Corbin, Rich, Reed, & Raj, 2011). One study found that it was the strongest direct predictor of perpetrating IPV among men (Fang & Corso, 2008). Factors such as shame and self-blame, emotional flooding during conflict, and PTSD symptoms serve as potential pathways from the abuse history to partner aggression, although the other sequelae described above undoubtedly also play a role (Feiring, Simon, & Cleland, 2009; Feiring, Simon, Cleland, & Barrett, 2013; Kim, Talbot, & Cicchetti, 2009; Martinson, Sigmon, Craner, Rothstein, & McGillicuddy, 2013; Walker, Holman, & Busby, 2009).

On the other hand, secure maternal attachment moderates the effect of a CSA history on a young woman's eventual marital relationship (Liang et al., 2006). Moreover, the partner relationship moderates the effects of a CSA history on a woman's depression and parenting (Whiffen, Judd, & Aube, 1999; Wright, Fopma-Loy, & Fischer, 2005). For example, CSA survivors reported engaging in role reversal with their children only to the degree that they were dissatisfied with their current marital relationship (Alexander et al., 2000). Therefore, current attachment relationships both are impacted by CSA and also modify the effect of CSA on subsequent parenting.

Parenting

Children of mothers with a history of CSA are at increased risk for a variety of negative outcomes, starting with preterm delivery, maltreatment in general, poorer behavioral trajectories, and involvement with child protective services (Collishaw et al., 2007; Marcenko, Kemp, & Larson, 2000; Noll et al., 2009). CSA survivors are more likely to be psychologically and physically aggressive to their children and to display less parental warmth (Banyard, 1997; Barrett, 2010; Craig & Sprang, 2007; DiLillo, Tremblay, & Peterson, 2000; Mapp, 2006; Newcomb & Locke, 2001). Perhaps because their experience of CSA tends to be extrafamilial, fathers with a history of CSA are more likely to be rejecting than aggressive (Newcomb & Locke, 2001). Furthermore, daughters of CSA survivors are at increased risk for sexual victimization themselves, although rarely by their mother (Brodsky et al., 2008; Collin-Vezina & Cyr, 2003; Testa et al., 2011).

The reasons for this intergenerational connection are diverse and they include a mother's abuse of substances. In one sample, daughters of mothers who were CSA survivors and who abused drugs were almost 24 times more likely to be sexually abused themselves (McCloskey & Bailey, 2000). Furthermore, a sample of African American mother-daughter dyads in which approximately half of the daughters and half of the mothers had been sexually abused allowed a comparison of mothers with a history of CSA whose daughters either had or had not been sexually abused themselves as well as mothers without a history of CSA whose daughters had or had not been abused (Leifer, Kilbane, & Kalick, 2004). Among those variables significantly discriminating the four groups was the number of substances used by the mother. Thus, whether an abused mother's substance use reflected an attempt to self-medicate or her further engagement in risky behaviors, it had the effect of increasing her daughter's vulnerability to sexual victimization.

Mother-child attachment plays an even more important role in this cycle. Based on observations of mothers who were incest survivors and their toddlers, Sroufe and Ward (1980) noted that the internal working models (IWMs) apparently associated with the mother's history of abuse were reflected in seductive interactions with sons (seen in eight of nine dyads) as well as demeaning and shaming behavior toward daughters. When women with a history of CSA were unresolved in their state of mind regarding attachment, especially when the abuse was perpetrated by a parent (Madigan et al., 2012; Riggs & Jacobvitz, 2002), their interactions with their children resembled those described in Chapter 2. In particular, a mother's CSA history has been associated with helpless, passive, and withdrawn interactions with her child (Ballen, Demers, & Bernier, 2006; Lyons-Ruth & Block, 1996). This type of role reversal is associated with controlling-punitive behavior on the part of the child, reminiscent of the aggression and delinquency observed in the teen with a history of CSA. For example, daughters of incest survivors in one study reacted to their mothers with complaints of role reversal, a lack of affection toward their mothers, and a negative view of themselves (Voth & Tutty, 1999). Another study observed a different pattern of mother-child interactions more characteristic of the hostile intrusive parent (Moehler, Biringen, & Poustka, 2007). In their literature review, DiLillo and Damashek (2003) noted that the parenting of CSA survivors ranges from unclear generational boundaries to excessive permissiveness to the use of harsh physical punishment.

The dissociation so often seen in mothers who are unresolved complicates the attachment relationship even further. It may contribute to the mother's poor monitoring and supervision of the child, inconsistent discipline, and the use of corporal punishment (Collin-Vezina & Cyr, 2003; Collin-Vezina, Cyr, Pauze, & McDuff, 2005) and thus mediates between her trauma history and her daughter's (and perhaps son's) increased risk for sexual victimization. Furthermore, the dissociation may contribute to a mother's increased risk for revictimization herself by her partner (Crowell et al., 2010), thereby contributing to her child's risk for maltreatment (Barrett, 2010; Schuetze & Eiden, 2005).

These attachment dynamics can also be observed in the mother's ongoing relationship with her own family of origin. In a three-generation study of African American children, their mothers, and their grandmothers, CSA in the child was best predicted by the mother's experience of disrupted parenting during her childhood, the mother's current negative relationship with her own mother, and the mother's problems in adult functioning (Leifer, Kilbane, Jacobsen, & Grossman, 2004). A mother's relationship with her own family of origin is even more complicated than these data might imply in that reconciling or separating with this family may be either positive or negative depending on the nature of the abuse experience, including ancillary physical or emotional abuse by the non-offending parent(s). While attachment to this family of origin can interfere with a mother's protectiveness of her own children, an emotional cutoff from this family can lead to a sense of loss as well as deprivation of instrumental support. Therefore, the basis for the mother's decision about ongoing contact with her family is more illustrative of underlying attachment dynamics than is the existence of the contact. Thus, unresolved attachment relationships continue to exert a potent effect on the vulnerability of children generations later.

Finally, consistent with the notion of the multiproblem family, many of the parenting practices observed in mothers and the outcomes in their children may be as much due to family dynamics and environmental conditions as to the mother's history of CSA (Brodsky et al., 2008). As argued previously, to the extent that a young woman's history of abuse leads to teen pregnancy and an unpredictable household characterized by changes in family composition, the child's separations from parents, and lower SES (Barrett, 2009; Collishaw et al., 2007; Roberts et al., 2004), these factors in themselves could explain the development of disorganized attachment, behavioral disorganization, and serious behavioral problems in a child. For example, in addition to a mother's substance abuse, McCloskey and Bailey (2000) found that intimate partner violence, family isolation, residential mobility, and the presence of a stepfather in the home were all significant risk factors for a daughter's experience of sexual abuse. Other correlates of a history of CSA such as limited social support, lack of access to services, hospitalization of the mother for mental health issues arising from her abuse, and problems with employment (Alexander, 2011; Hooper & Koprowska, 2004) combine to create a harsh and unpredictable household for a child, independent of the occurrence of any abuse.

Angie's life is illustrative of how a history of CSA and preoccupied attachment combined to increase her risk for IPV and the continuation of an intergenerational cycle. Consistent with a classification of preoccupied attachment (passive subtype) on the AAI, her narrative was tangential, confusing, and meandering with frequent pauses and non sequiturs. Angie experienced intercourse by her father starting when she was approximately 7 and lasting until she was 15. She described him as strange and her IWM of him carried forward into adulthood in that she only felt comfortable around a man who didn't want her. She stated that her mother was always reading, inaccessible, unresponsive, and "just there." On the other hand, her mother became angry with her for disclosing her father's abuse at age 9, hitting her in the head with a cooking pot and treating her like "the other woman." (Angie's father was jailed for several years but started abusing her again when he was released from prison.) Other indications of Angie's perceived role reversal with her mother included having to forcibly remove her mother's boyfriends from the house when her mother had been drinking too much, following the imprisonment of Angie's father.

Although Angie saw herself and her two younger siblings as self-reliant, quiet, and obedient, she recounted numerous examples of her own significantly aggressive behavior. When she was upset as a child, she reported that she would talk her younger sister into hitting her 3-year-old younger brother and would then use her sister's behavior as an excuse to beat her in retaliation. On several occasions she hurt her enough to require the sister's hospitalization—for example, twice pushing her through a glass door. (One can only speculate on the long-term effect of this sibling aggression on her sister.)

Angie described her husband as similar to her mother—quiet with low self-esteem, except when he was drinking, which invariably led to their arguments and fights. She reported that her husband initiated the IPV the first 10 years of their marriage and she initiated it the last 8 years, after she began drinking. The violence was severe with the use of guns, knives, bottles, and bricks by both, and with both of them bearing scars all over their bodies. Her husband finally left the relationship when he reportedly worried aloud that she would kill him. She stated that he was a warm, affectionate father and was not abusive to their children.

Aside from the obvious problem of her children witnessing severe IPV between two alcoholic parents, Angie described other interactions with them that undoubtedly contributed to intergenerational cycles. She reported that she typically reacted to her children's distress by distancing herself from them, stating that she never allowed any crying, affection, or emotional closeness. She noted that she especially avoided a close relationship with her daughters for fear that they might disclose to her that they had been sexually abused—which indeed they eventually did (by someone from outside the family). She currently experiences much of the same role reversal with her children that she extended to her mother, describing her oldest daughter and her son as part-time mother and father to her when she is drinking or spending money too freely. Thus, this case study highlights the family environment frequently seen in incestuous families, the multiple risk factors of a history of maltreatment (sexual, physical, and emotional), abdication of caregiving, role reversal in which the parents' needs supersede those of the children, the impact of emotion dysregulation on sibling aggression and IPV, and the role of substance abuse as both an outcome of CSA and a contributor to IPV. Angie's distrust of both men and women and her preference for being alone have certainly also interfered with her ability to seek help and support from others.

Sexual Revictimization

One consequence of a history of CSA is an increased risk for physical abuse by one's partner and for physical abuse by multiple partners (Chapter 5). Many of the predictors of this revictimization are similar for both

IPV and sexual revictimization. However, this section focuses specifically on the relationship between a CSA history and sexual revictimization. The rate of adult sexual assault (ASA) among CSA survivors is substantial—with two to three times the increased risk (Arata, 2002; West, Williams, & Siegel, 2000). The effects of sexual revictimization are significant, too, with a cumulative effect of victimization experiences on emotion regulation, suicide attempts, and reproductive health concerns (Lau & Kristensen, 2010; Miner, Flitter, & Robinson, 2006; Walsh, DiLillo, & Scalora, 2011; West et al., 2000). Sexual revictimization also occurs in men who were abused as children with similar effects of psychological distress (Aosved, Long, & Voller, 2011).

Revictimization is predicted in part by the severity of the abuse experienced (Arata, 2002; Lau & Kristensen, 2010). What is perhaps more interesting is a consideration of the potential mediators between CSA and ASA. The most widely agreed-upon mediator is sexual behavior—the number of sexual partners, decreased sexual assertiveness, frequency of sex, and risky sex with a stranger (Bramsen et al., 2013; Fargo, 2009; Griffee et al., 2012; Messman-Moore, Walsh, & DiLillo, 2010; Santos-Iglesias & Sierra, 2012). As mentioned earlier, there are neurobiological and even evolutionary explanations for this increased sexual behavior. However, the risky sex may also arise from emotion dysregulation associated with the abuse (Messman-Moore et al., 2010). For example, in a longitudinal community-based study of a racially diverse sample of women, increased sexual contact was used as a strategy to reduce psychological distress and thus partially mediated the connection between CSA and ASA (Orcutt, Cooper, & Garcia, 2005). The use of alcohol as a similar attempt to blunt negative affect may also contribute to engaging in risky sex (Filipas & Ullman, 2006; Wilsnack, Wilsnack, Kristjanson, Vogeltanz-Holm, & Harris, 2004). Consistent with these studies, PTSD symptoms have been found to mediate between CSA and revictimization in a complex way. The cluster of numbing symptoms directly mediated between CSA and ASA while the effects of the reexperiencing, avoidance, and hyperarousal clusters were related to revictimization through their association with the abuse of alcohol (Ullman, Najdowski, & Filipas, 2009).

Research on information processing among CSA survivors also provides an explanation for this increased risk. In a longitudinal study of 8 months, young women were presented with written vignettes requiring them to decide when to leave a potentially risky situation. A history of

CSA was associated with either a more uncomfortable and sensitized reaction to the vignettes (i.e., leaving earlier) than even nonabused women or with a more desensitized response, leading the women to perceive danger much later than nonabused women (Messman-Moore & Brown, 2006). Not surprisingly, those women who exhibited a delayed response to the danger cues were more likely to have been revictimized in adulthood and to be victimized again in the intervening 8 months. The finding was more significant when the vignette referred to an acquaintance as opposed to a stranger, highlighting the fact that the vast majority of sexual assaults in both childhood and adulthood occur within relationships and not by strangers. Similarly, a study based on betrayal trauma theory used facial electromycography to detect the differential affective responsiveness of women with experiences of high-betrayal abuse, low-betrayal abuse, or no abuse at all (Reichmann-Decker, DePrince, & McIntosh, 2009). As compared to the other two groups, a history of high-betrayal trauma was associated with displaying more mimicry of happy faces, less mimicry of angry faces, and less affective modulation of startle when viewing pictures of men threatening women. The authors concluded that women with a history of high-betrayal trauma may have particular difficulties in assessing potential threat due to their motivation to maintain attachment relationships at all costs.

Finally, a comprehensive model of sexual revictimization, Read-React-Respond, was developed by Noll and Grych (2011). In this model, "Read" refers to evaluating the meaning of a situation which, as just noted, may be particularly challenging in interactions with acquaintances as opposed to strangers. The authors proposed that assessing a social interaction may be compromised by the heightened sexual activity and impulses common among many CSA survivors, by attachment that is characteristically anxious or preoccupied, by a deficit in reading others' and even one's own emotional responses, and in some cases by substance abuse. The "React" component of this model refers to the physiological arousal necessary to initiate a fight-or-flight response. Although individuals who have experienced a trauma are initially more likely to display a hypersensitive response due to the hyperarousal of the HPA axis, chronic abuse can lead to the downregulation and hypoarousal of the HPA axis. As a function of this effect, adults with a history of trauma may lack the physiological activation required to act assertively in a situation of threat. This phase of the model may also explain the bimodal response to threat observed by

Messman-Moore and Brown (2006) in their comparison of abuse survivors with nonabused women. Finally, as a function of a lack of knowledge of appropriate responses, the concern with maintaining a relationship with a threatening other, impairment due to the abuse of substances, and the triggering of dissociative responses, individuals may be unable to respond sufficiently. Therefore, the information-processing, attachment-related concerns, heightened sexual activities, and dysregulated physiological arousal observed in many CSA survivors may combine to significantly increase their risk for sexual revictimization.

Sexual Offending

Another problematic outcome of a history of CSA is an increased risk for sexual offending against others—both children and adults (Jespersen, Lalumiere, & Seto, 2009; Seto & Lalumiere, 2010). In fact, one survey of prisoners in Europe found that the experience of sexual abuse by a family member increased the odds of later sexual offending fourfold (Dudeck et al., 2012). Furthermore, family characteristics are often as determinant of sexual offending as is the abuse history, as evidenced by twin studies in which only one twin was sexually abused but both twins became offenders (Di Giacomo & Clerici, 2009). Parental loss appears to contribute to the connection between a CSA history and subsequent offending (Glasser et al., 2001; Thomas & Fremouw, 2009). Moreover, comparisons between those who sexually abuse adults and those who sexually abuse children highlight important differences in maltreatment history and attachment, as do comparisons between male and female perpetrators and comparisons between adolescent offenders against siblings versus nonsiblings.

Sexual Offenders Against Adults Versus Children

Rapists, or sexual offenders against adults, are more likely to have a history of physical abuse than sexual abuse, to have been exposed to parental violence and emotional abuse, and to have engaged as children in cruelty to animals (Di Giacomo & Clerici, 2009; Jespersen et al., 2009; Simons, Wurtele, & Durham, 2008). They are also more likely to be characterized by avoidant or dismissing attachment (Di Giacomo & Clerici, 2009; Simons et al., 2008; Stirpe, Abracen, Stermac, & Wilson, 2006). Consistent with this background, they tend to be more physically violent and psychopathic than offenders against children, typically with prior offenses for criminal behavior rather than sexual offending (Abracen, Looman, DiFazio, Kelly, & Stirpe, 2006; Scott, Lambie, Henwood, & Lamb, 2006; Whitaker et al., 2008; Young, Justice, & Erdberg, 2012).

Offenders against children present with a very different background. They are more likely to have been sexually abused than physically abused, and even within this group, a history of CSA is associated with more recidivism (Craissati, McClurg, & Browne, 2002a; Dennison & Leclerc, 2011; Di Giacomo & Clerici, 2009; Jespersen et al., 2009; Marshall, Serran, & Cortoni, 2000; Simons et al., 2008). One set of researchers found that approximately a third of their sample of adolescent offenders had been sexually abused by a female relative (Glasser et al., 2001).

The attachment dynamics and family context rounds out the picture with more anxious or preoccupied attachment, characterized by low levels of care combined with overprotectiveness by the mother (Craissati, McClurg, & Browne, 2002b; Di Giacomo & Clerici, 2009; McKillop, Smallbone, Wortley, & Andjic, 2012; Simons et al., 2008; Stirpe et al., 2006). In addition to the sexual abuse, the family environment is marked by heightened sexuality including an early exposure of the children in the home to pornography (Simons et al., 2008). As a consequence, the child displays early sex play, atypical sexual interests including sexual activities with animals, and the apparent use of sexual fantasies as an ineffective coping strategy to avoid or reduce the painful emotions stemming from the abuse (Craissati et al., 2002b; Maniglio, 2011b; Miner et al., 2010; Seto & Lalumiere, 2010; Simons et al., 2008).

The function of the sexual behavior also appears to differ between offenders against children and offenders against adults. Given the attachment anxiety, immaturity, and odd preoccupation with sexuality at a precociously early age, this child or adolescent is more likely to become isolated from peers, leading to loneliness and further alienation from potential partners. As a result, the withdrawal from peers and the retreat into the world of deviant sexual fantasies contribute to the adolescent's reliance upon children to meet his or her attachment-related needs for intimacy, emotional closeness, and sexuality (Maniglio, 2012; Miner et al., 2010). One important consequence of this dynamic is that the typical risk management treatment approach to sexual offending, which encourages (and even litigates) an avoidance of high-risk situations, will not be effective because it fails to address the attachment-related needs of this type of offender (Simons et al., 2008).

Male Versus Female Perpetrators

Both sexually abusive boys and girls are characterized by histories of extremely high rates of maltreatment, including CSA, and caregiver instability (Schwartz, Cavanaugh, Pimental, & Prentky, 2006). While sexual offending among males is also associated with a history of other experiences of violence in the home and delinquent peers, female offenders are more likely to have experienced severe CSA with multiple perpetrators (Schwartz et al., 2006; Sigurdsson, Gudjonsson, Asgeirsdottir, & Sigfusdottir, 2010). They are also more likely to self-medicate for their trauma history with sedatives and amphetamines (Sigurdsson et al., 2010). While the sexual abuse of children by females occurs at a much lower rate than that by males, it is not as uncommon as frequently assumed (19% of one large sample of adolescent sexual offenders; Schwartz et al., 2006) and is significant enough to deserve more attention and study.

Sibling Versus Nonsibling Sexual Abuse

Although approximately half of all victims of adolescent sex offenders are siblings, the topic of sibling incest has been relatively ignored (Latzman, Viljoen, Scalora, & Ullman, 2011). This is unfortunate for a number of reasons, not the least because it offers a window into the family and developmental risk factors that contribute to sexual offending. It is also unfortunate because sibling abuse leads to more negative outcomes for the victim than does nonsibling abuse (Carlson, 2011; Cyr, Wright, McDuff, & Perron, 2002). The adolescent offenders of siblings are even more likely to have a history of CSA than are offenders against nonsiblings (Latzman et al., 2011). Their abusive behavior is more severe, with penetration more likely (Cyr et al., 2002; Tidefors, Arvidsson, Ingevaldson, & Larsson, 2010). The family environment is also more dysfunctional, including exposure to IPV and pornography, alcohol abuse, emotionally unavailable parents, and an atmosphere of chaos (Cyr et al., 2002; Latzman et al., 2011; Phillips-Green, 2002). There are several typical dynamics—one in which two scared and neglected children provide nurturance and safety for each other within the context of a terrifying household. The second situation occurs when a sibling has a privileged position within the home to exert power without any fear of consequences by the parents, who may also be intimidated by this particular adolescent (Phillips-Green, 2002). In either of these scenarios, the parents have abdicated their caregiving. Thus, this type of maltreatment reflects not only the sexual abuse of a child but also the neglect of that child's (and that perpetrator's) needs for safety, structure, and nurturance.

RESILIENCE

A sizeable proportion of boys and girls who are sexually abused do not exhibit symptoms either as children or adults. Not surprisingly, they are often the children who were not as severely abused (e.g., perhaps a one-time incident of fondling by a nonrelative). On the other hand, some survivors of even severe abuse display resilience. Resilience has been operationalized in a variety of ways ranging from fewer symptoms of distress (Bryant-Davis, Ullman, Tsong, & Gobin, 2011; Greenfield & Marks, 2010) to "self-acceptance, positive relationships with others and environmental mastery" (McClure, Chavez, Agars, Peacock, & Matosian, 2008) to the "capacity to negotiate ordinary developmental tasks successfully in spite of cumulative adversity" (Eisold, 2005). Recognizing that the definition used and the developmental stage at which it is measured both lend themselves to the identification of different predictors, individuals who function without excess distress in spite of the adversity they have experienced can rightfully be considered to be resilient. Examining characteristics of these children, adolescents, and adults can provide direction for promising interventions.

As might be expected, the availability of attachment relationships emerges again and again among the reports and narratives of individuals of all different ages judged to be resilient. Relationships with nonoffending caregivers during childhood are particularly important in predicting short-term and long-term resilience (Collishaw et al., 2007; Lambie, Seymour, Lee, & Adams, 2002; Rosenthal, Feiring, & Taska, 2003; Spaccarelli & Kim, 1995; Williams & Nelson-Gardell, 2012). For example, in the study of African American mothers and daughters referred to earlier (Leifer, Kilbane, & Kalick, 2004), what differentiated abuse discontinuity mothers (i.e., CSA survivors whose children were not abused) from no abuse discontinuity mothers (their children were abused) was their recollection of more positive relationships with their own mothers and more continuity of these relationships, even though they acknowledged that these attachment relationships had been unstable in childhood. In fact, the contrast between their description of their relationships with their mothers in childhood and their current attachment security suggests that many of these abuse discontinuity mothers were undoubtedly "earned-secure."

By adolescence, good peer relationships are both a sign of resilience and a predictor of continued resilience into adulthood for both males and females (Collishaw et al., 2007; Edmond, Auslander, Etze, & Bowland, 2006; Lambie et al., 2002; Rosenthal et al., 2003). In adulthood, supportive partner relationships are associated with resilience and they moderate the impact of an abuse history on parenting (Collishaw et al., 2007; DuMont et al., 2007; Wright et al., 2005). Having a sense of belonging to a supportive community of others, including those with shared experiences, is also both an outcome of resilience and a correlate of future adjustment (Banyard & Williams, 2007; Greenfield & Marks, 2010). Moreover, interactions with others in safe relationships (such as in group therapy) foster the development of other healthy relationships by providing a forum for learning how to set boundaries, control anger during stressful interchanges, build trust, and develop intimacy (Kia-Keating, Sorsoli, & Grossman, 2010).

One of the most striking attributes of resilient individuals is their conscious awareness and acceptance of the occurrence of the abuse as well as its impact on their current functioning (Wright, Fopma-Loy, & Oberle, 2012). The descriptions of their attitudes with regard to their history are indistinguishable from the concept of coherence, assessed in the AAI. This coherence of their personal narrative may also involve the need and ability to derive meaning and understanding of the abuse, their own role as children who were not able to freely refuse, the perpetrator as responsible for his or her behavior, and the nonoffending parent(s) who for his or her own reasons may not have provided sufficient protection or empathy once the abuse was discovered (Bradley & Davino, 2007; Burton, 2004; Feinauer & Stuart, 1996; Grossman, Sorsoli, & Kia-Keating, 2006). What this meaning-making does not involve is a ruminative search for meaning (Silver, Boon, & Stones, 1983), more characteristic of preoccupied individuals who are stuck in an endless loop of asking why.

As a function of this awareness and understanding, resilient individuals reach turning points when they make conscious choices of how their history will not determine their future relationships, parenting, or sexual offending (Banyard & Williams, 2006; Kia-Keating, Grossman, Sorsoli, & Epstein, 2005; Wright, Fopma-Loy, et al., 2012). This process of developing a coherent narrative of one's experience necessarily evolves over time as reflective of stage of development and as the individual is confronted by trigger events such as new attachment relationships or stressful life events. However, the willingness to consider new interpretations while not being overwhelmed by them is the hallmark of the resilient individual and is associated with a hopeful, optimistic focus on the future (Edmond et al., 2006; Tarakeshar, Hansen, Kochman, Fox, & Sikkema, 2006; Williams & Nelson-Gardell, 2012). Interestingly, research suggests that religion and spirituality are associated positively with resilience for some and negatively for others (Bryant-Davis et al., 2011; Gall, 2006; Grossman et al., 2006).

Finally, research on coping suggests that, while avoidant coping is problematic, some degree of coping through distancing (such as minimization and refusing to dwell on the memories of abuse) is associated with greater resilience (Brand & Alexander, 2003; Cortes & Justicia, 2008; Himelein & McElrath, 1996; Wright et al., 2005). Confronting one's past without limitlessly pondering its effects is obviously the ideal and is characteristic of secure attachment. Nonetheless, it is important to note that the deactivating strategies of dismissing attachment are often less problematic than the hyperactivating strategies of preoccupied attachment.

IMPLICATIONS FOR TREATMENT

Both the research on resilience described above as well as research on the factors common across successful psychotherapy approaches emphasize the importance of relationships—with parents, partners, children, and therapists (Lambert & Cattani-Thompson, 1996). Thus, any approach to therapy with the abuse survivor needs to foster a strong therapeutic alliance allowing the development of the client's secure base behavior—namely, the safety, willingness, and ability to explore and alter models of self, others, and relationships. Given the past history of betrayal among abuse survivors, it is also important for the therapist to be sensitive to the need for a sequenced, phased, progressive treatment that initially emphasizes alliance building and support (Courtois, 2012). Liotti (2006) similarly emphasized the need for a phase-oriented approach in working with dissociative individuals, focusing on achieving attachment security before addressing trauma symptoms. Safety is not just relevant to the client's contacts outside of the session but also within the therapy room given that reenactment dynamics may surface in session (Carey, 1997). Given the risk for revictimization, even by the therapist, the therapist needs to help the CSA survivor develop a new and adequate IWM of protection (Thomas, 2005).

Both dialectical behavior therapy and transference-focused psychotherapy (TFP) have been used with significant success with trauma survivors diagnosed with BPD; however, TFP was even more useful than dialectical behavior therapy with regard to the alleviation of aggression and verbal assault against others (Clarkin, Levy, Lenzenweger, & Kernberg, 2007). Furthermore, while structured and cognitive behavioral therapy approaches may work better with regard to specific PTSD symptoms, treatment approaches for the CSA survivor that focus on interpersonal processes are more effective with regard to attachment relationships and overall social functioning (Alexander, Neimeyer, & Follette, 1991; Taylor & Harvey, 2010). Given the particular pertinence of aggression, attachment, and overall social functioning to the risks for problematic parenting, revictimization, and sexual offending, therapeutic approaches focusing specifically on the attachment relationship should be considered in interventions with the CSA survivor.

Another benefit of TFP has been its success in changing narrative coherence and reflective functioning (Levy et al., 2006). As was noted in the section on resilience, developing a coherent awareness and understanding of one's history of trauma is associated with reduced risk both for maltreating one's children and for sexual offending (Kia-Keating et al., 2005; Wright, Fopma-Loy, et al., 2012). Therefore, approaches that focus on fostering this understanding are especially relevant to the prevention of cycles of violence. Of particular note is mentalization-based treatment, which attempts to foster a client's ability to represent the thoughts, feelings, beliefs, and desires in oneself and in others with whom the client has an attachment relationship (Fonagy & Bateman, 2007). Another approach that also aims to enhance this coherence as a psychotherapy outcome is narrative therapy, which seeks to help clients derive a balanced position between the deactivation of the attachment system characterizing dismissing individuals and the hyperactivation of the attachment system characterizing preoccupied individuals (Daniel, 2009).

An additional focus of approaches in preventing cycles of violence among CSA survivors is emotion regulation. As described in Chapter 2, video feedback treatment with the mother-child dyad fosters this attachment relationship by helping the mother engage in reflective functioning with her child and by helping her self-regulate in the face of the challenging task of parenting. Thus, these approaches are pertinent to interrupting the cycle of trauma associated with the parenting of CSA survivors.

With regard to the prevention of sexual revictimization, the information typically provided by date rape prevention programs is not sufficient (Noll & Grych, 2011). Instead, interventions need to specifically address the emotion dysregulation that increases an individual's risk for revictimization and for abusing others. In one model, Cloitre, Koenen, Cohen, and Han (2002) used a staged intervention consisting of two phases of eight sessions each. The first phase focused on helping clients learn how to identify and label their feelings, tolerate and manage negative affect, and then negotiate challenging interpersonal situations. The next phase consisted of modified prolonged exposure designed to reduce PTSD symptoms. Not only was the program successful in improving affect regulation and interpersonal skills and in decreasing PTSD symptoms, but the therapeutic alliance and affect regulation skills of Phase 1 predicted improvement in Phase 2. Another approach that similarly addresses the affect dysregulation, disorganized attachment, dissociation, and disorders of the self that are associated with a history of complex trauma is accelerated experiential dynamic psychotherapy, a model of treatment that has also been used to develop self-regulation and the integration of self-states within dissociative individuals (Gleiser, Ford, & Fosha, 2008; Lamagna & Gleiser, 2007).

Finally, couples therapy has an important role in addressing the interpersonal problems associated with a history of CSA (Nasim & Nadan, 2013). Even participating in individual or group therapy for CSA survivors may elicit current attachment issues in the couple relationship (Follette et al., 1991; Oz, 2001). Fortunately, couples therapy appears to be just as effective for couples in which a partner has a CSA history as for couples without this history (Anderson & Miller, 2006). In particular, emotionally focused therapy has been empirically successful in addressing the trauma symptoms, such as affect dysregulation, hypervigilance, and dissociation, that contribute to interpersonal problems in CSA survivors and their partners (Dalton, Greenman, Classen, & Johnson, 2013; MacIntosh, 2013; MacIntosh & Johnson, 2008).

In conclusion, the survivor of CSA is at increased risk for revictimization, sexual offending, and problematic parenting for a variety of reasons. Interventions with sexually abused children, adolescents, and adults all offer challenges unique to the respective developmental stage being addressed but also offer the opportunity to protect both the individual and other important people in that person's life from further harm.

CHAPTER 7

Special Populations

The focus of this chapter is on a variety of special populations whose actual or potential exposure to violence or trauma increases their family members' and offspring's risk. The specific topics include political violence (especially the Holocaust), combat exposure, critical incident exposure of police officers, foster care and adoption, and the impact of parental incarceration on children.

THE HOLOCAUST AND OTHER POLITICAL VIOLENCE

The Holocaust is the best-known example of political terrorism directed against a particular group. However, the traumatic effects of exposure to such violence have been observed and well documented in a variety of groups, including families in Northern Ireland (Merrilees et al., 2011; McGuigan & Shevlin, 2010), Israeli Arabs (Johnson et al., 2009), Native Americans (Tafoya & Del Vecchio, 2005), political detainees in postwar East Germany (Klinitzke, Bohm, Brahler, & Weissflog, 2012), and Armenian refugees (Karenian et al., 2011). Children exposed to such violence (as victims, witnesses, and, in the case of child soldiers, as both victims and perpetrators) are further traumatized by their physical or psychological lack of access to their parents. For example, Almqvist and Broberg (2003) recounted the stories of young Kosovar children who escaped from Macedonia with their mothers and who witnessed multiple rapes of their mothers. The children's PTSD symptoms and clinging behavior triggered their mothers' intrusive memories of the trauma, leading to the mothers' withdrawal, disengagement, and even emotional abandonment of their children. The authors argued that the mothers' internal representation of their own caregiving behavior was damaged as was their view of their children, leading to their frightened and frightening behavior (Main & Hesse, 1990) and abdication of caregiving (Solomon & George, 1999b). As a result of these disorganized attachment relationships, the children developed controlling, punitive, and aggressive behavior.

Beyond these descriptions of clear attachment disruptions on parents and children experiencing political terrorism, research on the Holocaust has explored whether and under what conditions this trauma was transmitted to subsequent generations. Thus, it constitutes a model of the intergenerational transmission of trauma.

Some research (including meta-analyses) has found evidence of poorer adjustment, a higher incidence of PTSD, health problems, anxiety, low self-esteem, inhibition of aggression, and relational ambivalence among children of Holocaust survivors, while acknowledging the general resilience of these individuals (Barel, van IJzendoorn, Sagi-Schwartz, & Bakermans-Kranenburg, 2010; Gangi, Talamo, & Gerracuti, 2009; Shrira, Palgi, Ben-Ezra, & Shmotkin, 2011). Other researchers have noted the presence of traumatic stress and lack of resolution in the parents or grandparents who themselves experienced the Holocaust, but no notable transgenerational effects in their children or grandchildren (Bachar, Cale, Eisenberg, & Dasberg, 1994; Sagi-Schwartz, van IJzendoorn, & Bakermans-Kranenburg, 2008; Sagi-Schwartz, van IJzendoorn, et al., 2003).

Other research has found that many children and even grandchildren were adversely affected by the experiences of their elders. Children and grandchildren of survivors have reported experiencing intrusive memories, PTSD, anger, and irritability (Giladi & Bell, 2013; Iliceto et al., 2012; Kellermann, 2001; Letzter-Pouw & Werner, 2012; Yehuda, Schmeidler, Giller, Siever, & Binder-Brynes, 1998). Problems of individuation and separation have been observed, as have role reversal, excessive filial piety, and guilt (Anderson, Fields, & Dobb, 2013; Bar-On et al., 1998; Brom, Kfir, & Dasberg, 2001; Kellermann, 2001; Scharf, 2007; Scharf & Mayseless, 2011). Significantly, adult offspring of Holocaust survivors with PTSD described more emotional abuse and neglect as children than did a comparison group, pointing to possible intergenerational cycles of maltreatment among parents with a diagnosis of PTSD (Yehuda, Halligan, & Grossman, 2001). Furthermore, even when not abused, these children were more likely to be diagnosed with PTSD and depression, suggesting the intergenerational transmission of trauma even in the absence of maltreatment (Yehuda, Halligan, & Bierer, 2001; Yehuda, Schmeidler, Wainberg, Binder-Brynes, & Duvdevani, 1998).

The interactional effects of the Holocaust and current stressors were most notable in a study of Israeli soldiers in the 1982 Lebanon War, whose parents had either experienced or not experienced the Holocaust (Solomon, Kotler, & Mikulincer, 1989). Two and three years after the war, those soldiers who were children of Holocaust survivors were significantly more likely to exhibit PTSD symptoms following combat exposure than were comparison soldiers. On the other hand, a 20-year follow-up of the same sample revealed lower rates of trauma among the second-generation survivors than among comparison soldiers, suggesting the possible transmission of positive as well as negative trauma outcomes (Dekel, Solomon, & Rozenstreich, 2013).

What then explains the intergenerational effects observed among some, but not all, children and grandchildren of Holocaust survivors? First, epigenesis may play a role. PTSD and other psychiatric diagnoses were more prevalent among adult children of mothers, but not fathers, who were Holocaust survivors diagnosed with PTSD (Yehuda et al., 2008). These results could also reflect the typical primacy of the attachment relationship with the mother. However, lower mean cortisol levels among children whose mothers (but not fathers) had Holocaust-related PTSD and dissociation may indicate exposure either in utero or early in life to vulnerability to developing PTSD in response to stress (van IJzendoorn, Fridman, Bakermans-Kranenburg, & Sagi-Schwartz, 2013; Yehuda et al., 2007).

Not surprisingly, attachment dynamics may play an important role in the transmission of Holocaust-related trauma to children. Bar-On et al. (1998) made the case that attachment theory is uniquely relevant to the core issues of attachment, separation, and loss associated with the experience of the Holocaust. Indeed, studies of the attachment of offspring of Holocaust survivors have found a range of effects, including a higher than expected incidence of insecure attachment, disoriented thought regarding trauma, and poor reflective functioning, but also relatively high rates of secure attachment (Caviglia, Fiocco, & Dazzi, 2004; Sagi, van IJzendoorn, Joels, & Scharf, 2002; Sossin, 2007). In a sample of children who had lost both parents in the Holocaust, 56% exhibited unresolved loss and trauma. Moreover, several exhibited indicators of failed mourning, consisting of an absence or denial of grief (Sagi-Schwartz, Koren-Karie, & Joels, 2003).

Consistent with the research on attachment relationships among Holocaust survivors is the research on parent-child communication in this group. The absence of informative verbal communication about a mother's experience of trauma in the Holocaust was predictive of an adult child's interpersonal distress and inhibited affiliation (Wiseman et al., 2002), an effect also observed by Giladi and Bell (2013). In fact, Schwab (2009) speculated that family secrets and taboos among parents who survived the Holocaust but lost a child sometimes led to the birth of a "replacement child" who would bear the burden of the parent's unresolved loss. Conversely, preoccupation with the Holocaust, as exhibited either by descendants of Holocaust survivors with strong Jewish identification or by members of the ultraorthodox community irrespective of their grandparents' Holocaust status, predicted PTSD symptoms and the intergenerational transfer of this type of trauma (Perlstein & Motta, 2013; Wohl & Van Bavel, 2011). Thus, both denial (i.e., disorganized attachment's "conspiracy of silence"; Bar-On et al., 1998) and preoccupation may preclude the coherent understanding and acceptance of one's own and one's parent's trauma that is necessary for its resolution and for a secure parent-child attachment relationship.

Barel et al. (2010) speculated as to why intergenerational patterns of trauma would not be more prevalent among people whose experience was so severe. They argued, first of all, that because the Holocaust was not inflicted by parents on their children, it did not inherently involve a disruption of the attachment relationship. (The unresolved loss experienced by child survivors of the Holocaust is clearly a counterpoint to this perspective.) Furthermore, they hypothesized that those who survived may have been genetically protected from the intense reactions of stress. Finally, the ongoing acknowledgment, including formal memorials and social support of survivors, may have facilitated the resolution of trauma. Therefore, both societally and individually, "after-trauma care" may have decreased the impact of the Holocaust for many individuals and may serve as a guide for the healing of other groups and individuals affected by political violence (van der Hal-van Raalte, van IJzendoorn, & Bakermans-Kranenburg, 2007).

COMBAT EXPOSURE

The long-term suffering of soldiers exposed to combat has rightfully commanded attention within our country. However, the negative impact of war is not limited to the soldier, given that 56% of 1.5 million military service members are married and 2 million American children have at least one military parent (Anderson, Amanor-Boadu, Stith, & Foster, 2013; Cohen & Cozza, 2012). In fact, three of five deployed soldiers have spouses and/or children (Esposito-Smythers et al., 2011). These family members are themselves subject to the short-term, long-term, and potentially intergenerational effects of war.

The Experience of Soldiers

A large body of research has concluded that combat exposure contributes to the development of PTSD. Namely, (1) feeling in great danger of death, (2) being shot or seriously injured, (3) having prior violence experiences, and (4) personally seeing someone wounded, killed, or dead all increase the likelihood of receiving a diagnosis of PTSD (Phillips, Leard-Mann, Gumbs, & Smith, 2010). While a diagnosis of PTSD is generally presumed to reflect a severe fear reaction, more recent research has suggested the relevance of moral injury as an explanation for the many long-term psychological, biological, behavioral, and relational consequences of war (Litz et al., 2009). Moral injury refers to the harmful effects of events "such as perpetrating, failing to prevent, or bearing witness to acts that transgress deeply held moral beliefs and expectations" (Litz et al., 2009, p. 695). Instead of fear, its prime affect is shame, leading to withdrawal, thereby reinforcing the expectations of censure, rejection, and shame. Whether the impact is that of fear or shame, neurobiological studies of veterans have found concrete evidence of the negative impact of combat, including higher blood serotonin levels associated with behavioral irritability and other indicators of HPA axis dysregulation (Golier, Caramanica, & Yehuda, 2012; Lande, Banks-Williams, & Fileta, 2012).

The experience of soldiers with more recent wartime exposures is even more complicated than that of World War II, Korea, and Vietnam veterans because the nature of military service has changed. Multiple and lengthy deployments are more common with an absence of safety "outside the wire" or away from base and increased absence of safety inside the base, as cases of military sexual trauma have become more prevalent (Basham, 2008; Maguen, Luxton, Skopp, & Madden, 2012; Phillips et al., 2010). Predeployment vulnerabilities have become more relevant in recent conflicts than in the Vietnam War given our current all-volunteer military as opposed to a service including draftees (Vogt et al., 2011). Relational concerns have also increased as a larger percentage of recruits are women (Vogt et al., 2011). Thus, current wartime experiences are more similar to chronic trauma than the acute but well-delineated determinants of a traditional diagnosis of PTSD (Basham, 2008).

Combat Exposure, Childhood Trauma, PTSD, and Increased Aggression

The rates of violent behavior among male and female soldiers are high. One study found that 41% of a nationally representative sample of male Vietnam veterans and 32% of female Vietnam veterans were aggressive (Taft, Monson, Hebenstreit, King, & King, 2009). PTSD often mediates the effect of combat exposure on aggression (Hassija, Jakupcak, Maguen, & Shipherd, 2012; Jakupcak et al., 2007; Lenhardt, Howard, Taft, Kaloupek, & Keane, 2012; Renshaw & Kiddie, 2012; Stappenbeck, Hellmuth, Simpson, & Jakupcak, 2013; Taft, Street, Marshall, Dowdall, & Riggs, 2007; Taft, Vogt, Marshall, Panuzio, & Niles, 2007; Wright, Foran, Wood, Eckford, & McGurk, 2012).

However, a history of childhood trauma frequently also plays a role. First, as might be expected with a volunteer military, many of whom enlisted during periods of economic recession, recruits have higher rates of child sexual abuse (half of females in one large sample) and child physical abuse (half of both males and females in the same sample) than the population overall (Rosen & Martin, 1996). In another active-duty sample of army soldiers, 46% had a history of child physical abuse alone and 25% had a history of both child physical abuse and child sexual abuse; as might be expected, this child maltreatment history predicted more severe PTSD symptoms (Seifert, Polusny, & Murdoch, 2011). Furthermore, 90% of a sample of child or spouse abuse offenders in the army had a history of perpetrating maltreatment prior to their entry into the service (McCarroll, Ursano, Fan, & Newby, 2004). Similarly high rates of childhood trauma and nonmilitary trauma in adulthood have been observed in veterans with PTSD (Clancy et al., 2006). Furthermore, from an attachment perspective, predeployment unresolved loss or trauma was associated with the development of PTSD among veterans (Harari et al., 2009). Thus, preexisting trauma and adverse childhood experiences may have either an additive or interactive effect with combat exposure in increasing the risk for PTSD and the severity of PTSD symptoms (Dedert et al., 2009; Fritch, Mishkind, Reger, & Gahm, 2010; Gahm, Lucenko, Retzlaff, & Fukuda, 2007; Iversen et al., 2008; Owens et al., 2009; Phillips et al., 2010; Sareen et al., 2013; Stein et al., 2005; Van Voorhees et al., 2012).

Childhood trauma increases not only an individual's traumatic response to combat, but also vulnerability to other kinds of trauma such as sexual coercion and harassment (Murdoch et al., 2010; Rosen & Martin, 1998), an experience unfortunately so common to both men and women in today's military that it is receiving attention in the popular press (e.g., Matthews, 2013) and specialized treatment units in veterans' hospitals. Another infrequent but abhorrent outcome of a severe history of childhood trauma or a history of dissociation is the perpetration of war-zone atrocities (Ford, 1999; Schapiro, Glynn, Foy, & Yavorsky, 2002). In fact, the proneness to shame associated with the witnessing and perpetration of atrocities and with the development of moral injury (Litz et al., 2009) may be rooted for some individuals in their history of abuse (see Chapter 6). Therefore, the current military comprises many individuals who are already vulnerable to the triggering of traumatic responses during combat because of their own history of child maltreatment and other predeployment traumas. This both increases the risk for intergenerational cycles of violence and obviates any clear attribution to the effects of combat alone.

Impact on Families

Deployment

Most research on the damaging effects of war on soldiers has focused on the impact of combat exposure; however, families of soldiers experience stress and anxiety almost as soon as notifications of deployment are announced. As mentioned previously, multiple deployments in recent conflicts have led to a "cycle of deployment" for families as they prepare for and adjust to change again and again (Riggs & Riggs, 2011). From an attachment perspective, spouses and children must face threats to their sense of security due to the presumably temporary absence of the soldier. Not only is the family's sense of threat or danger exacerbated if the soldier is deployed to a combat zone, but depending upon the prior relationship or age of the child, the deployment may be experienced by family members as actual abandonment. Thus, it may trigger attachment anxieties.

Stressors such as loneliness, worry, anxiety, loss of emotional support, role overload, financial strain, and role conflicts are common among partners and depend in part upon the length of deployments (de Burgh, White, Fear, & Iversen, 2011; Esposito-Smythers et al., 2011). These stressors may be adequately addressed in securely attached partners, but may overwhelm someone with insecure attachment (Riggs & Riggs, 2011). Children respond differently to stressors based on their age, the nature of their attachment with both parents, and the overall functioning of the family (Riggs & Riggs, 2011). However, the prevalence of children's negative reactions was highlighted in a study of 5–12-year-old children with a deployed parent (Flake, Davis, Johnson, & Middleton, 2009). It found that 39% of the sample exhibited internalizing symptoms; 29% had externalizing symptoms; 56% had trouble sleeping; and 14% had school-related problems. As noted by Cozza (2011), military children often deal with prolonged moderate levels of distress and intermittent periods of high anxiety, a sense of loss of the deployed parent, and frequently the psychological absence of the nondeployed parent, who may be preoccupied with the partner's deployment.

In fact, deployment obviously affects the parenting of the nondeployed parent, which explains much of the variance in military children's symptoms (Pemberton, Kramer, Borrego, & Owen, 2013). Many of the negative intergenerational effects of deployment on children are due to the much higher rates of child maltreatment by the nondeployed parent. In a sample of approximately 1,800 families, rates of maltreatment and neglect by female civilian parents were three to four times higher during periods of deployment (Gibbs, Martin, Kupper, & Johnson, 2007).

Ambiguous Loss

Deployment during wartime necessarily involves either a conscious or unconscious anticipation of possible loss. Sometimes this loss is actual. For example, in a sample of Vietnam combat veterans with PTSD, 40% had an attachment classification of unresolved loss, which exacerbated PTSD avoidance or numbing symptoms (Nye et al., 2008). The families of soldiers may obviously also experience the loss of the soldier through death (Gewirtz, Erbes, Polusny, Forgatch, & DeGarmo, 2011). Even this experience may be different than for grieving nonmilitary families, depending upon the preceding length of deployment and the circumstances of the death (Cozza, 2011).

However, deployment has also been compared to the concept of ambiguous loss, in which a physically absent family member may be perceived as psychologically present or a physically present family member may be perceived as psychologically absent (see Chapter 2; Boss & Greenberg, 1984; Riggs & Riggs, 2011). Boss (1999) argued that both possibilities lead to boundary ambiguity and a fluctuation between hope and hopelessness. The nature of this boundary ambiguity was explored in a sample of reservists and their families following the reservists' return from Iraq (Faber, Willerton, Clymer, MacDermid, & Weiss, 2008). The authors described deployment as "ambiguous absence" associated with a family's worries about the soldier's safety, the stress arising from the redistribution of roles and responsibilities during the deployment, and anticipatory worries about the eventual reunion. They described reunion as "ambiguous presence," in which both family members and soldiers found that the resumption of roles, responsibilities, and even communication was either avoided or led to conflict.

Consistent with Hill's (1949) study of World War II soldiers and their families, the rigid internal and external boundaries of "closed-ranks" families may deal efficiently with the deployment and thus may avoid the ambiguous absence described above. However, these families may have more difficulty with the ambiguous presence associated with reunion and reintegration (Faber et al., 2008; Riggs & Riggs, 2011). In contrast, the weak external and internal boundaries of "open-ranks" families maintain the bond to the absent parent but are less successful in reorganizing the family to foster the nondeployed parent's assumption of decision making and authority within the family; these families are also more susceptible to enmeshment and parent-child role reversal (Riggs & Riggs, 2011). Thus, preexisting boundary rigidity and dissolution can interact with deployment to pose particular challenges to military families (Chapter 3). In fact, given the prevalence of this ambiguous loss for military families, their resilience may be best conceptualized as a tolerance for ambiguity (Boss, 2013).

The Soldier's Experience of Reunion With the Family

Basham portrayed the soldier's typical experience of returning home:

> Inevitably, when a warrior returns home, he or she returns as a changed individual. . . . Soldiers learn to control fears and suppress emotions, to

master the art of deception while cunningly devising ways to survive, and to parse information while restricting communication. As they gain physical strength, endurance, and quickness to respond to dangerous situations, they also develop the capacity to respond immediately and instantly with violent lethal force. They maintain a vigilant watchful stance at all times, preparing to respond to danger and recognize that the fixed rules of hierarchy can be broken when they pose a threat to safety. (2008, p. 87)

Basham (2008) concluded that soldiers also often begin to relate to intimate others and to the world through the lens of the "victim-victimizer-bystander" triangle first mentioned by Judith Herman (1992) as a way to describe the experience of the incest survivor. This process is associated with shattered trust and disrupted attachment relationships and is a challenge for both soldier and family.

Effects of Reunion and PTSD on Families

All military families must deal with reintegrating the absent parent or partner into the family (Faber et al., 2008). Given that both partners and their children may have had their own histories of trauma, insecure attachment, or problematic family functioning even before the deployment, the impact of a returning soldier's PTSD or depression is overlaid on prior experiences. Adjustment to a soldier's return home may be particularly problematic in dual-trauma couples, although the reciprocal triggering of PTSD-like symptoms of hyperarousal, avoidance, and numbing may occur even among partners without a history of trauma (Basham, 2008).

Combat exposure and subsequent PTSD contribute to family distress and higher rates of divorce (Galovski & Lyons, 2004; Monson, Fredman, & Taft, 2011; Taft, Schumm, Panuzio, & Monson, 2008). A meta-analysis found that PTSD predicted partners' psychological distress, especially in military populations, among female partners and when trauma was experienced in the distant past, emphasizing either the additive or interactive role of childhood trauma (Lambert, Engh, Hasbun, & Holzer, 2012). As would be expected from the literature on combat exposure's contribution to aggression and partner conflict, it also increases the risk for intimate partner violence (IPV; Foster et al., 2010). For example, a meta-analysis concluded that the association between PTSD and IPV was stronger among the military and males, especially for severe IPV (Taft, Watkins, Stafford, Street, & Monson, 2011). However, PTSD was also strongly associated with aggression by both female veterans and the female partners of veterans (Gold et al., 2007; LaMotte, Taft, Weatherill, Scott, & Eckhardt, 2014). In another sample of female Vietnam veterans, even aside from PTSD, women were more likely to be physically aggressive than were their male partners (Dutra, de Blank, Scheiderer, & Taft, 2012). In fact, only half of the women had physically aggressive partners. Therefore, given the prevalence of physical aggression in both male and female soldiers, mutual IPV is a particular risk in dual-military couples.

Combat exposure and PTSD also increase the risk for parenting problems and child maltreatment by both the soldier and the nondeployed spouse (Berz, Taft, Watkins, & Monson, 2008; Cozza, 2011; Foster et al., 2010; Gibbs, Martin, Clinton-Sherrod, Walters, & Johnson, 2011). In a longitudinal study of National Guard soldiers, PTSD predicted poorer couple adjustment and parenting problems at follow-up (Gewirtz, Polusny, DeGarmo, Khaylis, & Erbes, 2010). In a large sample of active-duty U.S. Air Force parents with substantiated cases of child maltreatment, milder forms of maltreatment were less common post-deployment but more severe forms of maltreatment (i.e., child sexual abuse and severe child neglect) were more common post-deployment (Thomsen et al., 2014). Furthermore, children respond to the increased stress, anxiety, and hostility (and perhaps maltreatment) by parents with their own hostility, behavior problems, and violent behavior (Glenn et al., 2002; Gold et al., 2007). This then contributes to reciprocal dynamics between the parent's PTSD and family interactions, greatly increasing the risk for severe family violence and intergenerational consequences (Esposito-Smythers et al., 2011; Gewirtz et al., 2010; Monson et al., 2011; Pemberton et al., 2013).

Longer-Term Intergenerational Effects

Clearly, individual, couple, and family dynamics that increase the risk for family violence increase the risk for cycles of violence and trauma. Few longitudinal studies have explicitly examined this in a military population. However, there is some evidence that a parent's combat experience may interact with an adult child's subsequent combat exposure to increase his or her risk for PTSD. Namely, Vietnam veterans whose fathers had combat exposure in World War II were significantly likely to have more severe PTSD symptoms than were those Vietnam veterans whose fathers had not been exposed to combat (Rosenheck & Fontana, 1998). The results mirror the findings of Solomon et al. (1989) comparing the military offspring of Holocaust survivors with parents who had not experienced the Holocaust. Unfortunately, neither of these studies examined the possible mediating role of family violence, a factor that both follows from and increases the risk for combat-related PTSD. In addition to problematic family dynamics (Dekel & Goldblatt, 2008), the increased intergenerational risk for PTSD (and its consequences) could be associated with genetic factors, such as polymorphisms or the risk for epigenetic effects due to the stress experienced by mothers whose partners have been deployed. Whatever the combination of causes, there is clearly a significant propensity for intergenerational cycles of violence and trauma among individuals already at risk for violent behavior because of their own history of trauma even before they are confronted with the terrors of war.

Implications for Treatment

Any intervention that can reduce the symptoms stemming from combat-related PTSD is relevant to interrupting intergenerational cycles in military families. To that end, a variety of treatment approaches have been adapted to a military population. For example, cognitive-behavioral conjoint therapy for PTSD is a 15-session manual-based treatment consisting of psychoeducation about the impact of PTSD on relationship functioning, behavioral interventions focused on communication and problem solving, and cognitive interventions related to PTSD and relationship distress (Monson et al., 2011). Other treatments that have also been used with military families include parent-child interaction therapy, shown to be effective in reducing abusive parenting by coaching parents in their interactions with children (Pemberton et al., 2013). The parent management training-Oregon model has been adapted for use with military families (after deployment: adaptive parenting tools; Gewirtz et al., 2011), with a focus on the resilience of military families, attending to typical family stressors associated with deployment, and enhancing emotion regulation in parent-child interactions.

Given the role of childhood traumas in increasing the risk for deployment-related PTSD, it is shortsighted to ignore preexisting factors in the soldier, the nondeployed parent, and even children within the family. Therefore, even prevention interventions should assess the existence of childhood trauma. As noted by Yehuda, Flory, Southwick, and Charney (2006), a soldier's resolution of prior trauma, attachment, and relationships in childhood protects against a negative reaction to combat. It is likely that resolution of similar issues in nondeployed spouses would also facilitate their reaction to deployment.

An attachment and family systems approach is also advisable following deployment in order to address the myriad issues confronting the military family (Basham, 2008; Riggs & Riggs, 2011). Given the relevance of moral injury to the development of PTSD, a secure family base that facilitates meaning making and fosters and articulates family belief systems may be the best way to navigate a soldier's return to normalcy. The principles of psychological first aid are consistent with this perspective and include the following key principles: (a) establishing a sense of safety, (b) promoting calming and self-soothing, (c) building a sense of self and community efficacy, (d) fostering connectedness, and (e) promoting a sense of hope (Cozza, 2011). Another intervention that has been used with military couples to accomplish similar goals is emotionally focused therapy (Chapter 3; Johnson, 2002; Rheem, Woolley, & Johnson, 2011; Sneath & Rheem, 2011).

In conclusion, even in the context of ubiquitous worries and concerns among military families, including the uncontrollable external factors of war, most military families find ways to adapt to the stresses of deployment and reunion (Peterson, Park, & Castro, 2011). Future research should seek to identify the characteristics of those families who survive and thrive.

LAW ENFORCEMENT

As with soldiers in the military, the impact of PTSD on police officers is often quite severe, leading to depression following exposure to trauma, deficits in social cognition and emotion regulation, and significantly more feelings of personal threat and vulnerability upon subsequent exposure to critical incidents (Carlier, Lamberts, & Gersons, 2000; Martin, Marchand, & Boyer, 2009; Mazza et al., 2012). Psychophysiological studies also provide evidence of the underlying effects of PTSD on brain functioning in terms of reduced hippocampal volume and lower levels of basal cortisol on awakening (Lindauer et al., 2004; Neyland et al., 2005; Shucard et al., 2012).

One of the most consistently observed correlates of PTSD in police officers is peritraumatic dissociation, referring to depersonalization, derealization, and disorientation experienced at the time of trauma exposure, which leads to dysregulated physiological arousal (Carlier, Lamberts, Fouwels, & Gersons, 1996; Hodgins, Creamer, & Bell, 2001; Maia et al., 2011; Martin, Marchand, Boyer, & Martin, 2009; Pole, 2008; Sijbrandij et al., 2007). Other research has emphasized the role of negative affect, either by itself or in interaction with peritraumatic dissociation in predicting PTSD and increased distress over time (Apfel et al., 2008; Galatzer-Levy et al., 2013; Maia et al., 2011).

However, the dissociation and negative affect cannot be attributed only to the current critical incident. Instead, preexisting vulnerability factors help explain the development of PTSD in reaction to a subsequent exposure to trauma. For example, Pole et al. (2009) conducted a longitudinal study of police cadets' exaggerated physiological reactivity to startling sounds within a background of threat. They found that the severity of subsequent PTSD symptoms was predicted by the following: greater subjective fear under low threat, greater sympathetic nervous system reactivity to explicit threat, and failure to adapt to repeated aversive stimuli — in other words, all preexisting traits associated with prior experiences of trauma. Moreover, trait dissociation, assessed during academy training and associated with prior trauma exposure, predicted peritraumatic dissociation and, along with peritraumatic dissociation, accounted for the impact of subsequent critical incidents on the development of PTSD symptoms (McCaslin et al., 2008). Therefore, a history of trauma prior to employment as a police officer appears to increase an officer's vulnerability for both peritraumatic dissociation and PTSD symptoms when he or she is later confronted by a highly stressful situation.

This preexisting trauma was typically experienced in childhood. For example, one-fifth of a sample of first-responder police and firefighters involved in relief efforts after Hurricane Katrina reported a history of physical abuse before age 18 (Komarovskaya et al., 2014). This early victimization was associated with PTSD symptoms, peritraumatic dissociation, depression, and sleep problems. Similarly, a history of childhood trauma predicted work-related depression and work-related PTSD (Follette, Polusny, & Milbeck, 1994; Wang et al., 2010). Finally, a history of childhood trauma was associated with an increased catecholamine response (a risk factor for anxiety disorders) to a video depicting police officers' exposure to critical incidents (Otte et al., 2005). Therefore, police recruits with a history of childhood trauma may be at increased risk for PTSD and other symptoms when subsequently exposed to stress in the line of duty.

Whether or not this vulnerability leads to impaired judgment and performance on the job (LeBlanc, Regehr, Jelley, & Barath, 2007), it has implications for family violence. High rates of family violence, alcohol abuse, family disruption, and psychological problems are prevalent among police officers (Clark-Miller & Brady, 2013; Kruger & Valltos, 2002). As with any adult, a history of child physical abuse increases police officers' risk for abusing their spouses and children (Valentine, Oehme, & Martin, 2012; Zavala, 2013). However, the job characteristics of policing make this connection even more likely. Work stressors such as sleep deprivation and exposure to critical incidents are not only common but are associated with adverse outcomes such as depression and IPV (Charles, Slaven, et al., 2011; Gershon, Barocas, Canton, Li, & Vlahov, 2009). Stressful events on the job and interactions with the perpetrators of violence also contribute to the authoritarian spillover seen in violent partner relationships (Anderson & Lo, 2011). Finally, compassion fatigue among detectives who work with traumatized individuals, such as children who are victims of sexual assault, has been correlated with PTSD symptoms (Lane, Lating, Lowry, & Martino, 2010), which is itself a risk factor for aggression toward others.

Given these stressors that are endemic to the practice of law enforcement, it is necessary to identify factors that ameliorate the connections between trauma exposure, PTSD, and aggressive behavior. For example, social support may protect against the impact of a history of trauma on police officers' reaction to current stress (Carlier, Lamberts, & Gersons, 1997; Maia et al., 2011; Martin, Marchand, Boyer, & Martin, 2009; Pole, 2008; Stephens & Long, 1999; Stephens, Long, & Miller, 1997). Moreover, in a prospective study of protective factors for PTSD among police officers, beliefs of greater benevolence of the world predicted fewer PTSD symptoms after 2 years of police service (Yuan et al., 2011). The fact that gender may affect police officers' reactions to critical incidents and to different types of social support suggests that further research is required to determine how best to intervene with police officers (Bär, Pahlike, Dahm, Weiss, & Heuft, 2004; Gehrke & Violanti, 2006; Lane et al., 2010; Lilly, Pole, Best, Metzler, & Marmar, 2009; Pole, 2008; Violanti & Gehrke, 2004).

In the meantime, even though certain police officers may be vulnerable to the development of PTSD because of preexisting trauma exposure, a number of interventions have been identified that are successful in ameliorating these symptoms. For example, mindfulness-based interventions lead to reduced PTSD symptoms (Chopko & Schwartz, 2013) as does the use of eye movement desensitization and reprocessing therapy (Keenan & Royle, 2007). A study of police officers employing functional MRIs found that psychotherapy resulted in fewer PTSD symptoms and decreased arousal during traumatic memory retrieval (Peres et al., 2011). The use of emotionally focused therapy may be particularly useful for couples in which one partner is a police officer or first responder (Johnson & Faller, 2011). Among other things, it helps couples confront the attachment-related anxieties that arise in both partners as a consequence of the very real dangers and personal threat that law enforcement entails. Moreover, it helps partners learn to disclose and to listen to the narratives of traumatic events stemming from the practice of law enforcement.

Sam grew up with his mother, father and three younger brothers. Three of his grandparents had experienced significant abuse as children as had his mother and his father. He described his mother (who has bipolar disorder) as rageful against him, as blaming him even for misbehavior by his siblings, and as inciting his father's excessive punishment, including beatings with bullwhips and electric cords until he bled. For example, after one incident of quarreling at the dinner table with his younger brother when he was 12 years old, his mother threw a plate of food at him, punched him and pushed his face into his plate. Sam called the police on her; when his father came home from work, he sent Sam out into the winter cold from 8 p.m. until 4 a.m. to shovel neighbors' walks. In another incident, his younger brothers knocked down the Christmas tree when Sam was outside with his father. Nonetheless, at his mother's urgings, his father beat all of the children, including Sam. He reported that even more hurtful than the physical abuse, however, was the verbal abuse by his mother who frequently stated that she wished he had never been born.

Triangulation seemed to be a common family dynamic with Sam's father accusing him of siding with his mother and comparing him unfavorably to his mother. Particularly severe abuse of Sam and his next-to-youngest sib was associated with his parents' especially notable marital conflict at the times of their respective births. (The second-oldest and youngest sons were born at times of relative calm during the parents' relationship and these sons were somewhat less subject to maltreatment.) Sam stated that he was not close to either parent, but felt emotionally supported growing up by his maternal grandmother and his paternal grandfather, with whom he lived at ages 4–6 years old when his parents temporarily separated. Sam entered the Navy at age 18 for four years and returned home to attend college until he fought physically with his inebriated father who was threatening Sam's mother with a shotgun. At that point, he moved to the East Coast and joined a metropolitan police force.

Sam's attachment to his grandparents appears to have provided him with some degree of earned security, as revealed also in his valuing of his current attachment relationships. Nonetheless, ongoing effects of his abuse interact with the stresses of critical incident exposures on his job. For example, his long-term role of protector to his younger brothers has translated into especially severe rage reactions as a police officer toward negligent or abusive parents. Furthermore, his emotion dysregulation from childhood has contributed to excessive risk-taking in his job—e.g., confronting ten people by himself in a dark alley, engaging in a 110 mph car chase down a two-lane road, going into a burning building for a child who died. Consequently, he has experienced significant panic attacks and sometimes drinks to self-medicate. Although he attempts to control his drinking, it contributes to marital conflict as does a tendency to see similarities between his mother and his wife. (For example, he appears to react to his wife's leaving the house for several hours after an argument as reminiscent of his mother abandoning him for several years when he was four years old.)

Sam is currently in therapy and is aware of the impact of his childhood on his current behavior. He has made a conscious decision to not physically discipline his children. However, ongoing issues remain (including his risk for alcohol abuse) and, given no known IPV (assessed individually with each partner), he and his wife would be prime candidates for an intervention such as emotionally focused therapy as a way both to work through his transference reactions to his wife and to benefit from what appears to be her general support.

FOSTER CARE AND ADOPTION

The need for foster care and adoption is great in the United States. More than a half million children were in formal foster care in 2006, with many more residing with relatives or neighbors (Dozier & Rutter, 2008). Around the same time, approximately 50,000 children were adopted from foster care with an additional 22,000 children adopted internationally (Dozier & Rutter, 2008). The experiences of being in foster care or adopted are also significant qualitatively and not just because of their numbers. By definition, both foster care and adoption follow from a major disruption in the primary attachment relationship. The impact of this attachment disruption on intergenerational cycles of violence and trauma is uncertain because of the challenge of separating the long-term effects of prior abuse, neglect, early neurobiological effects, genetic vulnerabilities, and institutionalization from the effects of the foster care or adoption itself. It is similarly challenging to distinguish the long-term impact of the adoptive or foster parent's prior loss or infertility that frequently precedes a decision to adopt from the nature of this parent-child relationship. As noted in one interview study, "grief was an important marker of the story of every adoptive couple" (Begue, 2013, p. 106). Therefore, it is speculative to suggest exactly how the process of foster care or adoption either contributes to or interrupts potential cycles of violence and trauma. Nonetheless, existing research does indicate what characteristics either protect or exacerbate the effects of this attachment disruption on children's behavior. Research can similarly propose how supportive adoption or foster care can overcome prior negative effects.

Prior to Adoption or Foster Care

Children are often placed in foster care because of severe abuse or neglect, both of which have long-term effects. As argued in Chapter 4, even a mother's history of stress (associated with the necessity of placing her child in foster care or giving up her child for adoption) can impact the child through the process of epigenesis. Similarly, foster or adoptive children are not exempt from other genetic effects associated with prenatal pregnancy risk (Pemberton et al., 2010). Furthermore, except when a child is placed in foster or adoptive care immediately after birth, the placement necessarily involves a separation from the parent, with important consequences for the child (Dozier & Rutter, 2008). Given that early placement tends to be associated with a mother's prenatal substance abuse while later placement tends to result from postnatal maltreatment (Dozier & Rutter, 2008), a child's age at entry into foster care or adoption may reflect different but not necessarily diminished risks.

Parent-Child Interactions in Foster or Adoptive Care

Parenting a foster child or adoptive child can be extremely challenging, even with an adequate understanding of attachment-related issues (Tyrrell & Dozier, 1999). However, with the possible exception of children with reactive attachment disorder (see below), parental characteristics appear to be more important than child characteristics in predicting child outcomes. That is, attachment security in children is predicted by parental attachment security, sensitivity, acceptance, and reflective functioning (Ackerman & Dozier, 2005; Steele et al., 2008; Stovall-McClough & Dozier, 2004; Verissimo, Salvaterra, Santos, & Santos, 2008). For the most part, caregivers' sensitivity to their foster children is similar no matter how challenging the child (Koren-Karie, Oppenheim, Yuval-Adler, & Mor, 2013). Consequently, even late-adopted children were seen to exhibit enhanced attachment security over time to the degree that their adoptive mothers had securely attached states of mind (Pace & Zavattini, 2011). Conversely, insecure attachment and unresolved mourning in adoptive parents who were assessed with the AAI prior to child placement in their homes predicted intense aggression in children's attachment story completions only 3 months into the placement (Steele et al., 2007).

Some studies have found that placement at a younger age either by itself or in interaction with the foster parent's secure attachment is associated with increased attachment security in the child (Bates & Dozier, 2002; Stovall & Dozier, 2000; Stovall-McClough & Dozier, 2004). However, other studies have found no effect of age on attachment quality in foster and adoptive children, suggesting that even older babies (2–4 years old in these samples) can become securely attached to their caregivers (Dozier, Stovall, Albus, & Bates, 2001; Verissimo & Salvaterra, 2006; Verissimo et al., 2008). A foster or adoptive parent's commitment to a child also has important ramifications for children's behavior and development (Dozier & Lindhiem, 2006; Dozier, Grasso, Lindhiem, & Lewis, 2007; Lindhiem & Dozier, 2007). Indeed, a foster mother's delight in her child (as a proxy for her commitment) has even been associated with her oxytocin levels and electrophysiological responses to the child (Bernard & Dozier, 2011; Bick, Dozier, Bernard, Grasso, & Simons, 2013). Given that approximately 8% of foster parents request the child's removal (Dozier & Rutter, 2008), and given that even the transition from a foster home to an adoptive home represents yet another experience of loss for a child (Lanyado, 2003), the issue of placement instability is not an insignificant problem. Moreover, placement instability is associated with adoptive children's reduced inhibitory control and oppositional behavior (Lewis, Dozier, Ackerman, & Sepulveda-Kozakowski, 2007) and therefore is relevant to later violent behavior. However, other than a finding of reduced parental commitment among foster mothers who had fostered more children in the past or who were caring for older children (Dozier & Lindhiem, 2006), it is not always clear whether the placement instability contributes to or results from child behavior problems and poor inhibitory control (Lindhiem & Dozier, 2007). This question of cause and effect is complicated further with regard to children exhibiting reactive attachment disorder (RAD).

Reactive Attachment Disorder

According to the *DSM-5*, RAD is characterized by "markedly disturbed and developmentally inappropriate attachment behaviors, in which a child rarely or minimally turns preferentially to an attachment figure for comfort, support, protection, and nurturance" (American Psychiatric Association, 2013, p. 266). These children are at least as impaired as those with autism spectrum disorder in their use of context, rapport, and pragmatic language skills (Sadiq et al., 2012). RAD has typically been observed in the behavior of children adopted from foreign orphanages in which they had received a lack of attention, warmth, and emotional responsiveness and instability of caregivers. As a function of the length of time spent in institutions such as these, children display indiscriminate friendliness, poor inhibitory control, noncompliance, and provocative, aggressive, and violent behaviors (Bruce, Tarullo, & Gunnar, 2009; Groark, McCall, & Fish, 2011). A small study of Ukrainian preschoolers raised either in an institution or with their families also suggested the relevance of a gene-environment interaction. Namely, children with the *ll* polymorphism of the serotonin receptor gene (5HTT) showed no impact of institutionalization on their attachment in the Strange Situation, while those with the *ss* or *sl* allele who were raised in an institution exhibited more disorganized and insecure attachment as compared to children raised in a family (Bakermans-Kranenburg, Dobrova-Krol, & van IJzendoorn, 2012). Furthermore, although usually associated with institutionalization, indiscriminate friendliness has been observed in maltreated foster children, with poor inhibitory control especially seen in children with multiple placements (Kay & Green, 2013; Minnis et al., 2013; Pears, Bruce, Fisher, & Kim, 2010).

There are actually two subtypes of RAD—the more well-known indiscriminately social/disinhibited type (now referred to as disinhibited social engagement disorder) and the emotionally withdrawn/inhibited type (American Psychiatric Association, 2013). Both types are associated with stable functional impairment over time and are not entirely independent of each other (Gleason et al., 2011; Zeanah et al., 2004). However, the latter type appears to respond fairly quickly to enhanced caregiving while the former shows less resolution with foster care and enhanced caregiving (Gleason et al., 2011; Smyke et al., 2012). The disinhibited type is often comorbid with activity, impulsivity, and ADHD, although it is diagnostically distinct from ADHD (Gleason et al., 2011).

The relevance of RAD (and especially indiscriminate friendliness) to potential cycles of violence can be seen in the high rates of insecure and disorganized attachment among children with this diagnosis (Chisholm, 1998; Kocovska et al., 2012; Minnis et al., 2009; van den Dries, Juffer, van IJzendoorn, Bakermans-Kranenburg, & Alink, 2012). In fact, in an interview study, 9–14-year-olds with RAD appeared to respond to their experiences of rejection and insecurity with a self-described trust of strangers, with a craving for kindness, and with attempts at control over others (Bennett, Espie, Duncan, & Minnis, 2009), suggesting vulnerability to either revictimization or to reactive violence in subsequent relationships. On the other hand, half of a sample of adolescents with RAD was described as Cannot Classify on the AAI, with evidence of a very different interpersonal dynamic of extreme derogation and extreme detachment (Goldwyn & Hugh-Jones, 2011). Children with this indiscriminately social behavior are also likely to display behavior problems, victimization by peers, and bullying of others (Chisholm, 1998; Raaska et al., 2012). Needless to say, their parents described significantly more parenting stress (Chisholm, 1998).

Nonetheless, postadoption parenting matters. The emotional availability of adoptive parents of postinstitutionalized children at 18 months predicted the children's emotional understanding several years later (Garvin, Tarullo, Ryzin, & Gunnar, 2012). Similarly, adoptive mothers' sensitivity was associated with less indiscriminate friendliness in their children, although former foster children were more responsive to their adoptive mothers than were formerly institutionalized children (van den Dries et al., 2012). In light of the importance of parental availability and sensitivity for a particularly challenged population (i.e., children who have been institutionalized), interventions for foster and adoptive parents in general emphasize the newly formed parent-child attachment relationship.

Implications for Intervention

The best-researched treatment for foster families is the attachment and biobehavioral catch-up (ABC) intervention developed by Mary Dozier and her colleagues. She noted three frequent occurrences in foster families that hamper adjustment (Dozier, Higley, Albus, & Nutter, 2002). First, because of foster children's common behavioral signals that elicit nonnurturing responses, even normally nurturing caregivers need to learn to reinterpret the child's signals and avoid responding in kind. Second, some caregivers require extra help in providing nurturance to their foster children. Third, because of the behavioral and biobehavioral dysregulation that often accompanies attachment disruptions, caregivers may need help in learning how to provide their foster children with a predictable interpersonal environment. In randomized clinical trials, children whose parents received the experimental intervention were compared to children whose parents received an educational intervention. The ABC condition led to significantly less avoidant attachment behaviors, lower cortisol levels, and stronger cognitive flexibility relative to children in the control condition (Dozier et al., 2006, 2009; Lewis-Morrarty, Dozier, Bernard, Terracciano, & Moore, 2012). The intervention also resulted in foster mothers' increased sensitivity over time, with their initial attachment security predictive of their levels of reflective functioning during the intervention (Bick & Dozier, 2013; Bick, Dozier, & Moore, 2012). Therefore, intervening explicitly with the components of both children's and foster parents' attachment-related behaviors that often prove problematic in this population has quantifiable behavioral and neurobiological outcomes that are associated with a secure parent-child relationship and that would presumably also reduce children's vulnerabilities in the future.

In conclusion, the study of foster and adoptive families represents an opportunity to assess the long-term effects of attachment disruptions (and often preexisting neurobiological and genetic vulnerabilities) when children are no longer residing with the maltreating family. In other words, although the focus of adoption studies has typically been the assessment of genetic effects, the same studies can provide much-needed information on the role of caregiving by parents who are not biologically related. Furthermore, insights gained from intervening with foster or adoptive children are undoubtedly applicable to maltreated or neglected children raised at home. Finally, the phenomenon of the postinstitutionalized child with RAD represents the most extreme prototype of neglect and inattention, if not also maltreatment. Clearly, more longitudinal studies of these children are needed to assess the long-term impact of this extreme deprivation on their future relationships and their vulnerability to revictimization and violent behavior. Therefore, as an important population in itself and as a proxy for other populations with attachment-related issues, the study of foster or adoptive families warrants more attention.

INCARCERATION OF PARENTS

The number of children of incarcerated parents in the United States is high, with a conservative estimate of more than 3 million children (Cassidy, Poehlmann, & Shaver, 2010). This issue is relevant to the intergenerational transmission of violence and trauma for several reasons. First, although the impact of having had an incarcerated parent on one's own parenting has not yet been explored longitudinally, the impact on a child's criminal and antisocial behavior may be a good proxy for that adult child's risk for maltreating his or her own child or partner. Second, the fear, trauma, and unresolved loss suffered by a child whose parent is imprisoned are evidence at a minimum of a cycle of trauma if not actual violence. Third, the impact of parental incarceration on a child's vulnerability for maltreatment by a substitute caregiver is substantial. At the same time, many affected children display a resilience that is both heartening and that helps inform intervention programs that have been developed to minimize their risk. Therefore, while the prevalence of imprisonment of adults in the United States poses a significant burden to children, research highlights ways to interrupt intergenerational cycles in this population.

Impact on Children's Externalizing Behavior

Research consistently demonstrates that parental incarceration is associated with a child's delinquency, risky behaviors, youth crime, and illegal drug use (Aaron & Dallaire, 2010; Dallaire, 2007a; Kjellstrand & Eddy, 2011; Murray, Loeber, & Pardini, 2012; Ou & Reynolds, 2010; Roettger & Swisher, 2011; Roettger, Swisher, Kuhl, & Chavez, 2011). The incarceration also predicts an adult child's involvement in the criminal justice system, reoffending, and higher levels of anger and prison violence among second-generation prisoners whose parents (and particularly mothers) had previously been incarcerated (Huebner & Gustafson, 2007; Kjelsberg & Friestad, 2008; Novero, Loper, & Warren, 2011; Tasca, Rodriguez, & Zatz, 2011). In fact, one review concluded that children of incarcerated parents were six times more likely to become involved in the criminal justice system themselves (Purvis, 2013). Only one study looked explicitly at family violence, finding an association between parental incarceration and family victimization (Aaron & Dallaire, 2010).

The import of these findings is even greater given that the results cannot be attributed to other correlated factors. For example, a study of relevant genetic polymorphisms concluded that genetics may explain a child's eventual arrest, but not eventual incarceration (Miller & Barnes, 2013). Furthermore, a meta-analysis of 40 studies found an overall effect of parental incarceration on children's antisocial behavior even controlling for parental criminality and children's antisocial behavior prior to the parent's incarceration (Murray, Farrington, & Sekol, 2012). Murray and his colleagues (Murray, Janson, & Farrington, 2007; Murray & Murray, 2008) noted that incarceration had less effect (as opposed to parental criminality) in Sweden and Australia than in the United States and United Kingdom. They attributed these cross-national differences to the existence of shorter prison sentences, more family-friendly prison policies, and more benign attitudes toward crime and punishment in the former than in the latter countries. Therefore, there appears to be something unique about parental incarceration separate from parental criminality that predicts children's violent behavior.

Impact on Children's Attachment and Experience of Trauma

There is no clear consensus as to whether parental incarceration is more damaging to boys or to girls (Cho, 2010; Foster & Hagan, 2013; Geller, Garfinkel, Cooper, & Mincy, 2009; Midgley & Lo, 2013). However, for both boys and girls, the process of incarceration of a parent is frequently preceded by a child's actual witnessing of the parent's arrest—an experience that can be especially terrifying to a young child (Murray & Murray, 2010). Not surprisingly, it is predictive of maladjustment in emotion regulation skills, anxiety, and depression (Dallaire & Wilson, 2010). In fact, in one study, one in four children who witnessed the arrest of a parent had significantly elevated PTSD symptoms (Phillips & Zhao, 2010).

Beyond the child's witnessing a parent's arrest, the loss of the parent (particularly the mother) is potentially even more damaging. For example, Bocknek, Sanderson, and Britner (2009) found that the ambiguous loss stemming from parental incarceration led to high rates of internalizing and externalizing behaviors as well as posttraumatic stress. One indicator of the potential long-term effects of this loss can be found in Corvo's (2006) study of male batterers. He noted that men's experience of separation and loss from an attachment figure during childhood was even more predictive of their violent behavior than was a history of maltreatment. Moreover, studies of attachment in the children of incarcerated parents have found much higher rates of insecure attachment and signs of disorganized attachment, including role reversal, bizarreness, and dissociation in children's family drawings (Dallaire, Ciccone, & Wilson, 2012; Poehlmann, 2005).

The attachment representations of parents mirror these disruptions. For example, 50% of a sample of incarcerated fathers in a minimum-security facility were either unresolved regarding loss or trauma or rated as Cannot Classify on the AAI (Fairchild, 2009). Furthermore, 9% of incarcerated women give birth while in prison (Chambers, 2009). Qualitative studies have recorded their feelings of emptiness, depression, and hostility associated with the themes of separation, attachment, and jealousy of substitute caregivers as well as indicators of unresolved loss and trauma (Borelli, Goshin, Joestl, Clark, & Byrne, 2010; Chambers, 2009; Hutchinson, Moore, Propper, & Mariaskinj, 2008). Reciprocally, a history of child maltreatment and insecure attachment contributes to women's incarceration, as mediated by their substance abuse and criminal behavior to support their drug use (Bowles, DeHart, & Webb, 2012), suggesting a mutual relationship between a history of insecure attachment's effect on risk for incarceration and incarceration's effect on a mother's insecure attachment—obviously both may compromise her caregiving.

Impact on Families and Children's Increased Risk for Maltreatment

Incarceration of a parent also affects a child less directly through its impact on the other parent and on the child's relationship with substitute caregivers. Consistent with the overall thesis of this book, adverse events experienced by individuals typically increase other family members' risk through the influence on the broader family system. Thus, a father's incarceration may affect a child through its repercussions for a mother's depression and decreased instrumental support (Turney, Schnittker, & Wildeman, 2012; Wildeman, Schnittker, & Turney, 2012). Similarly, a father's incarceration is associated with an infant's significantly increased risk of mortality (if the father is not abusive), presumably through its psychological and financial effects on a mother's pregnancy (Wildeman, 2012). On the other hand, if the father is abusive, the negative effects of his incarceration on his infant's mortality risk is cancelled, highlighting that all potentially adverse events are mediated through their influence on the family system.

A parent's incarceration and absence may also affect a child's well-being and risk for maltreatment to the degree that they expose the child to discrimination, social exclusion, violence, and abuse by others (Dawson, Jackson, & Nyamathi, 2012; Foster & Hagan, 2007). As described in Chapter 3, the absence of a biological father also greatly increases a child's risk for homelessness and for sexual abuse by nonbiological father figures (Foster & Hagan, 2007; Wildeman, 2014). Furthermore, children of incarcerated parents who are raised by grandparents are frequently subject to relationship violence and exhibit externalizing behaviors, due to the grandparents' depression, psychological distress, and fewer family resources (Kelley, Whitley, & Campos, 2011; Poehlmann et al., 2008). Of course, these substitute caregiving relationships do not develop in a vacuum and are greatly influenced by the prior relationship between the incarcerated parent and the caregiver as well as the caregiver's current family support system (Turanovic, Rodriguez, & Pratt, 2012).

Resilience in Children of Incarcerated Parents

In spite of the many stressors and risk factors associated with parental incarceration, many children and families display remarkable resilience. A series of studies has identified child- or family-level resilience processes that suggest useful strategies of intervention for interrupting cycles of violence and trauma within this population. One study focused on children's self-reported empathy, which protected them from engaging in the peer aggression often observed in children of incarcerated parents (Dallaire & Zeman, 2013). The depletion of current emotional resources within the family was seen as a primary reason for decreased parent/guardian-reported empathy in the child. Furthermore, consistent with an attachment perspective, separation from parents for any reason explained children's level of empathy more than did separation specifically due to parental incarceration.

Second, just as unresponsive or overly stressed grandparents may pose a risk to children of incarcerated parents, they are frequently an important source of resilience for children, depending on the nature of their relationship with the parent. For example, warmth and acceptance in an incarcerated mother's early attachment relationship with her own mother were predictive of a positive coparenting alliance with her mother which is associated with more positive mood indicators in the children (Loper & Clarke, 2013; Loper, Phillips, Nichols, & Dallaire, 2014). These coparenting alliances were also observed between recently released mothers, the caregiving grandmothers, and young children (McHale, Salman, Strozier, & Cecil, 2013). Therefore, as described in Chapter 3, just as coparenting between mothers and fathers serves as a protective factor for their children, coparenting between mothers and their own mothers is associated with increased resilience in the child. Third, emotion regulation was found to attenuate bullying, hostile teasing, and aggressive peer behavior in the children of incarcerated mothers (Myers et al., 2013), emphasizing the importance of interventions that facilitate children's emotion regulation.

Implications for Intervention

Parent-Child Contact

On one hand, increased parent-child contact (especially letter writing) has been associated with reduced parenting stress and reduced feelings of alienation among children (Shlafer & Poehlmann, 2010; Tuerk & Loper, 2006). On the other hand, in-prison contact between male prisoners and their family members had negative ramifications, especially if the prior relationship was poor (Vigne, Naser, Brooks, & Castro, 2005). Furthermore, visitation environments that are not child friendly were associated with representations of insecure attachment relationships in children (Poehlmann, 2005), suggesting that the child's fearfulness associated with the visit itself may transfer to the relationship with the parent. Therefore, Poehlmann, Dallaire, Loper, and Shear (2010) listed a number of recommendations for facilitating the visits between children and their incarcerated parents. Among other things, they suggested that corrections programs provide child- and family-friendly visitation, including limiting child visits behind Plexiglas and avoiding the frisking of very young children and other frightening procedures. They noted that improved parent-caregiver relationships and decreased parent and caregiver stress facilitated positive parent-child contact. They highlighted the importance of attending to children's needs for visitation based on their ages and for preparing and supporting children with regard to the visits, including helping them feel safe, especially if conflicts arise among family members regarding the visit. Finally, they suggested the use of remote forms of contact, such as letter writing, journals, and video conferencing. Many of these suggestions are consistent with the following actual interventions that have been assessed for their effectiveness.

Interventions

Parenting programs have been used with the goals of reducing parenting stress, facilitating better alliances with caregivers, increasing letter writing, and reducing mental health symptoms (Loper & Tuerk, 2011). Although dropout rates were high, incarcerated mothers who were randomly assigned to the treatment condition demonstrated significantly more improvement than did the wait-list group. Another parenting class, Parenting Inside Out, was similarly effective in improving parent adjustment, parent-caregiver relationships, and parenting prior to parents' release from prison (Eddy, Martinez, & Burraston, 2013).

Several other programs have focused more specifically on children and their relationships with their parents. For example, visit coaching makes use of family centers within prisons and jails to help incarcerated parents and the children's caregivers understand and manage the process of visitation and to support children in the visits (Beyer, Blumenthal-Guigui, & Krupat, 2010). Finally, a mentoring program just for children had high dropout rates but was successful in reducing internalizing and externalizing behaviors among children who remained in the program (Shlafer, Poehlmann, Coffino, & Hanneman, 2009). It should be noted, however, that the effectiveness of these programs for improving parent-child relationships remains to be demonstrated.

CONCLUSION

Certain commonalities can be seen in the special populations reviewed in this chapter. First, the concept of loss is prominent in the experience of foster and adoptive children and frequently in the experience of their new parents. Similarly, the concept of ambiguous loss (Boss, 1999) is relevant to survivors of political terrorism and combat exposure and to the children of incarcerated parents. Although not typically studied in conjunction with attachment theory's concept of unresolved loss, the parallels are striking, including the connection of each definition of loss to boundary ambiguity and role reversal within the family. Second, these topics generally refer to sources of violence and trauma external to the family, with the possible exception of incarceration, although its negative effects may be worsened by violence experienced within the prison system. Nonetheless, each of these sources of violence and trauma interacts with preexisting trauma and attachment relationships to determine the severity of their impact, both on the individual and on the individual's risk for continuing the cycle. Finally, just as the experiences described in this chapter affect family members to varying degrees, their resolution depends upon those same current attachment relationships. Even in occupations such as the military and law enforcement and in occurrences such as incarceration for which family relations are typically not even considered, their positive (or at least neutral) impact on society is integrally tied to the support that affected individuals receive from family members. Therefore, interrupting potential intergenerational cycles of violence and trauma is beneficial on a broader level to society as well as to children.

CHAPTER 8

Final Thoughts

Several other factors affect the experience of maltreatment and even its definition. First, culture is the broader milieu of the family and the parent-child relationship. A culture decides what is maltreatment and whether it will be recognized and condemned as such or alternatively approved. Although culture also regulates parent-child attachment behavior, it is remarkable how many similarities exist in different cultures around the world. Second, while the roles typically adopted by mothers and fathers in our society have some consistency (see Chapter 3), this too is changing along with gender roles and family structures. Third, the gender of the child also matters and is briefly reviewed. Part of this is undoubtedly due to socialization, but actual neurobiological differences and even the differential effects of life history on males and females also play a role. Fourth, the type of maltreatment certainly affects intergenerational cycles, but not always in ways that are presumed—emotional abuse and neglect are frequently even more important than physical abuse. Finally, children vary in their degree of resilience. Understanding the contributors to resilience can provide a basis for the development of interventions that are more likely to succeed.

CULTURE

The notion of culture encompasses many different levels of analysis, not the least of which is the family. However, norms within a country, region, subculture, and racial or ethnic group regarding violent behavior are clearly relevant for generalizing about cycles of trauma and violence.

Cross-cultural differences in perspectives on parenting and what constitutes appropriate methods of conflict resolution may also explain variations in intergenerational cycles. The following section gives a brief overview of these factors as well as a reminder to the reader of attending to these important contexts of violent behavior and the effects of trauma.

Cultural Views of Family Violence

Child Maltreatment

A variety of surveys have explored cultural variations in the definition of maltreatment, its prevalence, its risk factors, and its effects. Most notably, the International Society for Prevention of Child Abuse and Neglect (ISPCAN) conducts periodic surveys of key informants who are knowledgeable about child maltreatment issues within their respective countries. In a recent survey (ISPCAN, 2008), contacts were made with representatives from 75 countries, 52 of which were classified as developing countries. Among all but three respondents, physical abuse by parents or caregivers and sexual abuse (defined as incest, sexual touching, or pornography) were labeled as child abuse. Other behaviors labeled as maltreatment by more than 80% of all respondents included physical neglect (e.g., failure to provide adequate food, clothing, or shelter; abandonment or a child living on the street) and physical abuse in other settings (e.g., by other adults or within foster care or educational settings). On the other hand, physical discipline was significantly less likely to be endorsed as maltreatment by respondents from Africa and Asia. It should be noted that this survey referred to specific maltreatment and not to other experiences of trauma that have comparable effects on subsequent aggressive behavior. It should also be noted, as mentioned in Chapter 7, that cross-cultural differences in trauma and violence may be explained in part by a group's exposure to political violence and terrorism.

Other cross-cultural surveys have similarly attempted to identify what is meant by maltreatment. Comparisons within a convenience sample in the United States, Ghana, and Nigeria found varying degrees of consensus within countries and significant differences between countries and between races (Fakunmoju et al., 2013). Immigrants to Israel from the Caucasus and from European countries differed on the basis for defining parental behaviors as abusive, with respondents from the Caucasus more concerned with local norms and European immigrants more concerned with potential harm to the child (Shor, 1999).

The prevalence of child maltreatment was not explicitly addressed by the ISPCAN report. However, a majority of respondents overall and the majority of the six industrialized countries that keep official records reported increases in physical abuse, sexual abuse, neglect, and psychological maltreatment cases, perhaps reflecting in part an increase in the public's perception of maltreatment. Consistent with cross-cultural differences in the definitions of maltreatment, several surveys found higher prevalence rates of physical abuse in African and Asian countries (Leung, 2003; Mbagaa, Oburu, & Bakermans-Kranenburg, 2013). In a survey of post–communist bloc countries, higher rates of abuse were reported in rural regions (Sebre et al., 2004).

While common risk factors for abuse were noted in comparisons within cultural regions (e.g., Sebre et al., 2004), more comprehensive comparisons are obviously required to arrive at any conclusions about risk factors. Fairly similar effects of maltreatment were observed in a number of comparisons of countries, including Latin America, the Caribbean, the Philippines, Outer Mongolia, and the post–communist bloc countries (Kohrt, Kohrt, Waldman, Saltzman, & Carrion, 2004; Longman-Mills et al., 2013; Ramiro, Madrid, & Brown, 2010; Sebre et al., 2004). However, different pathways of effects were also observed, based on the perceptions of the parental behaviors in the respective countries (Mbagaa et al., 2013). For example, although arguably never warranted (cf., Straus, Douglas, & Medeiros, 2014), physical discipline that is administered within the context of a loving relationship will have less deleterious effects than that associated with parental anger, rejection, unpredictability, or rage. Furthermore, comparisons may need to focus on specific values associated with a given culture rather than the country or region. For example, Asian values rather than ethnicity predicted nondisclosure of sexual and emotional abuse by survivors of very close victim-perpetrator relationships (Foynes, Platt, Hall, & Freyd, 2014). These are the nuances that descriptive statistics on specific parental behaviors or on specific cultural groups do not explain.

Intimate Partner Violence

A child's exposure to intimate partner violence (IPV) also factors into intergenerational cycles of violence and the child's vicarious experience

of trauma. Cross-cultural comparisons have found high levels of acceptance of wife beating in Asian and African countries. One survey found
that 57% of female Indian respondents and 56% of male Turkish respondents endorsed IPV (Rani & Bonu, 2009). In another survey, 71% of
Zambian men and 68% of Kenyan men similarly justified the use of IPV
to punish women for failing to meet their domestic responsibilities
(Lawoko, 2008). Within the United States, the incidence and recurrence
of IPV are significantly higher among African Americans and Hispanics
(Caetano, Field, Ramisetty-Mikler, & McGrath, 2005). Furthermore,
interethnic couples in the United States are more likely to engage in
mutual IPV than are intraethnic couples (Chartier & Caetano, 2012).

Risk factors for IPV vary in different cultural groups, with legal married
status protecting women from IPV in most but not all of the 19 countries
studied (Bernards & Graham, 2013). For example, single women were
less likely to be victimized in India, where wife beating is so often
accepted. In addition to these community norms in India, individual-
level variables such as childlessness, economic hardship, and intergenerational transmission of violence as well as violent crime within the
community all contribute to physical and sexual IPV (Koenig, Stephenson, Ahmed, Jejeebhoy, & Campbell, 2006). Therefore, not only exposure to family violence, but also its risk factors and the meaning attributed
to the violence are likely to vary cross-culturally. Interventions to interrupt these cycles of violence need to be germane to the respective cultures.

Culture and Parent-Child Attachment

Parent-child attachment is probably one of the very few Western concepts
that was originally measured in a developing country. Mary Ainsworth's
classification of secure, avoidant, and anxious/ambivalent attachment in
toddlers was based on her observations of mothers and their children in
Uganda. She then followed up these observations with extensive in-home
evaluations of mothers and their children in Baltimore.

At this point, thousands of children all over the world have been
assessed in the Strange Situation and thousands more adults have been
administered the AAI. Therefore, many cross-cultural comparisons of
attachment theory have been conducted. As a way of organizing these
results, I refer to four basic assumptions put forth by van IJzendoorn and
Sagi-Schwartz (2008). The first assumption is the *universality hypothe-*

sis—that is, all infants will become attached to and will display secure base behavior and separation protest with one or more specific caregivers. Two surveys of child development experts and trained observers in a wide range of countries did indeed derive common descriptions of the optimally attached child and found that children from all the countries displayed secure base behavior (Posada et al., 1995, 2013). Individual studies in Japan, Korea, rural Bangladesh, and the Trobriand Islands came to a similar conclusion (Grossmann, Grossmann, & Keppler, 2005; Jin, Jacobvitz, Hazen, & Jung, 2012; Mizuta, Zahn-Waxler, Cole, & Hiruma, 1996; Super, Guldan, Ahmed, & Zeitlin, 2012).

The next assumption is the *normativity hypothesis*—that is, most children (and most adults) are securely attached as evidenced by their ability to settle more easily in a stressful situation than those who are insecurely attached (or for adults, as evidenced by their coherence on the AAI). This hypothesis was confirmed in samples of Korean, Italian, and African American children and in samples of Italian, Finnish, and German adults who were assessed on the Strange Situation and AAI, respectively (Cassiba, Sette, Bakermans-Kranenburg, & van IJzendoorn, 2013; Dexter, Wong, Stacks, Beeghly, & Barnett, 2013; Jin et al., 2012; Kouvo & Silven, 2010; Soares, Fremmer-Bombik, Grossmann, & Silva, 2000). Moreover, an examination of a large sample of AAIs found that distributions of attachment classifications were largely independent of language and country of origin (van IJzendoorn & Bakermans-Kranenburg, 2010).

The *sensitivity hypothesis*—that sensitive parenting leads to secure attachment in children—was confirmed in views of the ideal sensitive mother among Dutch, Moroccan, and Turkish mothers in the Netherlands and in observations of Mexican and African American mothers and their children (Dexter et al., 2013; Emmen, Malda, Mesman, Ekmekci, & van IJzendoorn, 2012; Gojman et al., 2012; Howes, Vu, & Hamilton, 2011). Finally, the *competence hypothesis*—that attachment security predicts a child's level of competence—was confirmed in a sample of Puerto Rican 5-year-olds, admittedly a more restricted test than the other assumptions (Gullon-Rivera, 2013).

While these broad characteristics of attachment behavior emerged in virtually every sample in which they were tested, cultural differences were also apparent. There was an overrepresentation of insecure attachment in a sample of Portuguese mothers and of avoidant attachment in nonclinical samples of Italian infants and an underrepresentation of unresolved loss among Italian adults (Cassibba et al., 2013; Soares et al., 2000; Vizziello, Calvo, & Simonelli, 2003). Both Korean and Japanese mothers and their children exhibited a preference for physical closeness, referred to in Japanese culture as *amae* (Behrens, 2010; Jin et al., 2012; Rothbaum, Rosen, Ujiie, & Uchida, 2002). However, it was less likely to be associated with internalizing disorders in Japanese children than in American children (Mizuta et al., 1996). Furthermore, the magnitude of gender differences in attachment security varied among different cultures (Pierrehumbert et al., 2009). Finally, many of the observed cultural differences were actually attributable to demographic characteristics, such as socioeconomic status, education level, family structure, family size, and poor health of the child (Ahnert, Meischner, & Schmidt, 2000; Emmen et al., 2012; Kouvo & Silven, 2010; Newland et al., 2013; Super et al., 2012). So what may sometimes appear to be cultural differences may actually be attributable to a poor specification of the sample being studied.

In conclusion, it should be noted that in spite of the many comparisons between cultures as to definitions and rates of maltreatment, parent-child attachment, and other family relationships, very little research has focused on the cross-cultural correlates of cycles of violence. In the absence of that, whether it be at the level of the individual, the dyad, the family, the neighborhood, or a broader delineation of culture, the norms and meanings ascribed to intimacy and conflict within family relationships need to be identified and articulated in order for viable interventions to be developed.

VARIATIONS IN FAMILY STRUCTURE

As same-sex marriage and same-sex parents' adoption of children or use of surrogacy are becoming much more prevalent, the issue of intergenerational transmission of trauma and violence should be considered in this population. IPV among same-sex couples has generally been ignored in our culture, because it doesn't conform with stereotypes about patriarchy (Nunan, 2004), because of secrecy and fear of retaliation among gay and lesbian couples (Jackson, 2007), and because gays and lesbians have often felt marginalized in even reporting partner abuse (Bograd, 2005). Similarly, little is known about rates of child abuse and other forms of family violence in this population although the impact of homophobia within families and within society is a significant form of trauma with potentially long-lasting effects. However, recent research on couple, parenting and family processes within gay and lesbian couples suggests the existence of few differences from heterosexual couples. For example, the children of lesbian mothers and gay fathers appear to be comparable to children of heterosexual parents in their levels of adjustment, socialization and attachment to their parents, with a similar range of parental functioning and parental stresses (Alexander, 2001; Averett, Nalavany, & Ryan, 2009; Erich, Hall, Kanenberg, & Case, 2009; Erich, Kanenberg, Case, Allen, & Bogdanos, 2009; Fond, Franc, & Purper-Ouakil, 2012). Similarly, the challenges, stresses and rewards of adoption appear to be comparable among lesbian, gay and heterosexual parents (Goldberg & Smith, 2013, 2014; Lavner, Waterman, & Peplau, 2014). In fact, recent research has found evidence of more child externalizing problems among the children of heterosexual parents (Golombok et al., 2014) and greater overall levels of co-parenting among lesbian and gay couples (Farr & Patterson, 2013). In any case, it can be safely said that much more research needs to be conducted with regard to the risk for intergenerational cycles of violence in this population.

Another type of family structure with a much longer history in our society is that of the single-parent family, described in Chapter 3 with regard to the absence of the biological father. Its unique challenges include increased rates of financial stresses and poverty, the frequent presence of non-biologically related father figures in the home, and/or the common social isolation of single mothers. Both intergenerational support and stressors are often more prevalent in this family structure with mothers and grandmothers enacting the same family dynamics of co-parenting versus parental conflict and boundary dissolution observed in the more traditional two-parent family structure. Although it is likely that the prevention of intergenerational cycles of family violence is primarily dependent upon the resolution of past trauma and supportive co-parenting, much more research is required to explore the impact of different types of family structures.

GENDER OF THE CHILD

As noted in Chapter 1, both males and females are subject to the ill effects of exposure to family violence, including intergenerational cycles of violence and trauma. However, certain gender differences do emerge, as a function of differences in the types of parenting experienced by sons and daughters, differences in the types of maltreatment experienced, differential effects of maltreatment on brain physiology, and different pathways to intergenerational cycles. The following is a brief review of some of the differences and similarities of experiences and behaviors of males and females.

Gender and Disorganized Attachment

The prevalence of disorganized attachment, controlling punitive and caregiving behavior, and frightened or frightening behaviors elicited from mothers does not appear to differ as a function of gender in low-risk middle-class samples, under low-level frightening conditions, or when the mother engages in withdrawal (David & Lyons-Ruth, 2005; Hennighausen et al., 2011; Moss et al., 2004). However, in high-risk samples, boys are more likely to respond to their mothers' abusive or disrupted behavior with disorganized and insecure behavior, while girls are more likely to respond with approach, affiliation, and compliance (Hazen et al., 2011; Lyons-Ruth, Bronfman, & Atwood, 1999). These gender differences may reflect the prevalence of "fight or flight" in males and of "tending and befriending" in females (David & Lyons-Ruth, 2005). Other observers have suggested that mothers may be more likely to engage in intrusive, negative, and even sexualized role-reversing behavior with their sons than with their daughters (Crockenberg, Leerkes, & Jo, 2008; Solomon & George, 2011; Sroufe & Ward, 1980).

Gender differences in the effects of disorganization have also emerged, with disorganized boys more likely than disorganized girls to exhibit externalizing and internalizing behaviors, social problems, and punitive-controlling behavior toward their mothers (Fearon, Bakermans-Kranenburg, van IJzendoorn, Lapsley, & Roisman, 2010; Hazen et al., 2011). Disorganized girls tend to exhibit more caregiving-controlling behavior (Hazen et al., 2011), although more externalizing behaviors were observed in the disorganized daughters of adolescent mothers (Munson, McMahon, & Spieker, 2001). Notably, research on gender differences in disorganized attachment fails to consider the impact of the father—his absence, his role in either marital conflict or support of the mother, his direct impact on his sons and daughters, and even his own attachment history. Mothers' role reversal with their sons was associated with the husband's history of role reversal (Chapter 3; Macfie, McElwain, et al., 2005). Therefore, without attending to this family context, conclusions regarding gender differences in attachment may be premature.

Gender, Maltreatment, and Its Effects

While it is sometimes assumed that maltreatment has vastly different effects on males and females, this assumption is often belied by research findings. For example, even though girls are more likely than boys to experience child sexual abuse (CSA), the outcomes are frequently comparable (Banyard, Williams, & Siegel, 2004; Dube et al., 2005; Jones et al., 2010; Menard & Pincus, 2012). Similarly, maltreatment leads to externalizing and aggressive behaviors in both males and females (Fang & Corso, 2008; Maschi, Morgen, Bradley, & Hatcher, 2008; Topitzes, Mersky, & Reynolds, 2012). However, differences do emerge in the pathways to the outcomes and sometimes in the specific nature of the outcomes. For example, while a history of CSA is associated with aggression in both males and females, some studies have found it to be more predictive of relationship aggression in girls and more predictive of IPV in young men (Cullerton-Sen et al., 2008; Fang & Corso, 2008). Rates of dating violence and IPV perpetration are comparable in men and women, even though the physical, psychological, and financial impact on women is often greater (Chapter 5). The connection between a history of maltreatment and violent behavior in men is often mediated by childhood aggression, adolescent problems, and emotion dysregulation (Fang & Corso, 2008; Gratz, Paulson, Jakupcak, & Tull, 2009; Topitzes et al., 2012). A similar connection between an abuse history and aggression in women is frequently associated with internalizing problems, as either a mediator, an outcome of the aggression, or a protective factor (Brensilver, Negriff, Mennenm, & Trickett, 2011; Maschi et al., 2008; Topitzes et al., 2012). This comparison also extends to parenting, with antisocial behavior more characteristic of abusive fathers and a maltreatment history and mental health problems more prevalent among abusive mothers (Chapter 3; Dixon et al., 2007).

Physiological effects of maltreatment have been seen to vary as a function of gender. For example, blunted cortisol levels are frequently more common in females and individuals engaging in relational aggression, with steep declines in cortisol levels more common among physical aggressors (Doom et al., 2013; Murray-Close et al., 2008). Autonomic nervous system hyperreactivity and hypersensitivity are more common among females, with hyporeactivity and atypical emotion more common among males (Chapter 4). Structural brain effects are more common (although not exclusive) in males with PTSD (De Bellis & Keshavan, 2003). Genetics may also play a role, with high heritability for callous-unemotional traits and physical aggression in boys as opposed to an environmental influence for callous-unemotional traits and dating violence perpetration in girls (Chapter 5; Barnes et al., 2010; Dodge, 2004; Fontaine, Rijsdijk, McCrory, & Viding, 2010). Even the role of substance abuse in IPV suggests physiological differences by gender, with men's aggression more affected by substance use and women's substance use associated more with self-medication for trauma symptoms.

Finally, in a metatheory consistent with life history theory, Martel (2013) proposed that gene × environment × sex interactions explained male biases in externalizing behaviors and female biases in internalizing behaviors. Namely, given the relevance of factors such as social dominance for males that facilitate their intrasex competition for reproductive success, boys may be more vulnerable to prenatal stressors that signal information about the broader ecological environment, with downstream effects on disinhibition, sensation-seeking, and externalizing disorders in childhood. In contrast, the relevance of interpersonal competence for intrasex competition, mate choice, and reproduction among females may increase their sensitivity to interpersonal stressors that often emerge during puberty. In particular, rising levels of ovarian hormones during puberty may interact with the HPA axis, cortisol, and oxytocin to increase sensitivity to the environment, negative emotionality, and rumination.

Martel (2013) noted that this model does not rule out comorbid externalizing and internalizing disorders in both males and females. This comorbidity may reflect the presence of multiple differential susceptibility genes (see Chapter 4) as well as early-occurring (even prenatal) ecological stressors and later-occurring interpersonal stressors. These children would not only experience more distress, but would be less likely to exhibit the high approach behaviors of pure externalizing disorders and the high effortful control behaviors of pure internalizing disorders. The similarity of the description of these children to those with disorganized attachment (especially behavioral disorganization) is striking and suggests a potentially useful model for some portion of the population engaging in intergenerational cycles of violence and trauma.

TYPES OF MALTREATMENT

Many descriptions of the intergenerational transmission of violence implicitly focus on the experience and then the perpetration of child physical abuse (CPA) as it is passed down from generation to generation. However, although CPA certainly has negative consequences (including less competent social behavior, anger, and unrealistic expectations of children; cf. Okado & Azar, 2011; Valentino, Cicchetti, Toth, & Rogosch, 2011; Waldinger et al., 2001), it is not necessarily the most damaging type of family stress for a child. For example, alcohol abuse in a large representative sample of adolescents was associated with all types or combinations of types of maltreatment except CPA-only (Shin, Edwards, Heeren, & Amodeo, 2009). The following brief review similarly suggests that other types of maltreatment and neglectful parenting may be even more relevant to intergenerational cycles.

CSA's unique and damaging effects warranted a whole chapter in this book. It is harmful to both girls and boys and it often occurs within one of the most dysfunctional and secretive sets of family dynamics characterizing any abusive family. It is not only predictive of dissociation, borderline personality disorder, and shame, but it is also associated with an experience of unresolved loss (Bailey, Moran, & Pederson, 2007). Thus, it encompasses emotional neglect as well as physical abuse, emotional abuse, and sexual exploitation. It disrupts normal developmental processes (social, cognitive, and even physical) in a manner that distinguishes it from other types of abuse. However, CSA refers to a wide range of events—therefore, its frequency, severity, developmental timing, relationship with the perpetrator, and response to disclosure all must be considered in evaluating its impact.

Child emotional abuse (also referred to as psychological or verbal abuse) not only leads to behavior problems, aggression, dissociation, and other types of psychopathology, but may also help account for the impact of CPA on conduct problems (Berzenski & Yates, 2011; Crawford & Wright, 2007; Dutra, Bureau, Holmes, Lyubchik, & Lyons-Ruth, 2009; English, Thompson, Graham, & Briggs, 2005). Moreover, psychological maltreatment has a much greater impact on adolescent problems than does CPA (Butaney, Pelcovitz, & Kaplan, 2011; Teicher, Samson, Polcari, & McGreenery, 2006). It is also clearly implicated in the subsequent perpetration of relationship violence and hostile parenting (Bailey, DeOliveira, Wolfe, Evans, & Hartwick, 2012; Berzenski & Yates, 2010).

Although children are more likely to come to the attention of child protective services because of supervisory or environmental neglect (Mennen, Kim, Sang, & Trickett, 2010), emotional neglect by a mother has significantly more negative outcomes, resulting in externalizing behaviors (especially with an experience of early neglect), substance abuse, cognitive and academic problems, internalizing behaviors, and poor interactions with peers (Chapple, Tyler, & Bersani, 2005; Chen, Propp, DeLara, & Corvo, 2011; Dubowitz et al., 2005; Fantuzzo, Perlman, & Dobbins, 2011; Hildyard & Wolfe, 2002; Kotch et al., 2008; Lounds, Borkowski, & Whitman, 2006; Manly, Lynch, Oshri, Herzog, & Wortel, 2013; Manly, Oshri, Lynch, Herzog, & Wortel, 2013). It is also associated with hostility and aggression against partners and one's children (Bailey et al., 2012; Okado & Azar, 2011; Straus & Savage, 2005). Its correlation with indiscriminate friendliness of children with reactive attachment disorder (Oliveira et al., 2012) suggests a possible link to increased risk for revictimization.

The impact of emotional neglect can also be seen in Lyons-Ruth's work on maternal withdrawal (Chapter 2). Maternal withdrawal is associated not only with punitive and disorganized behavior (Bureau et al., 2009a), but also with lower nonverbal cognition at age 5, substance abuse at age 20, and antisocial features at age 20 independent of the effects of childhood maltreatment (Pechtel, Woodman, & Lyons-Ruth, 2012; Shi et al., 2012). In fact, a widely used paradigm for experimentally stressing an infant is for the parent to adopt a still face in interactions with the child, pointing to the critical importance of face-to-face connections for the child (cf. Tronick, Als, Adamson, Wise, & Brazelton, 1978).

Of course, different types of maltreatment tend not to occur in isolation. Polyvictimization is more common and more damaging, leading to more trauma symptoms, externalizing behaviors, and more psychiatric problems overall (Arata, Langhinrichsen-Rohling, Bowers, & O'Brien, 2007; Arata, Langhinrichsen-Rohling, Bowers, & O'Farrill-Swails, 2005; Ford, Wasser, & Connor, 2011; Kim, Cicchetti, Rogosch, & Manly, 2009; Pears, Kim, & Fisher, 2008; Turner et al., 2010). It is associated with more severe abuse (Clemmons, DiLillo, Martinez, DeGue, & Jeffcott,

2003; Clemmons, Walsh, DiLillo, & Messman-Moore, 2007) as well as an increased risk for both the perpetration of violence and revictimization (Cort et al., 2011; Duke, Pettingell, McMorris, & Borowsky, 2010; Taylor et al., 2008).

Polyvictimization is also more likely to occur within a multiproblem family environment of recurrent crises, disorganization, the abandonment of parental functioning, and social isolation as well as frequent changes in residence and parental job status (Belsky et al., 2012; Gomez, Munoz, & Haz, 2007). Reminiscent of the background of the behaviorally disorganized child described in Chapter 2, Finkelhor and colleagues (2009) proposed that the most notable pathways to polyvictimization include living in a dangerous community, a dangerous family, and a chaotic multiproblem family, sometimes exacerbated by child vulnerabilities. What is thus most characteristic of both polyvictimization and a severe level of threat is unpredictability. Even more damaging than living in a harsh environment, unpredictability is highly correlated with the development of subsequent life strategies and risky behaviors that perpetuate cycles of violence and trauma (Belsky et al., 2012; Simpson et al., 2012). Therefore, instead of a notion of maltreatment as a catalog of the number of abusive events, it is more useful to think of maltreatment as a child's ongoing experience of threat and danger, occurring in the absence of a caregiver's attentiveness and emotional availability. This scenario results in a pattern of either hypervigilance or unemotionality that almost guarantees a continuation of a cycle of violence.

RESILIENCE

In addition to broadening our understanding of what constitutes maltreatment, we need to broaden our understanding of what constitutes resilience. A child's first and most important indicator of resilience is simply survival. Therefore, in a dangerous and unpredictable environment, supposedly dysfunctional behaviors are highly functional. Epigenetic changes in stress responsivity may help protect a fetus from the future effects of a dangerous environment. Seemingly contradictory behavior in a disorganized infant makes sense when the behavior of the parent is constantly changing. Dissociation allows a child to maintain connection with a severely abusive parent. Controlling and even aggressive behaviors are useful in helping to regulate the behavior and perhaps anxiety of an unpredictable parent. Fast and risky life history strategies help ensure one's reproductive capacity when life is short and uncertain.

In contrast, our standard notions of resilience are based upon the assumption of a relatively safe environment. If the environment truly does become safer, then previous strategies are no longer effective. However, in describing resilience, it is important to consider whether it is potentially dangerous to the individual (although perhaps not to others or to society) to discard these initial strategies if that individual remains in a harsh or unpredictable environment (Frankenhuis & Del Giudice, 2012). The following discussion of resilience proceeds in light of this caution.

Although typically encompassing a variety of domains of functioning, resilient behaviors in different domains are not necessarily highly correlated (Walsh, Dawson, & Mattingly, 2010). Furthermore, resilience varies as a function of stage of development and, as already stated, as a function of the environmental context (Bonanno & Mancini, 2008). However, in spite of these complications in assessing resilience, a useful definition was provided by Bradley and Davino (2007, p. 123), who referred to resilience as "the ability to derive meaning from traumatic events and to place the memories into context, ability to form meaningful relationships with others, and ability to regulate affect."

Neurobiological Contributors to Resilience

Certain genetic polymorphisms (e.g., the *ll* allele of 5HTTLPR) render children some degree of immunity from the negative effects of adversity (Chapter 4). Therefore, even though they may also reap less benefit from the influence of an exceptionally positive environment, these children would appear to be more resilient with regard to the experience of maltreatment. On the other hand, children with the opposite forms of these polymorphisms (e.g., the *ss* or *sl* allele of 5HTTLPR) are more responsive to parent-child treatment interventions such as video feedback or to enhanced foster care. Therefore, given optimal conditions, these children may be the most resilient of all. Other psychophysiological indicators of resilience in maltreated populations include higher morning cortisol levels and greater left hemispheric EEG activity; however, it is unclear whether these patterns are causally related to the resilience (Cicchetti & Rogosch, 2007; Curtis & Cicchetti, 2007; Linares et al., 2008).

Individual Contributors to Resilience

Aside from these neurobiological correlates of resilience, individual factors appear to be associated with resilience. Numerous studies have noted the role of gender in predicting resilience either as a main effect or in interaction with other variables, but without any clear conclusions. For example, many researchers have found females to be more resilient to the effects of maltreatment both generally and neurologically (Daining & DePanfilis, 2007; DuMont et al., 2007; McGloin & Widom, 2001; Samplin, Ikuta, Malhotra, Szeszko, & DeRosse, 2013). Other researchers have noted the resilience of boys, especially those with a higher IQ and no parental history of antisocial behavior (Campbell-Sills, Forde, & Stein, 2009; Jaffee et al., 2007).

As might be expected from the thesis of Chapter 2, other individual predictors of resilience include emotion regulation (Cloitre, Stovall-McClough, Zorbas, & Charuvastra, 2008; Schelble, Franks, & Miller, 2010) and correlates of reflective functioning (Narayanan, 2009). For example, a qualitative study highlighted a number of conscious mental strategies used by women who were abused as children to overcome the effects of their maltreatment, including redefining their abusers and family of origin and moving beyond the abuse without denying its impact (Hall et al., 2009). In essence, these individuals actively reflected upon their experiences and developed a coherent understanding of themselves and their past.

Another individual factor found to predict resilience among maltreated children is ego resiliency, referring to the ability and flexibility to adapt, plan, and work for a distant goal as well as to relax and reduce behavioral controls when the situation permits it (Block & Block, 2006). In contrast to the overcontol (internalizing behaviors) or undercontrol (externalizing behaviors) typically displayed by maltreated and disorganized children, ego resiliency among these children was associated with more positive outcomes (Flores, Cicchetti, & Rogosch, 2005; Manly, Lynch et al., 2013; Oshri, Rogosch, & Cicchetti, 2013; Shonk & Cicchetti, 2001; Smeekens, Riksen-Walraven, & Van-Bakel, 2009; Stams, Juffer, & van IJzendoorn, 2002).

Relational Contributors to Resilience

Interpersonal relationships both inside and outside the family reflect resilient functioning (Chapters 3 and 6). Clearly, nonmaltreated securely attached children are more likely to exhibit closeness to their caregivers and families and, by extension, to peers and future romantic partners. However, for many adults who were maltreated as children, resilience (as evidenced by interrupting the cycle of violence) may best be derived by escaping the influence of the abusive family of origin (Easterbrooks et al., 2011), and instead by relying upon alternative attachment figures.

Alternative attachment figures are frequently present in the backgrounds of individuals with earned security (Saunders et al., 2011; Zaccagnino, Cussino, Cook, Jacobvitz, & Veglia, 2011). Earned secure attachment refers to the display of a coherent perspective of relationships in spite of negative attachment experiences in childhood (Phelps, Belsky, & Crnic, 1998). It is associated with positive parenting and marital functioning, even under conditions of stress, and thus is a type of resilience (Paley, Cox, Burchinal, & Payne, 1999; Phelps et al., 1998). Although Roisman and his colleagues attributed the construct to the retrospective report of negative parenting by depressed securely attached individuals (Roisman, Fortuna, & Holland, 2006; Roisman, Fraley, & Belsky, 2007; Roisman, Padron, Sroufe, & Egeland, 2002), other researchers have noted its existence even when controlling for depression (Saunders et al., 2011). In either case, it emphasizes the primacy of one's current state of mind regarding attachment in the prediction of functioning (Haydon, Roisman, & Burt, 2012).

The fact that current attachment security and resilience can be impacted not only by caregivers but also by alternative sources of support speaks to the power of relationships in overcoming the effects of adversity. These sources of support may range from nonparental kin who serve as mentors to friendships (especially for women), to supportive partners, to therapists, to a perceived relationship with God, even to brief encounters with strangers (DuMont et al., 2007; Feldman, Conger, & Burzette, 2004; Granqvist, Mikulincer, & Shaver, 2010; Powers, Ressler, & Bradley, 2009; Roman, Hall, & Bolton, 2008; Southwick, Morgan, Vythilingam, & Charney, 2006). One way of characterizing these interactions is that they provided abused and neglected individuals with "'saw something in me' and 'no matter what' relationships" that they lacked in childhood (Roman et al., 2008).

Unfortunately, insecure attachment can interfere with the willingness and ability to elicit and benefit from these social supports. As opposed to securely attached individuals whose internal working models facilitate their seeking and eliciting social support from others (Bachman & Bippus, 2005; DeFronzo, Panzarella, & Butler, 2001), the self-sufficiency and negative expectations of dismissing individuals may interfere with their ability to get support from others, especially under conditions of stress (DeFronzo et al., 2001; Larose & Bernier, 2001). Preoccupied individuals appear to have limited expectations of receiving sufficient support as well as dissatisfaction with the support they do receive (Bachman & Bippus, 2005; Borelli, Goshin, et al., 2010; Cloitre et al., 2008; Larose & Bernier, 2001). Finally, the same dynamics that disrupt the disorganized child's and unresolved adult's relationships with others will typically preclude their engagement of others' support (Alexander & Anderson, 1994). Therefore, social support's potential contribution to the resilience of many insecure maltreated adolescents and adults may be deflected by individuals' reluctance or inability to solicit the support that they need.

Social Contextual Contributors to Resilience

Finally, the effects of family violence, disorganized attachment, and even genetic vulnerability (Chapter 4) may be exacerbated by a context of neighborhood disruption, social instability, and poverty. Thus, although generally attributed to individuals and families, cycles of violence are also a reflection of societal factors. These influences can be overcome, as shown by the positive outcomes of enhanced foster and adoptive parenting and successful interventions with at-risk mothers and their children (Chapters 2 and 7). Moreover, the social context may itself be the primary source of the trauma from which escape is difficult, the source of one's income, or the potential solution to the problem of trauma (Chapters 3 and 7). In any case, the social context cannot be ignored.

CONCLUSION

In conclusion, the effects of maltreatment, emotional neglect, family stress, and societal disruption on children can be immense. However, they occur within the context of attachment and family relationships. If we remember that children can survive almost any stress with the support of a caregiver, fostering these caregiving relationships is much more powerful than traditional treatments in interrupting intergenerational cycles and fending off a whole range of deleterious outcomes. Just as individuals differ in their response to stress, they also differ in their response to interventions. Therefore, given our limited resources, prevention and treatment efforts should be firmly grounded in an awareness of the many sources of variation in children's experience. In this way, we can be successful in interrupting intergenerational cycles of trauma and violence, which is ultimately the best form of prevention for future generations.

References

Aaron, L., & Dallaire, D. H. (2010). Parental incarceration and multiple risk experiences: Effects on family dynamics and children's delinquency. *Journal of Youth and Adolescence, 39*, 1471–1484.

Ablow, J. C., Measelle, J. R., Cowan, P. A., & Cowan, C. P. (2009). Linking marital conflict and children's adjustment: The role of young children's perceptions. *Journal of Family Psychology, 23*, 485–499.

Abracen, J., Looman, J., DiFazio, R., Kelly, T., & Stirpe, T. (2006). Patterns of attachment and alcohol abuse in sexual and violent non-sexual offenders. *Journal of Sexual Aggression, 12*, 19–30.

Abrams, K. Y., Rifkin, A., & Hesse, E. (2006). Examining the role of parental frightened/frightening subtypes in predicting disorganized attachment within a brief observational procedure. *Development and Psychopathology, 18*, 345–361.

Ackerman, B. P., & Brown, E. D. (2010). Physical and psychosocial turmoil in the home and cognitive development. In G. W. Evans & T. D. Wachs (Eds.), *Chaos and its influence on children's development: An ecological perspective* (pp. 35–47). Washington, DC: American Psychological Association.

Ackerman, J. P., & Dozier, M. (2005). The influence of foster parent investment on children's representations of self and attachment figures. *Journal of Applied Developmental Psychology, 26*, 507–520.

Adam, E. K., Gunnar, M. R., & Tanaka, A. (2004). Adult attachment, parent emotion, and observed parenting behavior: Mediator and moderator models. *Child Development, 75*, 110–122.

Agrawal, H. R., Gunderson, J., Holmes, B. M., & Lyons-Ruth, K. (2004). Attachment studies with borderline patients: A review. *Harvard Review of Psychiatry, 12*, 94–104.

Ahnert, L., Meischner, T., & Schmidt, A. (2000). Maternal sensitivity and attachment in East German and Russian family networks. In P. M. Crittenden, &

A. H. Claussen (Eds.), *The organization of attachment relationships: Maturation, culture, and context* (pp. 61–74). New York: Cambridge University Press.

Ainsworth, M. D. S., Blehar, M. C., Waters, E., & Wall, S. (1978). *Patterns of attachment: A psychological study of the strange situation.* Oxford, England: Lawrence Erlbaum.

Ainsworth, M. D. S., & Eichberg, C. G. (1991). Effects on infant-mother attachment of mother's unresolved loss of an attachment figure or other traumatic experience. In C. M. Parkes, J. Stevenson-Hinde, & P. Marris (Eds.), *Attachment across the life cycle* (pp. 160–183). New York: Tavistock/Routledge.

Alaggia, R., & Kirshenbaum, S. (2005). Speaking the unspeakable: Exploring the impact of family dynamics on child sexual abuse disclosures. *Families in Society, 86*, 227–234.

Alasaari, J. S., Lagus, M., Ollila, H. M., Toivola, A., Kivimaki, M., Vahtera, J., et al. (2012). Environmental stress affects DNA methylation of a CpG rich promoter region of serotonin transporter gene in a nurse cohort. *PLoS ONE, 7*, Article e45813.

Alexander, C. J. (2001). Developmental attachment and gay and lesbian adoptions. *Journal of Gay & Lesbian Social Services, 13*, 93-97.

Alexander, P. C. (1993). The differential effects of abuse characteristics and attachment in the prediction of long-term effects of sexual abuse. *Journal of Interpersonal Violence, 8*, 346–362.

Alexander, P. C. (2003). Parent-child role reversal: Development of a measure and test of an attachment theory model. *Journal of Systemic Therapies, 22*, 31–44.

Alexander, P. C. (2009). Childhood trauma, attachment, and abuse by multiple partners. *Psychological Trauma, 1*, 78–88.

Alexander, P. C. (2011). Child maltreatment, intimate partner violence, work interference and women's employment. *Journal of Family Violence, 26*, 255–261.

Alexander, P. C. (2014). Dual-trauma couples and intimate partner violence. *Psychological Trauma, 6*, 224-231.

Alexander, P. C., & Anderson, C. L. (1994). An attachment approach to psychotherapy with the incest survivor. *Psychotherapy: Theory, Research, Practice, Training, 31*, 665–675.

Alexander, P. C., & Anderson, C. L. (1997). Incest, attachment, and developmental psychopathology. In D. Cicchetti & S. L. Toth (Eds.), *Developmental perspectives on trauma: Theory, research, and intervention.* Rochester symposium on developmental psychology, Vol. 8 (pp. 343–377). Rochester, NY: University of Rochester Press.

Alexander, P. C., Anderson, C. L., Brand, B., Schaeffer, C., Grelling, B. Z., & Kretz, L. (1998). Adult attachment and long-term effects in survivors of incest. *Child Abuse and Neglect, 22*, 45–81.

Alexander, P. C., Morris, E., Tracy, A., & Frye, A. (2010). Stages of change and the group treatment of batterers: A randomized clinical trial. *Violence and Victims, 25,* 571–587.

Alexander, P. C., Neimeyer, R. A., & Follette, V. M. (1991). Group therapy for women sexually abused as children: A controlled study and investigation of individual differences. *Journal of Interpersonal Violence, 6,* 218–231.

Alexander, P. C., Teti, L., & Anderson, C. L. (2000). Child sexual abuse history and role reversal in parenting. *Child Abuse and Neglect, 24,* 829–838.

Alexander, P. C., Tracy, A., Radek, M., & Koverola, C. (2009). Predicting stages of change in battered women. *Journal of Interpersonal Violence, 24,* 1652–1672.

Alexander, P. C., & Warner, S. (2003). Attachment theory and family systems theory as frameworks for understanding the intergenerational transmission of family violence. In P. Erdman & T. Caffery (Eds.), *Attachment and family systems: Conceptual, empirical, and therapeutic relatedness* (pp. 241–257). New York: Brunner-Routledge.

Alexandre, G. C., Nadanovsky, P., Moraes, C. L., & Reichenheim, M. (2010). The presence of a stepfather and child physical abuse, as reported by a sample of Brazilian mothers in Rio de Janeiro. *Child Abuse and Neglect, 34,* 959–966.

Ali, N., & Pruessner, J. C. (2012). The salivary alpha amylase over cortisol ratio as a marker to assess dysregulations of the stress systems. *Physiology and Behavior, 106,* 65–72.

Alink, L. R. A., Cicchetti, D., Kim, J., & Rogosch, F. A. (2012). Longitudinal associations among child maltreatment, social functioning, and cortisol regulation. *Developmental Psychology, 48,* 224–236.

Almqvist, K., & Broberg, A. G. (2003). Young children traumatized by organized violence together with their mothers: The critical effects of damaged internal representations. *Attachment and Human Development, 5,* 367–380.

Alpert, J. L., Brown, L. S., & Courtois, C. A. (1998). Symptomatic clients and memories of childhood abuse: What the trauma and child sexual abuse literature tells us. *Psychology, Public Policy and Law, 4,* 941–995.

Alvergne, A., Faurie, C., & Raymond, M. (2008). Developmental plasticity of human reproductive development: Effects of early family environment in modern-day France. *Physiology and Behavior, 95,* 625–632.

Amanor-Boudu, Y., Stith, S. M., Miller, M. S., Cook, J., Allen, L., & Gorzek, M. (2011). Impact of dating violence on male and female college students. *Partner Abuse, 2,* 323–343.

American Psychiatric Association. (2013). *Diagnostic and statistical manual of mental disorders* (5th ed.). Washington, DC: American Psychiatric Publishing.

Andersen, S. L., & Teicher, M. H. (2009). Desperately driven and no brakes: Developmental stress exposure and subsequent risk for substance abuse. *Neuroscience and Biobehavioral Reviews, 33,* 516–524.

Anderson, A. S., & Lo, C. C. (2011). Intimate partner violence within law enforcement families. *Journal of Interpersonal Violence, 26,* 1176–1193.

Anderson, C. L., & Alexander, P. C. (1996). The relationship between attachment and dissociation in adult survivors of incest. *Psychiatry, 59,* 240–254.

Anderson, J. R., Amanor-Boadu, Y., Stith, S. M., & Foster, R. E. (2013). Resilience in military marriages experiencing deployment. In D. S. Becvar (Ed), *Handbook of family resilience* (pp. 105–118). New York: Springer.

Anderson, K. A., Fields, N. L., & Dobb, L. A. (2013). Caregiving and early life trauma: Exploring the experiences of family caregivers to aging Holocaust survivors. *Family Relations, 62,* 366–377.

Anderson, K. L. (2002). Perpetrator or victim? Relationships between intimate partner violence and well-being. *Journal of Marriage and Family, 64,* 851–863.

Anderson, S. R., & Miller, R. B. (2006). The effectiveness of therapy with couples reporting a history of childhood sexual abuse: An exploratory study. *Contemporary Family Therapy, 28,* 353–366.

Aosved, A. C, Long, P. J., & Voller, E. K. (2011). Sexual revictimization and adjustment in college men. *Psychology of Men and Masculinity, 12,* 285–296.

Apfel, B., McCaslin, S., Inslicht, S., Metzler, T., Wang, Z., & Marmar, C. (2008, November). Impact of personality traits and negative affect on PTSD in a prospective study of police officers. Paper presented at the annual meeting of the International Society for Traumatic Stress Studies, Chicago, IL.

Appel, A. E., & Holden, G. W. (1998). The co-occurrence of spouse and physical child abuse: A review and appraisal. *Journal of Family Psychology, 12,* 578–599.

Appleyard, K., Egeland, B., van Dulmen, M. H., & Sroufe, L. A. (2005). When more is not better: The role of cumulative risk in child behavior outcomes. *Journal of Child Psychology and Psychiatry, 46,* 235–245.

Arata, C. M. (2000). From child victim to adult victim: A model for predicting sexual revictimization. *Child Maltreatment, 5,* 28–38.

Arata, C. M. (2002). Child sexual abuse and sexual revictimization. *Clinical Psychology: Science and Practice, 9,* 135–164.

Arata, C. M., Langhinrichsen-Rohling, J., Bowers, D., & O'Brien, N. (2007). Differential correlates of multi-type maltreatment among urban youth. *Child Abuse and Neglect, 31,* 393–415.

Arata, C. M., Langhinrichsen-Rohling, J., Bowers, D., & O'Farrill-Swails, L. (2005). Single versus multi-type maltreatment: An examination of the long-term effects of child abuse. *Journal of Aggression, Maltreatment and Trauma, 11*, 29–52.

Arregi, A., Azpiroz, A., Fano, E., & Garmendia, L. (2006). Aggressive behavior: Implications of dominance and subordination for the study of mental disorders. *Aggression and Violent Behavior, 11*, 394–413.

Arriaga, X. B., & Foshee, V. A. (2004). Adolescent dating violence: Do adolescents follow in their friends', or their parents', footsteps? *Journal of Interpersonal Violence, 19*, 162–184.

Austin, M. A., Riniolo, T. D., & Porges, S. W. (2007). Borderline personality disorder and emotion regulation: Insights from the polyvagal theory. *Brain and Cognition, 65*, 69–76.

Averett, P., Nalavany, B., & Ryan, S. (2009). An evaluation of gay/lesbian and heterosexual adoption. *Adoption Quarterly, 12*, 129-151.

Avery-Leaf, S., Cascardi, M., O'Leary, K. D., & Cano, A. (1997). Efficacy of a dating violence prevention program on attitudes justifying aggression. *Journal of Adolescent Health, 21*, 11–17.

Ayoub, C. C., Fischer, K. W., & O'Connor, E. E. (2003). Analyzing development of working models for disrupted attachments: The case of hidden family violence. *Attachment and Human Development, 5*, 97–119.

Babcock, J. C., Green, C. E., & Robie, C. (2004). Does batterers' treatment work? A meta-analytic review of domestic violence treatment outcome research. *Clinical Psychology Review, 23*, 1023–1053.

Babcock, J. C., Jacobson, N. S., Gottman, J. M., & Yerington, T. P. (2000). Attachment, emotional regulation, and the function of marital violence: Differences between secure, preoccupied, and dismissing violent and nonviolent husbands. *Journal of Family Violence, 15*, 391–409.

Babcock, R. L., & DePrince, A. P. (2013). Factors contributing to ongoing intimate partner abuse: Childhood betrayal trauma and dependence on one's perpetrator. *Journal of Interpersonal Violence, 28*, 1385–1402.

Bachar, E., Cale, M., Eisenberg, J., & Dasberg, H. (1994). Aggression expression in grandchildren of Holocaust survivors: A comparative study. *Israel Journal of Psychiatry and Related Sciences, 31*, 41–47.

Bachman, G. F., & Bippus, A. M. (2005). Evaluation of supportive messages provided by friends and romantic partners: An attachment theory approach. *Communication Reports, 18*, 85–94.

Bailey, H. N., DeOliveira, C. A., Wolfe, V. V., Evans, E. M., & Hartwick, C. (2012). The impact of childhood maltreatment history on parenting: A comparison of maltreatment types and assessment methods. *Child Abuse and Neglect, 36*, 236–246.

Bailey, H. N., Moran, G., & Pederson, D. R. (2007). Childhood maltreatment, complex trauma symptoms, and unresolved attachment in an at-risk sample of adolescent mothers. *Attachment and Human Development, 9*, 139–161.

Bailey, H. N., Moran, G., Pederson, D. R., & Bento, S. (2007). Understanding the transmission of attachment using variable- and relationship-centered approaches. *Development and Psychopathology, 19*, 313–343.

Bakermans-Kranenburg, M. J., Dobrova-Krol, N., & van IJzendoorn, M. (2012). Impact of institutional care on attachment disorganization and insecurity of Ukrainian preschoolers: Protective effect of the long variant of the serotonin transporter gene (5HTT). *International Journal of Behavioral Development, 36*, 11–18.

Bakermans-Kranenburg, M. J., & van IJzendoorn, M. H. (2004). No association of the dopamine D4 receptor (DRD4) and -521 C/T promoter polymorphisms with infant attachment disorganization. *Attachment and Human Development, 6*, 211–218.

Bakermans-Kranenburg, M. J., & van IJzendoorn, M. H. (2008). Oxytocin receptor (OXTR) and serotonin transporter (5-HTT) genes associated with observed parenting. *Social Cognitive and Affective Neuroscience, 3*, 128–134.

Bakermans-Kranenburg, M. J., & van IJzendoorn, M. H. (2009). The first 10,000 adult attachment interviews: Distributions of adult attachment representations in clinical and non-clinical groups. *Attachment and Human Development, 11*, 223–263.

Bakermans-Kranenburg, M. J., van IJzendoorn, M. H., Caspers, K., & Philibert, R. (2011). DRD4 genotype moderates the impact of parental problems on unresolved loss or trauma. *Attachment and Human Development, 13*, 253–269.

Bakermans-Kranenburg, M. J., van IJzendoorn, M. H., & Juffer, F. (2003). Less is more: Meta-analyses of sensitivity and attachment interventions in early childhood. *Psychological Bulletin, 129*, 195–215.

Bakermans-Kranenburg, M. J., van IJzendoorn, M. H., & Juffer, F. (2005). Disorganized infant attachment and preventive interventions: A review and meta-analysis. *Infant Mental Health Journal, 26*, 191–216.

Bakermans-Kranenburg, M. J., van IJzendoorn, M. H., Mesman, J., Alink, L. R., & Juffer, F. (2008). Effects of an attachment-based intervention on daily cortisol moderated by dopamine receptor D4: A randomized control trial on 1- to 3-year-olds screened for externalizing behavior. *Development and Psychopathology, 20*, 805–820.

Bakermans-Kranenburg, M. J., van IJzendoorn, M. H., Pijlman, F. T., Mesman, J., & Juffer, F. (2008). Experimental evidence for differential susceptibility: Dopamine D4 receptor polymorphism (DRD4 VNTR) moderates intervention effects on toddlers' externalizing behavior in a randomized controlled trial. *Developmental Psychology, 44*, 293–300.

Ballen, N., Demers, I., & Bernier, A. (2006). A differential analysis of the sub-types of unresolved states of mind in the Adult Attachment Interview. *Journal of Psychological Trauma, 5*, 69–93.

Bandelow, B., Schmahl, C., Falkai, P., & Wedekind, D. (2010). Borderline personality disorder: A dysregulation of the endogenous opioid system. *Psychological Review, 117*, 623–636.

Bandura, A. (1973). *Aggression: A social learning analysis.* Englewood Cliffs, NJ: Prentice-Hall.

Bandura, A. (1977). *Social learning theory.* Englewood Cliffs, NJ: Prentice-Hall.

Bandyopadhvay, A., Deokar, A., & Omar, H. A. (2010). Adolescent dating violence: A comprehensive review. *International Journal of Child and Adolescent Health, 3*, 305–320.

Banyard, V. L. (1997). The impact of childhood sexual abuse and family functioning on four dimensions of women's later parenting. *Child Abuse and Neglect, 21*, 1095–1107.

Banyard, V. L., Cross, C., & Modecki, K. L. (2006). Interpersonal violence in adolescence: Ecological correlates of self-reported perpetration. *Journal of Interpersonal Violence, 21*, 1314–1332.

Banyard, V. L., & Williams, L. M. (2006). Women's voices on recovery: A multi-method study of the complexity of recovery from child sexual abuse. *Child Abuse and Neglect, 31*, 275–290.

Banyard, V. L., Williams, L. M., & Siegel, J. A. (2004). Childhood sexual abuse: A gender perspective on context and consequences. *Child Maltreatment, 9*, 223–238.

Bär, O., Pahlke, C., Dahm, P., Weiss, U., & Heuft, G. (2004). Secondary prevention for police officers involved in job-related psychological stressful or traumatic situations. *Zeitschrift für Psychosomatische Medizin und Psychotherapie, 50*, 190–202.

Baradon, T. (2010). Discussion: And what about fathers? In T. Baradon (Ed.), *Relational trauma in infancy: Psychoanalytic attachment and neuropsychological contributions to parent-infant psychotherapy* (pp. 130–135). New York: Routledge.

Barel, E., van IJzendoorn, M. H., Sagi-Schwartz, A., & Bakermans-Kranenburg, M. J. (2010). Surviving the Holocaust: A meta-analysis of the long-term sequelae of a genocide. *Psychological Bulletin, 136*, 677–698.

Baril, M. E., Crouter, A. C., & McHale, S. M. (2007). Processes linking adolescent well-being, marital love, and coparenting. *Journal of Family Psychology, 21*, 645–654.

Barker, E. D., Oliver, B. R., Viding, E., Salekin, R. T., & Maughan, B. (2011). The impact of prenatal maternal risk, fearless temperament and early parent-

ing on adolescent callous-unemotional traits: A 14-year longitudinal investigation. *Journal of Child Psychology and Psychiatry, 52,* 878–888.

Barnes, J. C., & Jacobs, B. A. (2013). Genetic risk for violent behavior and environmental exposure to disadvantage and violent crime: The case for gene-
environment interaction. *Journal of Interpersonal Violence, 28,* 92–120.

Barnes, J. C., TenEyck, M., Boutwell, B. B., & Beaver, K. M. (2013). Indicators
of domestic/intimate partner violence are structured by genetic and non-
shared environmental influences. *Journal of Psychiatric Research, 47,* 371–
376.

Bar-On, D., Eland, J., Kleber, R. J., Krell, R., Moore, Y., Sagi, A., Soriano, E.,
Suidfeld, P., van der Velden, P. G., & van IJzendoorn, M. H. (1998). Multigenerational perspectives on coping with the Holocaust experience: An
attachment perspective for understanding the developmental sequelae of
trauma across generations. *International Journal of Behavioral Development,
22,* 315–338.

Barrett, B. (2009). The impact of childhood sexual abuse and other forms of
childhood adversity on adulthood parenting. *Journal of Child Sexual Abuse,
18,* 489–512.

Barrett, B. (2010). Childhood sexual abuse and adulthood parenting: The mediating role of intimate partner violence. *Journal of Aggression, Maltreatment
and Trauma, 19,* 323–346.

Barry, R. A., Kochanska, G., & Philibert, R. A. (2008). G × E interaction in the
organization of attachment: Mothers' responsiveness as a moderator of children's genotypes. *Journal of Child Psychology and Psychiatry, 49,* 1313–1320.

Bartholomew, K., & Allison, C. J. (2006). An attachment perspective on abusive
dynamics in intimate relationships. In M. Mikulincer & G. S. Goodman
(Eds.), *Dynamics of romantic love: Attachment, caregiving, and sex* (pp. 102–
127). New York: Guilford.

Bartz, J. A., Zaki, J., Ochsner, K. N., Bolger, N., Kolevzon, A., Ludwig, N., &
Lydon, J. E. (2010). Effects of oxytocin on recollections of maternal care and
closeness. *Proceedings of the National Academy of Sciences of the United
States of America, 107,* 21371–21375.

Barzman, D. H., Patel, A., Sonnier, L., & Strawn, J. R. (2010). Neuroendocrine
aspects of pediatric aggression: Can hormone measures be clinically useful?
Neuropsychiatric Disease and Treatment, 6, 691–697.

Basham, K. (2008). Homecoming as safe haven or the new front: Attachment
and detachment in military couples. *Clinical Social Work Journal, 36,* 83–
96.

Bassuk, E., Dawson, R., & Huntington, N. (2006). Intimate partner violence in
extremely poor women: Longitudinal patterns and risk markers. *Journal of
Family Violence, 21,* 387–399.

Bates, B. C., & Dozier, M. (2002). The importance of maternal state of mind regarding attachment and infant age at placement to foster mothers' representations of their foster infants. *Infant Mental Health Journal, 23,* 417–431.

Batten, S. V., Follette, V. M., & Aban, I. B. (2001). Experiential avoidance and high-risk sexual behavior in survivors of child sexual abuse. *Journal of Child Sexual Abuse, 10,* 101–120.

Beach, S. R. H., Brody, G. H., Lei, M. K., Gibbons, F. X., Gerrard, M., Simons, R. L., et al. (2013). Impact of child sex abuse on adult psychopathology: A genetically and epigenetically informed investigation. *Journal of Family Psychology, 27,* 3–11.

Beaver, K. M., & Belsky, J. (2012). Gene-environment interaction and the intergenerational transmission of parenting: Testing the differential-susceptibility hypothesis. *Psychiatric Quarterly, 83,* 29–40.

Beaver, K. M., Shutt, J. E., Vaughn, M. G., DeLisi, M., & Wright, J. P. (2012). Genetic influences on measures of parental negativity and childhood maltreatment: An exploratory study testing for gene × environment correlations. *Journal of Contemporary Criminal Justice, 28,* 273–292.

Begle, A. M., Dumas, J. E., & Hanson, R. F. (2010). Predicting child abuse potential: An empirical investigation of two theoretical frameworks. *Journal of Clinical Child and Adolescent Psychology, 39,* 208–219.

Begue, F. (2013). Grief and adoption: Unconscious expectations of adoptive parents without problem of fertility. *Neuropsychiatrie de l'Enfance et de l'Adolescence, 61,* 106–117.

Behrens, K. Y. (2010). Amae through the eyes of Japanese mothers: Refining differences and similarities between attachment and amae. In P. Erdman & K.-M. Ng (Eds.), *Attachment: Expanding the cultural connections* (pp. 55–69). New York: Routledge.

Behringer, J., Reiner, I., & Spangler, G. (2011). Maternal representations of past and current attachment relationships, and emotional experience across the transition to motherhood: A longitudinal study. *Journal of Family Psychology, 25,* 210–219.

Belsky, J. (1993). Etiology of child maltreatment: A developmental-ecological analysis. *Psychological Bulletin, 114,* 413–434.

Belsky, J. (1997). Variation in susceptibility to environmental influence: An evolutionary argument. *Psychological Inquiry, 8,* 182–186.

Belsky, J., & Beaver, K. M. (2011). Cumulative-genetic plasticity, parenting and adolescent self-regulation. *Journal of Child Psychology and Psychiatry, 52,* 619–626.

Belsky, J., & Fearon, R. M. P. (2002). Infant-mother attachment security, contextual risk, and early development: A moderational analysis. *Development and Psychopathology, 14,* 293–310.

Belsky, J., & Pluess, M. (2009). Beyond diathesis stress: Differential susceptibility to environmental influences. *Psychological Bulletin, 135,* 885–908.

Belsky, J., Schlomer, G. L., & Ellis, B. J. (2012). Beyond cumulative risk: Distinguishing harshness and unpredictability as determinants of parenting and early life history strategy. *Developmental Psychology, 48,* 662–673.

Belsky, J., Steinberg, L., & Draper, P. (1991). Childhood experience, interpersonal development, and reproductive strategy: An evolutionary theory of socialization. *Child Development, 62,* 647–670.

Belsky, J., Steinberg, L., Houts, R. M., Halpern-Felsher, B. L., & NICHD Early Child Care Research Network. (2010). The development of reproductive strategy in females: Early maternal harshness, earlier menarche, and increased sexual risk taking. *Developmental Psychology, 46,* 120–128.

Bendersky, M., Bennett, D., & Lewis, M. (2006). Aggression at age 5 as a function of prenatal exposure to cocaine, gender, and environmental risk. *Journal of Pediatric Psychology, 31,* 71–84.

Bennett, J., Espie, C., Duncan, B., & Minnis, H. (2009). A qualitative exploration of children's understanding of indiscriminate friendliness. *Clinical Child Psychology and Psychiatry, 14,* 595–618.

Benson, M. J., Buehler, C., & Gerard, J. M. (2008). Interparental hostility and early adolescent problem behavior: Spillover via maternal acceptance, harshness, inconsistency, and intrusiveness. *Journal of Early Adolescence, 28,* 428–454.

Berger, L. M., Paxson, C., & Waldfogel, J. (2009). Mothers, men, and child protective services involvement. *Child Maltreatment, 14,* 263–276.

Bergman, K., Sarkar, P., Glover, V. G., & O'Connor, T. G. (2008). Quality of child-parent attachment moderates the impact of antenatal stress on child fearfulness. *Journal of Child Psychology and Psychiatry, 49,* 1089–1098.

Bergman, K., Sarkar, P., Glover, V., & O'Connor, T. G. (2010). Maternal prenatal cortisol and infant cognitive development: Moderation by infant-mother attachment. *Biological Psychiatry, 67,* 1026–1032.

Bergman, K., Sarkar, P., O'Connor, T. G., Modi, N., & Glover, V. (2007). Maternal stress during pregnancy predicts cognitive ability and fearfulness in infancy. *Journal of the American Academy of Child and Adolescent Psychiatry, 46,* 1454–1463.

Berlin, L. J., Cassidy, J., & Appleyard, K. (2008). The influence of early attachments on other relationships. In J. Cassidy & P. R. Shaver (Eds.), *Handbook of attachment: Theory, research and clinical applications* (2nd ed., pp. 333–347). New York: Guilford.

Bernard, K., & Dozier, M. (2011). This is my baby: Foster parents' feelings of commitment and displays of delight. *Infant Mental Health Journal, 32,* 251–262.

Bernards, S., & Graham, K. (2013). The cross-cultural association between marital status and physical aggression between intimate partners. *Journal of Family Violence, 28,* 403–418.

Bernier, A., Larose, S., & Boivin, M. (2007). Individual differences in adult attachment: Disentangling two assessment traditions. *European Journal of Developmental Psychology, 4,* 220–238.

Bernier, A., & Matte-Gagne, C. (2011). More bridges: Investigating the relevance of self-report and interview measures of adult attachment for marital and caregiving relationships. *International Journal of Behavioral Development, 35,* 307–316.

Bernier, A., & Meins, E. (2008). A threshold approach to understanding the origins of attachment disorganization. *Developmental Psychology, 44,* 969–982.

Berry, D., Deater-Deckard, K., McCartney, K., Wang, Z., & Petrill, S. A. (2013). Gene-environment interaction between dopamine receptor D4 7-repeat polymorphism and early maternal sensitivity predicts inattention trajectories across middle childhood. *Development and Psychopathology, 25,* 291–306.

Berz, J. B., Taft, C. T., Watkins, L. E., & Monson, C. M. (2008). Associations between PTSD symptoms and parenting satisfaction in a female veteran sample. *Journal of Psychological Trauma, 7,* 37–45.

Berzenski, S. R., & Yates, T. M. (2010). Research on intimate partner violence: A developmental process analysis of the contribution of childhood emotional abuse to relationship violence. *Journal of Aggression, Maltreatment and Trauma, 19,* 180–203.

Berzenski, S. R., & Yates, T. M. (2011). Classes and consequences of multiple maltreatment: A person-centered analysis. *Child Maltreatment, 16,* 250–261.

Bevan, E., & Higgins, D. J. (2002). Is domestic violence learned? The contribution of five forms of child maltreatment to men's violence and adjustment. *Journal of Family Violence, 17,* 223–245.

Beyer, M., Blumenthal-Guigui, R., & Krupat, T. (2010). Strengthening parent-child relationships: Visit coaching with children and their incarcerated parents. In Y. R. Harris, J. A. Graham, & G. J. Carpenter (Eds.), *Children of incarcerated parents: Theoretical, development, and clinical issues* (pp. 187–214). New York: Springer.

Bibou-Nakou, I., Tsiantis, J., Assimopoulos, H., & Chatzilambou, P. (2013). Bullying/victimization from a family perspective: A qualitative study of secondary school students' views. *European Journal of Psychology of Education, 28,* 53–71.

Bick, J., & Dozier, M. (2013). The effectiveness of an attachment-based intervention in promoting foster mothers' sensitivity toward foster infants. *Infant Mental Health Journal, 34,* 95–103.

Bick, J., Dozier, M., Bernard, K., Grasso, D., & Simons, R. (2013). Foster mother-infant bonding: Associations between foster mothers' oxytocin production, electrophysiological brain activity, feelings of commitment, and caregiving quality. *Child Development, 84,* 826–840.

Bick, J., Dozier, M., & Moore, S. (2012). Predictors of treatment use among foster mothers in an attachment-based intervention program. *Attachment and Human Development, 14,* 439–452.

Black, M. M., Oberlander, S. E., Lewis, T., Knight, E. D., Zolotor, A. J., Litrownik, A. J., et al. (2009). Sexual intercourse among adolescents maltreated before age 12: A prospective investigation. *Pediatrics, 124,* 941–949.

Blair, C., Berry, D., Mills-Koonce, R., & Granger, D. (2013). Cumulative effects of early poverty on cortisol in young children: Moderation by autonomic nervous system activity. *Psychoneuroendocrinology, 38,* 2666–2675.

Blair, M. M., Glynn, L. M., Sandman, C. A., & Davis, E. P. (2011). Prenatal maternal anxiety and early childhood temperament. *Stress: The International Journal on the Biology of Stress, 14,* 644–651.

Block, J., & Block, J. H. (2006). Venturing a 30-year longitudinal study. *American Psychologist, 71,* 315–327.

Bocknek, R. L., Sanderson, J., & Britner IV, P. A. (2009). Ambiguous loss and posttraumatic stress in school-age children of prisoners. *Journal of Child and Family Studies, 18,* 323–333.

Boden, J. M., Fergusson, D. M., & Horwood, L. J. (2012). Alcohol misuse and violent behavior: Findings from a 30-year longitudinal study. *Drug and Alcohol Dependence, 122,* 135–141.

Bogat, G. A., Levendosky, A. A., Theran, S., von Eye, A., & Davidson, W. S. (2003). Predicting the psychosocial effects of interpersonal partner violence (IPV): How much does a woman's history of IPV matter? *Journal of Interpersonal Violence, 18,* 1271–1291.

Bograd, M. (2005). Strengthening domestic violence theories: Intersections of race, class, sexual orientation, and gender. In N. J. Sokoloff & C. Pratt (Eds.), *Domestic violence at the margins: Readings on race, class, gender, and culture* (pp. 25-38). Piscataway, NJ: Rutgers University Press.

Bohlin, G., Eninger, L., Brocki, K. C., & Thorell, L. B. (2012). Disorganized attachment and inhibitory capacity: Predicting externalizing problem behaviors. *Journal of Abnormal Child Psychology, 40,* 449–458.

Bohlin, G., Hagekull, B., & Rydell, A.-M. (2000). Attachment and social functioning: A longitudinal study from infancy to middle childhood. *Social Development, 9,* 24–39.

Bohnke, R., Bertsch, K., Kruk, M. R., & Naumann, E. (2010). The relationship between basal and acute HPA axis activity and aggressive behavior in adults. *Journal of Neural Transmission, 117,* 629–637.

Bonanno, G. A. (2004). Loss, trauma, and human resilience: Have we underestimated the human capacity to thrive after extremely aversive events? *American Psychologist, 59,* 20–28.

Bonanno, G. A., & Mancini, A. D. (2008). The human capacity to thrive in the face of potential trauma. *Pediatrics, 121,* 369–375.

Booth-LaForce, C., Oh, W., Kim, A. H., Rubin, K. H., Rose-Krasnor, L., & Burgess, K. (2006). Attachment, self-worth, and peer-group functioning in middle childhood. *Attachment and Human Development, 8,* 309–325.

Borelli, J. L., David, D. H., Crowley, M. J., & Mayes, L. C. (2010). Links between disorganized attachment classification and clinical symptoms in school-aged children. *Journal of Child and family Studies, 19,* 243–256.

Borelli, J. L., Goshin, L., Joestl, S., Clark, J., & Byrne, M. W. (2010). Attachment organization in a sample of incarcerated mothers: Distribution of classifications and associations with substance abuse history, depressive symptoms, perceptions of parenting competency and social support. *Attachment and Human Development, 12,* 355–374.

Born, A. (2012). Relationship violence and teenage parents. *Journal of Infant, Child and Adolescent Psychotherapy, 11,* 368–375.

Bosch, N. M., Riese, H., Reijneveld, S. A., Bakker, M. P., Verhulst, F. C., Ormel, J., & Oldehinkel, A. J. (2012). Timing matters: Long term effects of adversities from prenatal period up to adolescence on adolescents' cortisol stress response. The TRAILS study. *Psychoneuroendocrinology, 37,* 1439–1447.

Boss, P. (1999). *Ambiguous loss: Learning to live with unresolved grief.* Cambridge, MA: Harvard University Press.

Boss, P. (2013). Resilience as tolerance for ambiguity. In D. S. Becvar (Ed.), *Handbook of family resilience* (pp. 285–297). New York: Springer.

Boss, P., & Greenberg, J. (1984). Family boundary ambiguity: A new variable in family stress theory. *Family Process, 23,* 535–546.

Bossarte, R. M., Simon, T. R., & Swahn, M. H. (2008). Clustering of adolescent dating violence, peer violence, and suicidal behavior. *Journal of Interpersonal Violence, 23,* 815–833.

Bourassa, C. (2007). Co-occurrence of interparental violence and child physical abuse and its effect on the adolescents' behavior. *Journal of Family Violence, 22,* 691–701.

Bouthillier, D., Julien, D., Dube, M., Belanger, I., & Hamelin, M. (2002). Predictive validity of adult attachment measures in relation to emotion regulation behaviors in marital interactions. *Journal of Adult Development, 9,* 291–305.

Boutwell, B. B., Beaver, K. M., Barnes, J. C., & Vaske, J. (2012). The developmental origins of externalizing behavioral problems: Parental disengagement and the role of gene-environment interplay. *Psychiatry Research, 197,* 337–344.

Bowes, L., Arseneault, L., Maughan, B., Taylor, A., Caspi, A., & Moffitt, T. E. (2009). School, neighborhood, and family factors are associated with children's bullying involvement: A nationally representative longitudinal study. *Journal of the American Academy of Child and Adolescent Psychiatry, 48*, 545–553.

Bowlby, J. (1982). *Attachment and loss: Vol. 1. Attachment.* New York: Basic Books. (Original work published 1969)

Bowlby, J. (1988). *A secure base: Parent-child attachment and healthy human development.* New York: Basic Books.

Bowles, M. A., DeHart, D., & Webb, J. R. (2012). Family influences on female offenders' substance use: The role of adverse childhood events among incarcerated women. *Journal of Family Violence, 27*, 681–686.

Bowman, K. G. (2007). When breastfeeding may be a threat to adolescent mothers. *Issues in Mental Health Nursing, 28*, 89–99.

Bradford, K., & Barber, B. K. (2005). Interparental conflict as intrusive family process. *Journal of Emotional Abuse, 5*, 143–167.

Bradford, K., Vaughn, L. B., & Barber, B. K. (2008). When there is conflict: Interparental conflict, parent-child conflict, and youth problem behaviors. *Journal of Family Issues, 29*, 780–805.

Bradley, R., & Davino, K. (2007). Interpersonal violence, recovery, and resilience in incarcerated women. *Journal of Aggression, Maltreatment and Trauma, 14*, 123–146.

Bramsen, R. H., Lasgaard, M., Koss, M. P., Shevlin, M., Elklit, A., & Banner, J. (2013). Testing a multiple mediator model of the effect of childhood sexual abuse on adolescent sexual victimization. *American Journal of Orthopsychiatry, 83*, 47–54.

Brand, B. L., & Alexander, P. C. (2003). Coping with incest: The relationship between recollections of childhood coping and adult functioning in female survivors of incest. *Journal of Traumatic Stress, 16*, 285–293.

Bratberg, G. H., Nilsen, T. I. L., Holmen, T. L., & Vatten, L. J. (2005). Sexual maturation in early adolescence and alcohol drinking and cigarette smoking in late adolescence: A prospective study of 2,129 Norwegian girls and boys. *European Journal of Pediatrics, 164*, 621–625.

Bratberg, G. H., Nilsen, T. I. L., Holmen, T. L., & Vatten, L. J. (2007). Perceived pubertal timing, pubertal status and the prevalence of alcohol drinking and cigarette smoking in early and late adolescence: A population based study of 8950 Norwegian boys and girls. *Acta Paediatrica, 96*, 292–295.

Brensilver, M., Negriff, S., Mennen, F. E., & Trickett, P. K. (2011). Longitudinal relations between depressive symptoms and externalizing behavior in adolescence: Moderating effects of maltreatment experience and gender. *Journal of Clinical Child and Adolescent Psychology, 40*, 607–617.

Bridges, L. J., Connell, J. P., & Belsky, J. (1988). Similarities and differences in infant-mother and infant-father interaction in the strange situation: A component process analysis. *Developmental Psychology, 24,* 92–100.

Briere, J. (1992). Methodological issues in the study of sexual abuse effects. *Journal of Consulting and Clinical Psychology, 60,* 196–203.

Britner, P. A., Marvin, R. S., & Pianta, R. C. (2005). Development and preliminary validation of the caregiving behavior system: Association with child attachment classification in the preschool Strange Situation. *Attachment and Human Development, 7,* 83–102.

Brodsky, B. S., Mann, J. J., Stanley, B., Tin, A., Oguendo, M., Birmaher, B., et al. (2008). Familial transmission of suicidal behavior: Factors mediating the relationship between childhood abuse and offspring suicide attempts. *Journal of Clinical Psychiatry, 69,* 584–596.

Brody, G. H., Chen, Y.-F., Yu, T., Beach, S. R. H., Kogan, S. M., Simons, R. L., et al. (2012). Life stress, the dopamine receptor gene, and emerging adult drug use trajectories: A longitudinal, multilevel, mediated moderation analysis. *Development and Psychopathology, 24,* 941–951.

Brody, G. H., Yu, T., Chen, Y., Kogan, S. M., Evans, G. W., Beach, S. R. H., et al. (2013a). Cumulative socioeconomic status risk, allostatic load, and adjustment: A prospective latent profile analysis with contextual and genetic protective factors. *Developmental Psychology, 49,* 913–927.

Brody, G. H., Yu, T., Chen, Y., Kogan, S. M., Evans, G. W., Windle, M., et al. (2013b). Supportive family environments, genes that confer sensitivity, and allostatic load among rural African American emerging adults: A prospective analysis. *Journal of Family Psychology, 27,* 22–29.

Brom, D., Kfir, R., & Dasberg, H. (2001). A controlled double-blind study on children of Holocaust survivors. *Israel Journal of Psychiatry and Related Sciences, 38,* 47–57.

Brown, G. L., Schoppe-Sullivan, S. J., Mangelsdorf, S. C., & Neff, C. (2010). Observed and reported supportive coparenting as predictors of infant-mother and infant-father attachment security. *Early Child Development and Care, 180,* 121–137.

Brown, J. (1998, July). *The Process of Change in Abused Women Scales (PROCAWS).* Paper presented at the Program Evaluation and Family Violence Research Conference, Durham, NH.

Brown, J., Cohen, P., Chen, H., Smailes, E., & Johnson, J. G. (2004). Sexual trajectories of abused and neglected youths. *Journal of Developmental and Behavioral Pediatrics, 25,* 77–82.

Brown, L. S., & Pantalone, D. (2011). Lesbian, gay, bisexual, and transgender issues in trauma psychology: A topic comes out of the closet. *Traumatology, 17,* 1–3.

Bruce, J., Fisher, P. A., Pears, K. C., & Levine, S. (2009). Morning cortisol levels in preschool-aged foster children: Differential effects of maltreatment type. *Developmental Psychobiology, 51,* 14–23.

Bruce, J., Tarullo, A. R., & Gunnar, M. R. (2009). Disinhibited social behavior among internationally adopted children. *Development and Psychopathology, 21,* 157–171.

Bryant-Davis, T., Ullman, S. E., Tsong, Y., & Gobin, R. (2011). Surviving the storm: The role of social support and religious coping in sexual assault recovery of African American women. *Violence Against Women, 17,* 1601–1618.

Buchheim, A., George, C., Liebl, V., Moser, A., & Benecke, C. (2007). Affective facial behavior of borderline patients during the adult attachment projective. *Zeitschrift für Psychosomatische Medizin und Psychotherapie, 53,* 339–354.

Buehler, C., Franck, K. L., & Cook, E. C. (2009). Adolescents' triangulation in marital conflict and peer relations. *Journal of Research on Adolescence, 19,* 669–689.

Buehler, C., & Gerard, J. M. (2002). Marital conflict, ineffective parenting, and children's and adolescents' maladjustment. *Journal of Marriage and Family, 64,* 78–92.

Buehler, C., & Welsh, D. P. (2009). A process model of adolescents' triangulation into parents' marital conflict: The role of emotional reactivity. *Journal of Family Psychology, 23,* 167–180.

Bureau, J.-F., Easterbrooks, M. A., & Lyons-Ruth, K. (2009a). Attachment disorganization and controlling behavior in middle childhood: Maternal and child precursors and correlates. *Attachment and Human Development, 11,* 265–284.

Bureau, J.-F., Easterbrooks, M. A., & Lyons-Ruth, K. (2009b). Maternal depressive symptoms in infancy: Unique contribution to children's depressive symptoms in childhood and adolescence? *Development and Psychopathology, 21,* 519–537.

Bureau, J.-F., & Moss, E. (2010). Behavioural precursors of attachment representations in middle childhood and links with child social adaptation. *British Journal of Developmental Psychology, 28,* 657–677.

Burt, S. A., Barnes, A. R., McGue, M., & Iacono, W. G. (2008). Parental divorce and adolescent delinquency: Ruling out the impact of common genes. *Developmental Psychology, 44,* 1668–1677.

Burton, L. (2007). Childhood adultification in economically disadvantaged families: A conceptual model. *Family Relations, 56,* 329–345.

Busch, A. L., & Lieberman, A. F. (2010). Mothers' Adult Attachment Interview ratings predict preschool children's IQ following domestic violence exposure. *Attachment and Human Development, 12,* 505–527.

Buss, C., Davis, E. P., Hobel, C. J., & Sandman, C. A. (2011). Maternal pregnancy-specific anxiety is associated with child executive function at 6–9 years age. *Stress: The International Journal on the Biology of Stress, 14,* 665–676.

Butaney, B., Pelcovitz, D., & Kaplan, S. (2011). Psychological maltreatment as a moderator for physical abuse and adolescent maladjustment: Implications for treatment and intervention. *Journal of Infant, Child and Adolescent Psychotherapy, 10,* 442–454.

Button, D. M., & Gealt, R. (2010). High risk behaviors among victims of sibling violence. *Journal of Family Violence, 25,* 131–140.

Byng-Hall, J. (1990). Attachment theory and family therapy: A clinical view. *Infant Mental Health Journal, 11,* 228–236.

Byng-Hall, J. (1995). Creating a secure family base: Some implications of attachment theory for family therapy. *Family Process, 34,* 45–58.

Byng-Hall, J. (1999). Family couple therapy: Toward greater security. In J. Cassidy & P. R. Shaver (Eds.), *Handbook of attachment: Theory, research and clinical applications* (pp. 625–645). New York: Guilford.

Byng-Hall, J. (2002). Relieving parentified children's burdens in families with insecure attachment patterns. *Family Process, 41,* 375–388.

Byng-Hall, J. (2008). The crucial roles of attachment in family therapy. *Journal of Family Therapy, 30,* 129–146.

Byrd-Craven, J., Auer, B. J., Granger, D. A., & Massey, A. R. (2012). The father-daughter dance: The relationship between father-daughter relationship quality and daughters' stress response. *Journal of Family Psychology, 26,* 87–94.

Caetano, R., Field, C. A., Ramisetty-Mikler, S., & McGrath, C. (2005). The 5-year course of intimate partner violence among white, black, and Hispanic couples in the United States. *Journal of Interpersonal Violence, 20,* 1039–1057.

Caldera, Y. M. (2004). Paternal involvement and infant-father attachment: A Q-set study. *Fathering, 2,* 191–210.

Caldera, Y. M., & Lindsey, E. W. (2006). Coparenting mother-infant interaction, and infant-parent attachment relationships in two-parent families. *Journal of Family Psychology, 20,* 275–283.

Campbell, A. (2008). Attachment, aggression and affiliation: The role of oxytocin in female social behavior. *Biological Psychology, 77,* 1–10.

Campbell-Sills, L., Forde, D. R., & Stein, M. B. (2009). Demographic and childhood environmental predictors of resilience in a community sample. *Journal of Psychiatric Research, 43,* 1007–1012.

Canton-Cortes, D., Cortes, M. R., & Canton, J. (2012). The role of traumagenic dynamics on the psychological adjustment of survivors of child sexual abuse. *European Journal of Developmental Psychology, 9,* 665–680.

Capaldi, D. M., & Clark, S. (1998). Prospective family predictors of aggression toward female partners for at-risk young men. *Developmental Psychology, 34,* 1175–1188.

Capaldi, D. M., Kim, H. K., & Shortt, J. W. (2004). Women's involvement in aggression in young adult romantic relationships: A developmental systems model. In M. Putallaz & K. L. Bierman (Eds.), *Aggression, antisocial behavior, and violence among girls* (pp. 223–241). New York: Guilford.

Capaldi, D. M., Knoble, N. B., Shortt, J. W., & Kim, H. K. (2012). A systematic review of risk factors for intimate partner violence. *Partner Abuse, 3,* 1–194.

Cappell, C., & Heiner, R. B. (1990). The intergenerational transmission of family aggression. *Journal of Family Violence, 5,* 135–152.

Carey, A. L. (1997). Survivor revictimization: Object relations dynamics and treatment implications. *Journal of Counseling and Development, 75,* 357–365.

Carlier, I. V. E., Lamberts, R. D., Fouwels, A. J., & Gersons, B. P. R. (1996). PTSD in relation to dissociation in traumatized police officers. *American Journal of Psychiatry, 153,* 1325–1328.

Carlier, I. V. E., Lamberts, R. D., & Gersons, B. P. R. (1997). Risk factors for posttraumatic stress symptomatology in police officers: A prospective analysis. *Journal of Nervous and Mental Disease, 185,* 498–506.

Carlier, I. V. E., Lamberts, R. D., & Gersons, B. P. R. (2000). The dimensionality of trauma: A multidimensional scaling comparison of police officers with and without posttraumatic stress disorder. *Psychiatry Research, 97,* 29–39.

Carlisle, N., & Rofes, E. (2007). School bullying: Do adult survivors perceive long-term effects? *Traumatology, 13,* 16–26.

Carlson, B. E. (2011). Sibling incest: Adjustment in adult women survivors. *Families in Society, 92,* 77–83.

Carlson, V., Cicchetti, D., Barnett, D., & Braunwald, K. (1989). Disorganized/disoriented attachment relationships in maltreated infants. *Developmental Psychology, 25,* 525–531.

Carney, M. M., & Barner, J. R. (2012). Prevalence of partner abuse: Rates of emotional abuse and control. *Partner Abuse, 3,* 286–335.

Carpenter, L. L., Shattuck, T. T., Tyrka, A. R., Geracioti, T. D., & Price, L. H. (2011). Effect of childhood physical abuse on cortisol stress response. *Psychopharmacology, 214,* 367–375.

Carpenter, L. L., Tyrka, A. R., Ross, N. S., Khoury, L., Anderson, G. M., & Price, L. H. (2009). Effect of childhood emotional abuse and age on cortisol responsivity in adulthood. *Biological Psychiatry, 66,* 69–75.

Carrado, M., George, M. J., Loxam, E., Jones, L., & Templar, D. (1996). Aggression in British heterosexual relationships: A descriptive analysis. *Aggressive Behavior, 22,* 401–415.

Casanueva, C. E., & Martin, S. L. (2007). Intimate partner violence during pregnancy and mothers' child abuse potential. *Journal of Interpersonal Violence*, 22, 603–622.

Casas, J. F., Weigel, S. M., Crick, N. R., Ostrov, J. M., Woods, K. E., Jansen Yeh, E. A., & Huddleston-Casas, C. A. (2006). Early parenting and children's relational and physical aggression in the preschool and home contexts. *Journal of Applied Developmental Psychology*, 27, 209–227.

Caspers, K. M., Paradiso, S., Yucuis, R., Troutman, B., Arndt, S., & Philibert, R. (2009). Association between the serotonin transporter promoter polymorphism (5-HTTLPR) and adult unresolved attachment. *Developmental Psychology*, 45, 64–76.

Caspi, A., Sugden, K., Moffitt, T. E., Taylor, A., Craig, I. W., Harrington, H. L., et al. (2003). Influence of life stress on depression: Moderation by a polymorphism in the 5-HTT gene. *Science*, 301, 386–389.

Cassibba, R., Sette, G., Bakermans-Kranenburg, M. J., & van IJzendoorn, M. H. (2013). Attachment the Italian way: In search of specific patterns of infant and adult attachments in Italian typical and atypical samples. *European Psychologist*, 18, 47–58.

Cassidy, J., & Berlin, L. J. (1994). The insecure/ambivalent pattern of attachment: Theory and research. *Child Development*, 65, 971–981.

Cassidy, J., & Mohr, J. J. (2001). Unsolvable fear, trauma, and psychopathology: Theory, research, and clinical considerations related to disorganized attachment across the life span. *Clinical Psychology: Science and Practice*, 8, 275–298.

Cassidy, J., Poehlmann, J., & Shaver, P. R. (2010). An attachment perspective on incarcerated parents and their children. *Attachment and Human Development*, 12, 285–288.

Castellano, R., Velotti, P., Crowell, J. A., & Zavattini, G. C. (2014). The role of parents' attachment configurations at childbirth on marital satisfaction and conflict strategies. *Journal of Child and Family Studies*, 23, 1011–1026..

Caviglia, G., Fiocco, B., & Dazzi, N. (2004). Intergenerational transmission of the trauma of Shoà: A study conducted by the Adult Attachment Interview. *Ricerca in Psicoterapia*, 7, 67–83.

Chambers, A. N. (2009). Impact of forced separation policy on incarcerated postpartum mothers. *Policy, Politics, and Nursing Practice*, 10, 204–211.

Champagne, F. A., & Curley, J. P. (2009). Epigenetic mechanisms mediating the long-term effects of maternal care on development. *Neuroscience and Biobehavioral Reviews*, 33, 593–600.

Chapple, C. L. (2003). Examining intergenerational violence: Violent role modeling or weak parental controls? *Violence and Victims*, 18, 143–162.

Chapple, C. L., Tyler, K. A., & Bersani, B. E. (2005). Child neglect and adolescent violence: Examining the effects of self-control and peer rejection. *Violence and Victims, 20,* 39–54.

Charles, D., Whitaker, D. J., Le, B., Swahn, M., & DiClemente, R. J. (2011). Differences between perpetrators of bidirectional and unidirectional physical intimate partner violence. *Partner Abuse, 2,* 344–364.

Charles, L. E., Slaven, J. E., Mnatsakanova, A., Ma, C., Violanti, J. M., Fekedulegn, D., et al. (2011). Association of perceived stress with sleep duration and sleep quality in police officers. *International Journal of Emergency Mental Health, 13,* 229–242.

Chartier, K. G., & Caetano, R. (2012). Intimate partner violence and alcohol problems in interethnic and intraethnic couples. *Journal of Interpersonal Violence, 27,* 1780–1801.

Chase, K. A., Treboux, D., O'Leary, K. D., & Strassberg, Z. (1998). Specificity of dating aggression and its justification among high-risk adolescents. *Journal of Abnormal Child Psychology, 26,* 467–473.

Chen, C. G., & Carolan, M. T. (2010). The phenomenon of comparative development between female survivors and their partners: Implications for couples therapy. *Contemporary Family Therapy, 32,* 396–411.

Chen, F. M., Lin, H. S., & Li, C. H. (2012). The role of emotion in parent-child relationships: Children's emotionality, maternal meta-emotion, and children's attachment security. *Journal of Child and Family Studies, 21,* 403–410.

Chen, W.-Y., Propp, J., DeLara, E., & Corvo, K. (2011). Child neglect and its association with subsequent juvenile drug and alcohol offense. *Child and Adolescent Social Work Journal, 28,* 273–290.

Cheng, S.-C., & Kuo, L.-A. (2008). Marital satisfaction and parent-child triangulation. *Bulletin of Educational Psychology, 40,* 220–238.

Chisholm, K. (1998). A three year follow-up of attachment and indiscriminate friendliness in children adopted from Romanian orphanages. *Child Development, 69,* 1092–1106.

Cho, R. M. (2010). Maternal incarceration and children's adolescent outcomes: Timing and dosage. *Social Service Review, 84,* 257–282.

Chopko, B. A., & Schwartz, R. C. (2013). The relation between mindfulness and posttraumatic stress symptoms among police officers. *Journal of Loss and Trauma, 18,* 1–9.

Chu, A., & DePrince, A. P. (2006). Development of dissociation: Examining the relationship between parenting, maternal trauma and child dissociation. *Journal of Trauma and Dissociation, 7,* 75–89.

Cicchetti, D., & Barnett, D. (1991). Attachment organization in maltreated preschoolers. *Development and Psychopathology, 3,* 397–411.

Cicchetti, D., & Rogosch, F. A. (2007). Personality, adrenal steroid hormones, and resilience in maltreated children: A multilevel perspective. *Development and Psychopathology, 19,* 787–809.

Cicchetti, D., Rogosch, F. A., Gunnar, M. R., & Toth, S. L. (2010). The differential impacts of early physical and sexual abuse and internalizing problems on daytime cortisol rhythm in school-aged children. *Child Development, 81,* 252–269.

Cima, M., Smeets, T., & Jelicic, M. (2008). Self-reported trauma, cortisol levels, and aggression in psychopathic and non-psychopathic prison inmates. *Biological Psychology, 78,* 75–86.

Clancy, C. P., Graybeal, A., Tompson, W. P., Badgett, K. S., Feldman, M. E., Calhoun, P. S., et al. (2006). Lifetime trauma exposure in veterans with military-related posttraumatic stress disorder: Association with current symptomatology. *Journal of Clinical Psychiatry, 67,* 1346–1353.

Clarkin, J. F., Levy, K. N., Lewnzenweger, M. F., & Kernberg, O. F. (2007). Evaluating three treatments for borderline personality disorder: A multiwave study. *American Journal of Psychiatry, 164,* 922–928.

Clark-Miller, J., & Brady, H. C. (2013). Critical stress: Police officer religiosity and coping with critical stress incidents. *Journal of Police and Criminal Psychology, 28,* 26–34.

Clemmons, J. C., DiLillo, D., Martinez, I. G., DeGue, S., & Jeffcott, M. (2003). Co-occurring forms of child maltreatment and adult adjustment reported by Latina college students. *Child Abuse and Neglect, 27,* 751–767.

Clemmons, J. C., Walsh, K., DiLillo, D., & Messman-Moore, T. L. (2007). Unique and combined contributions of multiple child abuse types and abuse severity to adult trauma symptomatology. *Child Maltreatment, 12,* 172–181.

Cleveland, H. H., Wiebe, R. P., & Rowe, D. C. (2005). Sources of exposure to smoking and drinking friends among adolescents: A behavioral-genetic evaluation. *Journal of Genetic Psychology, 166,* 153–169.

Cloitre, M., Koenen, K. C., Cohen, L. R., & Han, H. (2002). Skills training in affective and interpersonal regulation followed by exposure: A phase-based treatment for PTSD related to childhood abuse. *Journal of Consulting and Clinical Psychology, 70,* 1067–1074.

Cloitre, M., Stovall-McClough, C., Zorbas, P., & Charuvastra, A. (2008). Attachment organization, emotion regulation, and expectations of support in a clinical sample of women with childhood abuse histories. *Journal of Traumatic Stress, 21,* 282–289.

Clulow, C. (2007). John Bowlby and couple psychotherapy. *Attachment and Human Development, 9,* 343–353.

Coan, J. A. (2008). Toward a neuroscience of attachment. In J. Cassidy & P. R. Shaver (Eds.), *Handbook of attachment: Theory, research, and clinical applications* (pp. 241–265). New York: Guilford.

Coffey, P., Leitenberg, H., Henning, K., Turner, T., & Bennett, R. T. (1996). Mediators of the long-term impact of child sexual abuse: Perceived stigma, betrayal, powerlessness, and self-blame. *Child Abuse and Neglect, 20*, 447–455.

Cohen, J. A., & Cozza, S. J. (2012). Children in military families. In J. A. Cohen, A. P. Mannarino, & E. Deblinger (Eds.), *Trauma-focused CBT for children and adolescents: Treatment applications* (pp. 199–224). New York: Guilford.

Cohen, K. (2008). The movable genogram: Family intervention techniques toward breaking cycles of intergenerational conflict. In J. Hamel (Ed.), *Intimate partner and family abuse: A casebook of gender-inclusive therapy* (pp. 173–193). New York: Springer.

Cohin, E., & Miljkovitch, R. (2007). Development of attachment representations within love relationships: The role of childhood versus that of the partner. *Psychologie Francaise, 52*, 519–533.

Cohn, A. M., McCrady, B. S., Epstein, E. E., & Cook, S. M. (2010). Men's avoidance coping and female partner's drinking behavior: A high-risk context for partner violence? *Journal of Family Violence, 25*, 679–687.

Cohn, D. A., Silver, D. H., Cowan, C. P., Cowan, P. A., & Pearson, J. 1992. Working models of childhood attachment and couple relationships. *Journal of Family Issues, 13*, 432–449.

Coiro, M. J., & Emery, R. E. (1998). Do marriage problems affect fathering more than mothering? A quantitative and qualitative review. *Clinical Child and Family Psychology Review, 1*, 23–40.

Cole, P. M., Alexander, P. C., & Anderson, C. L. (1996). Dissociation in typical and atypical development: Examples from father–daughter incest survivors. In L. K. Michelson & W. J. Ray (Eds.), *Handbook of dissociation: Theoretical, empirical, and clinical perspectives* (pp. 69-89). New York: Plenum Press.

Collin-Vézina, D., & Cyr, M. (2003). Transmission of sexual violence: Description of the phenomenon and current understanding [in French]. *Child Abuse and Neglect, 27*, 489–507.

Collin-Vézina, D., Cyr, M., Pauze, R., & McDuff, P. (2005). The role of depression and dissociation in the link between childhood sexual abuse and later parental practices. *Journal of Trauma and Dissociation, 6*, 71–97.

Collishaw, S., Pickles, A., Messer, J., Rutter, M., Shearer, C., & Maughan, B. (2007). Resilience to adult psychopathology following childhood maltreatment: Evidence from a community sample. *Child Abuse and Neglect, 31*, 211–229.

Consedine, N. S., & Magai, C. (2003). Attachment and emotion experience in later life: The view from emotions theory. *Attachment and Human Development, 5*, 165–187.

Coohey, C., & Zhang, Y. (2006). The role of men in chronic supervisory neglect. *Child Maltreatment, 11*, 27–33.

Coolidge, F. L., & Anderson, L. W. (2002). Personality profiles of women in multiple abusive relationships. *Journal of Family Violence, 17*, 117–131.

Cort, N. A., Toth, S. L., Cerulli, C., & Rogosch, F. (2011). Maternal intergenerational transmission of childhood multitype maltreatment. *Journal of Aggression, Maltreatment and Trauma, 20*, 20–39.

Cortes, D. C., & Justicia, F. J. (2008). Child sexual abuse coping and long term psychological adjustment. *Psicothema, 20*, 509–515.

Cortes Arboleda, M. R., Canton-Cortes, D., & Duarte, J. C. (2011). Long term consequences of child sexual abuse: The role of the nature and continuity of abuse and family environment. *Psicología Conductual: Revista Internacional Clínica y de la Salud, 19*, 41–56.

Corvo, K. (2006). Violence, separation, and loss in the families of origin of domestically violent men. *Journal of Family Violence, 21*, 117–125.

Corvo, K., & Carpenter, E. H. (2000). Effects of parental substance abuse on current levels of domestic violence: A possible elaboration of intergenerational transmission processes. *Journal of Family Violence, 15*, 123–135.

Corvo, K., & deLara, E. (2010). Towards an integrated theory of relational violence: Is bullying a risk factor for domestic violence? *Aggression and Violent Behavior, 15*, 181–190.

Courtois, C. A. (2012). Retraumatization and complex traumatic stress: A treatment overview. In M. P. Duckworth & V. M. Follette (Eds.), *Retraumatization: Assessment, treatment and prevention* (pp. 163–190). New York: Routledge.

Courtois, C. A., & Ford, J. D. (2009). *Treating complex traumatic stress disorders: An evidence-based guide.* New York: Guilford.

Cowan, C. P., & Cowan, P. A. (2005). Two central roles for couple relationships: Breaking negative intergenerational patterns and enhancing children's adaptation. *Sexual and Relationship Therapy, 20*, 275–288.

Cowan, C. P., & Cowan, P. A. (2012). Prevention: Intervening with couples at challenging family transition points. In A. Balfour, M. Morgan, & C. Vincent (Es.), *How couple relationships shape our world: Clinical practice, research, and policy perspectives* (pp. 1-14). London, England: Karnac Books.

Cowan, C. P., Cowan, P. A., & Barry, J. (2011). Couples' groups for parents of preschoolers: Ten-year outcomes of a randomized trial. *Journal of Family Psychology, 25*, 240–250.

Cowan, C. P., Cowan, P. A., Pruett, M. K., & Pruett, K. (2007). An approach to preventing coparenting conflict and divorce in low-income families: Strengthening couple relationships and fostering fathers' involvement. *Family Process, 46*, 109–121.

Cowan, P. A., Bradburn, I., & Cowan, C. P. (2005). Parents' working models of attachment: The intergenerational context of parenting and children's adaptation to school. In P. A. Cowan, C. P. Cowan, J. C. Ablow, V. K. Johnson, & J. R. Measelle (Eds.), *The family context of parenting in children's adaptation to elementary school* (pp. 209–235). Mahwah, NJ: Lawrence Erlbaum.

Cowan, P. A., Cowan, C. P., Pruett, M. K., Pruett, K., & Wong, J. J. (2009). Promoting fathers' engagement with children: Preventive interventions for low-income families. *Journal of Marriage and Family, 71,* 663–679.

Cox, M. J., Paley, B., Payne, C. C., & Burchinal, M. (1999). The transition to parenthood: Marital conflict and withdrawal and parent-infant interactions. In M. J. Cox & J. Brooks-Gunn (Eds.), *Conflict and cohesion in families: Causes and consequences* (pp. 87–104). Mahwah, NJ: Lawrence Erlbaum.

Coyne, C. A., Langstrom, N., Rickert, M. E., Lichtenstein, P., & D'Onofrio, B. M. (2013). Maternal age at first birth and offspring criminality: Using the children of twins design to test causal hypotheses. *Development and Psychopathology, 25,* 17–35.

Cozza, S. J. (2011). Meeting the wartime needs of military children and adolescents. In J. I. Ruzek, P. P. Schnurr, J. J. Vasterling, & M. J. Friedman (Eds.), *Caring for veterans with deployment-related stress disorders* (pp. 171–190). Washington, DC: American Psychological Association.

Craig, C. D., & Sprang, G. (2007). Trauma exposure and child abuse potential: Investigating the cycle of violence. *American Journal of Orthopsychiatry, 77,* 296–305.

Craissati, J., McClurg, G., & Browne, K. (2002a). Characteristics of perpetrators of child sexual abuse who have been sexually victimized as children. *Sexual Abuse, 14,* 225–239.

Craissati, J., McClurg, G., & Browne, K. (2002b). The parental bonding experiences of sex offenders: A comparison between child molesters and rapists. *Child Abuse and Neglect, 26,* 909–921.

Crapanzano, A. M., Frick, P. J., Childs, K., & Terranova, A. M. (2011). Gender differences in the assessment, stability, and correlates to bullying roles in middle school children. *Behavioral Sciences and the Law, 29,* 677–694.

Crapanzano, A. M., Frick, P. J., & Terranova, A. M. (2010). Patterns of physical and relational aggression in a school-based sample of boys and girls. *Journal of Abnormal Child Psychology, 38,* 433–445.

Crawford, E., & Wright, M. O. (2007). The impact of childhood psychological maltreatment on interpersonal schemas and subsequent experiences of relationship aggression. *Journal of Emotional Abuse, 7,* 93–116.

Creasey, G. (2002). Associations between working models of attachment and conflict management behavior in romantic couples. *Journal of Counseling Psychology, 49,* 365–375.

Creasey, G. (2014). Conflict management behavior in dual trauma couples. *Psychological Trauma, 6,* 232-239.

Creswell, K. G., Sayette, M. A., Manuck, S. B., Ferrell, R. E., Hill, S. Y., & Dimoff, J. D. (2012). DRD4 polymorphism moderates the effect of alcohol consumption on social bonding. *PLoS ONE, 7,* Article e28914.

Crick, N. R., & Bigbee, M. A. (1998). Relational and overt forms of peer victimization: A multiinformant approach. *Journal of Consulting and Clinical Psychology, 66,* 337–347.

Crittenden, P. (2006). Why do inadequate parents do what they do? In O. Mayseless (Ed.), *Parenting representations: Theory, research and clinical implications* (pp. 388–433). London: Cambridge University Press.

Crittenden, P. M. (1997). Toward an integrative theory of trauma: A dynamic-maturation approach. In D. Cicchetti & S. L. Toth (Eds.), *Developmental perspectives on trauma: Theory, research, and intervention* (pp. 33–84). Rochester, NY: University of Rochester Press.

Crittenden, P. M. (2001). Organization, alternative organizations, and disorganization: Competing perspectives on the development of attachment among endangered children. *PsycCRITIQUES, 46,* 593–596.

Crittenden, P. M., & Dallos, R. (2009). All in the family: Integrating attachment and family systems theories. *Clinical Child Psychology and Psychiatry, 14,* 389–409.

Crittenden, P. M., Partridge, M. F., & Claussen, A. H. (1991). Family patterns of relationship in normative and dysfunctional families. *Development and Psychopathology, 3,* 491–512.

Crockenberg, S. C., Leerkes, E. M., & Jo, P. S. B. (2008). Predicting aggressive behavior in the third year from infant reactivity and regulation as moderated by maternal behavior. *Development and Psychopathology, 20,* 37–54.

Crockett, E. E., Holmes, B. M., Granger, D. A., & Lyons-Ruth, K. (2013). Maternal disrupted communication during face-to-face interaction at 4 months: Relation to maternal and infant cortisol among at-risk families. *Infancy, 18,* 1111-1134.

Crowell, J. A., Treboux, D., & Waters, E. (1999). The Adult Attachment Interview and the Relationship Questionnaire: Relations to reports of mothers and partners. *Personal Relationships, 6,* 1–18.

Crowell, J. A., Treboux, D., & Waters, E. (2002). Stability of attachment representations: The transition to marriage. *Developmental Psychology, 38,* 467–479.

Crowell, J. A., Warner, D. E., Davis, C. R., Marraccini, M., & Dearing, E. (2010). The influence of childhood adversity on mothers' behavior with preschoolers: Role of maternal attachment coherence, dissociative symptoms, and marital behaviors. *Research in Human Development, 7,* 274–291.

Cuevas, C. A., Finkelhor, D., Ormrod, R., & Turner, H. (2009). Psychiatric diagnosis as a risk marker for victimization in a national sample of children. *Journal of Interpersonal Violence, 24,* 636–652.

Cui, M., Durtschi, J. A., Donnellan, M. B., Lorenz, F. O., & Conger, R. D. (2010). Intergenerational transmission of relationship aggression: A prospective longitudinal study. *Journal of Family Psychology, 24,* 688–697.

Cullerton-Sen, C., Cassidy, A. R., Murray-Close, D., Cicchetti, D., Crick, N. R., & Rogosch, F. A. (2008). Childhood maltreatment and the development of relational and physical aggression: The importance of a gender-informed approach. *Child Development, 79,* 1736–1751.

Cummings, E. M., Keller, P. S., & Davies, P. T. (2005). Towards a family process model of maternal and paternal depressive symptoms: Exploring multiple relations with child and family functioning. *Journal of Child Psychology and Psychiatry, 46,* 479–489.

Curran, M., Hazen, N., Jacobvitz, D., & Feldman, A. (2005). Representations of early family relationships predict marital maintenance during the transition to parenthood. *Journal of Family Psychology, 19,* 189–197.

Curtis, W. J., & Cicchetti, D. (2007). Emotion and resilience: A multilevel investigation of hemispheric electroencephalogram asymmetry and emotion regulation in maltreated and nonmaltreated children. *Development and Psychopathology, 19,* 811–840.

Cyr, C., Euser, E. M., Bakermans-Kranenburg, M. J., & van IJzendoorn, M. H. (2010). Attachment security and disorganization in maltreating and high-risk families: A series of meta-analyses. *Development and Psychopathology, 22,* 87–108.

Cyr, M., McDuff, P., & Hebert, M. (2013). Support and profiles of nonoffending mothers of sexually abused children. *Journal of Child Sexual Abuse, 22,* 209–230.

Cyr, M., McDuff, P., & Wright, J. (2006). Prevalence and predictors of dating violence among adolescent female victims of child sexual abuse. *Journal of Interpersonal Violence, 21,* 1000–1017.

Cyr, M., Wright, J., McDuff, P., & Perron, A. (2002). Intrafamilial sexual abuse: Brother-sister incest does not differ from father-daughter and stepfather-stepdaughter incest. *Child Abuse and Neglect, 26,* 957–973.

Daigneault, I., Hebert, M., & McDuff, P. (2009). Men's and women's childhood sexual abuse and victimization in adult partner relationships: A study of risk factors. *Child Abuse and Neglect, 33,* 638–647.

Daining, C., & DePanfilis, D. (2007). Resilience of youth in transition from out-of-home care to adulthood. *Children and Youth Services Review, 29,* 1158–1178.

Daisy, N. V., & Hien, D. A. (2014). The role of dissociation in the cycle of violence. *Journal of Family Violence, 29,* 99–109.

Dallaire, D. H. (2007a). Children with incarcerated mothers: Developmental outcomes, special challenges and recommendations. *Journal of Applied Developmental Psychology, 28,* 15–24.

Dallaire, D. H. (2007b). Incarcerated mothers and fathers: A comparison of risks for children and families. *Family Relations, 56,* 440–453.

Dallaire, D. H., Ciccone, A., & Wilson, L. C. (2012). The family drawings of at-risk children: Concurrent relations with contact with incarcerated parents, caregiver behavior, and stress. *Attachment and Human Development, 14,* 161–183.

Dallaire, D. H., & Wilson, L. C. (2010). The relation of exposure to parental criminal activity, arrest, and sentencing to children's maladjustment. *Journal of Child and Family Studies, 19,* 404–418.

Dallaire, D. H., & Zeman, J. L. (2013). Relationship processes and resilience in children with incarcerated parents: II. Empathy as a protective factor for children with incarcerated parents. *Monographs of the Society for Research in Child Development, 78,* 7–25.

Dalton, E. J., Greenman, P. S., Classen, C. C., & Johnson, S. M. (2013). Nurturing connections in the aftermath of childhood trauma: A randomized controlled trial of emotionally focused couple therapy for female survivors of childhood abuse. *Couple and Family Psychology, 2,* 209–221.

Daniel, S. I. F. (2009). The developmental roots of narrative expression in therapy: Contributions from attachment theory and research. *Psychotherapy: Theory, Research, Practice, Training, 46,* 301–316.

Dankoski, M. E., Keiley, M. K., Thomas, V., Choice, P., Lloyd, S. A., & Seery, B. L. (2006). Affect regulation and the cycle of violence against women: New directions for understanding the process. *Journal of Family Violence, 21,* 327–339.

Daughters, S. B., Gorka, S. M., Matusiewicz, A., & Anderson, K. (2013). Gender specific effect of psychological stress and cortisol reactivity on adolescent risk taking. *Journal of Abnormal Child Psychology, 41,* 749–758.

David, D. H., & Lyons-Ruth, K. (2005). Differential attachment responses of male and female infants to frightening maternal behavior: Tend or befriend versus fight or flight? *Infant Mental Health Journal, 26,* 1–18.

Davies, P. T., & Cummings, E. M. (1994). Marital conflict and child adjustment: An emotional security hypothesis. *Psychological Bulletin, 116,* 387–411.

Davies, P. T., Harold, G. T., Goeke-Morey, M. C., & Cummings, E. M. (2002). Child emotional security and interparental conflict. *Monographs of the Society for Research in Child Development, 67,* vii–viii.

Davies, P. T., Sturge-Apple, M. L., & Cicchetti, D. (2011). Interparental aggression and children's adrenocortical reactivity: Testing an evolutionary model of allostatic load. *Development and Psychopathology, 23,* 801–814.

Davies, P. T., Sturge-Apple, M. L., Cicchetti, D., Manning, L. G., & Zale, E. (2009). Children's patterns of emotional reactivity to conflict as explanatory mechanisms in links between interpartner aggression and child physiological functioning. *Journal of Child Psychology and Psychiatry, 50,* 1384–1391.

Davies, P. T., Sturge-Apple, M. L., Woitach, M. J., & Cummings, E. M. (2009). A process analysis of the transmission of distress from interparental conflict to parenting: Adult relationship security as an explanatory mechanism. *Developmental Psychology, 45,* 1761–1773.

Daw, J., Shanahan, M., Harris, K. M., Smolen, A., Haberstick, B., & Boardman, J. D. (2013). Genetic sensitivity to peer behaviors: 5HTTLPR, smoking, and alcohol consumption. *Journal of Health and Social Behavior, 54,* 92–108.

Dawson, A., Jackson, D., & Nyamathi, A. (2012). Children of incarcerated parents: Insights to addressing a growing public health concern in Australia. *Children and Youth Services Review, 34,* 2433–2441.

Deater-Deckard, K., Dodge, K. A., & Sorbring, E. (2005). Cultural differences in the effects of physical punishment. In M. Rutter & M. Tienda (Eds.), *Ethnicity and causal mechanisms* (pp. 204–226). New York: Cambridge University Press.

Deater-Deckard, K., Ivy, L., & Petrill, S. A. (2006). Maternal warmth moderates the link between physical punishment and child externalizing problems: A parent-offspring behavior genetic analysis. *Parenting: Science and Practice, 6,* 59–78.

Deater-Deckard, K., Mullineaux, P. Y., Beekman, C., Petrill, S. A., Schatschneider, C., & Thompson, L. A. (2009). Conduct problems, IQ, and household chaos: A longitudinal multi-informant study. *Journal of Child Psychology and Psychiatry, 50,* 1301–1308.

Deater-Deckard, K., & O'Connor, T. G. (2000). Parent-child mutuality in early childhood: Two behavioral genetic studies. *Developmental Psychology, 36,* 561–570.

Deater-Deckard, K., & Petrill, S. A. (2004). Parent-child dyadic mutuality and child behavior problems: An investigation of gene-environment processes. *Journal of Child Psychology and Psychiatry, 45,* 1171–1179.

De Bellis, M. D., & Keshavan, M. S. (2003). Sex differences in brain maturation in maltreatment-related pediatric posttraumatic stress disorder. *Neuroscience and Biobehavioral Reviews, 27,* 103–117.

DeBoard-Lucas, R. L., Fosco, G. M., Raynor, S. R., & Grych, J. H. (2010). Interparental conflict in context: Exploring relations between parenting processes and children's conflict appraisals. *Journal of Clinical Child and Adolescent Psychology, 39,* 163–175.

de Burgh, H. T., White, C. J., Fear, N. T., & Iversen, A. C. (2011). The impact of deployment to Iraq or Afghanistan on partners and wives of military personnel. *International Review of Psychiatry, 23*, 192–200.

Dedert, E. A., Green, K. T., Calhoun, P. S., Yoash-Gantz, R., Taber, K. H., Mumford, M. M., et al. (2009). Association of trauma exposure with psychiatric morbidity in military veterans who have served since September 11, 2001. *Journal of Psychiatric Research, 43*, 830–836.

DeFronzo, R., Panzarella, C., & Butler, A. C. (2001). Attachment, support seeking, and adaptive inferential feedback: Implications for psychological health. *Cognitive and Behavioral Practice, 8*, 48–52.

Dekel, R., & Goldblatt, H. (2008). Is there intergenerational transmission of trauma? The case of combat veterans' children. *American Journal of Orthopsychiatry, 78*, 281–289.

Dekel, S., Solomon, Z., & Rozenstreich, E. (2013). Secondary salutogenic effects in veterans whose parents were Holocaust survivors? *Journal of Psychiatric Research, 47*, 266–271.

Del Giudice, M., Ellis, B. J., & Shirtcliff, E. A. (2011). The Adaptive Calibration Model of stress responsivity. *Neuroscience and Biobehavioral Reviews, 35*, 1562–1592.

Del Giudice, M., Hinnant, J. B., Ellis, B. J., & El-Sheikh, M. (2012). Adaptive patterns of stress responsivity: A preliminary investigation. *Developmental Psychology, 48*, 775–790.

Delsol, C., & Margolin, G. (2004). The role of family-of-origin violence in men's marital violence perpetration. *Clinical Psychology Review, 24*, 99–122.

Delsol, C., Margolin, G., & John, R. S. (2003). A typology of maritally violent men and correlates of violence in a community sample. *Journal of Marriage and Family, 65*, 635–651.

Dennison, S., & Leclerc, B. (2011). Developmental factors in adolescent child sexual offenders: A comparison of nonrepeat and repeat sexual offenders. *Criminal Justice and Behavior, 38*, 1089–1102.

Denson, T. F., Mehta, P. H., & Ho Tan, D. (2013). Endogenous testosterone and cortisol jointly influence reactive aggression in women. *Psychoneuroendocrinology, 38*, 416–424.

DeOliveira, C. A., Bailey, H. N., Moran, G., & Pederson, D. R. (2004). Emotion socialization as a framework for understanding the development of disorganized attachment. *Social Development, 13*, 437–467.

DeOliveira, C. A., Moran, G., & Pederson, D. R. (2005). Understanding the link between maternal adult attachment classifications and thoughts and feelings about emotions. *Attachment and Human Development, 7*, 153–170.

DePrince, A. P. (2005). Social cognition and revictimization risk. *Journal of Trauma and Dissociation, 6*, 125–141.

Desmarais, S. L., Reeves, K. A., Nicholls, T. L., Telford, R. P., & Fiebert, M. S. (2012). Prevalence of physical violence in intimate relationships, Part 2: Rates of male and female perpetration. *Partner Abuse, 3,* 170–198.

Devries, K. M., Child, J. C., Bacchus, L. J., Mak, J., Falder, G., Graham, K. et al. (2014). Intimate partner violence victimization and alcohol consumption in women: A systematic review and meta-analysis. *Addiction, 109,* 379-391.

de Vries-Bouw, M., Jansen, L., Cermeiren, R., Doreleijers, T., van de Ven, P., & Popma, A. (2012). Concurrent attenuated reactivity of alpha-amylase and cortisol is related to disruptive behavior in male adolescents. *Hormones and Behavior, 62,* 77–85.

Dexter, C. A., Wong, K., Stacks, A. M., Beeghly, M., & Barnett, D. (2013). Parenting and attachment among low-income African American and Caucasian preschoolers. *Journal of Family Psychology, 27,* 629–638.

Diamond, G., Creed, T., Gillham, J., Gallop, R., & Hamilton, J. L. (2012). Sexual trauma history does not moderate treatment outcome in attachment-based family therapy (ABFT) for adolescents with suicide ideation. *Journal of Family Psychology, 26,* 595–605.

Diamond, G., Siqueland, L., & Diamond, G. M. (2003). Attachment-based family therapy for depressed adolescents: Programmatic treatment development. *Clinical Child and Family Psychology Review, 6,* 107–127.

Diamond, G. S., Wintersteen, M. B., Brown, G. K., Diamond, G. M., Gallop, R., Shelef, K., & Levy, S. (2010). Attachment-based family therapy for adolescents with suicidal ideation: A randomized controlled trial. *Journal of the American Academy of Child and Adolescent Psychiatry, 49,* 122–131.

Diamond, L. M., & Cribbet, M. R. (2013). Links between adolescent sympathetic and parasympathetic nervous system functioning and interpersonal behavior over time. *International Journal of Psychophysiology, 88,* 339–348.

Diamond, L. M., Fagundes, C. P., & Cribbet, M. R. (2012). Individual differences in adolescents' sympathetic and parasympathetic functioning moderate associations between family environment and psychosocial adjustment. *Developmental Psychology, 48,* 918–931.

Dietz, D. M., LaPlant, Q., Watts, E. L., Hodes, G. E., Russo, S. J., Feng, J., et al. (2011). Paternal transmission of stress-induced pathologies. *Biological Psychiatry, 70,* 408–414.

Di Giacomo, E., & Clerici, M. (2009). Physical and sexual violence as risk factors for people who rape and commit a paedophilic act. *Minerva Psichiatrica, 50,* 339–342.

DiLillo, D., & Damashek, A. (2003). Parenting characteristics of women reporting a history of childhood sexual abuse. *Child Maltreatment, 8,* 319–333.

DiLillo, D., Giuffre, D., Tremblay, G. C., & Peterson, L. (2001). A closer look at the nature of intimate partner violence reported by women with a history of child sexual abuse. *Journal of Interpersonal Violence, 16*, 116–132.

DiLillo, D., Tremblay, G. D., & Peterson, L. (2000). Linking childhood sexual abuse and abusive parenting: The mediating role of maternal anger. *Child Abuse and Neglect, 24*, 767–779.

Dimitrova, N., Pierrehumbert, B., Glatz, N., Torrisi, R., Heinrichs, M., Halfon, O., & Chouchena, O. (2010). Closeness in relationships as a mediator between sexual abuse in childhood or adolescence and psychopathological outcome in adulthood. *Clinical Psychology and Psychotherapy, 17*, 183–195.

Dinger, U., Strack, M., Sachsse, T., & Schauenburg, H. (2009). *Psychotherapy: Theory, Research, Practice, Training, 46*, 277–290.

Dixon, L., Browne, K., Hamilton-Giachritsis, C., & Ostapuik, E. (2010). Differentiating patterns of aggression in the family. *Journal of Aggression, Conflict and Peace Research, 2*, 32–44.

Dixon, L., Hamilton-Giachritsis, C., Browne, K., & Ostapuik, E. (2007). The co-occurrence of child and intimate partner maltreatment in the family: Characteristics of the violent perpetrators. *Journal of Family Violence, 22*, 675–689.

Doan, S. N., Fuller-Rowell, T. E., & Evans, G. W. (2012). Cumulative risk and adolescents' internalizing and externalizing problems: The mediating roles of maternal responsiveness and self-regulation. *Developmental Psychology, 48*, 1529–1539.

Dodge, K. A. (2004). Public policy and the "discovery" of girls' aggressive behavior. In M. Putallaz & K. L. Bierman (Eds.), *Aggression, antisocial behavior, and violence among girls* (pp. 302–311). New York: Guilford.

Dodge, K. A., Pettit, G. S., Bates, J. E., & Valente, E. (1995). Social information-processing patterns partially mediate the effect of early physical abuse on later conduct problems. *Journal of Abnormal Psychology, 104*, 632–643.

D'Onofrio, B. M., Turkheimer, E., Emery, R. E., Slutske, W. S., Heath, A. C., Madden, P. A., & Martin, N. G. (2005). A genetically informed study of marital instability and its association with offspring psychopathology. *Journal of Abnormal Psychology, 114*, 570–586.

Doom, J. R., Cicchetti, D., Rogosch, F. A., & Dackis, M. N. (2013). Child maltreatment and gender interactions as predictors of differential neuroendocrine profiles. *Psychoneuroendocrinology, 38*, 1442–1454.

Downing, J., & Bellis, M. A. (2009). Early pubertal onset and its relationship with sexual risk taking, substance use and anti-social behavior: A preliminary cross-sectional study. *BMC Public Health 9*, 446.

Dozier, M., Grasso, D., Lindhiem, O., & Lewis, E. (2007). The role of caregiver commitment in foster care: Insights from the This Is My Baby Interview. In

D. Oppenheim & D. F. Goldsmith (Eds.), *Attachment theory in clinical work with children: Bridging the gap between research and practice* (pp. 90–108). New York: Guilford.

Dozier, M., Higley, E., Albus, K. E., & Nutter, A. (2002). Intervening with foster infants' caregivers: Targeting three critical needs. *Infant Mental Health Journal, 23*, 541–554.

Dozier, M., & Kobak, R. (1992). Psychophysiology in attachment interviews: Converging evidence for deactivating strategies. *Child Development, 63*, 1473–1480.

Dozier, M., & Lindhiem, O. (2006). This is my child: Differences among foster parents in commitment to their young children. *Child Maltreatment, 11*, 338–345.

Dozier, M., Lindhiem, O., Lewis, E., Bick, J., Bernard, K., & Peloso, E. (2009). Effects of a foster parent training program on young children's attachment behaviors: Preliminary evidence from a randomized clinical trial. *Child and Adolescent Social Work Journal, 26*, 321–332.

Dozier, M., Peloso, E., Lindhiem, O., Gordon, M. K., Manni, M., Sepulveda, S., et al. (2006). Developing evidence-based interventions for foster children: An example of a randomized clinical trial with infants and toddlers. *Journal of Social Issues, 62*, 767–785.

Dozier, M., & Rutter, M. (2008). Challenges to the development of attachment relationships faced by young children in foster and adoptive care. In J. Cassidy & P. R. Shaver (Eds.), *Handbook of attachment: Theory, research, and clinical applications* (2nd ed., pp. 698–717). New York: Guilford.

Dozier, M., Stovall, K. C., Albus, K. E., & Bates, B. (2001). Attachment for infants in foster care: The role of caregiver state of mind. *Child Development, 72*, 1467–1477.

Drury, S. S., Gleason, M. M., Theall, K. P., Smyke, A. T., Nelson, C. A., Fox, N. A., & Zeanah, C. H. (2012). Genetic sensitivity to the caregiving context: The influence of 5HTTLPR and BDNF Val66Met on indiscriminate social behavior. *Physiology and Behavior, 106*, 728–735.

Dube, S. R., Anda, R. F., Whitfield, C. L., Brown, D. W., Felitti, V. J., Dong, M., & Giles, W. H. (2005). Long-term consequences of childhood sexual abuse by gender of victim. *American Journal of Preventive Medicine, 28*, 430–438.

Dubo, E. D., Zanarini, M. C., Lewis, R. E., & Williams, A. A. (1997). Relationship between lifetime self-destructiveness and pathological childhood experiences. In M. C. Zanarini (Ed.), *Role of sexual abuse in the etiology of borderline personality disorder* (pp. 107–129). Arlington, VA: American Psychiatric Association.

Dubois-Comtois, K., Cyr, C., & Moss, E. (2011). Attachment behavior and mother-child conversations as predictors of attachment representations in middle childhood: A longitudinal study. *Attachment and Human Development, 13,* 335–357.

Dubois-Comtois, K., & Moss, E. (2008). Beyond the dyad: Do family interactions influence children's attachment representations in middle childhood. *Attachment and Human Development, 10,* 415–431.

Dubowitz, H. (2006). Where's Dad? A need to understand father's role in child maltreatment. *Child Abuse and Neglect, 30,* 461–465.

Dubowitz, H., Black, M. M., Cox, C. E., Kerr, M. A., Litrownik, A. J., Radhakrishna, A., et al. (2001). Father involvement and children's functioning at age 6 years: A multisite study. *Child Maltreatment, 6,* 300–309.

Dubowitz, H., Newton, R. R., Litrownik, A. J., Lewis, T., Briggs, E. C., Thompson, R., et al. (2005). Examination of a conceptual model of child neglect. *Child Maltreatment, 10,* 173–189.

Dudeck, M., Denkhahn, K., Spitzer, C., Barnow, S., Freyberger, H. J., & Grabe, H. J. (2012). Is there an association between intra-familiar sexual abuse and sexual offenses in later life? Findings of a European study of long-term prisoners. *Psychiatrische Praxis, 39,* 217–221.

Dufour, S., Lavergne, C., Larrivee, M.-C., & Trocme, N. (2008). Who are these parents involved in child neglect? A differential analysis by parent gender and family structure. *Children and Youth Services Review, 30,* 141–156.

Duke, N. N., Pettingell, S. L., McMorris, B. J., & Borowsky, I. W. (2010). Adolescent violence perpetration: Associations with multiple types of adverse childhood experiences. *Pediatrics, 125,* e778–e786.

DuMont, K. A., Widom, C. S., & Czaja, S. J. (2007). Predictors of resilience in abused and neglected children grown-up: The role of individual and neighborhood characteristics. *Child Abuse and Neglect, 31,* 255–274.

Dutra, L., Bureau, J.-F., Holmes, B., Lyubchik, A., & Lyons-Ruth, K. (2009). Quality of early care and childhood trauma: A prospective study of developmental pathways to dissociation. *Journal of Nervous and Mental Disease, 197,* 383–390.

Dutra, L., de Blank, G., Scheiderer, E., & Taft, C. (2012). Correlates of female veterans' perpetration of relationship aggression. *Psychological Trauma, 4,* 323–329.

Dykas, M. J., Ziv, Y., & Cassidy, J. (2008). Attachment and peer relations in adolescence. *Attachment and Human Development, 10,* 123–141.

Easterbrooks, M. A., Chaudhuri, J. H., Bartlett, J. D., & Coperman, A. (2011). Resilience in parenting among young mothers: Family and ecological risks and opportunities. *Children and Youth Services Review, 33,* 42–50.

Eaton, D. K., Davis, K. S., Barrios, L., Brener, N. D., & Noonan, R. K. (2007). Associations of dating violence victimization with lifetime participation, co-occurrence, and early initiation of risk behaviors among U. S. high school students. *Journal of Interpersonal Violence, 22,* 585–602.

Eddy, J. M., Martinez, C. R., & Burraston, B. (2013). Relationship processes and resilience in children with incarcerated parents: VI. A randomized controlled trial of a parent management training program for incarcerated parents: Proximal impacts. *Monographs of the Society for Research in Child Development, 78,* 75–93.

Edmond, T., Auslander, W., Elze, D., & Bowland, S. (2006). Signs of resilience in sexually abused adolescent girls in the foster care system. *Journal of Child Sexual Abuse, 15,* 1–28.

Edwards, J., & Alexander, P. C. (1992). The contribution of family background to the long-term adjustment of women sexually abused as children. *Journal of Interpersonal Violence, 7,* 306–320.

Edwards, K. M., Dixon, K. J., Gidycz, C. A., & Desai, A. D. (2014). Family-of-origin violence and college men's reports of intimate partner violence perpetration in adolescence and young adulthood: The role of maladaptive interpersonal patterns. *Psychology of Men and Masculinity, 15,* 234–240.

Egeland, B. (1988). Fathers and child abuse. *PsycCRITIQUES, 33,* 302–303.

Egeland, B., Jacobvitz, D., & Sroufe, L. A. (1988). Breaking the cycle of abuse. *Child Development, 59,* 1080–1088.

Ehrensaft, M. K. (2008). Intimate partner violence: Persistence of myths and implications for intervention. *Children and Youth Services Review, 30,* 276–286.

Ehrensaft, M. K. (2012, July). Early antisocial behavior and the prevention of intimate partner violence. Paper presented at the International Family Violence and Child Victimization Research Conference, Portsmouth, NH.

Ehrensaft, M. K., & Cohen, P. (2012). Contribution of family violence to the intergenerational transmission of externalizing behavior. *Prevention Science, 13,* 370–383.

Ehrensaft, M. K., Cohen, P., Brown, J., Smailes, E., Chen, H., & Johnson, J. G. (2003). Intergenerational transmission of partner violence: A 20-year prospective study. *Journal of Consulting and Clinical Psychology, 71,* 741–753.

Eiden, R. D., Ostrov, J. M., Colder, C. R., Leonard, K. E., Edwards, E. P., & Orrange-Torchia, T. (2010). Parent alcohol problems and peer bullying and victimization: Child gender and toddler attachment security as moderators. *Journal of Clinical Child and Adolescent Psychology, 39,* 341–350.

Eisold, B. K. (2005). Notes on lifelong resilience: Perceptual and personality factors implicit in the creation of a particular adaptive style. *Psychoanalytic Psychology, 22,* 411–425.

Elliston, D., McHale, J., Talbot, J., Parmley, M., & Kuersten-Hogan, R. (2008).

Withdrawal from coparenting interactions during early infancy. *Family Process, 47,* 481–499.

El-Sheikh, M., Arsiwalla, D. D., Hinnant, J. B., & Erath, S. A. (2011). Children's internalizing symptoms: The role of interactions between cortisol and respiratory sinus arrhythmia. *Physiology and Behavior, 103,* 225–232.

El-Sheikh, M., Buckhalt, J. A., Keller, P. S., Cummings, E. M., & Acebo, C. (2007). Child emotional insecurity and academic achievement: The role of sleep deprivation. *Journal of Family Psychology, 21,* 29–38.

El-Sheikh, M., Cummings, E. M., Kouros, C. D., Elmore-Staton, L., & Buckhalt, J. (2008). Marital psychological and physical aggression and children's mental and physical health: Direct, mediated, and moderated effects. *Journal of Consulting and Clinical Psychology, 76,* 138–148.

El-Sheikh, M., & Erath, S. A. (2011). Family conflict, autonomic nervous system functioning, and child adaptation: State of the science and future directions. *Development and Psychopathology, 23,* 703–721.

El-Sheikh, M., Hinnant, J. B., & Erath, S. (2011). Developmental trajectories of delinquency symptoms in childhood: The role of marital conflict and autonomic nervous system activity. *Journal of Abnormal Psychology, 120,* 16–32.

El-Sheikh, M., Keller, P. S., & Erath, S. A. (2007). Marital conflict and risk for child maladjustment over time: Skin conductance level reactivity as a vulnerability factor. *Journal of Abnormal Child Psychology, 35,* 715–727.

El-Sheikh, M., Kouros, C. D., Erath, S., Cummings, E. M., Keller, P., Staton, L., et al. (2009). Marital conflict and children's externalizing behavior: Interactions between parasympathetic and sympathetic nervous system activity. *Monographs of the Society for Research in Child Development, 74,* 1–69.

El-Sheikh, M., & Whitson, S. A. (2006). Longitudinal relations between marital conflict and child adjustment: Vagal regulation as a protective factor. *Journal of Family Psychology, 20,* 30–39.

Emmen, R. A. G., Malda, M., Mesman, J., Ekmekci, H., & van IJzendoorn, M. H. (2012). Sensitive parenting as a cross-cultural ideal: Sensitivity beliefs of Dutch, Moroccan, and Turkish mothers in the Netherlands. *Attachment and Human Development, 14,* 601–619.

English, D. J., Thompson, R., Graham, J. C., & Briggs, E. C. (2005). Toward a definition of neglect in young children. *Child Maltreatment, 10,* 190–206.

Ensor, R., Marks, A., Jacobs, L., & Hughes, C. (2010). Trajectories of antisocial behavior towards siblings predict antisocial behavior towards peers. *Journal of Child Psychology and Psychiatry, 51,* 1208–1216.

Erdmans, M. P., & Black, T. (2008). What they tell you to forget: From child sexual abuse to adolescent motherhood. *Qualitative Health Research, 18,* 77–89.

Erel, O., & Burman, B. (1995). Interrelatedness of marital relations and parent-child relations: A meta-analytic review. *Psychological Bulletin, 118,* 108–132.

Erich, S., Hall, S. K., Kanenberg, H., & Case, K. (2009). Early and late stage adolescence: Adopted adolescents' attachment to their heterosexual and lesbian/gay parents. *Adoption Quarterly, 12,* 152-170.

Erich, S., Kanenberg, H., Case, K., Allen, T., & Bogdanos, T. (2009). An empirical analysis of factors affecting adolescent attachment in adoptive families with homosexual and straight parents. *Children and Youth Services Review, 31,* 398-404.

Esposito-Smythers, C., Wolff, J., Lemmon, K. M., Bodzy, M., Swenson, R. R., & Spirito, A. (2011). Military youth and the deployment cycle: Emotional health consequences and recommendations for intervention. *Journal of Family Psychology, 25,* 497–507.

Essex, M. J., Boyce, W. T., Hertzman, C., Lam, L. L., Armstrong, J. M., Neumann, S. M. A., & Kobor, M. S. (2013). Epigenetic vestiges of early developmental adversity: Childhood stress exposure and DNA methylation in adolescence. *Child Development, 84,* 58–75.

Estes, L. S., & Tidwell, R. (2002). Sexually abused children's behaviours: Impact of gender and mother's experience of intra- and extra-familial sexual abuse. *Family Practice, 19,* 36–44.

Evans, G. W., & Kim, P. (2013). Childhood poverty, chronic stress, self-regulation, and coping. *Child Development Perspectives, 7,* 43–48.

Evans, G. W., Li, D., & Sepanski Whipple, S. (2013). Cumulative risk and child development. *Psychological Bulletin, 139,* 1342–1396.

Faber, A. J., Willerton, E., Clymer, S. R., MacDermid, S. M., & Weiss, H. M. (2008). Ambiguous absence, ambiguous presence: A qualitative study of military reserve families in wartime. *Journal of Family Psychology, 22,* 222–230.

Fairchild, S. R. (2009). Attachment representations and parental memories of incarcerated fathers. *Child and Adolescent Social Work Journal, 26,* 361–377.

Faith, M. A., Storch, E. A., Roberti, J. W., & Ledley, D. R. (2008). Recalled childhood teasing among non-clinical, non-college adults. *Journal of Psychopathology and Behavioral Assessment, 30,* 171–179.

Fakunmoju, S. B., Bammeke, F. O., Bosiakoh, T. A., Boakye Asante, R. K., Wooten, N. R., Hill, A. C., & Karpman, H. (2013). Perception and determination of child maltreatment: Exploratory comparisons across three countries. *Children and Youth Services Review, 35,* 1418–1430.

Falk, A. E., & Lee, S. S. (2012). Parenting behavior and conduct problems in children with and without attention-deficit/hyperactivity disorder (ADHD): Moderation by callous-unemotional traits. *Journal of Psychopathology and Behavioral Assessment, 34,* 172–181.

Fals-Stewart, W., Golden, J., & Schumacher, J. A. (2003). Intimate partner violence and substance use: A longitudinal day-to-day examination. *Addictive Behaviors, 28*, 1555–1574.

Fang, X., & Corso, P. S. (2007). Child maltreatment, youth violence, and intimate partner violence: Developmental relationships. *American Journal of Preventive Medicine, 33*, 281–290.

Fang, X., & Corso, P. S. (2008). Gender differences in the connections between violence experienced as a child and perpetration of intimate partner violence in young adulthood. *Journal of Family Violence, 23*, 303–313.

Fanti, K. A. (2013). Individual, social, and behavioral factors associated with co-occurring conduct problems and callous-unemotional traits. *Journal of Abnormal Child Psychology, 41*, 811–824.

Fanti, K. A., Demetriou, A. G., & Hawa, V. V. (2012). A longitudinal study of cyberbullying: Examining risk and protective factors. *European Journal of Developmental Psychology, 9*, 168–181.

Fanti, K. A., Frick, P. J., & Georgiou, S. (2009). Linking callous-unemotional traits to instrumental and non-instrumental forms of aggression. *Journal of Psychopathology and Behavioral Assessment, 31*, 285–298.

Fanti, K. A., & Munoz Centifanti, L. C. (2013). Childhood callous-unemotional traits moderate the relation between parenting distress and conduct problems over time. *Child Psychiatry and Human Development, 45*, 173–184.

Fantuzzo, J. W., Perlman, S. M., & Dobbins, E. K. (2011). Types and timing of child maltreatment and early school success: A population-based investigation. *Children and Youth Services Review, 33*, 1404–1411.

Fargo, J. D. (2009). Pathways to adult sexual revictimization: Direct and indirect behavioral risk factors across the lifespan. *Journal of Interpersonal Violence, 24*, 1771–1791.

Farr, R. H., & Patterson, C. J. (2013). Coparenting among lesbian, gay, and heterosexual couples: Associations with adopted children's outcomes. *Child Development, 84*, 1226–1240.

Fassler, I. R., Amodeo, M., Griffin, M. L., Clay, C. M., & Ellis, M. A. (2005). Predicting long-term outcomes for women sexually abused in childhood: Contribution of abuse severity versus family environment. *Child Abuse and Neglect, 29*, 269–284.

Fauchier, A., & Margolin, G. (2004). Affection and conflict in marital and parent-child relationships. *Journal of Marital and Family Therapy, 30*, 197–211.

Faust, J., Kenny, M. C., & Runyon, M. K. (1997). Differences in family functioning of sexually abused vs. nonabused enuretics. *Journal of Family Violence, 12*, 405–416.

Fearon, R. M. P., Bakermans-Kranenburg, M. J., & van IJzendoorn, M. H. (2010). Jealousy and attachment: The case of twins. In S. L. Hart & M.

Legerstee (Eds.), *Handbook of jealousy: Theory, research, and multidisciplinary approaches* (pp. 362–386). New York: Wiley-Blackwell.

Fearon, R. P., Bakermans-Kranenburg, M. J., van IJzendoorn, M. H., Lapsley, A.-M., & Roisman, G. I. (2010). The significance of insecure attachment and disorganization in the development of children's externalizing behavior: A meta-analytic study. *Child Development, 81,* 435–456.

Fearon, R. M. P., & Belsky, J. (2011). Infant-mother attachment and the growth of externalizing problems across the primary-school years. *Journal of Child Psychology and Psychiatry, 52,* 782–791.

Feerick, M. M., & Snow, K. L. (2005). The relationship between childhood sexual abuse, social anxiety, and symptoms of posttraumatic stress disorder in women. *Journal of Family Violence, 20,* 409–419.

Feinauer, L. L., & Stuart, D. A. (1996). Blame and resilience in women sexually abused as children. *American Journal of Family Therapy, 24,* 31–40.

Feinberg, M. E., Jones, D. E., Granger, D. A., & Bontempo, D. (2011). Relation of intimate partner violence to salivary cortisol among couples expecting a first child. *Aggressive Behavior, 37,* 492–502.

Feingold, A., Kerr, D. C. R., & Capaldi, D. M. (2008). Associations of substance use problems with intimate partner violence for at-risk men in long-term relationships. *Journal of Family Psychology, 22,* 429–438.

Feiring, C., Simon, V. A., & Cleland, C. M. (2009). Childhood sexual abuse, stigmatization, internalizing symptoms, and the development of sexual difficulties and dating aggression. *Journal of Consulting and Clinical Psychology, 77,* 127–137.

Feiring, C., Simon, V. A., Cleland, C. M., & Barrett, E. P. (2013). Potential pathways from stigmatization and externalizing behavior to anger and dating aggression in sexually abused youth. *Journal of Clinical Child and Adolescescent Psychology, 42,* 309–322.

Feldman, B. J., Conger, R. D., & Burzette, R. G. (2004). Traumatic events, psychiatric disorders, and pathways of risk and resilience during the transition to adulthood. *Research in Human Development, 1,* 259–290.

Feldman, C. M. (1997). Childhood precursors of adult interpartner violence. *Clinical Psychology: Science and Practice, 4,* 307–334.

Feldman, R., Gordon, I., Schneiderman, I., Weisman, O., & Zagoory-Sharon, O. (2010). Natural variations in maternal and paternal care are associated with systematic changes in oxytocin following parent-infant contact. *Psychoneuroendocrinology, 35,* 1133–1141.

Feldman, R., Gordon, I., & Zagoory-Sharon, O. (2011). Maternal and paternal plasma, salivary, and urinary oxytocin and parent-infant synchrony: Considering stress and affiliation components of human bonding. *Developmental Science, 14,* 752–761.

Fergusson, D. M., Horwood, L. J., & Lynskey, M. R. (1996). Childhood sexual abuse and psychiatric disorder in young adulthood. II. Psychiatric outcomes of childhood sexual abuse. *Journal of the American Academy of Child and Adolescent Psychiatry, 35,* 1365–1374.

Fergusson, D. M., Horwood, L. J., & Ridder, E. M. (2005). "Partner violence and mental health outcomes in a New Zealand birth cohort": Rejoinder. *Journal of Marriage and Family, 67,* 1131–1136.

Figula, E., Margitics, F., Pauwlik, Z., & Szatmari, A. (2011). School bullying: Background factors of the victims, bullies, bully-victims in family socialization. *Mentalhigienees Pszichoszomatika, 12,* 47–72.

Filipas, H. H., & Ullman, S. E. (2006). Child sexual abuse, coping responses, self-blame, posttraumatic stress disorder, and adult sexual revictimization. *Journal of Interpersonal Violence, 21,* 652–672.

Finger, B., Hans, S. L., Bernstein, V. J., & Cox, S. M. (2009). Parent relationship quality and infant-mother attachment. *Attachment and Human Development, 11,* 285–306.

Finger, B., Kachadourian, L. K., Molnar, D. S., Eiden, R. D., Edwards, E. P., & Leonard, K. E. (2010). Alcoholism, associated risk factors, and harsh parenting among fathers: Examining the role of marital aggression. *Addictive Behaviors, 35,* 541–548.

Finkelhor, D., & Browne, A. (1986). The traumatic impact of child sexual abuse: A conceptualization. *Annual Progress in Child Psychiatry and Child Development, 19,* 632–648.

Finkelhor, D., Ormrod, R., Turner, H., & Holt, M. (2009). Pathways to polyvictimization. *Child Maltreatment, 14,* 316–329.

Finkelhor, D., Turner, H., & Ormrod, R. (2006). Kids' stuff: The nature and impact of peer and sibling violence on younger and older children. *Child Abuse and Neglect, 30,* 1401–1421.

Finnegan, R. A., Hodges, E. V. E., & Perry, D. G. (1998). Victimization by peers: Associations with children's reports of mother-child interaction. *Journal of Personality and Social Psychology, 75,* 1076–1086.

Finzi, R., Fam, A., Har-Even, D., Schnit, D., & Weizman, A. (2001). Attachment styles and aggression in physically abused and neglected children. *Journal of Youth and Adolescence, 30,* 769–786.

Fivaz-Depeursinge, E. (2008). Infant's triangular communication in "two for one" versus "two against one" family triangles: Case illustrations. *Infant Mental Health Journal, 29,* 189–202.

Fivaz-Depeursinge, E., & Corboz-Warnery, A. (1999). *The primary triangle: A developmental systems view of mothers, fathers, and infants.* New York: Basic Books.

Fivaz-Depeursinge, E., Frascarolo, F., Lopes, F., Dimitrova, N., & Favez, N.

(2007). Parents-child role reversal in trilogue play: Case studies of trajectories from pregnancy to toddlerhood. *Attachment and Human Development, 9,* 17–31.

Fivaz-Depeursinge, E., Lopes, F., Python, M., & Favez, N. (2009). Coparenting and toddler's interactive styles in family coalitions. *Family Process, 48,* 500–516.

Flake, E. M., Davis, B. E., Johnson, P. L., & Middleton, L. S. (2009). The psychosocial effects of deployment on military children. *Journal of Developmental and Behavioral Pediatrics, 30,* 271–278.

Flores, E., Cicchetti, D., & Rogosch, F. A. (2005). Predictors of resilience in maltreated and nonmaltreated Latino children. *Developmental Psychology, 41,* 338–351.

Flykt, M., Kanninen, K., Sinkkonen, J., & Punamaki, R.-L. (2010). Maternal depression and dyadic interaction: The role of maternal attachment style. *Infant and Child Development, 19,* 530–550.

Follette, V. M., Alexander, P. C., & Follette, W. C. (1991). Individual predictors of outcome in group treatment for incest victims. *Journal of Consulting and Clinical Psychology, 59,* 150–155.

Follette, V. M., Polusny, M. M., & Milbeck, K. (1994). Mental health and law enforcement professionals: Trauma history, psychological symptoms, and impact of providing services to child sexual abuse survivors. *Professional Psychology: Research and Practice, 25,* 275–282.

Fonagy, P. (1999). Male perpetrators of violence against women: An attachment theory perspective. *Journal of Applied Psychoanalytic Studies, 1,* 7–27.

Fonagy, P., & Bateman, A. W. (2007). Mentalizing and borderline personality disorder. *Journal of Mental Health, 16,* 83–101.

Fonagy, P., Leigh, T., Steele, M., Steele, H., Kennedy, R., Mattoon, G., et al. (1996). The relation of attachment status, psychiatric classification, and response to psychotherapy. *Journal of Consulting and Clinical Psychology, 64,* 22–31.

Fonagy, P., Target, M., & Gergely, G. (2000). Attachment and borderline personality disorder: A theory and some evidence. *Psychiatric Clinics of North America, 23,* 103–122.

Fond, G., Franc, N., & Purper-Ouakil, D. (2012). Homosexual parenthood and child development: Present data. *L'Encéphale: Revue de psychiatrie clinique biologique et thérapeutique, 38,* 10–15.

Fontaine, N. M. G., Rijsdijk, F. V., McCrory, E. J. P., & Viding, E. (2010). Etiology of different developmental trajectories of callous-unemotional traits. *Journal of the American Academy of Child and Adolescent Psychiatry, 49,* 656–664.

Ford, J. D. (1999). Disorders of extreme stress following war-zone military trauma: Associated features of posttraumatic stress disorder or comorbid but distinct syndromes? *Journal of Consulting and Clinical Psychology, 67*, 3–12.

Ford, J. D., & Saltzman, W. (2009). Family systems therapy. In C. A. Courtois & J. D. Ford (Eds.), *Treating complex traumatic stress disorders: An evidence-based guide* (pp. 391–414). New York: Guilford.

Ford, J. D., Wasser, T., & Connor, D. F. (2011). Identifying and determining the symptom severity associated with polyvictimization among psychiatrically impaired children in the outpatient setting. *Child Maltreatment, 16*, 216–226.

Foroughe, M. F., & Muller, R. T. (2011). Dismissing (avoidant) attachment and trauma in dyadic parent-child psychotherapy. *Psychological Trauma, 3*, 1–8.

Forsman, M., Lichtenstein, P., Andershed, H., & Larsson, H. (2008). Genetic effects explain the stability of psychopathic personality from mid- to late adolescence. *Journal of Abnormal Psychology, 117*, 606–617.

Fortunato, C. K., Gatzke-Kopp, L. M., & Ram, N. (2013). Associations between respiratory sinus arrhythmia reactivity and internalizing and externalizing symptoms are emotion specific. *Cognitive, Affective and Behavioral Neuroscience, 13*, 238–251.

Fosco, G. M., & Grych, J. H. (2008). Emotional, cognitive, and family systems mediators of children's adjustment to interparental conflict. *Journal of Family Psychology, 22*, 843–854.

Fosco, G. M., & Grych, J. H. (2010). Adolescent triangulation into parental conflicts: Longitudinal implications for appraisals and adolescent-parent relations. *Journal of Marriage and Family, 72*, 254–266.

Foshee, V. A., Bauman, K. E., Arriaga, X. B., Helms, R. W., Koch, G. G., & Linder, G. F. (1998). An evaluation of Safe Dates, an adolescent dating violence prevention program. *American Journal of Public Health, 88*, 45–50.

Foshee, V. A., Benefield, T. S., Ennett, S. T., Bauman, K. E., & Suchindran, C. (2004). Longitudinal predictors of serious physical and sexual dating violence victimization during adolescence. *Preventive Medicine, 39*, 1007–1016.

Foster, H., & Hagan, J. (2007). Incarceration and intergenerational social exclusion. *Social Problems, 54*, 399–433.

Foster, H., & Hagan, J. (2013). Maternal and paternal imprisonment in the stress process. *Social Science Research, 42*, 650–669.

Foster, R. E., Stone, F. P., Linkh, D. J., Besetsny, L. K., Collins, P. S., Saha, T., et al. (2010). Substantiation of spouse and child maltreatment reports as a function of referral source and maltreatment type. *Military Medicine, 175*, 560–565.

Fox, N. A., & Hanes, A. A. (2008). Studying the biology of human attachment. In J. Cassidy & P. R. Shaver (Eds.), *Handbook of attachment: Theory, research and clinical applications* (pp. 217–240). New York: Guilford.

Foynes, M. M., Platt, M., Hall, G. C. N., & Freyd, J. J. (2014). The impact of Asian values and victim–perpetrator closeness on the disclosure of emotional, physical, and sexual abuse. *Psychological Trauma, 6*, 134–141.

Fraedrich, E. M., Lakatos, K., & Spangler, G. (2010). Brain activity during emotion perception: The role of attachment representation. *Attachment and Human Development, 12*, 231–248.

Fraley, R. C. (2002). Attachment stability from infancy to adulthood: Meta-analysis and dynamic modeling of developmental mechanisms. *Personality and Social Psychology Review, 6*, 123–151.

Francisco, M. A., Hicks, K., Powell, J., Styles, K., Tabor, J. L., & Hulton, L. J. (2008). The effect of childhood sexual abuse on adolescent pregnancy: An integrative research review. *Journal for Specialists in Pediatric Nursing, 13*, 237–248.

Franck, K. L., & Buehler, C. (2007). A family process model of marital hostility, parental depressive affect, and early adolescent problem behavior: The roles of triangulation and parental warmth. *Journal of Family Psychology, 21*, 614–626.

Frankenhuis, W. E., & Del Giudice, M. (2012). When do adaptive developmental mechanisms yield maladaptive outcomes? *Developmental Psychology, 48*, 628–642.

Franklin, C. A., & Kercher, G. A. (2012). The intergenerational transmission of intimate partner violence: Differentiating correlates in a random community sample. *Journal of Family Violence, 27*, 187–199.

Freud, S. (1953). Fragment of an analysis of a case of hysteria. In J. Strachey (Ed. and Trans.), *The standard edition of the complete psychological works of Sigmund Freud* (Vol. 7, pp. 1–122). London: Hogarth. (Original work published 1905)

Freyd, J. J. (1996). *Betrayal trauma: The logic of forgetting childhood abuse.* Cambridge, MA: Harvard University Press.

Freyd, J. J., DePrince, A. P., & Zurbriggen, E. L. (2001). Self-reported memory for abuse depends upon victim-perpetrator relationship. *Journal of Trauma and Dissociation, 2*, 5–16.

Freyd, J. J., Klest, B., & Allard, C. B. (2005). Betrayal trauma: Relationship to physical health, psychological distress, and a written disclosure intervention. *Journal of Trauma and Dissociation, 6*, 83–104.

Fridman, A., Bakermans-Kranenburg, M. J., Sagi-Schwartz, A., & van IJzendoorn, M. H. (2011). Coping in old age with extreme childhood trauma: Aging Holocaust survivors and their offspring facing new challenges. *Aging and Mental Health, 15*, 232–242.

Friend, J., Langhinrichsen-Rohling, J., & Eichold II, B. H. (2011). Same-day substance use in men and women charged with felony domestic violence offenses. *Criminal Justice and Behavior, 38,* 619–633.

Friesen, M. D., Woodward, L. J., Horwood, L. J., & Fergusson, D. M. (2010). Childhood exposure to sexual abuse and partnership outcomes at age 30. *Psychological Medicine, 40,* 679–688.

Frigerio, A., Costantino, E., Ceppi, E., & Barone, L. (2013). Adult Attachment Interviews of women from low-risk, poverty, and maltreatment risk samples: Comparisons between the hostile/helpless and traditional AAI coding systems. *Attachment & Human Development, 15,* 424-442.

Fritch, A. M., Mishkind, M., Reger, M. A., & Gahm, G. A. (2010). The impact of childhood abuse and combat-related trauma on postdeployment adjustment. *Journal of Traumatic Stress, 23,* 248–254.

Fritz, P. A. T., Slep, A. M. S., & O'Leary, K. D. (2012). Couple-level analysis of the relation between family-of-origin aggression and intimate partner violence. *Psychology of Violence, 2,* 139–153.

Frosch, C. A., & Mangelsdorf, S. C. (2001). Marital behavior, parenting behavior, and multiple reports of preschoolers' behavior problems: Mediation or moderation? *Developmental Psychology, 37,* 502–519.

Frosch, C. A., Mangelsdorf, S. C., & McHale, J. L. (2000). Marital behavior and the security of preschooler-parent attachment relationships. *Journal of Family Psychology, 14,* 144–161.

Gabalda, M. K., Thompson, M. P., & Kaslow, N. J. (2010). Risk and protective factors for psychological adjustment among low-income, African American children. *Journal of Family Issues, 31,* 423–444.

Gagne, M.-H., Drapeau, S., Melancon, C., Saint-Jacques, M.-C., & Lepine, R. (2007). Links between parental psychological violence, other family disturbances, and children's adjustment. *Family Process, 46,* 523–542.

Gahm, G. A., Lucenko, B. A., Retzlaff, P., & Fukuda, S. (2007). Relative impact of adverse events and screened symptoms of posttraumatic stress disorder and depression among active duty soldiers seeking mental health care. *Journal of Clinical Psychology, 63,* 199–211.

Galatzer-Levy, I. R., Brown, A. D., Henn-Haase, C., Metzler, T. J., Neylan, T. C., & Marmar, C. R. (2013). Positive and negative emotion prospectively predict trajectories of resilience and distress among high-exposure police officers. *Emotion, 13,* 545–553.

Galbaud du Fort, G., Boothroyd, L. J., Bland, R. C., Newman, S. C., & Kakuma, R. (2002). Spouse similarity for antisocial behavior in the general population. *Psychological Medicine, 32,* 1407–1416.

Gall, T. L. (2006). Spirituality and coping with life stress among adult survivors of childhood sexual abuse. *Child Abuse and Neglect, 30,* 829–844.

Galovski, T., & Lyons, J. A. (2004). Psychological sequelae of combat violence: A review of the impact of PTSD on the veteran's family and possible interventions. *Aggression and Violent Behavior, 9,* 477–501.

Gangi, S., Talamo, A., & Ferracuti, S. (2009). The long-term effects of extreme war-related trauma on the second generation of Holocaust survivors. *Violence and Victims, 24,* 687–700.

Garber, B. D. (2011). Parental alienation and the dynamics of the enmeshed parent-child dyad: Adultification, spousification, and infantilization. *Family Court Review, 49,* 322–335.

Gardner, S., Loya, T., & Hyman, C. (2014). Familylive: Parental skill building for caregivers with interpersonal trauma exposures. *Clinical Social Work Journal, 42,* 81–89.

Garvin, M. C., Tarullo, A. R., Ryzin, M. V., & Gunnar, M. R. (2012). Postadoption parenting and socioemotional development in postinstitutionalized children. *Development and Psychopathology, 24,* 35–48.

Gaudineau, A., Ehlinger, V., Vayssiere, C., Jouret, B., Arnaud, C., & Godeau, E. (2010). Factors associated with early menarche: Results from the French Health Behaviour in School-aged Children (HBSC) study. *BMC Public Health, 10,* 175.

Gehrke, A., & Violanti, J. M. (2006). Gender differences and posttraumatic stress disorder: The role of trauma type and frequency of exposure. *Traumatology, 12,* 229–235.

Geller, A., Garfinkel, I., Cooper, C. E., & Mincy, R. B. (2009). Parental incarceration and child well-being: Implications for urban families. *Social Science Quarterly, 90,* 1186–1202.

George, C., & Solomon, J. (2008). The caregiving system: A behavioral systems approach to parenting. In J. Cassidy & P. R. Shaver (Eds.), *Handbook of attachment: Theory, research, and clinical applications* (2nd ed., pp. 833–856). New York: Guilford.

George, C., & Solomon, J. (2011). Caregiving helplessness: The development of a screening measure for disorganized maternal caregiving. In J. Solomon & C. George (Eds.), *Disorganized attachment and caregiving* (pp. 133–166). New York: Guilford.

Gerard, J. M., Krishnakumar, A., & Buehler, C. (2006). Marital conflict, parent-child relations, and youth maladjustment: A longitudinal investigation of spillover effects. *Journal of Family Issues, 27,* 951–975.

Gershon, R. R. M., Barocas, B., Canton, A. N., Li, X., & Vlahov, D. (2009). Mental, physical, and behavioral outcomes associated with perceived work stress in police officers. *Criminal Justice and Behavior, 36,* 275–289.

Gervai, J., Novak, A., Lakatos, K., Toth, I., Danis, I., Ronai, Z., et al. (2007). Infant genotype may moderate sensitivity to maternal affective communications: Attachment disorganization, quality of care, and the DRD4 polymorphism. *Social Neuroscience, 2,* 307–319.

Gewirtz, A. H., Erbes, C. R., Polusny, M. A., Forgatch, M. S., & DeGarmo, D. S. (2011). Helping military families through the deployment process: Strategies to support parenting. *Professional Psychology, 42,* 56–62.

Gewirtz, A. H., Polusny, M. A., DeGarmo, D. S., Khaylis, A., & Erbes, C. R. (2010). Posttraumatic stress symptoms among National Guard soldiers deployed to Iraq: Associations with parenting behaviors and couple adjustment. *Journal of Consulting and Clinical Psychology, 78,* 599–610.

Ghiassi, V., Dimaggio, G., & Brune, M. (2010). Dysfunctions in understanding other minds in borderline personality disorder: A study using cartoon pictures stories. *Psychotherapy Research, 20,* 657–667.

Gibbons, F. X., Roberts, M. E., Gerrard, M., Li, Z., Beach, S. R. H., Simons, R. L., et al. (2012). The impact of stress on the life history strategies of African American adolescents: Cognitions, genetic moderation, and the role of discrimination. *Developmental Psychology, 48,* 722–739.

Gibbs, D. A., Martin, S. L., Clinton-Sherrod, M., Walters, J. L. H., & Johnson, R. E. (2011). Child maltreatment within military families. In S. M. Wadsworth & D. Riggs (Eds.), *Risk and resilience in U.S. military families* (pp. 111–130). New York: Springer Science + Business Media.

Gibbs, D. A., Martin, S. L., Kupper, L. L., & Johnson, R. E. (2007). Child maltreatment in enlisted soldiers' families during combat-related deployments. *JAMA, 298,* 528–535.

Giladi, L., & Bell, T. S. (2013). Protective factors for intergenerational transmission of trauma among second and third generation Holocaust survivors. *Psychological Trauma, 5,* 384–391.

Gilissen, R., Bakermans-Kranenburg, M. J., van IJzendoorn, M. H., & Linting, M. (2008). Electrodermal reactivity during the Trier Social Stress Test for Children: Interaction between the serotonin transporter polymorphism and children's attachment representation. *Developmental Psychobiology, 50,* 615–625.

Gladstone, G. L., Parker, G. B., & Malhi, G. S. (2006). Do bullied children become anxious and depressed adults? A cross-sectional investigation of the correlates of bullying and anxious depression. *Journal of Nervous and Mental Disease, 194,* 201–208.

Glaesmer, H., Reichmann-Radulescu, A., Brahler, E., Kuwert, P., & Muhtz, C. (2011). Transgenerational trauma transmission: Traumatic experiences from World War II in Germany. *Trauma und Gewalt, 5,* 330–343.

Glasser, M., Kolvin, I., Campbell, D., Glasser, A., Leitch, I., & Farrelly, S. (2001). Cycle of child sexual abuse: Links between being a victim and becoming a perpetrator. *British Journal of Psychiatry, 179,* 482–494.

Gleason, M. M., Fox, N. A., Drury, S., Smyke, A., Egger, H. L., Nelson III, C. A., et al. (2011). Validity of evidence-derived criteria for reactive attachment disorder: Indiscriminately social/disinhibited and emotionally withdrawn/inhibited types. *Journal of the American Academy of Child and Adolescent Psychiatry, 50,* 216–231.

Gleiser, K., Ford, J. D., & Fosha, D. (2008). Contrasting exposure and experiential therapies for complex posttraumatic stress disorder. *Psychotherapy: Theory, Research, Practice, Training, 45,* 340–360.

Glenn, D. M., Beckham, J. C., Feldman, M. E., Kirby, A. C., Hertzberg, M. A., & Moore, S. D. (2002). Violence and hostility among families of Vietnam veterans with combat-related posttraumatic stress disorder. *Violence and Victims, 17,* 473–489.

Glover, M. B., Mullineaux, P. Y., Deater-Deckard, K., & Petrill, S. A. (2010). Parents' feelings towards their adoptive and non-adoptive children. *Infant and Child Development, 19,* 238–251.

Glover, V. (2011). Annual research review: Prenatal stress and the origins of psychopathology: An evolutionary perspective. *Journal of Child Psychology and Psychiatry, 52,* 356–367.

Gobin, R. L., & Freyd, J. J. (2009). Betrayal and revictimization: Preliminary findings. *Psychological Trauma, 1,* 242–257.

Godbout, N., Lussier, Y., & Sabourin, S. (2006). Early abuse experiences and subsequent gender differences in couple adjustment. *Violence and Victims, 21,* 744–760.

Godbout, N., Sabourin, S., & Lussier, Y. (2007). The relation between sexual abuse undergone during childhood and male marital satisfaction. *Canadian Journal of Behavioural Science, 39,* 46–59.

Gojman, S., Millan, S., Carlson, E., Sanchez, G., Rodarte, A., Gonzalez, P., & Hernandez, G. (2012). Intergenerational relations of attachment: A research synthesis of urban/rural Mexican samples. *Attachment and Human Development, 14,* 553–566.

Gold, J. I., Taft, C. T., Keehn, M. G., King, D. W., Kind, L. A., & Samper, R. E. (2007). PTSD symptom severity and family adjustment among female Vietnam veterans. *Military Psychology, 19,* 71–81.

Goldberg, A. E., & Smith, J. Z. (2013). Predictors of psychological adjustment in early placed adopted children with lesbian, gay, and heterosexual parents. *Journal of Family Psychology, 27,* 431–442.

Goldberg, A. E., & Smith, J. Z. (2014). Predictors of parenting stress in lesbian, gay, and heterosexual adoptive parents during early parenthood. *Journal of Family Psychology, 28,* 125–137.

Goldberg, S., Benoit, D., Blokland, K., & Madigan, S. (2003). Atypical maternal behavior, maternal representations, and infant disorganized attachment. *Development and Psychopathology, 15,* 239–257.

Goldstein, S. E., Chesir-Teran, D., & McFaul, A. (2008). Profiles and correlates of relational aggression in young adults' romantic relationships. *Journal of Youth and Adolescence, 37,* 251–265.

Goldwyn, R., & Hugh-Jones, S. (2011). Using the Adult Attachment Interview to understand reactive attachment disorder: Findings from a 10-case adolescent sample. *Attachment and Human Development, 13,* 169–191.

Golier, J. A., Caramanica, K., & Yehuda, R. (2012). Neuroendocrine response to CRF stimulation in veterans with and without PTSD in consideration of war zone era. *Psychoneuroendocrinology, 37,* 350–357.

Golinelli, D., Longshore, D., & Wenzel, S. L. (2009). Substance use and intimate partner violence: Clarifying the relevance of women's use and partners' use. *Journal of Behavioral Health Services and Research, 36,* 199–211.

Golombok, S., Mellish, L., Jennings, S., Casey, P., Tasker, F., & Lamb, M. E. (2014). Adoptive gay father families: Parent–child relationships and children's psychological adjustment. *Child Development, 85,* 456–468.

Gomez, E., Munoz, M. M., & Haz, A. M. (2007). Multiproblem families at social risk: Characteristics and intervention. *Psykhe, 16,* 43–54.

Goodman, G., Bartlett, R. C., & Stroh, M. (2013). Mothers' borderline features and children's disorganized attachment representations as predictors of children's externalizing behavior. *Psychoanalytic Psychology, 30,* 16–36.

Goodyear, R. K., Newcomb, M. D., & Locke, T. F. (2002). Pregnant Latina teenagers: Psychosocial and developmental determinants of how they select and perceive the men who father their children. *Journal of Counseling Psychology, 49,* 187–201.

Gordis, E. B., Feres, N., Olezeski, C. L., Rabkin, A. N., Ari, N., & Trickett, P. K. (2010). Skin conductance reactivity and respiratory sinus arrhythmia among maltreated and comparison youth: Relations with aggressive behavior. *Journal of Pediatric Psychology, 35,* 547–558.

Gordis, E. B., Granger, D. A., Susman, E. J., & Trickett, P. K. (2006). Asymmetry between salivary cortisol and α-amylase reactivity to stress: Relation to aggressive behavior in adolescents. *Psychoneuroendocrinology, 31,* 976–987.

Gordis, E. B., Granger, D. A., Susman, E. J., & Trickett, P. K. (2008). Salivary alpha amylase-cortisol asymmetry in maltreated youth. *Hormones and Behavior, 53,* 96–103.

Gordon, I., Zagoory-Sharon, O., Leckman, J. F., & Feldman, R. (2010). Oxytocin and the development of parenting in humans. *Biological Psychiatry, 68,* 377–382.

Gover, A. R., Kaukinen, C., & Fox, K. A. (2008). The relationship between violence in the family of origin and dating violence among college students. *Journal of Interpersonal Violence, 23,* 1667–1693.

Govorko, D., Bekdash, R. A., Zhang, C., & Sarkar, D. K. (2012). Male germline transmits fetal alcohol adverse effect on hypothalamic proopiomelanocortin gene across generations. *Biological Psychiatry, 72,* 378–388.

Gowin, J. L., Green, C. E., Alcom III, J. L., Swann, A. C., Moeller, F. G., & Lane, S. D. (2013). The role of cortisol and psychopathy in the cycle of violence. *Psychopharmacology, 227,* 661–672.

Graham, A. M., Yockelson, M., Kim, H. K., Bruce, J., Pears, K. C., & Fisher, P. A. (2012). Effects of maltreatment and early intervention on diurnal cortisol slope across the start of school: A pilot study. *Child Abuse and Neglect, 36,* 666–670.

Graham, N., Kimonis, E. R., Wasserman, A. L., & Kline, S. M. (2012). Associations among childhood abuse and psychopathy facets in male sexual offenders. *Personality Disorders: Theory, Research, and Treatment, 3,* 66–75.

Granot, D., & Mayseless, O. (2012). Representations of mother-child attachment relationships and social-information processing of peer relationships in early adolescence. *Journal of Early Adolescence, 32,* 537–564.

Granqvist, P., Mikulincer, M., & Shaver, P. R. (2010). Religion as attachment: Normative processes and individual differences. *Personality and Social Psychology Review, 14,* 49–59.

Gratz, K. L., Paulson, A., Jakupcak, M., & Tull, M. T. (2009). Exploring the relationship between childhood maltreatment and intimate partner abuse: Gender differences in the mediating role of emotion dysregulation. *Violence and Victims, 24,* 68–82.

Gray, H. M., & Foshee, V. (1997). Adolescent dating violence: Differences between one-sided and mutually violent profiles. *Journal of Interpersonal Violence, 12,* 126–141.

Green Jr., H. D., Tucker, J. S., Wenzel, S. L., Golinelli, D., Kennedy, D. P., Ryan, G. W., & Zhou, A. J. (2012). Association of childhood abuse with homeless women's social networks. *Child Abuse and Neglect, 36,* 21–31.

Green, J., Stanley, C., & Peters, S. (2007). Disorganized attachment representation and atypical parenting in young school age children with externalizing disorder. *Attachment and Human Development, 9,* 207–222.

Green, R.-J., & Werner, P. D. (1996). Intrusiveness and closeness-caregiving: Rethinking the concept of family enmeshment. *Family Process, 35,* 115–136.

Greenfield, E. A., & Marks, N. F. (2010). Sense of community as a protective factor against long-term psychological effects of childhood violence. *Social Service Review, 84,* 129–147.

Grice, H. P. (1975). Logic and conversation. In D. Davidson & G. Harman (Eds.), *The logic of grammar* (pp. 64–153). Encino, CA: Dickinson.

Griffee, K., O'Keefe, S. L., Stroebel, S. S., Beard, K. W., Swindell, S., & Young D. H. (2012). On the brink of paradigm change? Evidence for unexpected predictive relationships among sexual addiction, masturbation, sexual experimentation, and revictimization, child sexual abuse, and adult sexual risk. *Sexual Addiction and Compulsivity, 19,* 225–264.

Griffing, S., Ragin, D. F., Sage, R. E., Madry, L., Bingham, L. E., & Primm, B. J. (2002). Domestic violence survivors' self-identified reasons for returning to abusive relationships. *Journal of Interpersonal Violence, 17,* 306–319.

Groark, C. J., McCall, R. B., & Fish, L. (2011). Characteristics of environments, caregivers, and children in three Central American orphanages. *Infant Mental Health Journal, 32,* 232–250.

Groh, A. M., & Roisman, G. I. (2009). Adults' autonomic and subjective emotional responses to infant vocalizations: The role of secure base script knowledge. *Developmental Psychology, 45,* 889–893.

Groh, A. M., Roisman, G. I., van IJzendoorn, M. H., Bakermans-Kranenburg, M. J., & Fearon, R. P. (2012). The significance of insecure and disorganized attachment for children's internalizing symptoms: A meta-analytic study. *Child Development, 83,* 591–610.

Grossman, F. K., Sorsoli, L., & Kia-Keating, M. (2006). A gale force wind: Meaning making by male survivors of childhood sexual abuse. *American Journal of Orthopsychiatry, 76,* 434–443.

Grossmann, K. E., Grossmann, K., & Keppler, A. (2005). Universal and culture-specific aspects of human behavior: The case of attachment. In W. Friedlmeier, P. Chakkarath, & B. Schwarz (Eds.), *Culture and human development: The importance of cross-cultural research for the social sciences* (pp. 75–97). Hove, England: Psychology Press/Erlbaum.

Guille, L. (2004). Men who batter and their children: An integrated review. *Aggression and Violent Behavior, 9,* 129–163.

Guinn, J. (2013). *Manson: The life and times of Charles Manson.* New York: Simon and Schuster.

Gullon-Rivera, A. L. (2013). Puerto Rican kindergartners' self-worth as coded from the Attachment Story Completion Task: Correlated with other self-evaluation measures and ratings of child behavior toward mothers and peers. *Attachment and Human Development, 15,* 1–23.

Gunderson, J. G., & Lyons-Ruth, K. (2008). BPD's interpersonal hypersensitivity phenotype: A gene-environment-developmental model. *Journal of Personality Disorders, 22,* 22–41.

Gunnar, M. R., Wenner, J. A., Thomas, K. M., Glatt, C. E., McKenna, M. C., & Clark, A. G. (2012). The brain-derived neurotrophic factor Val66Met polymorphism moderates early deprivation effects on attention problems. *Development and Psychopathology, 24,* 1215–1223.

Gustafsson, H. C., Cox, M. J., & Blair, C. (2012). Maternal parenting as a mediator of the relationship between intimate partner violence and effortful control. *Journal of Family Psychology, 26,* 115–123.

Guterman, N. B., Lee, Y., Lee, S. J., Waldfogel, J., & Rathouz, P. J. (2009). Fathers and maternal risk for physical child abuse. *Child Maltreatment, 14,* 277–290.

Haapasalo, J. (2000). Childhood maltreatment, behavior problems and adult psychiatric disorders: A trauma and attachment theory perspective. *Psykologia, 35,* 45–57.

Hackman, D. A., Betancourt, L. M., Brodsky, N. L., Hurt, H., & Farah, M. J. (2012). Neighborhood disadvantage and adolescent stress reactivity. *Frontiers in Human Neuroscience, 6,* Article 277.

Hadley, J. A., Holloway, E. L., & Mallinckrodt, B. (1993). Common aspects of object relations and self-representations in offspring from disparate dysfunctional families. *Journal of Counseling Psychology, 40,* 348–356.

Hall, J. M., Roman, M. W., Thomas, S. P., Travis, C. B., Powell, J., Tennison, C. R., et al. (2009). Thriving as becoming resolute in narratives of women surviving childhood maltreatment. *American Journal of Orthopsychiatry, 79,* 375–386.

Hamberger, L. K., Lohr, J. M., Bonge, D., & Tolin, D. F. (1996). A large sample empirical typology of male spouse abusers and its relationship to dimensions of abuse. *Violence and Victims, 11,* 277–292.

Hamel, J. (2005). *Gender-inclusive treatment of intimate partner abuse: A comprehensive approach.* New York: Springer.

Hamilton-Giachritsis, C. E., & Browne, K. D. (2005). A retrospective study of risk to siblings in abusing families. *Journal of Family Psychology, 19,* 619–624.

Harari, D., Bakermans-Kranenburg, M. J., de Kloet, C. S., Geuze, E., Vermetten, E., Westenberg, H. G. M., & van IJzendoorn, M. H. (2009). Attachment representations in Dutch veterans with and without deployment-related PTSD. *Attachment and Human Development, 11,* 515–536.

Hardaway, C. R., Wilson, M. N., Shaw, D. S., & Dishion, T. J. (2012). Family functioning and externalizing behavior among low-income children: Self-regulation as a mediator. *Infant and Child Development, 21,* 67–84.

Harden, K. P. (2014). Genetic influences on adolescent sexual behavior: Why genes matter for environmentally oriented researchers. *Psychological Bulletin, 140,* 434–465.

Hardy, M. S. (2001). Physical aggression and sexual behavior among siblings: A retrospective study. *Journal of Family Violence, 16,* 255–268.

Hare, A. L., Miga, E. M., & Allen, J. P. (2009). Intergenerational transmission of aggression in romantic relationships: The moderating role of attachment security. *Journal of Family Psychology, 23,* 808–818.

Harel, J., & Scher, A. (2003). Insufficient responsiveness in ambivalent mother-infant relationships: Contextual and affective aspects. *Infant Behavior and Development, 26*, 371–383.

Harkness, K. L., Stewart, J. G., & Wynne-Edwards, K. E. (2011). Cortisol reactivity to social stress in adolescents: Role of depression severity and child maltreatment. *Psychoneuroendocrinology, 36*, 173–181.

Harned, M. S. (2001). Abused women or abused men? An examination of the context and outcomes of dating violence. *Violence and Victims, 16*, 269–285.

Harold, G. T., Leve, L. D., Elam, K. K., Thapar, A., Neiderhiser, J. M., Natsuaki, M. N., et al. (2013). The nature of nurture: Disentangling passive genotype-environment correlation from family relationship influences on children's externalizing problems. *Journal of Family Psychology, 27*, 12–21.

Harwood, I. (2006). Head Start is too late: Integrating and applying infant observation studies, and attachment, trauma, and neurobiological research to groups with pregnant and new mothers. *International Journal of Group Psychotherapy, 56*, 5–28.

Hassija, C. M., Jakupcak, M., Maguen, S., & Shipherd, J. C. (2012). The influence of combat and interpersonal trauma on PTSD, depression, and alcohol misuse in U.S. Gulf War and OEF/OIF women veterans. *Journal of Traumatic Stress, 25*, 216–219.

Hawes, D. J., Dadds, M. R., Frost, A. D. J., & Hasking, P. A. (2011). Do childhood callous-unemotional traits drive change in parenting practices? *Journal of Clinical Child and Adolescent Psychology, 40*, 507–518.

Haydon, K. C., Roisman, G. I., & Burt, K. B. (2012). In search of security: The latent structure of the Adult Attachment Interview revisited. *Development and Psychopathology, 24*, 589–606.

Hazen, N. L., Jacobvitz, D., Higgins, K. N., Allen, S., & Jin, M. K. (2011). Pathways from disorganized attachment to later social-emotional problems: The role of gender and parent-child interaction patterns. In J. Solomon & C. George (Eds.), *Disorganized attachment and caregiving* (pp. 167–206). New York: Guilford.

Hazen, N., Jacobvitz, D., & McFarland, L. (2005). Antecedents of boundary disturbances in families with young children: Intergenerational transmission and parent-infant caregiving patterns. *Journal of Emotional Abuse, 5*, 85–110.

Hebert, M., Collin-Vezina, D., Daigneault, I., Parent, N., & Tremblay, C. (2006). Factors linked to outcomes in sexually abused girls: A regression tree analysis. *Comprehensive Psychiatry, 47*, 443–455.

Hebert, M., Tremblay, C., Parent, N., Daignault, I. V., & Piche, C. (2006). Correlates of behavioral outcomes in sexually abused children. *Journal of Family Violence, 21*, 287–299.

Heins, M., Simons, C., Lataster, T., Pfeifer, S., Versmissen, D., Lardinois, M., et al. (2011). Childhood trauma and psychosis: A case-control and case-sibling comparison across different levels of genetic liability, psychopathology, and type of trauma. *American Journal of Psychiatry, 168*, 1286–1294.

Hendy, H. M., Weiner, K., Bakerofskie, J., Eggen, D., Gustitus, C., & McLeod, K. C. (2003). Comparison of six models for violent romantic relationships in college men and women. *Journal of Interpersonal Violence, 18*, 645–665.

Hennighausen, K. H., Bureau, J.-F., David, D. H., Holmes, B. M., & Lyons-Ruth, K. (2011). Disorganized attachment behavior observed in adolescence: Validation in relation to Adult Attachment Interview classifications at age 25. In J. Solomon & C. George (Eds.), *Disorganized attachment and caregiving* (pp. 207–244). New York: Guilford.

Herer, Y., & Mayseless, O. (2000). Emotional and social adjustment of adolescents who show role-reversal in the family. *Megamot, 40*, 413–441.

Herman, J. L. (1992). *Trauma and recovery.* New York: Basic Books.

Hermans, E. J., Ramsey, N. F., & van Honk, J. (2008). Exogenous testosterone enhances responsiveness to social threat in the neural circuitry of social aggression in humans. *Biological Psychiatry, 63*, 263–270.

Herrenkohl, T. I., Catalano, R. F., Hemphill, S. A., & Toumbourou, J. W. (2009). Longitudinal examination of physical and relational aggression as precursors to later problem behaviors in adolescents. *Violence and Victims, 24*, 3–19.

Hesse, E., & Main, M. (1999). Second generation effects of unresolved trauma in nonmaltreating parents: Dissociated, frightening, and threatening parental behavior. *Psychoanalytic Inquiry, 19*, 481–540.

Hesse, E., & Main, M. (2006). Frightened, threatening and dissociative parental behavior in low-risk samples: Description, discussion, and interpretations. *Development and Psychopathology, 18*, 309–343.

Hetzel, M. D., & McCanne, T. R. (2005). The roles of peritraumatic dissociation, child physical abuse, and child sexual abuse in the development of posttraumatic stress disorder and adult victimization. *Child Abuse and Neglect, 29*, 915–930.

Heyman, R. E., & Slep, A. M. S. (2002). Do child abuse and interparental violence lead to adulthood family violence? *Journal of Marriage and Family, 64*, 864–870.

Hicks, B. M., Johnson, W., Durbin, C. E., Blonigen, D. M., Iacono, W. G., & McGue, M. (2013). Gene-environment correlation in the development of adolescent substance abuse: Selection effects of child personality and mediation via contextual risk factors. *Development and Psychopathology, 25*, 119–132.

Higgins, D. J. (2004). The importance of degree versus type of maltreatment: A cluster analysis of child abuse types. *Journal of Psychology: Interdisciplinary and Applied, 138,* 303–324.

Hilburn-Cobb, C. (2004). Adolescent psychopathology in terms of multiple behavioral systems: The role of attachment and controlling strategies and frankly disorganized behavior. In L. Atkinson & S. Goldberg (Eds.), *Attachment issues in psychopathology and intervention* (pp. 95–135). Mahwah, NJ: Lawrence Erlbaum.

Hildyard, K. L., & Wolfe, D. A. (2002). Child neglect: Developmental issues and outcomes. *Child Abuse and Neglect, 26,* 679–695.

Hill, A. (2003). Issues facing brothers of sexually abused children: Implications for professional practice. *Child and Family Social Work, 8,* 281–290.

Hill, R. (1949). *Families under stress: Adjustment to the crises of war separation and return.* Oxford: Harper.

Hilt, L. M., Cha, C. B., & Nolen-Hoeksema, S. (2008). Nonsuicidal self-injury in young adolescent girls: Moderators of the distress-function relationship. *Journal of Consulting and Clinical Psychology, 76,* 63–71.

Himelein, M. J., & McElrath, J. V. (1996). Resilient child sexual abuse survivors: Cognitive coping and illusion. *Child Abuse and Neglect, 20,* 747–758.

Hines, D. A., Kantor, G. K., & Holt, M. K. (2006). Similarities in siblings' experiences of neglectful parenting behaviors. *Child Abuse and Neglect, 30,* 619–637.

Hines, D. A., & Saudino, K. J. (2009). Psychological and physical aggression in couples: Causes and interventions. In K. D. O'Leary & E. M. Woodin (Eds.), *Psychological and physical aggression in couples: Causes and interventions* (pp. 141–162). Washington, DC: American Psychological Association.

Hodgins, G. A., Creamer, M., & Bell, R. (2001). Risk factors for posttrauma reactions in police officers: A longitudinal study. *Journal of Nervous and Mental Disease, 189,* 541–547.

Hoffman, K. L., Kiecolt, K. J., & Edwards, J. N. (2005). Physical violence between siblings: A theoretical and empirical analysis. *Journal of Family Issues, 26,* 1103–1130.

Holt, M. K., Finkelhor, D., & Kantor, G. K. (2007). Hidden forms of victimization in elementary students involved in bullying. *School Psychology Review, 36,* 345–360.

Holt, M. K., Kantor, G. K., & Finkelhor, D. (2009). Parent-child concordance about bullying involvement and family characteristics related to bullying and peer victimization. *Journal of School Violence, 8,* 42–63.

Holtzworth-Munroe, A. (1992). Social skill deficits in maritally violent men: Interpreting the data using a social information-processing model. *Clinical Psychology Review, 12,* 605–617.

Holtzworth-Munroe, A., & Hutchinson, G. (1993). Attributing negative intent to wife behavior: The attributions of maritally violent versus nonviolent men. *Journal of Abnormal Psychology, 102,* 206–211.

Holtzworth-Munroe, A., & Meehan, J. C. (2004). Typologies of men who are maritally violent: Scientific and clinical implications. *Journal of Interpersonal Violence, 19,* 1369–1389.

Holtzworth-Munroe, A., Meehan, J. C., Herron, K., Rehman, U., & Stuart, G. L. (2000). Testing the Holtzworth-Munroe and Stuart (1994) batterer typology. *Journal of Consulting and Clinical Psychology, 68,* 1000–1019.

Holtzworth-Munroe, A., Meehan, J. C., Herron, K., Rehman, U., & Stuart, G. L. (2003). Do subtypes of maritally violent men continue to differ over time? *Journal of Consulting and Clinical Psychology, 71,* 728–740.

Holtzworth-Munroe, A., & Stuart, G. L. (1994). Typologies of male batterers: Three subtypes and the differences among them. *Psychological Bulletin, 116,* 476–497.

Holtzworth-Munroe, A., Stuart, G. L., & Hutchinson, G. (1997). Violent versus nonviolent husbands: Differences in attachment patterns, dependency, and jealousy. *Journal of Family Psychology, 11,* 314–331.

Homma, Y., Wang, N., Waewyc, E., & Kishor, N. (2011). The relationship between sexual abuse and risky sexual behavior among adolescent boys: A meta-analysis. *Journal of Adolescent Health, 51,* 18–24.

Hompes, T., Izzi, B., Gellens, E., Morreels, M., Fieuws, S., Pexsters, A., et al. (2013). Investigating the influence of maternal cortisol and emotional state during pregnancy on the DNA methylation status of the glucocorticoid receptor gene (nr3c1) promoter region in cord blood. *Journal of Psychiatric Research, 47,* 880–891.

Hong, J. S., Espelage, D. L., Grogan-Kaylor, A., & Allen-Meares, P. (2012). Identifying potential mediators and moderators of the association between child maltreatment and bullying perpetration and victimization in school. *Educational Psychology Review, 24,* 167–186.

Hooper, C.-A., & Koprowska, J. (2004). The vulnerabilities of children whose parents have been sexually abused in childhood: Towards a new framework. *British Journal of Social Work, 34,* 165–180.

Howes, P. W., Cicchetti, D., Toth, S. L., & Rogosch, F. A. (2000). Affective, organizational and relational characteristics of maltreating families: A systems perspective. *Journal of Family Psychology, 14,* 95–110.

Howes, C., Vu, J. A., & Hamilton, C. (2011). Mother-child attachment representation and relationships over time in Mexican-heritage families. *Journal of Research in Childhood Education, 25,* 228–247.

Huebner, B. M., & Gustafson, R. (2007). The effect of maternal incarceration on adult offspring involvement in the criminal justice system. *Journal of Criminal Justice, 35,* 283–296.

Hughes, P., Turton, P., Hopper, E., McGauley, G. A., & Fonagy, P. (2001). Disorganised attachment behavior among infants born subsequent to stillbirth. *Journal of Child Psychology and Psychiatry, 42,* 791–801.

Hughes, P., Turton, P., Hopper, E., McGauley, G. A., & Fonagy, P. (2004). Factors associated with the unresolved classification of the Adult Attachment Interview in women who have suffered stillbirth. *Development and Psychopathology, 16,* 215–230.

Hughes, P., Turton, P., McGauley, G. A., & Fonagy, P. (2006). Factors that predict infant disorganization in mothers classified as U in pregnancy. *Attachment and Human Development, 8,* 113–122.

Hulette, A. C., Kaehler, L. A., & Freyd, J. J. (2011). Intergenerational associations between trauma and dissociation. *Journal of Family Violence, 26,* 217–225.

Hutchinson, K. C., Moore, G. A., Propper, C. B., & Manaskin, A. (2008). Incarcerated women's psychological functioning during pregnancy. *Psychology of Women Quarterly, 32,* 440–453.

Huth-Bocks, A., Krause, K., Ahlfs-Dunn, S., Gallagher, E., & Scott, S. (2013). Relational trauma and posttraumatic stress symptoms among pregnant women. *Psychodynamic Psychiatry, 41,* 277–301.

Huth-Bocks, A. C., Levendosky, A. A., Theran, S. A., & Bogat, G. A. (2004). The impact of domestic violence on mothers' prenatal representations of their infants. *Infant Mental Health Journal, 25,* 79–98.

Huth-Bocks, A. C., Theran, S. A., Levendosky, A. A., & Bogat, C. A. (2011). A social-contextual understanding of concordance and discordance between maternal prenatal representations of the infant and infant-mother attachment. *Infant Mental Health Journal, 32,* 405–426.

Iliceto, P., Candilera, G., Funaro, D., Pompili, M., Kaplan, K. J., & Markus-Kaplan, M. (2012). Hopelessness, temperament, anger and interpersonal relationships in Holocaust (Shoah) survivors' grandchildren. *Journal of Religion and Health, 51,* 233–234.

International Society for the Prevention of Child Abuse and Neglect (ISPCAN). (2008). *World Perspectives On Child Abuse* (8th ed.).Aurora, CO: Author.

Ireland, J. L., & Power, C. L. (2004). Attachment, emotional loneliness, and bullying behavior: A study of adult and young offenders. *Aggressive Behavior, 30,* 298–312.

Iversen, A. C., Fear, N. T., Ehlers, A., Hughes, J. H., Hull, L., Earnshaw, M., et al. (2008). Risk factors for post-traumatic stress disorder among UK Armed Forces personnel. *Psychological Medicine, 38,* 511–522.

Iverson, K. M., Mercado, R., Carpenter, S. L., & Street, A. E. (2013). Intimate partner violence among women veterans: Previous interpersonal violence as a risk factor. *Journal of Traumatic Stress, 26*, 767–771.

Izard, C., & Kobak, R. (1991). Emotion system functioning and emotion regulation. In J. Garber & K. Dodge (Eds.), *The development of affect regulation* (pp. 303–321). Cambridge: Cambridge University Press.

Jackson, N. A. (2007). Same-sex domestic violence: Myths, facts, correlates, treatment, and prevention strategies. In A. R. Roberts (Ed.), *Battered women and their families: Intervention strategies and treatment programs (3rd Ed.)* (pp. 451–470). New York: Springer Publishing.

Jacobvitz, D., Curran, M., & Moller, N. (2002). Measurement of adult attachment: The place of self-report and interview methodologies. *Attachment and Human Development, 4*, 207–215.

Jacobvitz, D., & Hazen, N. (1999). Developmental pathways from infant disorganization to childhood peer relationships. In J. Solomon & C. George (Eds.), *Attachment disorganization* (pp. 127–159). New York: Guilford.

Jacobvitz, D., Hazen, N., Curran, M., & Hitchens, K. (2004). Observations of early triadic family interactions: Boundary disturbances in the family predict symptoms of depression, anxiety, and attention-deficit/hyperactivity disorder in middle childhood. *Development and Psychopathology, 16*, 577–592.

Jacobvitz, D., Hazen, N., & Riggs, S. (1997, April). Disorganized mental processes in mothers, frightening/frightened caregiving, and disoriented/disorganized behavior in infancy. Paper presented at the biennial meeting of the Society for Research in Child Development, Washington, DC.

Jacobvitz, D., Leon, K., & Hazen, N. (2006). Does expectant mothers' unresolved trauma predict frightened/frightening maternal behavior? Risk and protective factors. *Development and Psychopathology, 18*, 363–379.

Jaffee, S. R., Caspi, A., Moffitt, T. E., Polo-Tomas, M., & Taylor, A. (2007). Individual, family, and neighborhood factors distinguish resilient from non-resilient maltreated children: A cumulative stressors model. *Child Abuse and Neglect, 31*, 231–253.

Jakupcak, M., Conybeare, D., Phelps, L., Hunt, S., Holmes, H. A., Felker, B., et al. (2007). Anger, hostility, and aggression among Iraq and Afghanistan war veterans reporting PTSD and subthreshold PTSD. *Journal of Traumatic Stress, 20*, 945–954.

James, J., Ellis, B. J., Schlomer, G. L., & Garber, J. (2012). Sex-specific pathways to early puberty, sexual debut, and sexual risk taking: Tests of an integrated evolutionary-developmental model. *Developmental Psychology, 48*, 687–702.

Jaycox, L. H., McCaffrey, D., Eiseman, B., Aronoff, J., Shelley, G. A., Collins, R. L., & Marshall, G. N. (2006). Impact of a school-based dating violence prevention program among Latino teens: Randomized controlled effectiveness trial. *Journal of Adolescent Health, 39,* 694–704.

Jespersen, A. F., Lalumiere, M. L., & Seto, M. C. (2009). Sexual abuse history among adult sex offenders and non-sex offenders: A meta-analysis. *Child Abuse and Neglect, 33,* 179–192.

Jin, M. K., Jacobvitz, D., Hazen, N., & Jung, S. H. (2012). Maternal sensitivity and infant attachment security in Korea: Cross-cultural validation of the Strange Situation. *Attachment and Human Development, 14,* 33–44.

Johnson, M. P. (1995). Patriarchal terrorism and common couple violence: Two forms of violence against women. *Journal of Marriage and the Family, 57,* 283–294.

Johnson, M. P. (2006a). Apples and oranges in child custody disputes: Intimate terrorism vs. situational couple violence. *Journal of Child Custody, 2,* 43–52.

Johnson, M. P. (2006b). Conflict and control: Gender symmetry and asymmetry in domestic violence. *Violence Against Women, 12,* 1003–1018.

Johnson, M. P. (2009). Differentiating among types of domestic violence: Implications for healthy marriages. In H. E. Peters & C. M. K. Dush (Eds.), *Marriage and family: Perspectives and complexities* (pp. 281–297). New York: Columbia University Press.

Johnson, M. P., & Leone, J. M. (2005). The differential effects of intimate terrorism and situational couple violence: Findings from the National Violence Against Women Survey. *Journal of Family Issues, 26,* 322–349.

Johnson, R. J., Canetti, D., Palmieri, P. A., Galea, S., Varley, J., & Hobfoll, S. E. (2009). A prospective study of risk and resilience factors associated with posttraumatic stress symptoms and depression symptoms among Jews and Arabs exposed to repeated acts of terrorism in Israel. *Psychological Trauma, 1,* 291–311.

Johnson, S. M. (2002). *Emotionally focused couple therapy with trauma survivors: Strengthening attachment bonds.* New York: Guilford.

Johnson, S. M. (2004). *The practice of emotionally focused couple therapy: Creating connection.* New York: Brunner/Routledge.

Johnson, S. M., & Courtois, C. A. (2009). Couple therapy. In C. A. Courtois & J. D. Ford (Eds.), *Treating complex traumatic stress disorders: An evidence-based guide* (pp. 371–390). New York: Guilford.

Johnson, S. M., & Faller, G. (2011). Dancing with the dragon of trauma: EFT with couples who stand in harm's way. In J. L. Furrow, S. M. Johnson, & B. A. Bradley (Eds.), *The emotionally focused casebook: New directions in treating couples* (pp. 165–192). New York: Routledge.

Johnson, V. K., Cowan, P. A., & Cowan, C. P. (1999). Children's classroom behavior: The unique contribution of family organization. *Journal of Family Psychology, 13,* 355–371.

Johnston, J. R., Walters, M. G., & Olesen, N. W. (2005). Is it alienating parenting, role reversal or child abuse? A study of children's rejection of a parent in child custody disputes. *Journal of Emotional Abuse, 5,* 191–218.

Jones, D. J., Runyan, D. K., Lewis, T., Litrownik, A. J., Black, M. M., Wiley, T., et al. (2010). Trajectories of childhood sexual abuse and early adolescent HIV/AIDS risk behaviors: The role of other maltreatment, witnessed violence, and child gender. *Journal of Clinical Child and Adolescent Psychology, 39,* 667–680.

Jones, L. (1998). The Minnesota School Curriculum Project: A statewide domestic violence prevention project in secondary schools. In B. Levy (Ed.), *Dating violence: Young women in danger* (pp. 258–266). Seattle, WA: Seal Press.

Joosen, K. J., Mesman, J., Bakermans-Kranenburg, M. J., & van IJzendoorn, M. H. (2013). Maternal overreactive sympathetic nervous system responses to repeated infant crying predicts risk for impulsive harsh discipline of infants. *Child Maltreatment, 18,* 252–263.

Jordan, B. K., Schlenger, W. E., Caddell, J. M., & Fairbank, J. A. (1997). Etiological factors in a sample of convicted women felons in North Carolina. In M. C. Zanarini (Ed.), *Role of sexual abuse in the etiology of borderline personality disorder* (pp. 45–69). Arlington, VA: American Psychiatric Association.

Jurist, E. L., & Meehan, K. B. (2009). Attachment, mentalization, and reflective functioning. In J. H. Obegi & E. Berant (Eds.), *Attachment theory and research in clinical work with adults* (pp. 71–93). New York: Guilford.

Kalmuss, D. (1984). The intergenerational transmission of marital aggression. *Journal of Marriage and the Family, 46,* 11–20.

Kar, H. L., & O'Leary, K. D. (2010). Gender symmetry or asymmetry in intimate partner victimization? Not an either/or answer. *Partner Abuse, 1,* 152–168.

Karakurt, G., Keiley, M., & Posada, G. (2013). Intimate relationship aggression in college couples: Family-of-origin violence, egalitarian attitude, attachment security. *Journal of Family Violence, 28,* 561–575.

Karenian, H., Liyaditis, M., Karenian, S., Zafiriadis, K., Bochtsou, V., & Xenitidis, K. (2011). Collective trauma transmission and traumatic reactions among descendants of Armenian refugees. *International Journal of Social Psychiatry, 57,* 327–337.

Karpman, S. (1968). Fairy tales and script drama analysis. *Transactional Analysis Bulletin, 7,* 39–43.

Katerndahl, D., Burge, S., & Kellogg, N. (2005). Predictors of development of adult psychopathology in female victims of childhood sexual abuse. *Journal of Nervous and Mental Disease, 193,* 258–264.

Katz, J., Petracca, M., & Rabinowitz, J. (2009). A retrospective study of daughters' emotional role reversal with parents, attachment anxiety, excessive reassurance-seeking, and depressive symptoms. *American Journal of Family Therapy, 37,* 185–195.

Katz, J., & Tirone, V. (2008). Childhood sexual abuse predicts women's unwanted sexual interactions and sexual satisfaction in adult romantic relationships. In M. J. Smith (Ed.), *Child sexual abuse: Issues and challenges* (pp. 67–86). Hauppauge, NY: Nova Science.

Katz, L. F., & Gottman, J. M. (1996). Spillover effects of marital conflict: In search of parenting and coparenting mechanisms. In J. P. McHale & P. A. Cowan (Eds.), *Understanding how family-level dynamics affect children's development: Studies of two-parent families* (pp. 57–76). San Francisco, CA: Jossey-Bass.

Katz, L. F., & Low, S. M. (2004). Marital violence, co-parenting, and family-level processes in relation to children's adjustment. *Journal of Family Psychology, 18,* 372–382.

Kaufman, J., & Zigler, E. (1987). Do abused children become abusive parents? *American Journal of Orthopsychiatry, 57,* 186–192.

Kay, C., & Green, J. (2013). Reactive attachment disorder following early maltreatment: Systematic evidence beyond the institution. *Journal of Abnormal Child Psychology, 41,* 571–581.

Keenan, P., & Royle, L. (2007). Vicarious trauma and first responders: A case study utilizing eye movement desensitization and reprocessing (EMDR) as the primary treatment modality. *International Journal of Emergency Mental Health, 9,* 291–298.

Keenan-Miller, D., Hammen, C., & Brennan, P. (2007). Adolescent psychosocial risk factors for severe intimate partner violence in young adulthood. *Journal of Consulting and Clinical Psychology, 75,* 456–463.

Kellerman, N. P. F. (2001). Psychopathology in children of Holocaust survivors: A review of the research literature. *Israel Journal of Psychiatry and Related Sciences, 38,* 36–46.

Kelley, S. J., Whitley, D. M., & Campos, P. E. (2011). Behavior problems in children raised by grandmothers: The role of caregiver distress, family resources, and the home environment. *Children and Youth Services Review, 33,* 2138–2145.

Kelly, B. C., Izienicki, H., Bimbi, D. S., & Parsons, J. T. (2011). The intersection of mutual partner violence and substance use among urban gays, lesbians, and bisexuals. *Deviant Behavior, 32,* 379–404.

Kelly, J. B., & Johnson, M. P. (2008). Differentiation among types of intimate partner violence: Research update and implications for interventions. *Family Court Review, 46,* 476–499.

Kelly, R. J., & El-Sheikh, M. (2011). Marital conflict and children's sleep: Reciprocal relations and socioeconomic effects. *Journal of Family Psychology, 25*, 412–422.

Kemp, A., Green, B. L., Hovanitz, C., & Rawlings, E. I. (1995). Incidence and correlates of posttraumatic stress disorder in battered women. *Journal of Interpersonal Violence, 10*, 43–55.

Kendler, K. S., Bulik, C. M., Silberg, J., Hettema, J. M., Myers, J., & Prescott, C. A. (2000). Childhood sexual abuse and adult psychiatric and substance use disorders in women: An epidemiological and cotwin control analysis. *Archives of General Psychiatry, 57*, 953–959.

Kennedy, J. H. (2008). Is maternal behavior in the strange situation related to infant attachment? *Journal of Early Childhood and Infant Psychology, 4*, 83–92.

Kerig, P. K. (2005). Revisiting the construct of boundary dissolution: A multidimensional perspective. *Journal of Emotional Abuse, 5*(2–3), 5–42.

Kernsmith, P. (2006). Gender differences in the impact of family of origin violence on perpetrators of domestic violence. *Journal of Family Violence, 21*, 163–171.

Kessel Schneider, S., O'Donnell, L., Stueve, A., & Coulter, R. W. S. (2012). Cyberbullying, schoolbullying, and psychological distress: A regional census of high school students. *American Journal of Public Health, 102*, 171–177.

Ketring, S. A., & Feinauer, L. L. (1999). Perpetrator-victim relationship: Long-term effects of sexual abuse for men and women. *American Journal of Family Therapy, 27*, 109–120.

Kia-Keating, M., Grossman, F. K., Sorsoli, L., & Epstein, M. (2005). Containing and resisting masculinity: Narratives of renegotiation among resilient male survivors of childhood sexual abuse. *Psychology of Men and Masculinity, 6*, 169–185.

Kia-Keating, M., Sorsoli, L., & Grossman, F. K. (2010). Relational challenges and recovery processes in male survivors of childhood sexual abuse. *Journal of Interpersonal Violence, 25*, 666–683.

Killgore, W. D. S., Cotting, D. I., Thomas, J. L., Cox, A. L., McGurk, D., Vo, A. H., et al. (2008). Post-combat invincibility: Violent combat experiences are associated with increased risk-taking propensity following deployment. *Journal of Psychiatric Research, 42*, 1112–1121.

Kim, H. K., Pears, K. C., Fisher, P. A., Connelly, C. D., & Landsverk, J. A. (2010). Trajectories of maternal harsh parenting in the first 3 years of life. *Child Abuse and Neglect, 34*, 897–906.

Kim, J. (2009). Type-specific intergenerational transmission of neglectful and physically abusive parenting behaviors among young parents. *Children and Youth Services Review, 31*, 761–767.

Kim, J., Cicchetti, D., Rogosch, F. A., & Manly, J. T. (2009). Child maltreatment and trajectories of personality and behavioral functioning: Implications for the development of personality disorder. *Development and Psychopathology*, *21*, 889–912.

Kim, J., Talbot, N. L., & Cicchetti, D. (2009). Childhood abuse and current interpersonal conflict: The role of shame. *Child Abuse and Neglect, 33*, 362–371.

Kim, K., & Smith, P. K. (1999). Family relations in early childhood and reproductive development. *Journal of Reproductive and Infant Psychology, 17*, 133–148.

Kimonis, E. R., Cross, B., Howard, A., & Donoghue, K. (2013). Maternal care, maltreatment and callous-unemotional traits among urban male juvenile offenders. *Journal of Youth and Adolescence, 42*, 165–177.

Kimonis, E. R., Frick, P. J., Cauffman, E., Goldweber, A., & Skeem, J. (2012). Primary and secondary variants of juvenile psychopathy differ in emotional processing. *Development and Psychopathology, 24*, 1091–1103.

Kimonis, E. R., Frick, P. J., Munoz, L. C., & Aucoin, K. J. (2008). Callous-unemotional traits and the emotional processing of distress cues in detained boys: Testing the moderating role of aggression, exposure to community violence, and histories of abuse. *Development and Psychopathology, 20*, 569–589.

Kinsfogel, K. M., & Grych, J. H. (2004). Interparental conflict and adolescent dating relationships: Integrating cognitive, emotional and peer influences. *Journal of Family Psychology, 18*, 505–515.

Kjellstrand, J. M., & Eddy, J. M. (2011). Mediators of the effect of parental incarceration on adolescent externalizing behaviors. *Journal of Community Psychology, 39*, 551–565.

Kjelsberg, E., & Friestad, C. (2008). Social adversities in first-time and repeat prisoners. *International Journal of Social Psychiatry, 54*, 514–526.

Klahr, A. M., & Burt, S. A. (2013). Elucidating the etiology of individual differences in parenting: A meta-analysis of behavioral genetic research. *Psychological Bulletin, 140*, 544–586.

Klahr, A. M., McGue, M., Iacono, W. G., & Burt, S. A. (2011). The association between parent-child conflict and adolescent conduct problems over time: Results from a longitudinal adoption study. *Journal of Abnormal Psychology, 120*, 46–56.

Klahr, A. M., Thomas, K. M., Hopwood, C. J., Klump, K. L., & Burt, S. A. (2013). Evocative gene-environment correlation in the mother-child relationship: A twin study of interpersonal processes. *Development and Psychopathology, 25*, 105–118.

Klinitzke, G., Bohm, M., Brahler, E., & Weissflog, G. (2012). Anxiety, depression, somatoform symptoms and posttraumatic stress in the offspring of political detainees in Eastern Germany (1945–1989). *Psychotherapie Psychosomatik Medizinische Psychologie, 62*, 18–24.

Knous-Westfall, H. M., Ehrensaft, M. K., MacDonell, K. W., & Cohen, P. (2012). Parental intimate partner violence, parenting practices, and adolescent peer bullying: A prospective study. *Journal of Child and Family Studies, 21*, 754–766.

Kochanska, G., Philibert, R. A., & Barry, R. A. (2009). Interplay of genes and early mother-child relationship in the development of self-regulation from toddler to preschool age. *Journal of Child Psychology and Psychiatry, 50*, 1331–1338.

Kochenderfer-Ladd, B. (2003). Identification of aggressive and asocial victims and the stability of their peer victimization. *Merrill-Palmer Quarterly, 49*, 401–425.

Kocovska, E., Puckering, C., Follan, M., Smillie, M., Gorski, C., Barnes, J., et al. (2012). Neurodevelopmental problems in maltreated children referred with indiscriminate friendliness. *Research in Developmental Disabilities, 33*, 1560–1565.

Koenig, M. A., Stephenson, R., Ahmed, S., Jejeebhoy, S. J., & Campbell, J. (2006). Individual and contextual determinants of domestic violence in North India. *American Journal of Public Health, 96*, 132–138.

Kohl, P. L., Edleson, J. L., English, D. J., & Barth, R. P. (2005). Domestic violence and pathways into child welfare services: Findings from the National Survey of Child and Adolescent Well-Being. *Children and Youth Services Review, 27*, 1167–1182.

Kohrt, H. E., Kohrt, B. A., Waldman, I., Saltzman, K., & Carrion, V. G. (2004). An ecological-transactional model of significant risk factors for child psychopathology in Outer Mongolia. *Child Psychiatry and Human Development, 35*, 163–181.

Kok, R., Bakermans-Kranenburg, M. J., van IJzendoorn, M. H., Velders, F. P., Linting, M., Jaddoe, V. W. V., et al. (2013). The role of maternal stress during pregnancy, maternal discipline, and child COMT Val158Met genotype in the development of compliance. *Developmental Psychobiology, 55*, 451–464.

Komarovskaya, I., Brown, A. D., Galatzer-Levy, I. R., Madan, A., Henn-Haase, C., Teater, J., et al. (2014). Early physical victimization is a risk factor for posttraumatic stress disorder symptoms among Mississippi police and firefighter first responders to Hurricane Katrina. *Psychological Trauma, 6*, 92–96.

Koren-Karie, N., Oppenheim, D., & Getzler-Yosef, R. (2008). Shaping children's internal working models through mother-child dialogues: The importance of resolving past maternal trauma. *Attachment and Human Development, 10*, 465–483.

Koren-Karie, N., Oppenheim, D., Yuval-Adler, S., & Mor, H. (2013). Emotion dialogues of foster caregivers with their children: The role of the caregivers, above and beyond child characteristics, in shaping the interactions. *Attachment and Human Development, 15,* 175–188.

Koren-Karie, N., Sagi-Schwartz, A., & Joels, T. (2003). Absence of Attachment Representations (AAR) in the adult years: The emergence of a new AAI classification in catastrophically traumatized Holocaust child survivors. *Attachment and Human Development, 5,* 381–397.

Koss, K. J., George, M. R. W., Bergman, K. N., Cummings, E. M., Davies, P. T., & Cicchetti, D. (2011). Understanding children's emotional processes and behavioral strategies in the context of marital conflict. *Journal of Experimental Child Psychology, 109,* 336–352.

Kotch, J. B., Lewis, T., Hussey, J. M., English, D., Thompson, R., Litrownik, A. J., et al. (2008). Importance of early neglect for childhood aggression. *Pediatrics, 121,* 725–731.

Kouvo, A. M., & Silven, M. (2010). Finnish mother's and father's attachment representations during child's first year predict psychosocial adjustment in preadolescence. *Attachment and Human Development, 12,* 529–549.

Kretchmar, M. D., & Jacobvitz, D. B. (2002). Observing mother-child relationships across generations: Boundary patterns, attachment and the transmission of caregiving. *Family Process, 41,* 351–374.

Kretschmer, T., & Pike, A. (2009). Young children's sibling relationship quality: Distal and proximal correlates. *Journal of Child Psychology and Psychiatry, 50,* 581–589.

Krishnakumar, A., & Buehler, C. (2000). Interparental conflict and parenting behaviors: A meta-analytic review. *Family Relations, 49,* 25–44.

Kroneman, L. M., Hipwell, A. E., Loeber, R., Koot, H. M., & Pardini, D. A. (2011). Contextual risk factors as predictors of disruptive behavior disorder trajectories in girls: The moderating effect of callous-unemotional features. *Journal of Child Psychology and Psychiatry, 52,* 167–175.

Kruger, K. J., & Valltos, N. G. (2002). Dealing with domestic violence in law enforcement relationships. *FBI Lawa Enforcement Bulletin, 71,* 1–7.

Kumpulainen, K., & Rasanen, E. (2000). Children involved in bullying at elementary school age: Their psychiatric symptoms and deviance in adolescence: An epidemiological sample. *Child Abuse and Neglect, 24,* 1567–1577.

Kwong, M. J., Bartholomew, K., Henderson, A. J. Z., & Trinke, S. J. (2003). The intergenerational transmission of relationship violence. *Journal of Family Psychology, 17,* 288–301.

Labonte, B., Suderman, M., Maussion, G., Navaro, L., Yerko, V., Maher, I., et al. (2012). Genome-wide epigenetic regulation by early-life trauma. *JAMA Psychiatry, 69,* 722–731.

Lackey, C. (2003). Violent family heritage, the transition to adulthood, and later partner violence. *Journal of Family Issues, 24*, 74–98.

Lackey, C., & Williams, K. R. (1995). Social bonding and the cessation of partner violence across generations. *Journal of Marriage and the Family, 57*, 295–305.

Ladd, G. W., & Ladd, B. K. (1998). Parenting behaviors and parent-child relationships: Correlates of peer victimization in kindergarten? *Developmental Psychology, 34*, 1450–1458.

Lakatos, K., Nemoda, Z., Birkas, E., Ronai, Z., Kovacs, E., Ney, K., et al. (2003). Association of D4 dopamine receptor gene and serotonin transporter promoter polymorphisms with infants' response to novelty. *Molecular Psychiatry, 8*, 90–97.

Lakatos, K., Nemoda, Z., Toth, I., Ronai, Z., Ney, K., Sasvari-Szekely, M., & Gervai, J. (2002). Further evidence for the role of the dopamine D4 receptor (DRD4) gene in attachment disorganization: Interaction of the exon III 48-bp repeat and the -521 C/T promoter polymorphisms. *Molecular Psychiatry, 7*, 27–31.

Lamagna, J., & Gleiser, K. A. (2007). Building a secure internal attachment: An intra-relational approach to ego strengthening and emotional processing with chronically traumatized clients. *Journal of Trauma and Dissociation, 8*, 25–52.

Lambert, J. E., Engh, R., Hasbun, A., & Holzer, J. (2012). Impact of posttraumatic stress disorder on the relationship quality and psychological distress of intimate partners: A meta-analytic review. *Journal of Family Psychology, 26*, 729–737.

Lambert, M. J., & Cattani-Thompson, K. (1996). Current findings regarding the effectiveness of counseling: Implications for practice. *Journal of Counseling and Development, 74*, 601–608.

Lambie, I., Seymour, F., Lee, A., & Adams, P. (2002). Resiliency in the victim-offender cycle in male sexual abuse. *Sexual Abuse, 14*, 31–48.

LaMotte, A. D., Taft, C. T., Weatherill, R. P., Scott, J. P., & Eckhardt, C. I. (2014). Examining intimate partner aggression assessment among returning veterans and their partners. *Psychological Assessment, 26*, 8-15.

Lamoureux, B. E., Palmieri, P. A., Jackson, A. P., & Hobfoll, S. E. (2012). Child sexual abuse and adulthood-interpersonal outcomes: Examining pathways for intervention. *Psychological Trauma, 4*, 605–613.

Landa, S., & Duschinsky, R. (2013). Crittenden's dynamic-maturational model of attachment and adaptation. *Review of General Psychology, 17*, 326–338.

Lande, R. G., Banks-Williams, L., & Fileta, B. (2012). The forensic assessment of combat-related irritability with whole blood serotonin levels: A pilot study. *Journal of Forensic Psychiatry and Psychology, 23*, 654–663.

Lane, E. J., Lating, J. M., Lowry, J. L., & Martino, T. P. (2010). Differences in compassion fatigue, symptoms of posttraumatic stress disorder and relationship satisfaction, including sexual desire and functioning, between male and female detectives who investigate sexual offenses against children: A pilot study. *International Journal of Emergency Mental Health, 12,* 257–266.

Langeland, W., & Dijkstra, S. (1995). Breaking the intergenerational transmission of child abuse: Beyond the mother-child relationship. *Child Abuse Review, 4,* 4–13.

Langhinrichsen-Rohling, J., McCullars, A., & Misra, T. A. (2012). Motivations for men and women's intimate partner violence perpetration: A comprehensive review. *Partner Abuse, 3,* 429–468.

Langhinrichsen-Rohling, J., Misra, T. A., Selwyn, C., & Rohling, M. L. (2012). Rates of bidirectional versus unidirectional intimate partner violence across samples, sexual orientations, and race/ethnicities: A comprehensive review. *Partner Abuse, 3,* 199–230.

Langhinrichsen-Rohling, J., Neidig, P., & Thorn, G. (1995). Violent marriages: Gender differences in levels of current violence and past abuse. *Journal of Family Violence, 10,* 159–176.

Lanyado, M. (2003). The emotional tasks of moving from fostering to adoption: Transitions, attachment, separation and loss. *Clinical Child Psychology and Psychiatry, 8,* 337–349.

Lapierre, S. (2010). Striving to be "good" mothers: Abused women's experiences of mothering. *Child Abuse Review, 19,* 342–357.

Larose, S., & Bernier, A. (2001). Social support processes: Mediators of attachment state of mind and adjustment in late adolescence. *Attachment and Human Development, 3,* 96–120.

Larson, J. H., & Lamont, C. (2005). The relationship of childhood sexual abuse to the marital attitudes and readiness for marriage of single young adult women. *Journal of Family Issues, 26,* 415–430.

Larsson, H., Andershed, H., & Lichtenstein, P. (2006). A genetic factor explains most of the variation in the psychopathic personality. *Journal of Abnormal Psychology, 115,* 221–230.

Larsson, H., Viding, E., & Plomin, R. (2008). Callous-unemotional traits and antisocial behavior: Genetic, environmental, and early parenting characteristics. *Criminal Justice and Behavior, 35,* 197–211.

Latzman, N. E., Viljoen, J. L., Scalora, M. J., & Ullman, D. (2011). Sexual offending in adolescence: A comparison of sibling offenders and nonsibling offenders across domains of risk and treatment need. *Journal of Child Sexual Abuse, 20,* 245–263.

Lau, M., & Kristensen, E. (2010). Sexual revictimization in a clinical sample of women reporting childhood sexual abuse. *Nordic Journal of Psychiatry, 64,* 4–10.

Laurent, H. K., Ablow, J. C., & Measelle, J. (2012). Taking stress response out of the box: Stability, discontinuity, and temperament effects on HPA and SNS across social stressors in mother-infant dyads. *Developmental Psychology, 48,* 35–45.

Lavner, J. A., Waterman, J., & Peplau, L. A. (2014). Parent adjustment over time in gay, lesbian, and heterosexual parent families adopting from foster care. *American Journal of Orthopsychiatry, 84,* 46–53.

Lavoie, F., Vezina, L., Piche, C., & Boivin, M. (1995). Evaluation of a prevention program for violence in teen dating relationships. *Journal of Interpersonal Violence, 10,* 516–525.

Lawing, K., Frick, P. J., & Cruise, K. R. (2010). Differences in offending patterns between adolescent sex offenders high or low in callous-unemotional traits. *Psychological Assessment, 22,* 298–305.

Lawoko, S. (2008). Predictors of attitudes toward intimate partner violence: A comparative study of men in Zambia and Kenya. *Journal of Interpersonal Violence, 23,* 1056–1074.

Lawrence, E., Orengo-Aguayo, R., Langer, A., & Brock, R. L. (2012). The impact and consequences of partner abuse on partners. *Partner Abuse, 3,* 406–428.

LeBlanc, V. R., Rehehr, C., Jelley, R. B., & Barath, I. (2007). Does posttraumatic stress disorder (PTSD) affect performance? *Journal of Nervous and Mental Disease, 195,* 701–704.

Lee, H. Y., Lightfoot, E., & Edleson, J. L. (2008). Differences among battered mothers in their involvement with child protection services: Could the perpetrator's biological relationship to the child have an impact? *Children and Youth Services Review, 30,* 1189–1197.

Lee, Y., & Guterman, N. B. (2010). Young mother-father dyads and maternal harsh parenting behavior. *Child Abuse and Neglect, 34,* 874–885.

Leen, E., Sorbring, E., Mawer, M., Holdsworth, E., Helsing, B., & Bowen, E. (2013). Prevalence, dynamic risk factors and the efficacy of primary interventions for adolescent dating violence: An international review. *Aggression and Violent Behavior, 18,* 159–174.

Leerkes, E. M., & Crockenberg, S. C. (2006). Antecedents of mothers' emotional and cognitive responses to infant distress: The role of family, mother, and infant characteristics. *Infant Mental Health Journal, 27,* 405–428.

Leifer, M., Kilbane, T., Jacobsen, T., & Grossman, G. (2004). A three-generational study of transmission of risk for sexual abuse. *Journal of Clinical Child and Adolescent Psychology, 33,* 662–672.

Leifer, M., Kilbane, T., & Kalick, S. (2004). Vulnerability or resilience to intergenerational sexual abuse: The role of maternal factors. *Child Maltreatment, 9,* 78–91.

Leist, T., & Dadds, M. R. (2009). Adolescents' ability to read different emotional faces relates to their history of maltreatment and type of psychopathology. *Clinical Child Psychology and Psychiatry, 14,* 237–250.

Lemery-Chalfant, K., Kao, K., Swann, G., & Goldsmith, H. H. (2013). Child-hood temperament: Passive gene-environment correlation, gene-environment interaction, and the hidden importance of the family environment. *Development and Psychopathology, 25,* 51–63.

Lemitre, S. (2008). Trauma and psychopathy: Integrating the psychoanalytical and neuropsychological approaches. *Revue Francophone du Stress et du Trauma, 8,* 27–33.

Lenhardt, J. M., Howard, J. M., Taft, C. T., Kaloupek, D. G., & Keane, T. M. (2012). Examining aggression in male Vietnam veterans who receive VA services: The role of traumatic events and combat exposure. *Journal of Traumatic Stress, 25,* 461–464.

Leon, K., & Rudy, D. (2005). Family processes and children's representations of parentification. *Journal of Emotional Abuse, 5*(2–3), 111–142.

Letzter-Pouw, S., & Werner, P. (2012). The relationship between loss of parents in the Holocaust, intrusive memories, and distress among child survivors. *American Journal of Orthopsychiatry, 82,* 201–208.

Leung, D. (2003, August). Cross-cultural differences on the Conflict Tactics Scale: Parent-Child Version. Paper presented at the annual meeting of the American Psychological Association, Toronto, Canada.

Levendosky, A. A., Bogat, G. A., & Huth-Bocks, A. C. (2011). The influence of domestic violence on the development of the attachment relationship between mother and young child. *Psychoanalytic Psychology, 28,* 512–527.

Levendosky, A. A., Leahy, K. L., Bogat, G. A., Davidson, W. S., & von Eye, A. (2006). Domestic violence, maternal parenting, maternal mental health, and infant externalizing behavior. *Journal of Family Psychology, 20,* 544–552.

Levy, K. N., Meehan, K. B., Kelly, K. M., Reynoso, J. S., Weber, M., Clarkin, J. F., & Kernberg, O. F. (2006). Change in attachment patterns and reflective function in a randomized control trial of transference-focused psychotherapy for borderline personality disorder. *Journal of Consulting and Clinical Psychology, 74,* 1027–1040.

Lewis, E. E., Dozier, M., Ackerman, J., & Sepulveda-Kozakowski, S. (2007). The effect of placement instability on adopted children's inhibitory control abilities and oppositional behavior. *Developmental Psychology, 43,* 1415–1427.

Lewis-Morrarty, E., Dozier, M., Bernard, K., Terracciano, S. M., & Moore, S. V.

(2012). Cognitive flexibility and theory of mind outcomes among foster children: Preschool follow-up results of a randomized clinical trial. *Journal of Adolescent Health, 51*, S17–S22.

Liang, B., Williams, L. M., & Siegel, J. A. (2006). Relational outcomes of childhood sexual trauma in female survivors: A longitudinal study. *Journal of Interpersonal Violence, 21*, 42–57.

Lilly, M. M., Pole, N., Best, S. R., Metzler, T., & Marmar, C. R. (2009). Gender and PTSD: What can we learn from female police officers? *Journal of Anxiety Disorders, 23*, 767–774.

Linares, L. O., Stovall-McClough, K. C., Li, M., Morin, N., Silva, R., Albert, A., & Cloitre, M. (2008). Salivary cortisol in foster children: A pilot study. *Child Abuse and Neglect, 32*, 665–670.

Lindauer, R. J. L., Vlieger, E.-J., Jalink, M., Olff, M., Carlier, I. V. E., Majoie, C. B. L. M., den Heeten, G. J., & Gersons, B. P. R. (2004). Smaller hippocampal volume in Dutch police officers with posttraumatic stress disorder. *Biological Psychiatry, 56*, 356–363.

Linder, J. R., & Collins, W. A. (2005). Parent and peer predictors of physical aggression and conflict management in romantic relationships in early adulthood. *Journal of Family Psychology, 19*, 252–262.

Lindhiem, O., & Dozier, M. (2007). Caregiver commitment to foster children: The role of child behavior. *Child Abuse and Neglect, 31*, 361–374.

Lindsey, E. W., Caldera, Y. M., & Tankersley, L. (2009). Marital conflict and the quality of young children's peer play behavior: The mediating and moderating role of parent-child emotional reciprocity and attachment security. *Journal of Family Psychology, 23*, 130–145.

Liotti, G. (1992). Disorganized/disoriented attachment in the etiology of the dissociative disorders. *Dissociation, 5*, 196–204.

Liotti, G. (2006). A model of dissociation based on attachment theory and research. *Journal of Trauma and Dissociation, 7*, 55–73.

Liotti, G. (2008). Trauma, dissociation, and disorganized attachment: Three strands of a single braid. *Psychotherapy: Research, Practice, Training, 41*, 472–486.

Liotti, G. (2011). Attachment disorganization and the controlling strategies: An illustration of the contributions of attachment theory to developmental psychopathology and to psychotherapy integration. *Journal of Psychotherapy Integration, 21*, 232–252.

Lipsky, S., Caetano, R., & Roy-Byrne, P. (2011). Triple jeopardy: Impact of partner violence perpetration, mental health and substance use on perceived unmet need for mental health care among men. *Social Psychiatry and Psychiatric Epidemiology, 46*, 843–852.

Lipsky, S., Caetano, R., Field, C. A., & Larkin, G. L. (2005). Is there a relationship between victim and partner alcohol use during an intimate partner violence event? Findings from an urban emergency department study of abused women. *Journal of Studies on Alcohol, 66*, 407–412.

Litz, B. T., Stein, N., Delaney, E., Lebowitz, L., Nash, W. P., Silva, C., & Maguen, S. (2009). Moral injury and moral repair in war veterans: A preliminary model and intervention strategy. *Clinical Psychology Review, 29*, 695–706.

Locke, T. F., & Newcomb, M. (2004). Child maltreatment, parent alcohol- and drug-related problems, polydrug problems, and parenting practices: A test of gender differences and four theoretical perspectives. *Journal of Family Psychology, 18*, 120–134.

Loehlin, J. C. (2010). Is there an active gene-environment correlation in adolescent drinking behavior? *Behavior Genetics, 40*, 447–451.

Lohman, B. J., Neppl, T. K., Senia, J. M., & Schofield, T. J. (2013). Understanding adolescent and family influences on intimate partner psychological violence during emerging adulthood and adulthood. *Journal of Youth and Adolescence, 42*, 500–517.

Loney, B. R., Huntenburg, A., Counts-Allan, C., & Schmeelk, K. M. (2007). A preliminary examination of the intergenerational continuity of maternal psychopathic features. *Aggressive Behavior, 33*, 14–25.

Longman-Mills, S., Gonzalez, W. Y., Melendez, M. O., Garcia, M. R., Gomez, J. D., Juarez, C. G., et al. (2013). Exploring child maltreatment and its relationship to alcohol and cannabis use in selected Latin American and Caribbean countries. *Child Abuse and Neglect, 37*, 77–85.

Loos, M. E., & Alexander, P. C. (2001). Dissociation and the processing of threat related information: An attachment theory perspective on maintenance factors in dissociative pathology. *Maltrattamento e abuse all-infanzia, 3*, 61–83.

Loper, A. B., & Clarke, C. N. (2013). Relationship processes and resilience in children with incarcerated parents: IV. Attachment representations of imprisoned mothers as related to child contact and the caregiving alliance: The moderating effect of children's placement with maternal grandmothers. *Monographs of the Society for Research in Child Development, 78*, 41–56.

Loper, A. B., Phillips, V., Nichols, E. B., & Dallaire, D. H. (2014). Characteristics and effects of the co-parenting alliance between incarcerated parents and child caregivers. *Journal of Child and Family Studies, 23*, 225–241.

Loper, A. B., & Tuerk, E. H. (2011). Improving the emotional adjustment and communication patterns of incarcerated mothers: Effectiveness of a prison parenting intervention. *Journal of Child and Family Studies, 20*, 89–101.

Lopez-Duran, N. L., Olson, S. L., Hajal, N. J., Felt, B. T., & Vazquez, D. M. (2009). Hypothalamic pituitary adrenal axis functioning in reactive and proactive aggression in children. *Journal of Abnormal Child Psychology, 37,* 169–182.

Lounds, J. J., Borkowski, J. G., & Whitman, T. L. (2006). The potential for child neglect: The case of adolescent mothers and their children. *Child Maltreatment, 11,* 281–294.

Lovallo, W. R. (2013). Early life adversity reduces stress reactivity and enhances impulsive behavior: Implications for health behaviors. *International Journal of Psychophysiology, 90,* 8–16.

Lovegrove, P. J., Henry, K. L., & Slater, M. D. (2012). Examination of the predictors of latent class typologies of bullying involvement among middle school students. *Journal of School Violence, 11,* 75–93.

Low, N., Cui, L., & Merikangas, K. R. (2007). Spousal concordance for substance use and anxiety disorders. *Journal of Psychiatric Research, 41,* 942–951.

Luebbe, A. M., Elledge, L. C., Kiel, E. J., & Stoppelbein, L. (2012). Cortisol predicts behavioral dysregulation and length of stay among children admitted for psychiatric inpatient treatment. *Journal of Clinical Child and Adolescent Psychology, 41,* 227–238.

Lustenberger, Y., Fenton, B. T., Rothen, S., Vandeleur, C. L., Gamma, F., Matthey, M.-L., et al. (2008). Spouse similarity in recollections of parenting received: A study in a nonclinical sample. *Swiss Journal of Psychology, 67,* 165–176.

Lynne, S. D., Graber, J. A., Nichols, T. R., Brooks-Gunn, J., & Botvin, G. J. (2007). Links between pubertal timing, peer influences, and externalizing behaviors among urban students followed through middle school. *Journal of Adolescent Health, 40,* 181.e7–181.13.

Lyons-Ruth, K. (1996). Attachment relationships among children with aggressive behavior problems: The role of disorganized early attachment patterns. *Journal of Consulting and Clinical Psychology, 64,* 64–73.

Lyons-Ruth, K. (2008). Contributions of the mother-infant relationship to dissociative, borderline, and conduct symptoms in young adulthood. *Infant Mental Health Journal, 29,* 203–218.

Lyons-Ruth, K., & Block, D. (1996). The disturbed caregiving system: Relations among childhood trauma, maternal caregiving, and infant affect and attachment. *Infant Mental Health Journal, 17,* 257–275.

Lyons-Ruth, K., Bronfman, E., & Atwood, G. (1999). A relational diathesis model of hostile-helpless states of mind: Expressions in mother-infant interaction. In J. Solomon & C. George (Eds.), *Attachment disorganization* (pp. 33–70). New York: Guilford.

Lyons-Ruth, K., Bronfman, E., & Parsons, E. (1999). Maternal frightened, frightening or atypical behavior and disorganized infant attachment patterns. *Monographs of the Society for Research on Child Development, 64,* 67–96.

Lyons-Ruth, K., Bureau, J.-F., Holmes, B., Easterbrooks, A., & Brooks, N. H. (2013). Borderline symptoms and suicidality/self-injury in late adolescence: Prospectively observed relationship correlates in infancy and childhood. *Psychiatry Research, 206,* 273–281.

Lyons-Ruth, K., Easterbrooks, M. A., & Cibelli, C. D. (1997). Infant attachment strategies, infant mental lag, and maternal depressive symptoms: Predictors of internalizing and externalizing problems at age 7. *Developmental Psychology, 33,* 681–692.

Lyons-Ruth, K., & Jacobvitz, D. (1999). Attachment disorganization: Unresolved loss, relational violence, and lapses in behavioral and attentional strategies. In J. Cassidy & P. R. Shaver (Eds.), *Handbook of attachment: Theory, research, and clinical applications* (pp. 520–554). New York: Guilford.

Lyons-Ruth, K., Melnick, S., Bronfman, E., Sherry, S., & Llanas, L. (2004). Hostile-helpless relational models and disorganized attachment patterns between parents and their young children: Review of research and implications for clinical work. In L. Atkinson & S. Goldberg (Eds.), *Attachment issues in psychopathology and intervention* (pp. 65–94). Mahwah, NJ: Lawrence Erlbaum.

Lyons-Ruth, K., Melnick, S., Patrick, M., & Hobson, R. P. (2007). A controlled study of hostile-helpless states of mind among borderline and dysthymic women. *Attachment and Human Behavior, 9,* 1–16.

Lyons-Ruth, K., Repacholi, B., McLeod, S., & Silva, E. (1991). Disorganized attachment behavior in infancy: Short-term stability, maternal and infant correlates, and risk-related subtypes. *Development and Psychopathology, 3,* 377–396.

Lyons-Ruth, K., & Spielman, E. (2004). Disorganized infant attachment strategies and helpless-fearful profiles of parenting: Integrating attachment research with clinical intervention. *Infant Mental Health Journal, 25,* 318–335.

Lyons-Ruth, K., Yellin, C., Melnick, S., & Atwood, G. (2003). Childhood experiences of trauma and loss have different relations to maternal unresolved and hostile-helpless states of mind on the AAI. *Attachment and Human Development, 5,* 330–352.

Lyons-Ruth, K., Yellin, C., Melnick, S., & Atwood, G. (2005). Expanding the concept of unresolved mental states: Hostile/helpless states of mind on the Adult Attachment Interview are associated with disrupted mother-infant communication and infant disorganization. *Development and Psychopathology, 17,* 1–23.

MacDonald, K. (2012). Cutting nature at its joints: Toward an evolutionarily informed theory of natural types of conduct disorder. *Journal of Social, Evolutionary, and Cultural Psychology, 6,* 260–291.

Macfie, J., Houts, R. M., McElwain, N. L., & Cox, M. J. (2005). The effect of father-toddler and mother-toddler role reversal on the development of behavior problems in kindergarten. *Social Development, 14,* 514–531.

Macfie, J., Houts, R. M., Pressel, A. S., & Cox, M. J. (2008). Pathways from infant exposure to marital conflict to parent-toddler role reversal. *Infant Mental Health Journal, 29,* 297–319.

Macfie, J., McElwain, N. L., Houts, R. M., & Cox, M. J. (2005). Intergenerational transmission of role reversal between parent and child: Dyadic and family systems internal working models. *Attachment and Human Development, 7,* 51–65.

MacIntosh, H. B. (2013). Dissociative identity disorder and the process of couple therapy. *Journal of Trauma and Dissociation, 14,* 84–96.

MacIntosh, H. B., & Johnson, S. (2008). Emotionally focused therapy for couples and childhood sexual abuse survivors. *Journal of Marital and Family Therapy, 34,* 298–315.

MacKenzie, M. J., Kotch, J. B., & Lee, L.-C. (2011). Toward a cumulative ecological risk model for the etiology of child maltreatment. *Children and Youth Services Review, 33,* 1638–1647.

MacManus, D., Dean, K., Jones, M., Rona, R. J., Greenberg, N., Hull, L., et al. (2013). Violent offending by UK military personnel deployed to Iraq and Afghanistan: A data linkage cohort study. *Lancet, 381,* 907–917.

MacMillan, H. L., Georgiades, K., Duku, E. K., Shea, A., Steiner, M., Niec, A., et al. (2009). Cortisol response to stress in female youths exposed to childhood maltreatment: Results of the Youth Mood Project. *Biological Psychiatry, 66,* 62–68.

Madigan, S., Bakermans-Kranenburg, M. J., van IJzendoorn, M. H., Moran, G., Pederson, D. R., & Benoit, D. (2006). Unresolved states of mind, anomalous parental behavior, and disorganized attachment: A review and meta-analysis of a transmission gap. *Attachment and Human Development, 8,* 89–111.

Madigan, S., Hawkins, E., Goldberg, S., & Benoit, D. (2006). Reduction of disrupted caregiver behavior using Modified Interaction Guidance. *Infant Mental Health Journal, 27,* 509–527.

Madigan, S., Moran, G., & Pederson, D. R. (2006). Unresolved states of mind, disorganized attachment relationships, and disrupted interactions of adolescent mothers and their infants. *Developmental Psychology, 42,* 293–304.

Madigan, S., Vaillancourt, K., McKibbon, A., & Benoit, D. (2012). The reporting of maltreatment experiences during the Adult Attachment Interview in a sample of pregnant adolescents. *Attachment and Human Development, 14,* 119–143.

Madigan, S., Voci, S., & Benoit, D. (2011). Stability of atypical caregiver behaviors over six years and associations with disorganized infant-caregiver attachment. *Attachment and Human Development, 13,* 237–252.

Madsen, C. A., Stith, S. M., Thomsen, C. J., & McCollum, E. E. (2012). Violent couples seeking therapy: Bilateral and unilateral violence. *Partner Abuse*, 3, 43–58.

Maguen, S., Luxton, D. D., Skopp, N. A., & Madden, E. (2012). Gender differences in traumatic experiences and mental health in active duty soldiers redeployed from Iraq and Afghanistan. *Journal of Psychiatric Research, 46*, 311–316.

Maia, D. B., Marmar, C. R., Henn-Haase, C., Nobrega, A., Fiszman, A., Marques-Portella, C., Mendlowicz, M. V., Coutinho, E. S. F., & Figueira, I. (2011). Predictors of PTSD symptoms in Brazilian police officers: The synergy of negative affect and peritraumatic dissociation. *Revista Brasileira de Psiquiatria, 33*, 362–366.

Main, M. (1977). Analysis of a peculiar form of reunion behaviour seen in some day-care children. In R. Webb (Ed.), *Social development in childhood* (pp. 33–78). Baltimore, MD: Johns Hopkins University Press.

Main, M. (2000). The organized categories of infant, child, and adult attachment: Flexible vs. inflexible attention under attachment-related stress. *Journal of the American Psychoanalytic Association, 48*, 1055–1096.

Main, M., & Cassidy, J. (1988). Categories of response to reunion with the parent at age 6: Predictable from infant attachment classifications and stable over a 1-month period. *Developmental Psychology, 24*, 415–426.

Main, M., & Goldwyn, R. (1998). *Adult attachment scoring and classification system*. Version 6.3. Unpublished manuscript, University of California at Berkeley.

Main, M., & Hesse, E. (1990). Parents' unresolved traumatic experiences are related to infant disorganized attachment status: Is frightened and/or frightening parental behavior the linking mechanism? In M. T. Greenberg, D. Cicchetti, & E. M. Cummings (Eds.), *Attachment in the preschool years* (pp. 161–182). Chicago: University of Chicago Press.

Main, M., Kaplan, N., & Cassidy, J. (1985). Security in infancy, childhood, and adulthood: A move to the level of representation. *Monographs of the Society for Research in Child Development, 50*, 66–104.

Main, M., & Solomon, J. (1986). Discovery of an insecure-disorganized/disoriented attachment pattern. In T. B. Brazelton & M. W. Yogman (Eds.), *Affective development in infancy* (pp. 95–124). Westport, CT: Ablex.

Main, M., & Solomon, J. (1990). Procedures for identifying infants as disorganized/disoriented during the Ainsworth Strange Situation. In M. T. Greenberg, D. Cicchetti, & E. M. Cummings (Eds.), *Attachment in the preschool years: Theory, research, and intervention* (pp. 121–160). Chicago: University of Chicago Press.

Malik, S., Sorenson, S. B., & Aneshensel, C. S. (1997). Community and dating violence among adolescents: Perpetration and victimization. *Journal of Adolescent Health, 21,* 291–302.

Malone, J. C., Levendosky, A. A., Dayton, C. J., & Bogat, G. A. (2010). Understanding the "ghosts in the nursery" of pregnant women experiencing domestic violence: Prenatal maternal representations and histories of childhood maltreatment. *Infant Mental Health Journal, 31,* 432–454.

Maniglio, R. (2011a). The role of child sexual abuse in the etiology of substance-related disorders. *Journal of Addictive Diseases, 30,* 216–228.

Maniglio, R. (2011b). The role of childhood trauma, psychological problems, and coping in the development of deviant sexual fantasies in sexual offenders. *Clinical Psychology Review, 31,* 748–756.

Maniglio, R. (2012). The role of parent-child bonding, attachment, and interpersonal problems in the development of deviant sexual fantasies in sexual offenders. *Trauma, Violence, and Abuse, 13,* 83–96.

Manly, J. T., Lynch, M., Oshri, A., Herzog, M., & Wortel, S. N. (2013). The impact of neglect on initial adaptation to school. *Child Maltreatment, 18,* 155–170.

Manly, J. T., Oshri, A., Lynch, M., Herzog, M., & Wortel, S. (2013). Child neglect and the development of externalizing behavior problems: Associations with maternal drug dependence and neighborhood crime. *Child Maltreatment, 18,* 17–29.

Mapp, S. C. (2006). The effects of sexual abuse as a child on the risk of mothers physically abusing their children: A path analysis using systems theory. *Child Abuse and Neglect, 30,* 1293–1310.

Marazziti, D., Del Debbio, A., Roncaglia, I., Bianchi, C., Piccinni, A., & Dell'Osso, L. (2008). Neurotrophins and attachment. *Clinical Neuropsychiatry, 5,* 100–106.

Marcenko, M. O., Kemp, S. P., & Larson, N. C. (2000). Childhood experiences of abuse, later substance use, and parenting outcomes among low-income mothers. *American Journal of Orthopsychiatry, 70,* 316–326.

Marcus, R. F. (2012). Patterns of intimate partner violence in young adult couples: Nonviolent, unilaterally violent, and mutually violent couples. *Violence and Victims, 27,* 299–314.

Marcynyszyn, L. A., Evans, G. W., & Eckenrode, J. (2008). Family instability during early and middle adolescence. *Journal of Applied Developmental Psychology, 29,* 380–392.

Margolin, G., Christensen, A., & John, R. S. (1996). The continuance and spillover of everyday tensions in distressed and nondistressed families. *Journal of Family Psychology, 10,* 304–321.

Margolin, G., & Gordis, E. B. (2003). Co-occurrence between marital aggression and parents' child abuse potential: The impact of cumulative stress. *Violence and Victims, 18*, 243–258.

Margolin, G., Gordis, E. B., & Oliver, P. H. (2004). Links between marital and parent-child interactions: Moderating role of husband-to-wife aggression. *Development and Psychopathology, 16*, 753–771.

Marshall, D. B., English, D. J., & Stewart, A. J. (2001). The effect of fathers or father figures on child behavioral problems in families referred to child protective services. *Child Maltreatment, 6*, 290–299.

Marshall, W. L., Serran, G. A., & Cortoni, F. A. (2000). Childhood attachments, sexual abuse, and their relationship to adult coping in child molesters. *Sexual Abuse, 12*, 17–26.

Martelo, M. M. (2013). Sexual selection and sex differences in the prevalence of childhood externalizing and adolescent internalizing disorders. *Psychological Bulletin, 139*, 1221–1259.

Martin, M., Marchand, A., & Boyer, R. (2009). Traumatic events in the workplace: Impact on psychopathology and healthcare use of police officers. *International Journal of Emergency Mental Health, 11*, 165–176.

Martin, M., Marchand, A., Boyer, R., & Martin, N. (2009). Predictors of the development of posttraumatic stress disorder among police officers. *Journal of Trauma and Dissociation, 10*, 451–468.

Martinson, A. A., Sigmon, S. T., Craner, J., Rothstein, E., & McGillicuddy, M. (2013). Processing of intimacy-related stimuli in survivors of sexual trauma: The role of PTSD. *Journal of Interpersonal Violence, 28*, 1886–1908.

Marvin, R. S., & Stewart, R. B. (1990). A family systems framework for the study of attachment. In M. T. Greenberg, D. Cicchetti, & E. M. Cummings (Eds.), *Attachment in the preschool years: Theory, research, and intervention* (pp. 51–86). Chicago: University of Chicago Press.

Marvin, R. S., & Whelan, W. F. (2003). Disordered attachments: Toward evidence-based clinical practice. *Attachment and Human Development, 5*, 283–288.

Maschi, T., Morgen, K., Bradley, C., & Hatcher, S. S. (2008). Exploring gender differences on internalizing and externalizing behavior among maltreated youth: Implications for social work action. *Child and Adolescent Social Work Journal, 25*, 531–547.

Mashoodh, R., Franks, B., Curley, J. P., & Champagne, F. A. (2012). Paternal social enrichment effects on maternal behavior and offspring growth. *Proceedings of the National Academy of Sciences, 109* (Suppl. 2), 17232–17238.

Matthews, M. F. (2013, November 25). The untold story of military sexual assault. *New York Times*, A23.

Mayseless, O. (1998). Maternal caregiving strategy: A distinction between the ambivalent and the disorganized profile. *Infant Mental Health Journal, 19,* 20–33.

Mayseless, O., Bartholomew, K., Henderson, A., & Trinke, S. (2004). "I was more her mom than she was mine": Role reversal in a community sample. *Family Relations, 53,* 78–86.

Mayseless, O., & Scharf, M. (2007). Adolescents' attachment representations and their capacity for intimacy in close relationships. *Journal of Research on Adolescence, 17,* 23–50.

Mayseless, O., & Scharf, M. (2009). Too close for comfort: Inadequate boundaries with parents and individuation in late adolescent girls. *American Journal of Orthopsychiatry, 79,* 191–202.

Mazza, M., Giusti, L., Albanese, A., Mariano, M., Pino, M. C., & Roncone, R. (2012). Social cognition disorders in military police officers affected by posttraumatic stress disorder after the attack of An-Nasiriyah in Iraq 2006. *Psychiatry Research, 198,* 248–252.

Mbagaa, C., Oburu, P., & Bakermans-Kranenburg, M. J. (2013). Child physical abuse and neglect in Kenya, Zambia and the Netherlands: A cross-cultural comparison of prevalence, psychopathological sequelae and mediation by PTSS. *International Journal of Psychology, 48,* 95–107.

McCarroll, J. E., Ursano, R. J., Fan, Z., & Newby, J. H. (2004). Patterns of spouse and child maltreatment by discharged U.S. Army soldiers. *Journal of the American Academy of Psychiatry and the Law, 32,* 53–62.

McCaslin, S. E., Inslicht, S. S., Metzler, T. J., Henn-Haase, C., Maguen, S., Neyland, T. C., et al. (2008). Trait dissociation predicts posttraumatic stress disorder symptoms in a prospective study of urban police officers. *Journal of Nervous and Mental Disease, 196,* 912–918.

McCloskey, L. (1997). The continuum of harm: Girls and women at risk for sexual abuse across the lifespan. In D. Cicchetti & S. L. Toth (Eds.), *Developmental perspectives on trauma: Theory, research and intervention* (pp. 553–578). Rochester, NY: University of Rochester Press.

McCloskey, L. A., & Bailey, J. A. (2000). The intergenerational transmission of risk for child sexual abuse. *Journal of Interpersonal Violence, 15,* 1019–1035.

McClure, F. H., Chavez, D. V., Agars, M. D., Peacock, M. J., & Matosian, A. (2008). Resilience in sexually abused women: Risk and protective factors. *Journal of Family Violence, 23,* 81–88.

McCrory, E., De Brito, S. A., & Viding, E. (2010). Research review: The neurobiology and genetics of maltreatment and adversity. *Journal of Child Psychology and Psychiatry, 51,* 1079–1095.

McDonald, R., Jouriles, E. N., Rosenfield, D., & Leahy, M. M. (2012). Children's questions about interparent conflict and violence: What's a mother to say? *Journal of Family Psychology, 26,* 95–104.

McDonell, J., Ott, J., & Mitchell, M. (2010). Predicting dating violence victimization and perpetration among middle and high school students in a rural southern community. *Children and Youth Services Review, 32*, 1458–1463.

McElwain, N. L., Cox, M. J., Burchinal, M. R., & Macfie, J. (2003). Differentiating among insecure mother-infant attachment classifications: A focus on child-friend interaction and exploration during solitary play at 36 months. *Attachment and Human Development, 5*, 136–164.

McGloin, J. M., & Widom, C. S. (2001). Resilience among abused and neglected children grown up. *Development and Psychopathology, 13*, 1021–1038.

McGuigan, K., & Shevlin, M. (2010). Longitudinal changes in posttraumatic stress in relation to political violence (Bloody Sunday). *Traumatology, 16*, 1–6.

McHale, J. P. (1995). Coparenting and triadic interactions during infancy: The roles of marital distress and child gender. *Developmental Psychology, 31*, 985–996.

McHale, J. P. (2007). When infants grow up in multiperson relationship services. *Infant Mental Health Journal, 28*, 370–392.

McHale, J. P., & Fivaz-Depeursinge, E. (1999). Understanding triadic and family group interactions during infancy and toddlerhood. *Clinical Child and Family Psychology Review, 2*, 107–127.

McHale, J., Fivaz-Depeursinge, E., Dickstein, S., Robertson, J., & Daley, M. (2008). New evidence for the social embeddedness of infants' early triangular capacities. *Family Process, 47*, 415–463.

McHale, J. P., Salman, S., Strozier, A., & Cecil, D. K. (2013). Relationship processes and resilience in children with incarcerated parents: V. Triadic interactions in mother-grandmother coparenting systems following maternal release from jail. *Monographs of the Society for Research in Child Development, 78*, 57–74.

McIntyre, J. K., & Widom, C. S. (2011). Childhood victimization and crime victimization. *Journal of Interpersonal Violence, 26*, 640–663.

McKillop, N., Smallbone, S., Wortley, R., & Andjic, I. (2012). Offenders' attachment and sexual abuse onset: A test of theoretical propositions. *Sexual Abuse, 24*, 591–610.

McMahon, T. J., & Luthar, S. S. (2007). Defining characteristics and potential consequences of caretaking burden among children living in urban poverty. *American Journal of Orthopsychiatry, 77*, 267–281.

McMillen, C., & Zuravin, S. (1997). Attributions of blame and responsibility for child sexual abuse and adult adjustment. *Journal of Interpersonal Violence, 12*, 30–48.

Meckelmann, V. (2008). Childhood experiences, pubertal timing, and reproductive strategies of adolescent girls: A prospective longitudinal study. *Psychologie in Erziehung und Unterricht, 55*, 211–222.

Meins, E., Fernyhough, C., deRosnay, M., Arnott, B., Leekam, S. R., & Turner, M. (2012). Mind-mindedness as a multidimensional construct: Appropriate and nonattuned mind-related comments independently predict infant-mother attachment in a socially diverse sample. *Infancy, 17,* 393–415.

Melas, P. A., Wei, Y., Wong, C. C. Y., Sjoholm, L. K., Aberg, E., Mill, J., et al. (2013). Genetic and epigenetic associations of MAOA and NR3C1 with depression and childhood adversities. *International Journal of Neuropsychopharmacology, 16,* 1513–1528.

Mele, M., Roberts, J. C., & Wolfer, L. (2011). Men who seek protection orders against female intimate partners. *Partner Abuse, 2,* 61–75.

Menard, K. S., & Pincus, A. L. (2012). Predicting overt and cyber stalking perpetration by male and female college students. *Journal of Interpersonal Violence, 27,* 2183–2207.

Mendle, J., Leve, L. D., Van Ryzin, M., Natsuaki, M. N., & Ge, X. (2011). Associations between early life stress, child maltreatment, and pubertal development among girls in foster care. *Journal of Research on Adolescence, 21,* 871–880.

Mennen, F. E., Kim, K., Sang, J., & Trickett, P. K. (2010). Child neglect: Definition and identification of youth's experiences in official reports of maltreatment. *Child Abuse and Neglect, 34,* 647–658.

Merrilees, C. E., Cairns, E., Goeke-Morey, M. C., Schermerhom, A. C., Shirlow, P., & Cummings, E. M. (2011). Associations between mothers' experience with the Troubles in Northern Ireland and mothers' and children's psychological functioning: The moderating role of social identity. *Journal of Community Psychology, 39,* 60–75.

Messman-Moore, T. L., & Brown, A. L. (2006). Risk perception, rape, and sexual revictimization: A prospective study of college women. *Psychology of Women Quarterly, 30,* 1159–1172.

Messman-Moore, T. L., Walsh, K. L., & DiLillo, D. (2010). Emotion dysregulation and risky sexual behavior in revictimization. *Child Abuse and Neglect, 34,* 967–976.

Midgley, E. K., & Lo, C. C. (2013). The role of a parent's incarceration in the emotional health and problem behaviors of at-risk adolescents. *Journal of Child and Adolescent Substance Abuse, 22,* 85–103.

Mikulincer, M. (1998). Adult attachment style and individual differences in functional versus dysfunctional experiences of anger. *Journal of Personality and Social Psychology, 74,* 513–524.

Mileva-Seitz, V., Kennedy, J., Atkinson, L., Steiner, M., Levitan, R., Matthews, S. G., et al. (2011). Serotonin transporter allelic variation in mothers predicts maternal sensitivity, behavior and attitudes toward 6-month-old infants. *Genes, Brain and Behavior, 10,* 325–333.

Miller, H. V., & Barnes, J. C. (2013). Genetic transmission effects and intergenerational contact with the criminal justice system: A consideration of three dopamine polymorphisms. *Criminal Justice and Behavior, 40,* 671–689.

Miller-Johnson, S., Winn, D.-M., Coie, J., Maumary-Gremaud, A., Hyman, C., Terry, R., & Lochman, J. (1999). Motherhood during the teen years: A developmental perspective on risk factors for childbearing. *Development and Psychopathology, 11,* 85–100.

Milot, T., Lorent, A., St-Laurent, D., Bernier, A., Tarabulsy, G., Lemelin, J-P., & Ethier, L. S. (2014). Hostile-helpless state of mind as further evidence of adult disorganized states of mind in neglecting families. *Child Abuse & Neglect,* No Pagination Specified.

Miner, M. H., Flitter, J. M. K., & Robinson, B. E. (2006). Association of sexual revictimization with sexuality and psychological function. *Journal of Interpersonal Violence, 21,* 503–524.

Miner, M. H., Robinson, B. E., Knight, R. A., Berg, D., Romine, R. S., & Netland, J. (2010). Understanding sexual perpetration against children: Effects of attachment style, interpersonal involvement, and hypersexuality. *Sexual Abuse, 22,* 58–77.

Minnis, H., Green, J., O'Connor, T. G., Liew, A., Glaser, D., Taylor, E., et al. (2009). An exploratory study of the association between reactive attachment disorder and attachment narratives in early school-age children. *Journal of Child Psychology and Psychiatry, 50,* 931–942.

Minnis, H., Macmillan, S., Pritchett, R., Young, D., Wallace, B., Butcher, J., et al. (2013). Prevalence of reactive attachment disorder in a deprived population. *British Journal of Psychiatry, 202,* 342–346.

Minuchin, S. (1974). *Families and family therapy.* Cambridge, MA: Harvard University Press.

Mizuta, I., Zahn-Waxler, C., Cole, P. M., & Hiruma, N. (1996). A cross-cultural study of preschoolers' attachment: Security and sensitivity in Japanese and US dyads. *International Journal of Behavioral Development, 19,* 141–159.

Moehler, E., Biringen, Z., & Poustka, L. (2007). Emotional availability in a sample of mothers with a history of abuse. *American Journal of Orthopsychiatry, 77,* 624–628.

Molidor, C., & Tolman, R. M. (1998). Gender and contextual factors in adolescent dating violence. *Violence Against Women, 4,* 180–194.

Monk, C., Spicer, J., & Champagne, F. A. (2012). Linking prenatal maternal adversity to developmental outcomes in infants: The role of epigenetic pathways. *Development and Psychopathology, 24,* 1361–1376.

Monson, C. M., Fredman, S. J., & Taft, C. T. (2011). Couple and family issues and interventions for veterans of the Iraq and Afghanistan wars. In J. I. Ruzek, P. P. Schnurr, J. J. Vasterling, & M. J. Friedman (Eds.), *Caring for veterans with deployment-related stress disorders* (pp. 151–169). Washington, DC: American Psychological Association.

Moore, D. R., & Florsheim, P. (2008). Interpartner conflict and child abuse risk among African American and Latino adolescent parenting couples. *Child Abuse and Neglect, 32,* 463–475.

Moran, G., Bailey, H. N., Gleason, K., DeOliveira, C. A., & Pederson, D. R. (2008). Exploring the mind behind unresolved attachment: Lessons from and for attachment-based interventions with infants and their traumatized mothers. In H. Steele & M. Steele (Eds.), *Clinical applications of the Adult Attachment Interview* (pp. 371–398). New York: Guilford.

Moran, G., Pederson, D. R., & Krupka, A. (2005). Maternal unresolved attachment status impedes the effectiveness of interventions with adolescent mothers. *Infant Mental Health Journal, 26,* 231–249.

Moriceau, S., & Sullivan, R. M. (2005). Neurobiology of infant attachment. *Developmental Psychobiology, 47,* 230–242.

Morrill, M. I., Hines, D. A., Mahmood, S., & Cordova, J. V. (2010). Pathways between marriage and parenting for wives and husbands: The role of coparenting. *Family Process, 49,* 59–73.

Moss, E., Bureau, J.-F., St-Laurent, D., & Tarabulsy, G. M. (2011). Understanding disorganized attachment at preschool and school age: Examining divergent pathways of disorganized and controlling children. In J. Solomon & C. George (Eds.), *Disorganized attachment and caregiving* (pp. 52–79). New York: Guilford.

Moss, E., Cyr, C., & Dubois-Comtois, K. (2004). Attachment at early school age and developmental risk: Examining family contexts and behavior problems of controlling-caregiving, controlling-punitive, and behaviorally disorganized children. *Developmental Psychology, 40,* 519–532.

Moss, E., Dubois-Comtois, K., Cyr, C., Tarabulsy, G. M., St-Laurent, D., & Bernier, A. (2011). Efficacy of a home-visiting intervention aimed at improving maternal sensitivity, child attachment, and behavioral outcomes for maltreated children: A randomized control trial. *Development and Psychopathology, 23,* 195–210.

Moss, E., Smolla, N., Guerra, I., Mazzarello, T., Chayer, D., & Berthiaume, C. (2006). Attachment and self-reported internalizing and externalizing behavior problems in a school period. *Canadian Journal of Behavioural Science, 38,* 142–157.

Moss, E., Thibaudeau, P., Cyr, C., & Rousseau, D. (2001, April). Controlling attachment and child management of parental emotion. Paper presented at the biennial meeting of the Society for Research in Child Development, Minneapolis, MN.

Mrug, S., Elliott, M., Gilliland, M. J., Grunbaum, J. A., Tortolero, S. R., Cuccaro, P., & Schuster, M. (2008). Positive parenting and early puberty in girls. *Archives of Pediatrics and Adolescent Medicine, 162,* 781–786.

Munoz, L. C., Pakalniskiene, V., & Frick, P. J. (2011). Parental monitoring and youth behavior problems: Moderation by callous-unemotional traits over time. *European Child and Adolescent Psychiatry, 20,* 261–269.

Munson, J. A., McMahon, R. J., & Spieker, S. J. (2001). Structure and variability in the developmental trajectory of children's externalizing problems: Impact of infant attachment, maternal depressive symptomatology, and child sex. *Development and Psychopathology, 13,* 277–296.

Murdoch, M., Pryor, J. B., Polusny, M. A., Wall, M. M., Ripley, D. C., & Gackstetter, G. D. (2010). The association between military sexual stress and psychiatric symptoms after controlling for other stressors. *Journal of Psychiatric Research, 44,* 1129–1136.

Murray, J., Farrington, D. P., & Sekol, I. (2012). Children's antisocial behavior, mental health, drug use, and educational performance after parental incarceration: A systematic review and meta-analysis. *Psychological Bulletin, 138,* 175–210.

Murray, J., Janson, C.-G., & Farrington, D. P. (2007). Crime in adult offspring of prisoners: A cross-national comparison of two longitudinal samples. *Criminal Justice and Behavior, 34,* 133–149.

Murray, J., Loeber, R., & Pardini, D. (2012). Parental involvement in the criminal justice system and the development of youth theft, marijuana use, depression, and poor academic performance. *Criminology, 50,* 255–302.

Murray, J., & Murray, L. (2010). Parental incarceration, attachment and child psychopathology. *Attachment and Human Development, 12,* 289–309.

Murray-Close, D., Han, G., Cicchetti, D., Crick, N. R., & Rogosch, F. A. (2008). Neuroendocrine regulation and physical and relational aggression: The moderating roles of child maltreatment and gender. *Developmental Psychology, 44,* 1160–1176.

Murray-Close, D., Holland, A. S., & Roisman, G. I. (2012). Autonomic arousal and relational aggression in heterosexual dating couples. *Personal Relationships, 19,* 203–218.

Murrell, A. R., Christoff, K. A., & Henning, K. R. (2007). Characteristics of domestic violence offenders: Associations with childhood exposure to violence. *Journal of Family Violence, 22,* 523–532.

Mychasiuk, R., Schmold, N., Ilnytskyy, S., Kavalchuk, O., Kolb, B., & Gibb, R. (2011). Prenatal bystander stress alters brain, behavior, and the epigenome of developing rat offspring. *Developmental Neuroscience, 33,* 159–169.

Myers, B. J., Mackintosh, V. H., Kuznetsova, M. I., Lotze, G. M., Best, A. M., & Ravindran, N. (2013). Relationship processes and resilience in children with incarcerated parents: III. Teasing, bullying, and emotion regulation in children of incarcerated mothers. *Monographs of the Society for Research in Child Development, 78,* 26–40.

Myers, H. F., Wyatt, G. E., Loeb, T. B., Carmona, J. V., Warda, U., Longshore, D., et al. (2006). Severity of child sexual abuse, post-traumatic stress and risky sexual behaviors among HIV-positive women. *AIDS and Behavior, 10,* 191–199.

Najdowski, C. J., & Ullman, S. E. (2009). Prospective effects of sexual victimization on PTSD and problem drinking. *Addictive Behaviors, 34,* 965–968.

Nakashi-Eisikovits, O., Dutra, L., & Westen, D. (2002). Relationship between attachment patterns and personality pathology in adolescents. *Journal of the American Academy of Child and Adolescent Psychiatry, 41,* 1111–1123.

Nally, D. (2003, August). Barriers to treating nonabused siblings in sexual abuse treatment programs. Paper presented at the annual meeting of the American Psychological Association, Toronto, Canada.

Narang, D. S., & Contreras, J. M. (2000). Dissociation as a mediator between child abuse history and adult abuse potential. *Child Abuse and Neglect, 24,* 653–665.

Narayan, A. (2009). Resilience, metacognition and complexity. *Journal of the Indian Academy of Applied Psychology, 35,* 112–118.

Narayan, A. J., Englund, M. M., Carlson, E. A., & Egeland, B. (2014). Adolescent conflict as a developmental process in the prospective pathway from exposure to interparental violence to dating violence. *Journal of Abnormal Child Psychology, 42,* 239–250.

Narusyte, J., Andershed, A.-K., Neiderhiser, J. M., & Lichtenstein, P. (2007). Aggression as a mediator of genetic contributions to the association between negative parent-child relationships and adolescent antisocial behavior. *European Child and Adolescent Psychiatry, 16,* 128–137.

Nasim, R., & Nadan, Y. (2013). Couples therapy with childhood sexual abuse survivors (CSA) and their partners: Establishing a context for witnessing. *Family Process, 52,* 36–377.

Natsuaki, M. N., Leve, L. D., & Mendle, J. (2011). Going through the rites of passage: Timing and transition of menarche, childhood sexual abuse, and anxiety symptoms in girls. *Journal of Youth and Adolescence, 40,* 1357–1370.

Nauha, S., & Silven, M. (2000). Does childhood attachment predict the choice of spouse? *Psykologia, 35,* 71–82.

Nederhof, E., Belsky, J., Ormel, J., & Oldehinkel, A. J. (2012). Effects of divorce on Dutch boys' and girls' externalizing behavior in gene × environment perspective: Diathesis stress or differential susceptibility in Dutch Tracking Adolescents' Individual Lives Survey study. *Development and Psychopathology, 24,* 929–939.

Nelson, E. M., & Spieker, S. J. (2013). Intervention effects on morning and stimulated cortisol responses among toddlers in foster care. *Infant Mental Health Journal, 34,* 211–221.

Newcomb, M. D., & Locke, T. F. (2001). Intergenerational cycle of maltreatment: A popular concept obscured by methodological limitations. *Child Abuse and Neglect, 25,* 1219–1240.

Newland, L. A., Chen, H.-H., Coyl-Shepherd, D. D., Liang, Y.-C., Carr, E. R., Dykstra, E., & Gapp, S. C. (2013). Parent and child perspectives on mothering and fathering: The influence of ecocultural niches. *Early Child Development and Care, 183,* 534–552.

Newland, L. A., Coyl, D. D., & Freeman, H. (2008). Predicting preschoolers' attachment security from fathers' involvement, internal working models, and use of social support. *Early Child Development and Care, 178,* 785–801.

Neyland, T. C., Brunet, A., Pole, N., Best, S. R., Metzler, T. J., Yehuda, R., & Marmar, C. R. (2005). PTSD symptoms predict waking salivary cortisol levels in police officers. *Psychoneuroendocrinology, 30,* 373–381.

Nicolson, N. A., Davis, M. C., Kruszewski, D., & Zautra, A. J. (2010). Childhood maltreatment and diurnal cortisol patterns in women with chronic pain. *Psychosomatic Medicine, 72,* 471–480.

Noland, V. J., Liller, K. D., McDermott, R. J., Coulter, M. L., & Seraphine, A. E. (2004). Is adolescent sibling violence a precursor to college dating violence? *American Journal of Health Behavior, 28* (Suppl. 1), S13–S23.

Noll, J. G. (2008). Sexual abuse of children: Unique in its effects on development? *Child Abuse and Neglect, 32,* 603–605.

Noll, J. G., & Grych, J. H. (2011). Read-react-respond: An integrative model for understanding sexual revictimization. *Psychology of Violence, 1,* 202–215.

Noll, J. G., Haralson, K. J., Butler, E. M., & Shenk, C. E. (2011). Childhood maltreatment, psychological dysregulation, and risky sexual behaviors in female adolescents. *Journal of Pediatric Psychology, 36,* 743–752.

Noll, J. G., Trickett, P. K., Harris, W. W., & Putnam, F. W. (2009). The cumulative burden borne by offspring whose mothers were sexually abused as children: Descriptive results from a multigenerational study. *Journal of Interpersonal Violence, 24,* 424–449.

Novero, C. M., Loper, A. B., & Warren, J. I. (2011). Second-generation prisoners: Adjustment patterns for inmates with a history of parental incarceration. *Criminal Justice and Behavior, 38,* 761–778.

Nunan, A. (2004). Domestic violence among homosexual couples: The second closet? *PSICO, 35,* 69–78.

Nunes, S. O. V., Watanabe, M. A. E., Morimoto, H. K., Moriya, R., & Reiche, E. M. V. (2010). The impact of childhood sexual abuse on activation of immunological and neuroendocrine response. *Aggression and Violent Behavior, 15,* 440–445.

Nuttall, A. K., Valentino, K., & Borkowski, J. G. (2012). Maternal history of parentification, maternal arm responsiveness, and children's externalizing behavior. *Journal of Family Psychology, 26,* 767–775.

Nye, E. C., Katzman, J., Bell, J. B., Kilpatrick, J., Krainard, M., & Haaland, K. Y. (2008). Attachment organization in Vietnam combat veterans with posttraumatic stress disorder. *Attachment and Human Development, 10,* 41–57.

Obsuth, I., Hennighausen, K., Brumariu, L. E., & Lyons-Ruth, K. (2014). Disorganized behavior in adolescent–parent interaction: Relations to attachment state of mind, partner abuse, and psychopathology. *Child Development, 85,* 370-387.

O'Connor, E., Bureau, J.-F., McCartney, K., & Lyons-Ruth, K. (2011). Risks and outcomes associated with disorganized/controlling patterns of attachment at age three years in the National Institute of Child Health and Human Development study of early child care and youth development. *Infant Mental Health Journal, 32,* 450–472.

O'Connor, E. E., Collins, B. A., & Supplee, L. (2012). Behavior problems in late childhood: The roles of early maternal attachment and teacher-child relationship trajectories. *Attachment and Human Development, 14,* 265–288.

O'Connor, E., & McCartney, K. (2006). Testing associations between young children's relationships with mothers and teachers. *Journal of Educational Psychology, 98,* 87–98.

O'Connor, T. G., Bergman, K., Sarkar, P., & Glover, V. (2013). Prenatal cortisol exposure predicts infant cortisol response to acute stress. *Developmental Psychobiology, 55,* 145–155.

O'Connor, T. G., Caprariello, P., Blackmore, E. R., Gregory, A. M., Glover, V., & Fleming, P. (2007). Prenatal mood disturbance predicts sleep problems in infancy and toddlerhood. *Early Human Development, 83,* 451–458.

O'Connor, T. G., Deater-Deckard, K., Fulker, D., Rutter, M., & Plomin, R. (1998). Genotype-environment correlations in late childhood and early adolescence: Antisocial behavioral problems and coercive parenting. *Developmental Psychology, 34,* 970–981.

Oddone Paolucci, E., Genuis, M. L., & Violato, C. (2001). A meta-analysis of the published research on the effects of child sexual abuse. *Journal of Psychology, 135,* 17–36.

O'Donnell, K. J., Glover, V., Jenkins, J., Browne, D., Ben-Shlomo, Y., Golding, J., & O'Connor, T. G. (2013). Prenatal maternal mood is associated with altered diurnal cortisol in adolescence. *Psychoneuroendocrinology, 38,* 1630–1638.

Ogawa, J., Sroufe, A., Weinfield, N., Carlson, E., & Egeland, B. (1997). Development and the fragmented self: Longitudinal study of dissociative symptomatology in a non-clinical sample. *Development and Psychopathology, 9,* 855–879.

Okado, Y., & Azar, S. T. (2011). The impact of extreme emotional distance in the mother-child relationship on the offspring's future risk of maltreatment perpetration. *Journal of Family Violence, 26,* 439–452.

O'Keefe, M. (1998). Factors mediating the link between witnessing interparental violence and dating violence. *Journal of Family Violence, 13,* 39–57.

O'Leary, P., Coohey, C., & Easton, S. D. (2010). The effect of severe child sexual abuse and disclosure on mental health during adulthood. *Journal of Child Sexual Abuse, 19,* 275–289.

Olff, M., Frijling, J. L., Kubzansky, L. D., Bradley, B., Ellenbogen, M. A., Cardoso, C., et al. (2013). The role of oxytocin in social bonding, stress regulation and mental health: An update on the moderating effects of context and inter-individual differences. *Psychoneuroendocrinology, 38,* 1883–1894.

Oliveira, P. S., Soares, I., Martins, C., Silva, J. R., Marques, S., Baptista, J., & Lyons-Ruth, K. (2012). Indiscriminate behavior observed in the strange situation among institutionalized toddlers: Relations to caregiver report and to early family risk. *Infant Mental Health Journal, 33,* 187–196.

Oliver, J. E. (1993). Intergenerational transmission of child abuse: Rates, research, and clinical implications. *American Journal of Psychiatry, 150,* 1315–1324.

Olsson, C. A., Byrnes, G. B., Lotfi-Miri, M., Collins, V., Williamson, R., Patton, C., & Anney, R. J. L. (2005). Association between 5-HTTLPR genotypes and persisting patterns of anxiety and alcohol use: Results from a 10-year longitudinal study of adolescent mental health. *Molecular Psychiatry, 10,* 868–876.

Olweus, D. (1978). *Aggression in the schools: Bullies and whipping boys.* Oxford: Hemisphere.

Oosterlaan, J., Geurts, H. M., Knol, D. L., & Sergeant, J. A. (2005). Low basal salivary cortisol is associated with teacher-reported symptoms of conduct disorder. *Psychiatry Research, 134,* 1–10.

Orcutt, H. K., Cooper, M. L., & Garcia, M. (2005). Use of sexual intercourse to reduce negative affect as a prospective mediator of sexual revictimization. *Journal of Traumatic Stress, 18,* 729–739.

O'Rinn, S., Lishak, V., Muller, R. T., & Classen, C. (2012). A preliminary examination of perceptions of betrayal and its association with memory disturbances among survivors of childhood sexual abuse. *Psychological Trauma, 5,* 343–349.

Ornstein, P. A., Ceci, S. J., & Loftus, E. F. (1998). Comment on Alpert, Brown, and Courtois (1998): The science of memory and the practice of psychotherapy. *Psychology, Public Policy and Law, 4,* 996–1010.

Oshri, A., Rogosch, F. A., & Cicchetti, D. (2013). Child maltreatment and mediating influences of childhood personality types on the development of adolescent psychopathology. *Journal of Clinical Child and Adolescent Psychology,* 42, 287–301.

Otte, C., Neyland, T. C., Pole, N., Metzler, T., Best, S., Henn-Haase, C., et al. (2005). Association between childhood trauma and catecholamine response to psychological stress in police academy recruits. *Biological Psychiatry, 57,* 27–32.

Ou, S.-R., & Reynolds, A. J. (2010). Childhood predictors of young adult male crime. *Children and Youth Services Review, 32,* 1097–1107.

Out, D., Bakermans-Kranenburg, M. J., van Pelt, J., & van IJzendoorn, M. H. (2012). Salivary α-amylase and intended harsh caregiving in response to infant crying: Evidence for physiological hyperreactivity. *Child Maltreatment, 17,* 295–305.

Owen, M. T., & Cox, M. J. (1997). Marital conflict and the development of infant-parent attachment relationships. *Journal of Family Psychology, 11,* 152–164.

Owens, E. B., Shaw, D. S., Giovannelli, J., Garcia, M. M., & Yaggi, K. (1999). Factors associated with behavioral competence at school among young boys from multi-problem low-income families. *Early Education and Development, 10,* 135–162.

Owens, G. P., Dashevsky, B., Chard, K. M., Mohamed, S., Hall, U., Heppner, P. S., & Baker, D. G. (2009). The relationship between childhood trauma, combat exposure, and posttraumatic stress disorder in male veterans. *Military Psychology, 21,* 114–125.

Oz, S. (2001). When the wife was sexually abused as a child: Marital relations before and during her therapy for abuse. *Sexual and Relationship Therapy, 16,* 287–298.

Pace, C. S., & Zavattini, G. C. (2011). "Adoption and attachment theory": The attachment models of adoptive mothers and the revision of attachment patterns of their late-adopted children. *Child: Care, Health and Development, 37,* 82–88.

Palesh, O. G., Looney, E., Batiuchok, D., Koopman, C., Ginzburg, K., Bui, M., et al. (2008). Empirical support for a conceptual model of posttraumatic stress disorder among survivors of child sexual abuse. In T. I. Richardson & M. V. Williams (Eds.), *Child abuse and violence* (pp. 43–57). Hauppauge, NY: Nova Science.

Paley, B., Cox, M. J., Burchinal, M. R., & Payne, C. C. (1999). Attachment and marital functioning: Comparison of spouses with continuous-secure, earned-secure, dismissing, and preoccupied attachment stances. *Journal of Family Psychology, 13,* 580–597.

Paley, B., Cox, M. J., Kanoy, K. W., Harter, K. S. M., Burchinal, M., & Margand, N. A. (2005). Adult attachment and marital interaction as predictors of whole family interactions during the transition to parenthood. *Journal of Family Psychology, 19*, 420–429.

Parade, S. H., & Leerkes, E. M. (2011). Marital aggression predicts infant orienting toward mother at six months. *Infant Behavior and Development, 34*, 235–238.

Pardini, D., Stepp, S., Hipwell, A., Stouthamer-Loeber, M., & Loeber, R. (2012). The clinical utility of the proposed DSM-5 callous-unemotional subtype of conduct disorder in young girls. *Journal of the American Academy of Child and Adolescent Psychiatry, 51*, 62–73.

Paris, J. Z., & Frank, H. (1997). Parameters of childhood sexual abuse in female patients. In M. C. Zanarini (Ed.), *Role of sexual abuse in the etiology of borderline personality disorder* (pp. 15–28). Arlington, VA: American Psychiatric Association.

Pasalich, D. S., Dadds, M. R., Hawes, D. J., & Brennan, J. (2011). Do callous-unemotional traits moderate the relative importance of parental coercion versus warmth in child conduct problems? An observational study. *Journal of Child Psychology and Psychiatry, 52*, 1308–1315.

Pasalich, D. S., Dadds, M. R., Hawes, D. J., & Brennan, J. (2012). Attachment and callous-unemotional traits in children with early-onset conduct problems. *Journal of Child Psychology and Psychiatry, 53*, 838–845.

Pauli-Pott, U., Friedel, S., Hinney, A., & Hebebrand, J. (2009). Serotonin transporter gene polymorphism (5-HTTLPR), environmental conditions, and developing negative emotionality and fear in early childhood. *Journal of Neural Transmission, 116*, 503–512.

Pears, K. C., Bruce, J., Fisher, P. A., & Kim, H. K. (2010). Indiscriminate friendliness in maltreated foster children. *Child Maltreatment, 15*, 64–75.

Pears, K. C., & Capaldi, D. M. (2001). Intergenerational transmission of abuse: A two-generational prospective study of an at-risk sample. *Child Abuse and Neglect, 25*, 1439–1461.

Pears, K. C., Kim, H. K., & Fisher, P. A. (2008). Psychosocial and cognitive functioning of children with specific profiles of maltreatment. *Child Abuse and Neglect, 32*, 958–971.

Pechtel, P., Woodman, A., & Lyons-Ruth, K. (2012). Early maternal withdrawal and nonverbal childhood IQ as precursors for substance use disorder in young adulthood: Results of a 20-year prospective study. *International Journal of Cognitive Therapy, 5*, 316–329.

Pederson, D. R., Gleason, K. E., Moran, G., & Bento, S. (1998). Maternal attachment representations, maternal sensitivity, and the infant-mother attachment relationship. *Developmental Psychology, 34*, 925–933.

Peled, E., & Gil, I. B. (2011). The mothering perceptions of women abused by their partner. *Violence Against Women, 17*, 457–479.

Pemberton, C. K., Neiderhiser, J. M., Leve, L. D., Natsuaki, M. N., Shaw, D. S., Reiss, D., & Ge, X. (2010). Influence of parental depressive symptoms on adopted toddler behaviors: An emerging developmental cascade of genetic and environmental effects. *Development and Psychopathology, 22,* 803–818.

Pemberton, J. R., Kramer, T. L., Borrego, J., & Owen, R. R. (2013). Kids at the VA? A call for evidence-based parenting interventions for returning veterans. *Psychological Services, 10,* 194–202.

Pence, E., & Paymar, M. (1993). *Education groups for men who batter: The Duluth model.* New York: Springer.

Pener-Tessler, R., Avinun, R., Uzefovsky, F., Edelman, S., Ebstein, R. P., & Knafo, A. (2013). Boys' serotonin transporter genotype affects maternal behavior through self-control: A case of evocative gene-environment correlation. *Development and Psychopathology, 25,* 151–162.

Peres, J. F. P., Foerster, B., Santana, L. G., Fereira, M. D., Nasello, A. G., Savoia, M., et al. (2011). Police officers under attack: Resilience implications of an fMRI study. *Journal of Psychiatric Research, 45,* 727–734.

Peris, T. S., & Emery, R. E. (2005). Redefining the parent-child relationship following divorce: Examining the risk for boundary dissolution. *Journal of Emotional Abuse, 5,* 169–189.

Peris, T. S., Goeke-Morey, M. C., Cummings, E. M., & Emergy, R. E. (2008). Marital conflict and support seeking by parents in adolescence: Empirical support for the parentification construct. *Journal of Family Psychology, 22,* 633–642.

Perlstein, P., & Motta, R. W. (2013). An investigation of potential Holocaust-related secondary trauma in the third generation. *Traumatology, 19,* 95–106.

Perry, D. G., Kusel, S. J., & Perry, L. C. (1988). Victims of peer aggression. *Developmental Psychology, 24,* 807–814.

Peter, T., Roberts, L. W., & Buzdugan, R. (2008). Suicidal ideation among Canadian youth: A multivariate analysis. *Archives of Suicide Research, 12,* 263–275.

Peters, D. K., & Range, L. M. (1996). Self-blame and self-destruction in women sexually abused as children. *Journal of Child Sexual Abuse, 5,* 19–33.

Peterson, C., Park, N., & Castro, C. A. (2011). Assessment for the U.S. Army comprehensive soldier fitness program: The global assessment tool. *American Psychologist, 66,* 10–18.

Phelps, J. L., Belsky, J., & Crnic, K. (1998). Earned security, daily stress, and parenting: A comparison of five alternative models. *Development and Psychopathology, 10,* 21–38.

Phillips, C. J., LeardMann, C. A., Gumbs, G. R., & Smith, B. (2010). Risk factors for posttraumatic stress disorder among deployed US male Marines. *BMC Psychiatry, 10,* Article 52.

Phillips, S. D., & Zhao, J. (2010). The relationship between witnessing arrests and elevated symptoms of posttraumatic stress: Findings from a national study of children involved in the child welfare system. *Children and Youth Services Review, 32,* 1246–1254.

Phillips-Green, M. J. (2002). Sibling incest. *Family Journal, 10,* 195–202.

Pierrehumbert, B., Santelices, M. P., Ibanez, M., Alberdi, M., Ongari, B., Roskam, I., et al. (2009). Gender and attachment representations in the preschool years: Comparisons between five countries. *Journal of Cross-Cultural Psychology, 40,* 543–566.

Pietromonaco, P. R., & Barrett, L. (1997). Working models of attachment and daily social interactions. *Journal of Personality and Social Psychology, 73,* 1409–1423.

Pietromonaco, P. R., & Barrett, L. F. (2000). The internal working models concept: What do we really know about the self in relation to others? *Review of General Psychology, 4,* 155–175.

Piotrowski, C. C. (2011). Patterns of adjustment among siblings exposed to intimate partner violence. *Journal of Family Psychology, 25,* 19–28.

Pittman, J. F., & Buckley, R. R. (2006). Comparing maltreating fathers and mothers in terms of personal distress, interpersonal functioning, and perceptions of family climate. *Child Abuse and Neglect, 30,* 481–496.

Platje, E., Jansen, L. M. C., Raine, A., Branje, S. J. T., Doreleijers, T. A. H., de Vries-Bouw, M., et al. (2013). Longitudinal associations in adolescence between cortisol and persistent aggressive or rule-breaking behavior. *Biological Psychology, 93,* 132–137.

Poehlmann, J. (2005). Representations of attachment relationships in children of incarcerated mothers. *Child Development, 76,* 679–696.

Poehlmann, J., Dallaire, D., Loper, A. B., & Shear, L. D. (2010). Children's contact with their incarcerated parents: Research findings and recommendations. *American Psychologist, 66,* 575–598.

Poehlmann, J., Park, J., Bouffiou, L., Abrahams, J., Shlafer, R., & Hahn, E. (2008). Representations of family relationships in children living with custodial grandparents. *Attachment and Human Development, 10,* 165–188.

Pole, N. (2008). Predictors of PTSD symptoms in police officers: From childhood to retirement. In D. L. Delahanty (Ed.), *The psychobiology of trauma and resilience across the lifespan* (pp. 47–67). Lanham, MD: Jason Aronson.

Pole, N., Neyland, T. C., Otte, C., Henn-Haase, C., Metzler, T. J., & Marmar, C. R. (2009). Prospective prediction of posttraumatic stress disorder symptoms using fear potentiated auditory startle responses. *Biological Psychiatry, 65,* 235–240.

Popma, A., Vermeiren, R., Geluk, C. A. M. L., Rinne, T., van den Brink, W., Knol, D. L., et al. (2007). Cortisol moderates the relationship between testosterone and aggression in delinquent male adolescents. *Biological Psychiatry, 61*, 405–411.

Porges, S. W. (1997). Emotion: An evolutionary by-product of the neural regulation of the autonomic nervous system. *Annals of the New York Academy of Sciences, 807*, 62–77.

Porges, S. W. (2007). The polyvagal perspective. *Biological Psychology, 74*, 116–143.

Posada, G., Gao, Y., Wu, F., Posada, R., Tascon, M., Schoelmerich, A., et al. (1995). The secure-base phenomenon across cultures: Children's behavior, mother's preferences, and experts' concepts. *Monographs of the Society for Research in Child Development, 60*, 27–48.

Posada, G., Lu, T., Trumbell, J., Kaloustian, G., Trudel, M., Plata, S. J., et al. (2013). Is the secure base phenomenon evident here, there, and anywhere? A cross-cultural study of child behavior and experts' definitions. *Child Development, 84*, 1896–1905.

Poustka, L., Maras, A., Hohm, E., Fellinger, J., Holtmann, M., Banaschewski, T., et al. (2010). Negative association between plasma cortisol levels and aggression in a high-risk community sample of adolescents. *Journal of Neural Transmission, 117*, 621–627.

Power, C., Thomas, L., Li, L., & Hertzman, C. (2012). Childhood psychosocial adversity and adult cortisol patterns. *British Journal of Psychiatry, 201*, 199–206.

Powers, A., Ressler, K. J., & Bradley, R. G. (2009). The protective role of friendship on the effects of childhood abuse and depression. *Depression and Anxiety, 26*, 46–53.

Pregeli, P., & Videtic, A. (2010). Possible involvement of epigenetic mechanisms in the neurobiology of PTSD. In B. K. Wiederhold (Ed.), *Coping with posttraumatic stress disorder in returning troops: Wounds of war II* (pp. 3–12). NATO Science for Peace and Security Series E: Human and Societal Dynamics, Vol. 68. Amsterdam: IOS Press.

Pretorius, I.-M. (2010). Genetic and environmental contributors to the intergenerational transmission of trauma and disorganized attachment relationships. In T. Baradon (Ed.), *Relational trauma in infancy: Psychoanalytic, attachment and neuropsychological contributors to parent-infant psychotherapy* (pp. 6–18). New York: Routledge.

Prospero, M., & Kim, M. (2009). Mutual partner violence: Mental health symptoms among female and male victims in four racial/ethnic groups. *Journal of Interpersonal Violence, 24*, 2039–2056.

Purvis, M. (2013). Paternal incarceration and parenting programs in prison: A review paper. *Psychiatry, Psychology and Law, 20*, 9–28.

Putallaz, M., Costanzo, P. R., Grimes, C. L., & Sherman, D. M. (1998). Intergenerational continuities and their influences on children's social development. *Social Development, 7,* 389–427.

Quas, J. A., Goodman, G. S., & Jones, D. P. H. (2003). Predictors of attributions of self-blame and internalizing behavior problems in sexually abused children. *Journal of Child Psychology and Psychiatry, 44,* 723–736.

Quigley, D. D., Jaycox, L. H., McCaffrey, D. F., & Marshall, G. N. (2006). Peer and family influences on adolescent anger expression and the acceptance of cross-gender aggression. *Violence and Victims, 21,* 597–610.

Raaska, H., Lapinleimu, H., Sinkkonen, J., Salmivalli, C., Matomaki, J., Makipaa, S., & Elovainio, M. (2012). Experiences of school bullying among internationally adopted children: Results from the Finnish Adoption (FINADO) study. *Child Psychiatry and Human Development, 43,* 592–611.

Raby, K. L., Cicchetti, D., Carlson, E. A., Cutuli, J. J., Englund, M. M., & Egeland, B. (2012). Genetic and caregiving-based contributions to infant attachment: Unique associations with distress reactivity and attachment security. *Psychological Science, 23,* 1016–1023.

Radhakrishna, A., Bou-Saada, I. E., Hunter, W. M., Catellier, D. J., & Kotch, J. B. (2001). Are father surrogates a risk factor for child maltreatment? *Child Maltreatment, 6,* 281–289.

Ramiro, L. S., Madrid, B. J., & Brown, D. W. (2010). Adverse childhood experiences (ACE) and health-risk behaviors among adults in a developing country setting. *Child Abuse and Neglect, 34,* 842–855.

Rani, M., & Bonu, S. (2009). Attitudes toward wife beating: A cross-country study in Asia. *Journal of Interpersonal Violence, 24,* 1371–1397.

Rapoza, K. A., & Baker, A. T. (2008). Attachment style, alcohol, and childhood experience of abuse: An analysis of physical violence in dating couples. *Violence and Victims, 23,* 52–65.

Raval, V., Goldberg, S., Atkinson, L., Benoit, D., Myhal, N., Poulton, L., et al. (2001). Maternal attachment, maternal responsiveness and infant attachment. *Infant Behavior and Development, 24,* 281–304.

Rea, J. G., & Rossman, B. B. R. (2005). Children exposed to interparental violence: Does parenting contribute to functioning over time? *Journal of Emotional Abuse, 5,* 1–28.

Reichmann-Decker, A., DePrince, A. P., & McIntosh, D. N. (2009). Affective responsiveness, betrayal, and childhood abuse. *Journal of Trauma and Dissociation, 10,* 276–296.

Reinemann, D. H. S., Stark, K. D., & Swearer, S. M. (2003). Family factors that differentiate sexually abused and nonabused adolescent psychiatric inpatients. *Journal of Interpersonal Violence, 18,* 471–489.

Reiner, I., & Spangler, G. (2010). Adult attachment and gene polymorphisms of the dopamine d4 receptor and serotonin transporter (5-HTT). *Attachment and Human Development, 12,* 209–229.

Renner, L. M., & Whitney, S. D. (2012). Risk factors for unidirectional and bidirectional intimate partner violence among young adults. *Child Abuse and Neglect, 36,* 40–52.

Renshaw, K. D., & Kiddie, N. S. (2012). Internal anger and external expressions of aggression in OEF/OIF veterans. *Military Psychology, 24,* 221–235.

Rheem, K. D., Woolley, S. R., & Johnson, S. M. (2011). Emotionally focused couple therapy: A military case study. In D. K. Carson & M. Casado-Kehoe (Eds.), *Case studies in couples therapy: Theory-based approaches* (pp. 191–204). New York: Routledge.

Rhule-Louie, D. M., & McMahon, R. J. (2007). Problem behavior and romantic relationships: Assortative mating, behavior contagion, and desistance. *Clinical Child and Family Psychology Review, 10,* 53–100.

Richmond, M. K., & Stocker, C. M. (2009). Associations between siblings' differential family experiences and differences in psychological adjustment. *European Journal of Developmental Science, 3,* 98–114.

Riggs, S. A., & Jacobvitz, D. (2002). Expectant parents' representations of early attachment relationships: Associations with mental health and family history. *Journal of Consulting and Clinical Psychology, 70,* 195–204.

Riggs, S. A., Jacobvitz, D., & Hazen, N. (2002). Adult attachment and history of psychotherapy in a normative sample. *Psychotherapy: Theory, Research, Practice, Training, 39,* 344–353.

Riggs, S. A., Paulson, A., Tunnell, E., Sahl, G., Atkison, H., & Ross, C. A. (2007). Attachment, personality, and psychopathology among adult inpatients: Self-reported romantic attachment style versus Adult Attachment Interview states of mind. *Development and Psychopathology, 19,* 263–291.

Riggs, S. A., & Riggs, D. S. (2011). Risk and resilience in military families experiencing deployment: The role of the family attachment network. *Journal of Family Psychology, 25,* 675–687.

Rivera-Rivera, L., Allen-Leigh, B., Rodríguez-Ortega, G., Chávez-Ayala, R., & Lazcano-Ponce, E. (2007). Prevalence and correlates of adolescent dating violence: Baseline study of a cohort of 7,960 male and female Mexican public school students. *Preventive Medicine, 44,* 477–484.

Rizq, R., & Target, M. (2010a). "If that's what I need, it could be what someone else needs." Exploring the role of attachment and reflective function in counseling psychologists' accounts of how they use personal therapy in clinical practice: A mixed methods study. *British Journal of Guidance and Counselling, 38,* 459–481.

Rizq, R., & Target, M. (2010b). "We had a constant battle." The role of attachment status in counseling psychologists' experiences of personal therapy: Some results from a mixed-methods study. *Counselling Psychology Quarterly*, 23, 343–369.

Robbins, T. W., & Everitt, B. J. (1999). Motivation and reward. In M. J. Zigmond, F. E. Bloom, S. C. Landys, J. L. Roberts, & L. R. Squire (Eds.), *Fundamental neuroscience* (pp. 1246–1260). San Diego: Academic Press.

Robboy, J., & Anderson, K. G. (2011). Intergenerational child abuse and coping. *Journal of Interpersonal Violence*, 26, 3526–3541.

Roberts, R., O'Connor, T., Dunn, J., & Golding, J. (2004). The effects of child sexual abuse in later family life: Mental health, parenting and adjustment of offspring. *Child Abuse and Neglect*, 28, 525–545.

Rodgers, A. B., Morgan, C. P., Bronson, S. L., Revello, S., & Bale, T. L. (2013). Paternal stress exposure alters sperm microRNA content and reprograms offspring HPA stress axis regulation. *Journal of Neuroscience*, 33, 9003–9012.

Roelofs, K., Keijers, G. P., Hoogduin, K. A., Naring, G. W., & Moene, F. C. (2002). Childhood abuse in patients with conversion disorder. *American Journal of Psychiatry*, 159, 1908–1913.

Roettger, M. E., & Swisher, R. R. (2011). Associations of fathers' history of incarceration with sons' delinquency and arrest among black, white, and Hispanic males in the United States. *Criminology*, 49, 1109–1147.

Roettger, M. E., Swisher, R. R., Kuhl, D. C., & Chavez, J. (2011). Paternal incarceration and trajectories of marijuana and other illegal drug use from adolescence into young adulthood: Evidence from longitudinal panels of males and females in the United States. *Addiction*, 106, 121–132.

Roisman, G. I., Fortuna, K., & Holland, A. (2006). An experimental manipulation of retrospectively defined earned and continuous attachment security. *Child Development*, 77, 59–71.

Roisman, G. I., Fraley, R. C., & Belsky, J. (2007). A taxometric study of the Adult Attachment Interview. *Developmental Psychology*, 43, 675–686.

Roisman, G. I., Holland, A., Fortuna, K., Fraley, R. C., Clausell, E., & Clarke, A. (2007). The Adult Attachment Interview and self-reports of attachment style: An empirical rapprochement. *Journal of Personality and Social Psychology*, 92, 678–697.

Roisman, G. I., Padron, E., Sroufe, L. A., & Egeland, B. (2002). Earned-secure attachment status in retrospect and prospect. *Child Development*, 73, 1204–1219.

Roman, M. W., Hall, J. M., & Bolton, K. S. (2008). Nurturing natural resources: The ecology of interpersonal relationships in women who have thrived despite childhood maltreatment. *Advances in Nursing Science*, 31, 184–197.

Romans, S. E., Martin, M., Gendall, K., & Herbison, G. P. (2003). Age of men-arche: The role of some psychosocial factors. *Psychological Medicine, 33,* 933–939.

Rosen, L. N., & Martin, L. (1996). The measurement of childhood trauma among male and female soldiers in the U.S. Army. *Military Medicine, 161,* 342–345.

Rosen, L. N., & Martin, L. (1998). Childhood maltreatment history as a risk fac-tor for sexual harassment among U.S. Army soldiers. *Violence and Victims, 13,* 269–286.

Rosenbaum, A., & Leisring, P. A. (2003). Beyond power and control: Towards an understanding of partner abusive men. *Journal of Comparative Family Stud-ies, 34,* 7–22.

Rosenheck, R., & Fontana, A. (1998). Warrior fathers and warrior sons: Intergen-erational aspects of trauma. In Y. Danieli (Ed.), *International handbook of multigenerational legacies of trauma* (pp. 225–242). New York: Plenum.

Rosenthal, S., Feiring, C., & Taska, L. (2003). Emotional support and adjust-ment over a year's time following sexual abuse discovery. *Child Abuse and Neglect, 27,* 641–661.

Ross, J., & Fuertes, J. (2010). Parental attachment, interparental conflict, and young adults' emotional adjustment. *Counseling Psychologist, 38,* 1050–1077.

Rothbaum, F., Rosen, K., Ujiie, T., & Uchida, N. (2002). Family systems theory, attachment theory and culture. *Family Process, 41,* 328–350.

Rubin, K. H., Dwyer, K. M., Booth-LaForce, C., Kim, A. H., Burgess, K. B., & Rose-Krasnor, L. (2004). Attachment, friendship and psychosocial function-ing in early adolescence. *Journal of Early Adolescence, 24,* 326–356.

Rusiecki, J. A., Byrne, C., Galdzicki, Z., Srikantan, V., Chen, L., Poulin, M., et al. (2013). PTSD and DNA methylation in select immune function gene pro-moter regions: A repeated measures case-control study of U.S. military service members. *Frontiers in Psychiatry, 4,* Article 56.

Rylands, A. J., Hinz, R., Jones, M., Holmes, S. E., Feldmann, M., Brown, G., et al. (2012). Pre- and postsynaptic serotonergic differences in males with extreme levels of impulsive aggression without callous unemotional traits: A positron emission tomography study using ^{11}C-DASB and ^{11}C-MDL100907. *Biological Psychiatry, 72,* 1004–1011.

Sadeh, N., Javdani, S., Jackson, J. J., Reynolds, E. K., Potenza, M. N., Gelernter, J., et al. (2010). Serotonin transporter gene associations with psychopathic traits in youth vary as a function of socioeconomic resources. *Journal of Abnor-mal Psychology, 119,* 604–609.

Sadiq, F. A., Slator, L., Skuse, D., Law, J., Gillberg, C., & Minnis, H. (2012). Social use of language in children with reactive attachment disorder and autism spectrum disorders. *European Child and Adolescent Psychiatry, 21,* 267–276.

Sadowski, H., Trowell, J., Kolvin, I., Weeramanthri, T., Berelowitz, M., & Gilbert, L. H. (2003). Sexually abused girls: Patterns of psychopathology and exploration of risk factors. *European Child and Adolescent Psychiatry, 12,* 221–230.

Saewyc, E. M., Pettingell, S., & Magee, L. L. (2003). The prevalence of sexual abuse among adolescents in school. *Journal of School Nursing, 19,* 266–272.

Sagi, A., van IJzendoorn, M. H., Joels, T., & Scharf, M. (2002). Disorganized reasoning in Holocaust survivors. *American Journal of Orthopsychiatry, 72,* 194–203.

Sagi-Schwartz, A., Koren-Karie, N., & Joels, T. (2003). Failed mourning in the Adult Attachment Interview: The case of Holocaust child survivors. *Attachment and Human Development, 5,* 398–408.

Sagi-Schwartz, A., van IJzendoorn, M. H., & Bakermans-Kranenburg, M. J. (2008). Does intergenerational transmission of trauma skip a generation? No meta-analytic evidence for tertiary traumatization with third generation of Holocaust survivors. *Attachment and Human Development, 10,* 105–121.

Sagi-Schwartz, A., van IJzendoorn, M. H., Grossmann, K. E., Joels, T., Scharf, M., Koren-Karie, N., & Alkalay, S. (2003). Attachment and traumatic stress in female Holocaust child survivors and their daughters. *American Journal of Psychiatry, 160,* 1086–1092.

Salzman, J. P., Salzman, C., & Wolfson, A. N. (1997). Relationship of childhood abuse and maternal attachment to the development of borderline personality disorder. In M. C. Zanarini (Ed.), *Role of sexual abuse in the etiology of borderline personality disorder* (pp. 71–91). Arlington, VA: American Psychiatric Association.

Samek, D. R., & Rueter, M. A. (2011). Considerations of elder sibling closeness in predicting younger sibling substance use: Social learning versus social bonding explanations. *Journal of Family Psychology, 25,* 931–941.

Samplin, E., Ikuta, T., Malhotra, A. K., Szeszko, P. R., & DeRosse, P. (2013). Sex differences in resilience to childhood maltreatment: Effects of trauma history on hippocampal volume, general cognition and subclinical psychosis in healthy adults. *Journal of Psychiatric Research, 47,* 1174–1179.

Santos-Iglesias, P., & Sierra, J. C. (2012). Sexual victimization among Spanish college women and risk factors for sexual revictimization. *Journal of Interpersonal Violence, 27,* 3468–3485.

Sareen, J., Henriksen, C. A., Bolton, S.-L., Afifi, T. O., Stein, M. B., & Asmundson, G. J. G. (2013). Adverse childhood experiences in relation to mood and anxiety disorders in a population-based sample of active military personnel. *Psychological Medicine, 43,* 73–84.

Saunders, R., Jacobvitz, D., Zaccagnino, M., Beverung, L. M., & Hazen, N. (2011). Pathways to earned security: The role of alternative support figures. *Attachment and Human Development, 13*, 403–420.

Schaeffer, C. M., Alexander, P. C., Bethke, K., & Kretz, L. S. (2005). Predictors of child abuse potential among military parents: Comparing mothers and fathers. *Journal of Family Violence, 20*, 123–129.

Schapiro, J. A., Glynn, S. M., Foy, D. W., & Yavorsky, D. (2002). Participation in war-zone atrocities and trait dissociation among Vietnam veterans with combat-related posttraumatic stress disorder. *Journal of Trauma and Dissociation, 3*, 107–114.

Scharf, M. (2007). Long-term effects of trauma: Psychosocial functioning of the second and third generation of Holocaust survivors. *Development and Psychopathology, 19*, 603–622.

Scharf, M., & Mayseless, O. (2011). Disorganizing experiences in second- and third-generation Holocaust survivors. *Qualitative Health Research, 21*, 1539–1553.

Schauenburg, H., Buchheim, A., Beckh, K., Nolte, T., Brenk-Franz, K., Leichsenring, F., et al. (2010). The influence of psychodynamically oriented therapists' attachment representations on outcome and alliance in inpatient psychotherapy. *Psychotherapy Research, 20*, 193–202.

Schechter, D. S., Coates, S. W., Kaminer, T., Coots, T., Zeanah Jr., C. H., Davies, M., et al. (2008). Distorted maternal mental representations and atypical behavior in a clinical sample of violence-exposed mothers and their toddlers. *Journal of Trauma and Dissociation, 9*, 123–147.

Schechter, D. S., Zygmunt, A., Coates, S. W., Davies, M., Trabka, K. A., McCaw, J., et al. (2007). Caregiver traumatization adversely impacts young children's mental representations on the MacArthur Story Stem Battery. *Attachment and Human Development, 9*, 187–205.

Schelble, J. L., Franks, B. A., & Miller, M. D. (2010). Emotion dysregulation and academic resilience in maltreated children. *Child and Youth Care Forum, 39*, 289–303.

Schermerhorn, A. C., Cummings, E. M., & Davies, P. T. (2008). Children's representations of multiple family relationships: Organizational structure and development in early childhood. *Journal of Family Psychology, 22*, 89–101.

Schindler, A., Thomasius, R., Sack, P.-M., Gemeinhardt, B., & Kustner, U. (2007). Insecure family bases and adolescent drug abuse: A new approach to family patterns of attachment. *Attachment and Human Development, 9*, 111–126.

Schnurr, M. P., & Lohman, B. J. (2008). How much does school matter? An examination of adolescent dating violence perpetration. *Journal of Youth and Adolescence, 37*, 266–283.

Schnurr, M. P., & Lohman, B. J. (2013). The impact of collective efficacy on risks for adolescents' perpetration of dating violence. *Journal of Youth and Adolescence, 42,* 518–535.

Schonbucher, V., Maier, T., Mohler-Kuo, M., Schnyder, U., & Landolt, M. A. (2012). Disclosure of child sexual abuse by adolescents: A qualitative in-depth study. *Journal of Interpersonal Violence, 27,* 3486–3513.

Schoppe, S. J., Mangelsdorf, S. C., & Frosch, C. A. (2001). Coparenting, family process, and family structure: Implications for preschoolers' externalizing behavior problems. *Journal of Family Psychology, 15,* 526–545.

Schoppe-Sullivan, S. J., Mangelsdorf, S. C., Frosch, C. A., & McHale, J. L. (2004). Associations between coparenting and marital behavior from infancy to the preschool years. *Journal of Family Psychology, 18,* 194–207.

Schore, A. N. (2002). Dysregulation of the right brain: A fundamental mechanism of traumatic attachment and the psychopathogenesis of posttraumatic stress disorder. *Australian and New Zealand Journal of Psychiatry, 36,* 9–30.

Schore, A. N. (2003). Early relational trauma, disorganized attachment, and the development of a predisposition to violence. In M. F. Solomon & D. J. Siegel (Eds.), *Healing trauma: Attachment, mind, body, and brain* (pp. 107–167). New York: Norton.

Schore, A. N. (2010). Relational trauma and the developing right brain. In T. Baradon (Ed.), *Relational trauma in infancy* (pp. 19–47). New York: Routledge.

Schuckit, M. A., Smith, T. L., Eng, M. Y., & Kunovac, J. (2002). Women who marry men with alcohol-use disorders. *Alcoholism: Clinical and Experimental Research, 26,* 1336–1343.

Schuengel, C., Bakermans-Kranenburg, M. J., & van IJzendoorn, M. (1999). Frightening maternal behavior linking unresolved loss and disorganized infant attachment. *Journal of Consulting and Clinical Psychology, 67,* 54–63.

Schuetze, P., & Eiden, R. D. (2005). The relationship between sexual abuse during childhood and parenting outcomes: Modeling direct and indirect pathways. *Child Abuse and Neglect, 29,* 645–659.

Schulz, M. S., Cowan, C. P., & Cowan, P. A. (2006). Promoting healthy beginnings: A randomized controlled trial of a preventive intervention to preserve marital quality during the transition to parenthood. *Journal of Consulting and Clinical Psychology, 74,* 20–31.

Schulz, M. S., Cowan, P. A., Pape, Cowan, C., & Brennan, R. T. (2004). Coming home upset: Gender, marital satisfaction, and the daily spillover of workday experience into couple interactions. *Journal of Family Psychology, 18,* 250–263.

Schulz-Heik, R. J., Rhee, S. H., Silvern, L. E., Haberstick, B. C., Hopfer, C., Lessem, J. M., & Hewitt, J. K. (2010). The association between conduct problems and maltreatment: Testing genetic and environmental mediation. *Behavior Genetics, 40,* 338–348.

Schumacher, J. A., & Holt, D. J. (2012). Domestic violence shelter residents' substance abuse treatment needs and options. *Aggression and Violent Behavior, 17,* 188–197.

Schumm, J. A., O'Farrell, T. J., Murphy, C. M., & Fals-Stewart, W. (2009). Partner violence before and after couples-based alcoholism treatment for female alcoholic patients. *Journal of Consulting and Clinical Psychology, 77,* 1136–1146.

Schwab, G. (2009). Replacement children: The transgenerational transmission of traumatic loss. *American Imago, 66,* 277–310.

Schwartz, B. K., Cavanaugh, D., Pimental, A., & Prentky, R. (2006). Descriptive study of precursors to sex offending among 813 boys and girls: Antecedent life experiences. *Victims and Offenders, 1,* 61–77.

Schwartz, J. A., & Beaver, K. M. (2011). Evidence of a gene × environment interaction between perceived prejudice and MAOA genotype in the prediction of criminal arrests. *Journal of Criminal Justice, 39,* 378–384.

Schwarz, B. (2009). Interparental conflict and adolescents' depressive mood in separated families: The role of triangulation. *Psychologie in Erziehung und Unterricht, 56,* 95–104.

Scott, D., Lambie, I., Henwood, D., & Lamb, R. (2006). Profiling stranger rapists: Linking offence behaviour to previous criminal histories using a regression model. *Journal of Sexual Aggression, 12,* 265–275.

Scott, K. L., Wolfe, D. A., & Wekerle, C. (2003). Maltreatment and trauma: Tracking the connections in adolescence. *Child and Adolescent Psychiatric Clinics, 12,* 211–230.

Sebre, S., Sprugevica, I., Novotni, A., Bonevski, D., Pakalniskiene, V., Popescu, D., et al. (2004). Cross-cultural comparisons of child-reported emotional and physical abuse: Rates, risk factors and psychosocial symptoms. *Child Abuse and Neglect, 28,* 113–127.

Seifer, R., Schiller, M., Sameroff, A. J., Resnick, S., & Riordan, K. (1996). Attachment, maternal sensitivity, and infant temperament during the first year of life. *Developmental Psychology, 32,* 12–25.

Seifert, A. E., Polusny, M. A., & Murdoch, M. (2011). The association between childhood physical and sexual abuse and functioning and psychiatric symptoms in a sample of U.S. Army soldiers. *Military Medicine, 176,* 176–181.

Seto, M. C., & Lalumiere, M. L. (2010). What is so special about male adolescent sexual offending? A review and test of explanations through meta-analysis. *Psychological Bulletin, 136,* 526–575.

Shaffer, A., & Sroufe, L. A. (2005). The developmental and adaptational implications of generational boundary dissolution: Findings from a perspective, longitudinal study. *Journal of Emotional Abuse, 5*(2–3), 67–84.

Shakoor, S., Jaffee, S. R., Bowes, L., Ouellet-Morin, I., Andreou, P., Happe, F., et al. (2012). A prospective longitudinal study of children's theory of mind and adolescent involvement in bullying. *Journal of Child Psychology and Psychiatry, 53*, 254–261.

Shannon, L., Logan, T. K., Cole, J., & Walker, R. (2008). An examination of women's alcohol use and partner victimization experiences among women with protective orders. *Substance Use and Misuse, 43*, 1110–1128.

Sharpe, D., & Taylor, J. K. (1999). An examination of variables from a social-developmental model to explain physical and psychological dating violence. *Canadian Journal of Behavioural Science, 31*, 165–175.

Shaver, P. R., Belsky, J., & Brennan, K. A. (2000). The Adult Attachment Interview and self-reports of romantic attachment: Associations across domains and methods. *Personal Relationships, 7*, 25–43.

Shaw, D. S., Owens, E. B., Vondra, J. I., & Keenan, K. (1996). Early risk factors and pathways in the development of early disruptive behavior problems. *Development and Psychopathology, 8*, 679–699.

Sherrill, A. M., Wyngarden, N., & Bell, K. M. (2011). Expected outcomes of dating violence: Perspectives from female perpetrators. *Partner Abuse, 2*, 404–426.

Shi, Z., Bureau, J.-F., Easterbrooks, M. A., Zhao, X., & Lyons-Ruth, K. (2012). Childhood maltreatment and prospectively observed quality of early care as predictors of antisocial personality disorder features. *Infant Mental Health Journal, 33*, 55–69.

Shields, A., & Cicchetti, D. (2001). Parental maltreatment and emotion dysregulation as risk factors for bullying and victimization in middle childhood. *Journal of Clinical Child Psychology, 30*, 349–363.

Shields, A., Ryan, R. M., & Cicchetti, D. (2001). Narrative representations of caregivers and emotion dysregulation as predictors of maltreated children's rejection by peers. *Developmental Psychology, 37*, 321–337.

Shin, S. H., Edwards, E., Heeren, T., & Amodeo, M. (2009). Relationship between multiple forms of maltreatment by a parent or guardian and adolescent alcohol use. *American Journal on Addictions, 18*, 226–234.

Shin, S. H., Hong, H. G., & Hazen, A. L. (2010). Childhood sexual abuse and adolescent substance use: A latent class analysis. *Drug and Alcohol Dependence, 109*, 226–235.

Shlafer, R. J., & Poehlmann, J. (2010). Attachment and caregiving relationships in families affected by parental incarceration. *Attachment and Human Development, 12*, 395–415.

Shlafer, R. J., Poehlmann, J., Coffino, B., & Hanneman, A. (2009). Mentoring children with incarcerated parents: Implications for research, practice, and policy. *Family Relations, 58,* 507–519.

Shoal, G. D., Giancola, P. R., & Kinilova, G. P. (2003). Salivary cortisol, personality, and aggressive behavior in adolescent boys: A 5-year longitudinal study. *Journal of the American Academy of Child and Adolescent Psychiatry, 42,* 1101–1107.

Shonk, S. M., & Cicchetti, D. (2001). Maltreatment, competency deficits, and risk for academic and behavioral maladjustment. *Developmental Psychology, 37,* 3–17.

Shor, R. (1999). Beyond a cross-cultural definition of child maltreatment: Comparing immigrants from the Caucasus and European countries of the former Soviet Union. *Early Child Development and Care, 150,* 1–15.

Shorey, R. C., Stuart, G. L., & Cornelius, T. L. (2011). Dating violence and substance use in college students: A review of the literature. *Aggression and Violent Behavior, 16,* 541–550.

Shrira, A., Palgi, Y., Ben-Izra, M., & Shmotkin, D. (2011). Transgenerational effects of trauma in midlife: Evidence for resilience and vulnerability in offspring of Holocaust survivors. *Psychological Trauma, 3,* 394–402.

Shucard, J. L., Cox, J., Shucard, D. W., Fetter, H., Chung, C., Ramasamy, D., & Violanti, J. (2012). Symptoms of posttraumatic stress disorder and exposure to traumatic stressors are related to brain structural volumes and behavioral measures of affective stimulus processing in police officers. *Psychiatry Research: Neuroimaging, 204,* 25–31.

Sigurdsson, J. F., Gudjonsson, G., Asgeirsdottir, B. B., & Sigfusdottir, I. D. (2010). Sexually abusive youth: What are the background factors that distinguish them from other youth? *Psychology, Crime and Law, 16,* 289–303.

Sijbrandij, M., Wittmann, L., Delahanty, D., Brunet, A., Olff, M., Opmeer, B., et al. (2007, November). New insights into peritraumatic dissociation and the prediction of posttraumatic stress disorder. Paper presented at the annual meeting of the International Society of Traumatic Stress Studies, Baltimore, MD.

Silk, K. R., Nigg, J. T., Westen, D., & Lohr, N. E. (1997). Severity of childhood sexual abuse, borderline symptoms, and familial environment. In M. C. Zanarini (Ed.), *Role of sexual abuse in the etiology of borderline personality disorder* (pp. 131–163). Arlington, VA: American Psychiatric Association.

Silver, R. L., Boon, C., & Stones, M. H. (1983). Searching for meaning in misfortune: Making sense of incest. *Journal of Social Issues, 39,* 81–101.

Simmons, C. A., Lehmann, P., & Cobb, N. (2008). Women arrested for partner violence and substance use: An exploration of discrepancies in the literature. *Journal of Interpersonal Violence, 23,* 707–727.

Simonelli, C. J., Mullis, T., Elliott, A. N., & Pierce, T. W. (2002). Abuse by siblings and subsequent experiences of violence within the dating relationship. *Journal of Interpersonal Violence, 17,* 103–121.

Simoneti, S., Scott, E. C., & Murphy, C. M. (2000). Dissociative experiences in partner-assaultive men. *Journal of Interpersonal Violence, 15,* 1262–1283.

Simons, D. A., Wurtele, S. K., & Durham, R. L. (2008). Developmental experiences of child sexual abusers and rapists. *Child Abuse and Neglect, 32,* 549–560.

Simons, R. L., & Lei, M. K. (2013). Enhanced susceptibility to context: A promising perspective on the interplay of genes and the social environment. In C. L. Gibson & M. D. Krohn (Eds.), *Handbook of life-course criminology: Emerging trends and directions for future research* (pp. 57–67). New York: Springer.

Simons, R. L., Lei, M. K., Beach, S. R. H., Brody, G. H., Philibert, R. A., & Gibbons, F. X. (2011). Social environment, genes, and aggression: Evidence supporting the differential susceptibility perspective. *American Sociological Review, 76,* 883–912.

Simons, R. L., Lei, M. K., Stewart, E. A., Beach, S. R. H., Brody, G. H., Philibert, R. A., & Gibbons, F. X. (2012). Social adversity, genetic variation, street code, and aggression: A genetically informed model of violent behavior. *Youth Violence and Juvenile Justice, 10,* 3–24.

Simons, R. L., Simons, L. G., Lei, M. K., Beach, S. R. H., Brody, G. H., Gibbons, F. X., & Philibert, R. A. (2013). Genetic moderation of the impact of parenting on hostility toward romantic partners. *Journal of Marriage and Family, 75,* 325–341.

Simpson, J. A., Griskevicius, V., Kuo, S. I.-C., Sung, S., & Collins, W. A. (2012). Evolution, stress, and sensitive periods: The influence of unpredictability in early versus late childhood on sex and risky behavior. *Developmental Psychology, 48,* 674–686.

Sims, E. N., Dodd, V. J. N., & Tejeda, M. J. (2008). The relationship between severity of violence in the home and dating violence. *Journal of Forensic Nursing, 4,* 166–173.

Skopp, N. A., McDonald, R., Manke, B., & Jouriles, E. N. (2005). Siblings in domestically violent families: Experiences of interparent conflict and adjustment problems. *Journal of Family Psychology, 19,* 324–333.

Slade, A., Sadler, L. S., & Mayes, L. C. (2005). Minding the baby: Enhancing parental reflective functioning in a nursing/mental health home visiting program. In L. J. Berlin, Y. Ziv, L. Amaya-Jackson, & M. T. Greenberg (Eds.), *Enhancing early attachments: Theory, research, intervention, and policy* (pp. 152–177). New York: Guilford.

Sleed, M., & Fonagy, P. (2010). Understanding disruptions in the parent-infant relationship: Do actions speak louder than words? In T. Baradon (Ed.), *Rela-*

tional trauma in infancy: Psychoanalytic, attachment and neuropsychological contributions to parent-infant psychotherapy (pp. 136–162). New York: Routledge.

Smeekens, S., Riksen-Walraven, J. M., & Van-Bakel, H. J. A. (2009). The predictive value of different infant attachment measures for socioemotional development at age 5 years. *Infant Mental Health Journal, 30,* 366–383.

Smith, C. A., Elwyn, L. J., Ireland, T. O., & Thornberry, T. P. (2010). Impact of adolescent exposure to intimate partner violence on substance use in early adulthood. *Journal of Studies on Alcohol and Drugs, 71,* 219–230.

Smith, H. J., Sheikh, H. I., Dyson, M. W., Olino, T. M., Laptook, R. S., Durbin, C. E., et al. (2012). Parenting and child DRD4 genotype interact to predict children's early emerging effortful control. *Child Development, 83,* 1932–1944.

Smith, P. H., Homish, G. G., Leonard, K. E., & Cornelius, J. R. (2012). Intimate partner violence and specific substance use disorders: Findings from the National Epidemiologic Survey on Alcohol and Related Conditions. *Psychology of Addictive Behaviors, 26,* 236–245.

Smyke, A. T., Zeanah, C. H., Gleason, M. M., Drury, S. S., Fox, N. A., Nelson, C. A., & Guthrie, D. (2012). A randomized controlled trial comparing foster care and institutional care for children with signs of reactive attachment disorder. *American Journal of Psychiatry, 169,* 508–514.

Sneath, L., & Rheem, K. D. (2011). The use of emotionally focused couples therapy with military couples and families. In R. B. Everson & D. R. Figley (Eds.), *Families under fire: Systemic therapy with military families* (pp. 127–151). New York: Routledge.

Soares, I., Fremmer-Bombik, E., Grossmann, K. E., & Silva, M. C. (2000). Attachment representation in adolescence and adulthood: Exploring some intergenerational and intercultural issues. In P. K. Crittenden & A. H. Claussen (Eds.), *The organization of attachment relationships: Maturation, culture, and context* (pp. 325–342). New York: Cambridge University Press.

Sokolowski, M. S., Hans, S. L., Bernstein, V. J., & Cox, S. M. (2007). Mothers' representations of their infants and parenting behavior: Associations with personal and social-contextual variables in a high-risk sample. *Infant Mental Health Journal, 28,* 344–365.

Solomon, J., & George, C. (1999a). The development of attachment in separated and divorced families: Effects of overnight visitation, parent and couple variables. *Attachment and Human Development, 1,* 2–33.

Solomon, J., & George, C. (1999b). The place of disorganization in attachment theory: Linking classic observations with contemporary findings. In J. Solomon & C. George (Eds.), *Attachment disorganization* (pp. 3–32). New York: Guilford.

Solomon, J., & George, C. (2006). Intergenerational transmission of dysregu-lated maternal caregiving: Mothers describe their upbringing and childrear-ing. In O. Mayseless (Ed.), *Parenting representations: Theory, research, and clinical implications* (pp. 265–295). New York: Cambridge University Press.

Solomon, J., & George, C. (2011a). The disorganized attachment-caregiving sys-tem: Dysregulation of adaptive processes at multiple levels. In J. Solomon & C. George (Eds.), *Disorganized attachment and caregiving* (pp. 1–24). New York: Guilford.

Solomon, J., & George, C. (2011b). Disorganization of maternal caregiving across two generations: The origins of caregiving helplessness. In J. Solomon & C. George (Eds.), *Disorganized attachment and caregiving* (pp. 25–51). New York: Guilford.

Solomon, J., George, C., & De Jong, A. (1995). Children classified as control-ling at age six: Evidence of disorganized representational strategies and aggres-sion at home and at school. *Development and Psychopathology, 7,* 447–463.

Solomon, Z., Kotler, M., & Mikulincer, M. (1989). Combat related post-traumatic stress disorder among the second generation of Holocaust survivors: Transgenerational effects among Israeli soldiers. *Psychologia: Israel Journal of Psychology, 1,* 113–119.

Sorsoli, L., Kia-Keating, M., & Grossman, F. K. (2008). "I keep that hush-hush": Male survivors of sexual abuse and the challenges of disclosure. *Journal of Counseling Psychology, 55,* 333–345.

Sossin, K. M. (2007). Nonmentalizing states in early-childhood survivors of the Holocaust: Developmental considerations regarding treatment of child survi-vors of genocidal atrocities. *American Journal of Psychoanalysis, 67,* 68–81.

Sousa, L. (2005). Building on personal networks when intervening with multi-problem poor families. *Journal of Social Work Practice, 19,* 163–179.

Southwick, S. M., Morgan III, C. A., Vythilingam, M., & Charney, D. (2006). Mentors enhance resilience in at-risk children and adolescents. *Psychoana-lytic Inquiry, 26,* 577–584.

Spaccarelli, S., & Kim, S. (1995). Resilience criteria and factors associated with resilience in sexually abused girls. *Child Abuse and Neglect, 19,* 1171–1182.

Spangler, G., & Grossmann, K. E. (1993). Biobehavioral organization in securely and insecurely attached infants. *Child Development, 64,* 1439–1450.

Spangler, G., Johann, M., Ronai, Z., & Zimmermann, P. (2009). Genetic and environmental influence on attachment disorganization. *Journal of Child Psychology and Psychiatry, 50,* 952–961.

Spitzberg, B. J., Cupach, W. R., & Ciceraro, L. D. L. (2010). Sex differences in stalking and obsessive relational intrusion: Two meta-analyses. *Partner Abuse, 1,* 259–285.

Sroufe, L. A., & Fleeson, J. (1986). Attachment and the construction of relationships. In W. Hartup & Z. Rubin (Eds.), *Relationships and development* (pp. 51–71). New York: Cambridge University Press.

Sroufe, L. A., Jacobvitz, D., Mangelsdorf, S., DeAngelo, E., & Ward, M. J. (1985). Generational boundary dissolution between mothers and their preschool children: A relationship systems approach. *Child Development, 56,* 317–325.

Sroufe, L. A., & Ward, M. J. (1980). Seductive behavior of mothers of toddlers: Occurrence, correlates, and family origins. *Child Development, 51,* 1222–1229.

Stalans, L. J., & Ritchie, J. (2008). Relationship of substance use/abuse with psychological and physical intimate partner violence: Variations across living situations. *Journal of Family Violence, 23,* 9–24.

Stams, G.-J. M., Juffer, F., & van IJzendoorn, M. H. (2002). Maternal sensitivity, infant attachment, and temperament in early childhood predict adjustment in middle childhood: The case of adopted children and their biologically unrelated parents. *Developmental Psychology, 38,* 806–821.

Stappenbeck, C. A., Hellmuth, J. C., Simpson, T., & Jakupcak, M. (2014). The effects of alcohol problems, PTSD, and combat exposure on nonphysical and physical aggression among Iraq and Afghanistan war veterans. *Psychological Trauma, 6,* 65–72.

Starr, L. R., Hammen, C., Brennan, P. A., & Naiman, J. M. (2013). Relational security moderates the effect of serotonin transporter gene polymorphism (5-HTTLPR) on stress generation and depression among adolescents. *Journal of Abnormal Child Psychology, 41,* 379–388.

Steel, J., Sanna, L., Hammond, B., Whipple, J., & Cross, H. (2004). Psychological sequelae of childhood sexual abuse: Abuse-related characteristics, coping strategies, and attributional style. *Child Abuse and Neglect, 28,* 785–801.

Steele, M., Henderson, K., Hodges, J., Kanjuk, J., Hillman, S., & Steele, H. (2007). In the best interests of the late-placed child: A report from the attachment representations and adoption outcome study. In L. Mayes, P. Fonagy, & M. Target (Eds.), *Developmental science and psychoanalysis: Integration and innovation* (pp. 159–191). London: Karnac.

Steele, M., Kaniuk, J., Hodges, J., Asquith, K., Hillman, S., & Steele, H. (2008). Measuring mentalization across contexts: Links between representations of childhood and representations of parenting in an adoption sample. In E. L. Jurist, A. Slade, & S. Bergner (Eds.), *Mind to mind: Infant research, neuroscience, and psychoanalysis* (pp. 115–136). New York: Other Press.

Stein, A. L., Tran, G. Q., Lund, L. M., Haji, U., Dashevsky, B. A., & Baker, D. G. (2005). Correlates for posttraumatic stress disorder in Gulf War veterans: A retrospective study of main and moderating effects. *Journal of Anxiety Disorders, 19,* 861–876.

Stein, J. A., Milburn, N. G., Zane, J. I., Rotheram-Borus, M. J. (2009). Paternal and maternal influences on problem behaviors among homeless and runaway youth. *American Journal of Orthopsychiatry, 79,* 39–50.

Stephens, C., & Long, N. (1999). Posttraumatic stress disorder in the New Zealand police: The moderating role of social support following traumatic stress. *Anxiety, Stress and Coping, 12,* 247–264.

Stephens, C., Long, N., & Miller, I. (1997). The impact of trauma and social support on posttraumatic stress disorder: A study of New Zealand police officers. *Journal of Criminal Justice, 25,* 303–314.

Stirpe, T., Abracen, J., Stermac, L., & Wilson, R. (2006). Sexual offenders' state-of-mind regarding childhood attachment: A controlled investigation. *Sexual Abuse, 18,* 289–302.

Stith, S. M., McCollum, E. E., & Rosen, K. H. (2011). *Couples therapy for domestic violence: Finding safe solutions.* Washington, DC: American Psychological Association.

Stith, S. M., Rosen, K. H., McCollum, E. E., & Thomsen, C. J. (2004). Treating intimate partner violence within intact couple relationships: Outcomes of multi-couple versus individual couple therapy. *Journal of Marital and Family Therapy, 30,* 305–318.

Stith, S. M., Rosen, K. H., Middleton, K. A., Busch, A. L., Lundeberg, K., & Carlton, R. P. (2000). The intergenerational transmission of spouse abuse: A meta-analysis. *Journal of Marriage and the Family, 62,* 640–654.

Storch, E. A., Brassard, M. R., & Masia-Warner, C. L. (2003). The relationship of peer victimization to social anxiety and loneliness in adolescence. *Child Study Journal, 33,* 1–18.

Stovall, K. C., & Dozier, M. (2000). The development of attachment in new relationships: Single subject analyses for 10 foster infants. *Development and Psychopathology, 12,* 133–156.

Stovall-McClough, K. C., & Cloitre, M. (2006). Unresolved attachment, PTSD, and dissociation in women with childhood abuse histories. *Journal of Consulting and Clinical Psychology, 74,* 219–228.

Stovall-McClough, K. C., & Dozier, M. (2004). Forming attachments in foster care: Infant attachment behaviors during the first 2 months of placement. *Development and Psychopathology, 16,* 253–271.

Strathearn, L. (2011). Maternal neglect: Oxytocin, dopamine and the neurobiology of attachment. *Journal of Neuroendocrinology, 23,* 1054–1065.

Strathearn, L., Fonagy, P., Amico, J., & Montague, P. R. (2009). Adult attachment predicts maternal brain and oxytocin response to infant cues. *Neuropsychopharmacology, 34,* 2655–2666.

Straus, M. A. (2008). Dominance and symmetry in partner violence by male and female university students in 32 nations. *Children and Youth Services Review, 30,* 252–275.

Straus, M. A. (2011). Gender symmetry and mutuality in perpetration of clinical-level partner violence: Empirical evidence and implications for prevention and treatment. *Aggression and Violent Behavior, 16,* 279–288.

Straus, M. A., Douglas, E. M., & Medeiros, R. A. (2014). *The primordial violence: Spanking children, psychological development, violence, and crime.* New York: Routledge.

Straus, M. A., & Gozjolko, K. L. (2014). "Intimate terrorism" and gender differences in injury of dating partners by male and female university students. *Journal of Family Violence, 29,* 51–65.

Straus, M. A., & Savage, S. A. (2005). Neglectful behavior by parents in the life history of university students in 17 countries and its relation to violence against dating partners. *Child Maltreatment, 10,* 124–135.

Stroud, C. B., Durbin, C. E., Wilson, S., & Mendelsohn, K. A. (2011). Spillover to triadic and dyadic systems in families with young children. *Journal of Family Psychology, 25,* 919–930.

Stuart, G. L., Temple, J. R., Follansbee, K. W., Bucossi, M. M., Hellmuth, J. C., & Moore, T. M. (2008). The role of drug use in a conceptual model of intimate partner violence in men and women arrested for domestic violence. *Psychology of Addictive Behaviors, 22,* 12–24.

Sturge-Apple, M. L., Cicchetti, D., Davies, P. T., & Suor, J. H. (2012). Differential susceptibility in spillover between interparental conflict and maternal parenting practices: Evidence for OXTR and 5-HTT genes. *Journal of Family Psychology, 26,* 431–442.

Sturge-Apple, M. L., Davies, P. T., Cicchetti, D., & Cummings, E. M. (2009). The role of mothers' and fathers' adrenocortical reactivity in spillover between interparental conflict and parenting practices. *Journal of Family Psychology, 23,* 215–225.

Styron, T., & Janoff-Bulman, R. (1997). Childhood attachment and abuse: Long-term effects on adult attachment, depression and conflict resolution. *Child Abuse and Neglect, 21,* 1015–1023.

Subic-Wrana, C., Beetz, A., Wiltink, J., & Beutel, M. E. (2011). Unresolved attachment and remembered childhood trauma in patients undergoing psychosomatic inpatient treatment. *Zeitschrift für Psychosomatische Medizin und Psychotherapie, 57,* 325–342.

Suchman, N. E., DeCoste, C., Castiglioni, N., McMahon, T. J., Rousaville, B., & Mayes, L. (2010). The Mothers and Toddlers Program, an attachment-based parenting intervention for substance using women: Post-treatment results from a randomized clinical pilot. *Attachment and Human Development, 12,* 483–504.

Suchman, N. E., DeCoste, C., Rosenberger, P., & McMahon, T. J. (2012). Attachment-based intervention for substance-using mothers: A preliminary test of the proposed mechanisms of change. *Infant Mental Health Journal, 33,* 360–371.

Sulik, M. J., Eisenberg, N., Lemery-Chalfant, K., Spinrad, T. L., Silva, K. M., Eggum, N. D., et al. (2012). Interactions between serotonin transporter gene haplotypes and quality of mothers' parenting predict the development of children's noncompliance. *Developmental Psychology, 48,* 740–754.

Sullivan, M. W., Bennett, D. S., & Lewis, M. (2013). Individual differences in the cortisol responses of neglected and comparison children. *Child Maltreatment, 18,* 8–16.

Sullivan, T. P., Ashare, R. L., Jaquier, V., & Tennen, H. (2012). Risk factors for alcohol-related problems among victims of partner violence. *Substance Use and Misuse, 47,* 673–685.

Sullivan, T. P., Cavanaugh, C. E., Buckner, J. D., & Edmondson, D. (2009). Testing posttraumatic stress as a mediator of physical, sexual, and psychological intimate partner violence and substance problems among women. *Journal of Traumatic Stress, 22,* 575–584.

Sullivan, T. P., & Holt, L. J. (2008). PTSD symptom clusters are differentially related to substance use among community women exposed to intimate partner violence. *Journal of Traumatic Stress, 21,* 173–180.

Super, C. M., Guldan, G. S., Ahmed, N., & Zeitlin, M. (2012). The emergence of separation protest is robust under conditions of severe developmental stress in rural Bangladesh. *Infant Behavior and Development, 35,* 393–396.

Svedin, C. G., Back, C., & Soderback, S.-B. (2002). Family relations, family climate and sexual abuse. *Nordic Journal of Psychiatry, 56,* 355–362.

Swann, W. B., Hixon, J. G., Stein-Seroussi, A., & Gilbert, D. T. (1990). The fleeting gleam of praise: Cognitive processes underlying behavioral reactions to self-relevant feedback. *Journal of Personality and Social Psychology, 59,* 17–26.

Sweeting, H., Young, R., West, P., & Der, G. (2006). Peer victimization and depression in early-mid adolescence: A longitudinal study. *British Journal of Educational Psychology, 76,* 577–594.

Sweitzer, M. M., Halder, I., Flory, J. D., Craig, A. E., Gianaros, P. R., Ferrell, R. E., & Manuck, S. B. (2013). Polymorphic variation in the dopamine D4 receptor predicts delay discounting as a function of childhood socioeconomic status: Evidence for differential susceptibility. *Social Cognitive and Affective Neuroscience, 8,* 499–508.

Sylvers, P., Brennan, P. A., Lilienfeld, S. O., & Alden, S. A. (2010). Gender differences in autonomic indicators of antisocial personality disorder features. *Personality Disorders: Theory, Research, and Treatment, 1,* 87–96.

Tafoya, N., & Del Vecchio, A. (2005). Back to the future: An examination of the Native American Holocaust experience. In M. McGoldrick, J. Giordano, &

N. Garcia-Preto (Eds.), *Ethnicity and family therapy* (3rd ed., pp. 55–63). New York: Guilford.

Taft, C. T., Monson, C. M., Hebenstreit, C. L., King, D. W., & King, L. A. (2009). Examining the correlates of aggression among male and female Vietnam veterans. *Violence and Victims, 24*, 639–652.

Taft, C. T., Schumm, J. A., Panuzio, J., & Proctor, S. P. (2008). An examination of family adjustment among Operation Desert Storm veterans. *Journal of Consulting and Clinical Psychology, 76*, 648–656.

Taft, C. T., Street, A. E., Marshall, A. D., Dowdall, D. J., & Riggs, D. S. (2007). Posttraumatic stress disorder, anger, and partner abuse among Vietnam combat veterans. *Journal of Family Psychology, 21*, 270–277.

Taft, C. T., Vogt, D. W., Marshall, A. D., Panuzio, J., & Niles, B. L. (2007). Aggression among combat veterans: Relationships with combat exposure and symptoms of posttraumatic stress disorder, dysphoria, and anxiety. *Journal of Traumatic Stress, 20*, 135–145.

Taft, C. T., Watkins, L. E., Stafford, J., Street, A. E., & Monson, C. M. (2011). Posttraumatic stress disorder and intimate relationship problems: A meta-analysis. *Journal of Consulting and Clinical Psychology, 79*, 22–33.

Talbot, J. A., Baker, J. K., & McHale, J. P. (2009). Sharing the love: Prebirth adult attachment status and coparenting adjustment during early infancy. *Parenting: Science and Practice, 9*, 56–77.

Talge, N. M., Neal, C., & Glover, V. (2007). Antenatal maternal stress and long-term effects on child neurodevelopment: How and why? *Journal of Child Psychology and Psychiatry, 48*, 245–261.

Talley, C. (2009). Current effects of historical trauma: An epigenetic view. *Focus, 21*, 9.

Tancredy, C. M., & Fraley, R. C. (2006). The nature of adult twin relationships: An attachment-theoretical perspective. *Journal of Personality and Social Psychology, 90*, 78–93.

Tang, S. S. S., & Freyd, J. J. (2012). Betrayal trauma and gender differences in posttraumatic stress. *Psychological Trauma, 4*, 469–478.

Tarakeshwar, N., Hansen, N. B., Kochman, A., Fox, A., & Sikkema, K. J. (2006). Resiliency among individuals with childhood sexual abuse and HIV: Perspectives on addressing sexual trauma. *Journal of Traumatic Stress, 19*, 449–460.

Tasca, M., Rodriguez, N., & Zatz, M. S. (2011). Family and residential instability in the context of paternal and maternal incarceration. *Criminal Justice and Behavior, 38*, 231–247.

Taylor, C. A., Boris, N. W., Heller, S. S., Clum, G. A., Rice, J. C., & Zeanah, C. H. (2008). Cumulative experiences of violence among high-risk urban youth. *Journal of Interpersonal Violence, 23*, 1618–1635.

Taylor, C. A., Guterman, N. B., Lee, S. J., & Rathouz, P. J. (2009). Intimate partner violence, maternal stress, nativity, and risk for maternal maltreatment of young children. *American Journal of Public Health, 99,* 175–183.

Taylor, J. E., & Harvey, S. T. (2010). A meta-analysis of the effects of psychotherapy with adults sexually abused in childhood. *Clinical Psychology Review, 30,* 749–767.

Taylor, S. E., Way, B. M., Welch, W. T., Hilmert, C. J., Lehman, B. J., & Eisenberger, N. I. (2006). Early family environment, current adversity, the serotonin transporter promoter polymorphism, and depressive symptomatology. *Biological Psychiatry, 60,* 671–676.

Teicher, M. H., Anderson, C. M., Ohashi, K., & Polcari, A. (2013). Childhood maltreatment: Altered network centrality of cingulate, precuneus, temporal pole and insula. *Biological Psychiatry,* no pagination specified.

Teicher, M. H., & Samson, J. A. (2013). Childhood maltreatment and psychopathology: A case for ecophenotypic variants as clinically and neurobiologically distinct subtypes. *American Journal of Psychiatry, 170,* 1114–1133.

Teicher, M. H., Samson, J. A., Polcari, A., & McGreenery, C. E. (2006). Sticks, stones, and hurtful words: Relative effects of various forms of childhood maltreatment. *American Journal of Psychiatry, 163,* 993–1000.

Teicher, M. H., & Vitaliano, G. D. (2011). Witnessing violence toward siblings: An understudied but potent form of early adversity. *PLoS ONE, 6.*

Teisl, M., Rogosch, F. A., Oshri, A., & Cicchetti, D. (2012). Differential expression of social dominance as a function of age and maltreatment. *Developmental Psychology, 48,* 575–588.

Temple, J. R., Weston, R., Stuart, G. L., & Marshall, L. L. (2008). The longitudinal association between alcohol use and intimate partner violence among ethnically diverse community women. *Addictive Behaviors, 33,* 1244–1248.

Testa, M., Hoffman, J. H., & Livingston, J. A. (2011). Intergenerational transmission of sexual victimization vulnerability as mediated via parenting. *Child Abuse and Neglect, 35,* 363–371.

Testa, M., Livingston, J. A., & Leonard, K. E. (2003). Women's substance use and experiences of intimate partner violence: A longitudinal investigation among a community sample. *Addictive Behaviors, 28,* 1649–1664.

Teten, A. L., Schumacher, J. A., Bailey, S. D., & Kent, T. A. (2009). Male-to-female sexual aggression among Iraq, Afghanistan, and Vietnam veterans: Co-occurring substance abuse and intimate partner aggression. *Journal of Traumatic Stress, 22,* 307–311.

Teti, D. M. (1999). Conceptualizations of disorganization in the preschool years: An integration. In J. Solomon & C. George (Eds.), *Attachment disorganization* (pp. 213–242). New York: Guilford.

Teubert, D., & Pinquart, M. (2010). The association between coparenting and child adjustment: A meta-analysis. *Parenting: Science and Practice, 10,* 286–307.

Thomas, P. M. (2005). Dissociation and internal models of protection: Psychotherapy with child abuse survivors. *Psychotherapy: Theory, Research, Practice, Training, 42,* 20–36.

Thomas, T. A., & Fremouw, W. (2009). Moderating variables of the sexual "victim to offender cycle" in males. *Aggression and Violent Behavior, 14,* 382–387.

Thomsen, C. J., Rabenhorst, M. M., McCarthy, R. J., Milner, J. S., Travis, W. J., Foster, R. E., & Copeland, C. W. (2014). Child maltreatment before and after combat-related deployment among active-duty United States Air Force maltreating parents. *Psychology of Violence, 4,* 143-155.

Thornton, L. C., Frick, P. J., Crapanzano, A. M., & Terranova, A. M. (2013). The incremental utility of callous-unemotional traits and conduct problems in predicting aggression and bullying in a community sample of boys and girls. *Psychological Assessment, 25,* 366–378.

Tidefors, I., Arvidsson, H., Ingevaldson, S., & Larsson, M. (2010). Sibling incest: A literature review and a clinical study. *Journal of Sexual Aggression, 16,* 347–360.

Tiemeier, H., Velders, F. P., Szekely, E., Roza, S. J., Dieleman, G., Jaddoe, V. W. V., et al. (2012). The Generation R Study: A review of design, findings to date, and a study of the 5-HTTLPR by environmental interaction from fetal life onward. *Journal of the American Academy of Child and Adolescent Psychiatry, 51,* 1119–1135.

Timmer, S. G., Thompson, D., Culver, M. A., Urquiza, A. J., & Altenhofen, S. (2012). Mothers' physical abusiveness in a context of violence: Effects on the mother-child relationship. *Development and Psychopathology, 24,* 79–92.

Topitzes, J., Mersky, J. P., & Reynolds, A. J. (2012). From child maltreatment to violent offending: An examination of mixed-gender and gender-specific models. *Journal of Interpersonal Violence, 27,* 2322–2347.

Treboux, D., Crowell, J. A., & Waters, E. (2004). When "new" meets "old": Configurations of adult attachment representations and their implications for marital functioning. *Developmental Psychology, 40,* 295–314.

Trickett, P. K., Noll, J. G., & Putnam, F. W. (2011). The impact of sexual abuse on female development: Lessons from a multigenerational, longitudinal research study. *Development and Psychopathology, 23,* 453–476.

Tronick, E., Als, H., Adson, L., Wise, S., & Brazelton, T. B. (1978). The infant's response to entrapment between contradictory messages in face-to-face interaction. *Journal of the American Academy of Child Psychiatry, 17,* 1–13.

Tronick, E. Z., & Beeghly, M. (1999). Prenatal cocaine exposure, child development and the compromising effects of cumulative risk. *Clinics in Perinatology, 26,* 151–171.

Troy, M., & Sroufe, L. A. (1987). Victimization among preschoolers: Role of attachment relationship history. *Journal of the American Academy of Child and Adolescent Psychiatry, 26,* 166–172.

Tuerk, E. H., & Loper, A. B. (2006). Contact between incarcerated mothers and their children: Assessing parenting stress. *Journal of Offender Rehabilitation, 43,* 23–43.

Turanovic, J. J., Rodriguez, N., & Pratt, T. C. (2012). The collateral consequences of incarceration revisited: A qualitative analysis of the effects on caregivers of children of incarcerated parents. *Criminology, 50,* 913–959.

Turner, H. A., Finkelhor, D., Hamby, S. L., & Shattuck, A. (2013). Family structure, victimization, and child mental health in a nationally representative sample. *Social Science and Medicine, 87,* 39–51.

Turner, H. A., Finkelhor, D., & Ormrod, R. (2010). Poly-victimization in a national sample of children and youth. *American Journal of Preventive Medicine, 38,* 323–330.

Turner, H. A., Finkelhor, D., Ormrod, R., Hamby, S., Leeb, R. T., Mercy, J. A., & Holt, M. (2012). Family context, victimization, and child trauma symptoms: Variations in safe, stable, and nurturing relationships during early and middle childhood. *American Journal of Orthopsychiatry, 82,* 209–219.

Turney, K., Schnittker, J., & Wildeman, C. (2012). Those they leave behind: Paternal incarceration and maternal instrumental support. *Journal of Marriage and Family, 74,* 1149–1165.

Tyler, K. A., & Melander, L. A. (2012). Poor parenting and antisocial behavior among homeless young adults: Links to dating violence perpetration and victimization. *Journal of Interpersonal Violence, 27,* 1357–1373.

Tyrka, A. R., Price, L. H., Marsit, C., Walters, O. C., & Carpenter, L. L. (2012). Childhood adversity and epigenetic modulation of the leukocyte glucocorticoid receptor: Preliminary findings in healthy adults. *PLoS ONE, 7,* Article e30148.

Tyrrell, C., & Dozier, M. (1999). Foster parents' understanding of children's problematic attachment strategies: The need for therapeutic responsiveness. *Adoption Quarterly, 2,* 49–64.

Tzilos, G. K., Grekin, E. R., Beatty, J. R., Chase, S. K., & Ondersma, S. J. (2010). Commission versus receipt of violence during pregnancy: Associations with substance abuse variables. *Journal of Interpersonal Violence, 25,* 1928–1940.

Uddin, M., Aiello, A. E., Wildman, D. E., Koenen, K. C., Pawelec, G., de los Santos, R., et al. (2010). Epigenetic and immune function profiles associated with posttraumatic stress disorder. *Proceedings of the National Academy of Sciences, 107,* 9470–9475.

Ulbricht, J. A., Ganiban, J. M., Button, T. M. M., Feinberg, M., Reiss, D. & Neiderhiser, J. M. (2013). Marital adjustment as a moderator for genetic and environmental influences on parenting. *Journal of Family Psychology, 27,* 42–52.

Ullman, S. E. (2007). Relationship to perpetrator, disclosure, social reactions, and PTSD symptoms in child sexual abuse survivors. *Journal of Child Sexual Abuse, 16,* 19–36.

Ullman, S. E., Najdowski, C. J., & Filipas, H. H. (2009). Child sexual abuse, post-traumatic stress disorder, and substance use: Predictors of revictimization in adult sexual assault survivors. *Journal of Child Sexual Abuse, 18,* 367–385.

Underwood, M. K., Beron, K. J., Gentsch, J. K., Galperin, M. B., & Risser, S. D. (2008). Family correlates of children's social and physical aggression with peers: Negative interparental conflict strategies and parenting styles. *International Journal of Behavioral Development, 32,* 549–562.

Valentine, C., Oehme, K., & Martin, A. (2012). Correctional officers and domestic violence: Experiences and attitudes. *Journal of Family Violence, 27,* 531–545.

Valentino, K., Cicchetti, D., Toth, S. L., & Rogosch, F. A. (2011). Mother-child play and maltreatment: A longitudinal analysis of emerging social behavior from infancy to toddlerhood. *Developmental Psychology, 47,* 1280–1294.

Valois, R. F., Oeltmann, J. E., Waller, J., & Hussey, J. R. (1999). Relationship between number of sexual intercourse partners and selected health risk behaviors among public high school adolescents. *Journal of Adolescent Health, 25,* 328–335.

van den Dries, L., Juffer, F., van IJzendoorn, M. H., Bakermans-Kranenburg, M. J., & Alink, L. R. A. (2012). Infants' responsiveness, attachment, and indiscriminate friendliness after international adoption from institutions or foster care in China: Application of Emotional Availability Scales to adoptive families. *Development and Psychopathology, 24,* 49–64.

van den Hoofdakker, B. J., Nauta, M. H., Dijck-Brouwer, D. A. J., van der Veen-Mulders, L., Sytema, S., Emmelkamp, P. M. G., et al. (2012). Dopamine transporter gene moderates response to behavioral parent training in children with ADHD: A pilot study. *Developmental Psychology, 48,* 567–574.

van der Hal-van Raalte, E., van IJzendoorn, M. H., & Bakermans-Kranenburg, M. J. (2007). Quality of care after early childhood trauma and well-being in later life: Child Holocaust survivors reaching old age. *American Journal of Orthopsychiatry, 77,* 514–522.

van der Vegt, E. J. M., van der Ende, J., Kirschbaum, C., Verhulst, F. C., & Tiemeier, H. (2009). Early neglect and abuse predict diurnal cortisol patterns in adults: A study of international adoptees. *Psychoneuroendocrinology, 34,* 660–669.

Van de Wiel, N. M. H., van Goozen, S. H. M., Matthys, W., Snoek, H., & Van Engeland, H. (2004). Cortisol and treatment effect in children with disruptive behavior disorders: A preliminary study. *Journal of the American Academy of Child and Adolescent Psychiatry, 43,* 1011–1018.

van Goozen, S. H. M., Fairchild, G., Snoek, H., & Harold, G. T. (2007). The evidence for a neurobiological model of childhood antisocial behavior. *Psychological Bulletion, 133,* 149–182.

van IJzendoorn, M. (1995). Adult attachment representations, parental responsiveness, and infant attachment: A meta-analysis on the predictive validity of the Adult Attachment Interview. *Psychological Bulletin, 117,* 387–403.

van IJzendoorn, M. H., & Bakermans-Kranenburg, M. J. (1996). Attachment representations in mothers, fathers, adolescents, and clinical groups: A meta-analytic search for normative data. *Journal of Consulting and Clinical Psychology, 64,* 8–21.

van IJzendoorn, M. H., & Bakermans-Kranenburg, M. J. (2006). DRD47-repeat polymorphism moderates the association between maternal unresolved loss or trauma and infant disorganization. *Attachment and Human Development, 8,* 291–307.

van IJzendoorn, M. H., & Bakermans-Kranenburg, M. J. (2008). The distribution of adult attachment representations in clinical groups: A meta-analytic search for patterns of attachment in 105 AAI studies. In H. Steele & M. Steele (Eds.), *Clinical applications of the Adult Attachment Interview* (pp. 69–96). New York: Guilford.

van IJzendoorn, M. H., & Bakermans-Kranenburg, M. J. (2010). Invariance of adult attachment across gender, age, culture, and socioeconomic status? *Journal of Social and Personal Relationships, 27,* 200–208.

van IJzendoorn, M. H., Bakermans-Kranenburg, M. J., & Sagi-Schwartz, A. (2003). Are children of Holocaust survivors less well-adapted? A meta-analytic investigation of secondary traumatization. *Journal of Traumatic Stress, 16,* 459–469.

van IJzendoorn, M. H., Caspers, K., Bakermans-Kranenburg, M. J., Beach, S. R. H., & Philibert, R. (2010). Methylation matters: Interaction between methylation density and 5HTT genotype predicts unresolved loss or trauma. *Biological Psychiatry, 68,* 405–407.

van IJzendoorn, M. H., Fridman, A., Bakermans-Kranenburg, M. J., & Sagi-Schwartz, A. (2013). Aftermath of genocide: Holocaust survivors' dissociation moderates offspring level of cortisol. *Journal of Loss and Trauma, 18,* 64–80.

van IJzendoorn, M. H., Moran, G., Belsky, J., Pederson, D., Bakermans-Kranenburg, M. J., & Kneppers, K. (2000). The similarity of siblings' attachments to their mother. *Child Development, 71,* 1086–1098.

van IJzendoorn, M. H., & Sagi-Schwartz, A. (2008). Cross-cultural patterns of attachment: Universal and contextual dimensions. In J. Cassidy & P. R. Shaver (Eds.), *Handbook of attachment: Theory, research, and clinical applications* (2nd ed., pp. 880–905). New York: Guilford.

van IJzendoorn, M. H., Schuengel, C., & Bakermans-Kranenburg, M. J. (1999). Disorganized attachment in early childhood: Meta-analysis of precursors, concomitants, and sequelae. *Development and Psychopathology, 11,* 225–249.

van Santen, A., Vreeburg, S. A., Van der Does, A. J. W., Spinhoven, P., Zitman, F. G., & Penninx, B. W. J. H. (2011). Psychological traits and the cortisol awakening response: Results from the Netherlands Study of Depression and Anxiety. *Psychoneuroendocrinology, 36,* 240–248.

Van Voorhees, E. E., Dedert, E. A., Calhoun, P. S., Brancu, M., Runnals, J., & Beckham, J. C. (2012). Childhood trauma exposure in Iraq and Afghanistan war era veterans: Implications for posttraumatic stress disorder symptoms and adult functional social support. *Child Abuse and Neglect, 36,* 423–432.

Van Zeijl, J., Mesman, J., van IJzendoorn, M. H., Bakermans-Kranenburg, M. J., Juffer, F., Stolk, M. N., et al. (2006). Attachment-based intervention for enhancing sensitive discipline in mothers of 1- to 3-year-old children at risk for externalizing behavior problems: A randomized controlled trial. *Journal of Consulting and Clinical Psychology, 74,* 994–1005.

Veenema, A. H. (2009). Early life stress, the development of aggression and neuroendocrine and neurobiological correlates: What can we learn from animal models? *Frontiers in Neuroendocrinology, 30,* 497–518.

Velderman, M. K., Bakermans-Kranenburg, M. J., Juffer, F., & van IJzendoorn, M. H. (2006). Effects of attachment-based interventions on maternal sensitivity and infant attachment: Differential susceptibility of highly reactive infants. *Journal of Family Psychology, 20,* 266–274.

Velotti, P., Castellano, R., & Zavatini, G. C. (2011). Adjustment of couples following childbirth: The role of generalized and specific states of mind in an Italian sample. *European Psychologist, 16,* 1–10.

Ventura-Junca, R., & Herrera, L. M. (2012). Epigenetic alterations related to early-life stressful events. *Acta Neuropsychiatrica, 24,* 255–265.

Verissimo, M., & Salvaterra, F. (2006). Maternal secure-base scripts and children's attachment security in an adopted sample. *Attachment and Human Development, 8,* 261–273.

Verissimo, M., Salvaterra, F., Santos, A. J., & Santos, O. (2008). Maternal internal representation model and secure base behavior of the child in an adoptee sample. *Devenir, 20,* 347–359.

Viding, E., Blair, R. J. R., Moffitt, T. E., & Plomin, R. (2005). Evidence for substantial genetic risk for psychopathy in 7-year-olds. *Journal of Child Psychology and Psychiatry, 46,* 592–597.

Viding, E., Fontaine, N. M. G., Oliver, B. R., & Plomin, R. (2009). Negative parental discipline, conduct problems and callous-unemotional traits: Monozygotic twin differences study. *British Journal of Psychiatry, 195*, 414–419.

Viding, E., Frick, P. J., & Plomin, R. (2007). Aetiology of the relationship between callous-unemotional traits and conduct problems in childhood. *British Journal of Psychiatry, 190*(Suppl. 49), s33–s38.

Viding, E., & Jones, A. P. (2008). Cognition to genes via the brain in the study of conduct disorder. *Quarterly Journal of Experimental Psychology, 61*, 171–181.

Viding, E., Jones, A. P., Frick, P. J., Moffitt, T. E., & Plomin, R. (2008). Heritability of antisocial behaviour at 9: Do callous-unemotional traits matter? *Developmental Science, 11*, 17–22.

Viding, E., Simmonds, E., Petrides, K. V., & Frederickson, N. (2009). The contribution of callous-unemotional traits and conduct problems to bullying in early adolescence. *Journal of Child Psychology and Psychiatry, 50*, 471–481.

Vigil, J. M., Geary, D. C., & Byrd-Craven, J. (2005). A life history assessment of early childhood sexual abuse in women. *Developmental Psychology, 41*, 553–561.

Vigne, N. G. L., Naser, R. L., Brooks, L. E., & Castro, J. L. (2005). Examining the effect of incarceration and in-prison family contact on prisoners' family relationships. *Journal of Contemporary Criminal Justice, 21*, 314–335.

Violanti, J. M., & Gehrke, A. (2004). Police trauma encounters: Precursors of compassion fatigue. *International Journal of Emergency Mental Health, 6*, 75–80.

Vizziello, G. F., Calvo, V., & Simonelli, A. (2003). Secure and insecure attachment in early infancy in an intercultural perspective. *Età Evolutiva, 75*, 36–50.

Vogt, D., Smith, B., Elwy, R., Martin, J., Schultz, M., Drainoni, M.-L., & Eisen, S. (2011). Predeployment, deployment, and postdeployment risk factors for posttraumatic stress symptomatology in female and male OEF/OIF veterans. *Journal of Abnormal Psychology, 120*, 819–831.

Volling, B. L., Blandon, A. Y., & Kolak, A. M. (2006). Marriage, parenting, and the emergence of early self-regulation in the family system. *Journal of Child and Family Studies, 15*, 493–506.

Voth, P. F., & Tutty, L. M. (1999). Daughter's perceptions of being mothered by an incest survivor: A phenomenological study. *Journal of Child Sexual Abuse, 8*, 25–43.

Vullieza-Coady, L., Obsuth, I., Torreiro-Casal, M., Ellertsdottir, L., & Lyons-Ruth, K. (2013). Maternal role confusion: Relations to maternal attachment and mother–child interaction from infancy to adolescence. *Infant Mental Health Journal, 34*, 117-131.

Wagner, A. W., & Linehan, M. M. (1997). Biosocial perspective on the relationship of childhood sexual abuse, suicidal behavior, and borderline personality disorder. In M. C. Zanarini (Ed.), *Role of sexual abuse in the etiology of borderline personality disorder* (pp. 203–223). Arlington, VA: American Psychiatric Association.

Waldinger, R. J., Toth, S. L., & Gerber, A. (2001). Maltreatment and internal representations of relationships: Core relationship themes in the narratives of abused and neglected preschoolers. *Social Development, 10*, 41–58.

Waldron, M., Heath, A. C., Turkheimer, E. N., Emery, R. E., Nelson, E., Bucholz, K. K., et al. (2008). Childhood sexual abuse moderates genetic influences on age at first consensual sexual intercourse in women. *Behavior Genetics, 38*, 1–10.

Walker, E. C., Holman, T. B., & Busby, D. M. (2009). Childhood sexual abuse, other childhood factors, and pathways to survivors' adult relationship quality. *Journal of Family Violence, 24*, 397–406.

Walker, E. C., Sheffield, R., Larson, J. H., & Holman, T. B. (2011). Contempt and defensiveness in couple relationships related to childhood sexual abuse histories for self and partner. *Journal of Marital and Family Therapy, 37*, 37–50.

Waller, R., Gardner, F., & Hyde, L. W. (2013). What are the associations between parenting, callous-unemotional traits, and antisocial behavior in youth? A systematic review of evidence. *Clinical Psychology Review, 33*, 593–608.

Waller, R., Gardner, F., Hyde, L. W., Shaw, D. S., Dishion, T. J., & Wilson, M. N. (2012). Do harsh and positive parenting predict parent reports of deceitful-callous behavior in early childhood? *Journal of Child Psychology and Psychiatry, 53*, 946–953.

Walsh, K., DiLillo, D., & Scalora, M. J. (2011). The cumulative impact of sexual revictimization on emotion regulation difficulties: An examination of female inmates. *Violence Against Women, 17*, 1103–1118.

Walsh, S., Shulman, S., Bar-On, Z., & Tsur, A. (2006). The role of parentification and family climate in adaptation among immigrant adolescents in Israel. *Journal of Research on Adolescence, 16*, 321–350.

Walsh, W. A., Dawson, J., & Mattingly, M. J. (2010). How are we measuring resilience following childhood maltreatment? Is the research adequate and consistent? What is the impact on research, practice, and policy? *Trauma, Violence, and Abuse, 11*, 27–41.

Walton, M. A., Murray, R., Cunningham, R. M., Chermack, S. T., Barry, K. L., Booth, B. M., et al. (2009). Correlates of intimate partner violence among men and women in an inner city emergency department. *Journal of Addictive Diseases, 28*, 366–381.

Waltz, J., Babcock, J. C., Jacobson, N. S., & Gottman, J. M. (2000). Testing a typology of batterers. *Journal of Consulting and Clinical Psychology, 68*, 658–669.

Wampler, K. S., Shi, L., Nelson, B. S., & Kimball, T. G. (2003). The Adult Attachment Interview and observed couple interaction: Implications for an intergenerational perspective on couple therapy. *Family Process, 42*, 497–515.

Wang, D., Szyf, M., Benkelfat, C., Provencal, N., Turecki, G., Caramaschi, D., et al. (2012). Peripheral SLC6A4 DNA methylation is associated with in vivo measures of human brain serotonin synthesis and childhood physical aggression. *PLoS ONE, 7*, Article e39501.

Wang, Z., Inslicht, S. D., Metzler, T. J., Henn-Haase, C., McCaslin, S. E., Tong, H., et al. (2010). A prospective study of predictors of depression symptoms in police. *Psychiatry Research, 175*, 211–216.

Wanklyn, S. G., Ward, A. K., Cormier, N. S., Day, D. M., & Newman, J. E. (2012). Can we distinguish juvenile violent sex offenders, violent non-sex offenders, and versatile violent sex offenders based on childhood risk factors? *Journal of Interpersonal Violence, 27*, 2128–2143.

Ward, M. J., & Carlson, E. A. (1995). Associations among adult attachment representations, maternal sensitivity, and infant-mother attachment in a sample of adolescent mothers. *Child Development, 66*, 69–79.

Ward, M. J., Lee, S. S., & Polan, H. J. (2006). Attachment and psychopathology in a community sample. *Attachment and Human Development, 8*, 327–340.

Watson, B., & Halford, W. K. (2010). Classes of childhood sexual abuse and women's adult couple relationships. *Violence and Victims, 25*, 518–535.

Webster, L., & Hackett, R. K. (2011). An exploratory investigation of the relationships among representational security, disorganization and behavior ratings in maltreated children. In J. Solomon & C. George (Eds.), *Disorganized attachment and caregiving* (pp. 292–317). New York: Guilford.

Weeks, R., & Widom, C. S. (1998). Self-reports of early childhood victimization among incarcerated adult male felons. *Journal of Interpersonal Violence, 13*, 346–361.

Weinfield, N. S., Whaley, G. J. L., & Egeland, B. (2004). Continuity, discontinuity, and coherence in attachment from infancy to late adolescence: Sequelae of organization and disorganization. *Attachment and Human Development, 6*, 73–97.

Weinstock, L. M., & Whisman, M. A. (2004). The self-verification model of depression and interpersonal rejection in heterosexual dating relationships. *Journal of Social and Clinical Psychology, 23*, 240–259.

Weisz, A. N., & Black, B. M. (2001). Evaluating a sexual assault and dating violence prevention program for urban youths. *Social Work Research, 25*, 89–100.

Wekerle, C., Wolfe, D. A., Hawkins, D. L., Pittman, A.-L., Glickman, A., & Lovald, B. E. (2001). Childhood maltreatment, posttraumatic stress symptomatology, and adolescent dating violence: Considering the value of adolescent perceptions of abuse and a trauma meditational model. *Development and Psychopathology, 13,* 847–871.

Welles, S. L., Corbin, T. J., Rich, J. A., Reed, E., & Raj, A. (2011). Intimate partner violence among men having sex with men, women, or both: Early-life sexual and physical abuse as antecedents. *Journal of Community Health, 36,* 477–485.

Wells, M., & Jones, R. (2000). Childhood parentification and shame-proneness: A preliminary study. *American Journal of Family Therapy, 28,* 19–27.

West, C. M. (2012). Partner abuse in ethnic minority and gay, lesbian, bisexual, and transgender populations. *Partner Abuse, 3,* 336–357.

West, C. M., Williams, L. M., & Siegel, J. A. (2000). Adult sexual revictimization among black women sexually abused in childhood: A prospective examination of serious consequences of abuse. *Child Maltreatment, 5,* 49–57.

Whelan, D. J. (2003). Using attachment theory when placing siblings in foster care. *Child and Adolescent Social Work Journal, 20,* 21–36.

Whiffen, V. E., Judd, M. E., & Aube, J. A. (1999). Intimate relationships moderate the association between childhood sexual abuse and depression. *Journal of Interpersonal Violence, 14,* 940–954.

Whipple, N., Bernier, A., & Mageau, G. A. (2011). A dimensional approach to maternal attachment state of mind: Relations to maternal sensitivity and maternal autonomy support. *Developmental Psychology, 47,* 396–403.

Whisman, M. A. (2006). Childhood trauma and marital outcomes in adulthood. *Personal Relationships, 13,* 375–386.

Whisman, M. A. (2014). Dyadic perspectives in trauma and marital adjustment. *Psychological Trauma, 6,* 207–215.

Whitaker, D. J., Le, B., Hanson, R. K., Baker, C. K., McMahon, P. M., Ryan, G., et al. (2008). Risk factors for the perpetration of child sexual abuse: A review and meta-analysis. *Child Abuse and Neglect, 32,* 529–548.

White, H. R., & Widom, C. S. (2003). Intimate partner violence among abused and neglected children in young adulthood: The mediating effects of early aggression, antisocial personality, hostility and alcohol problems. *Aggressive Behavior, 29,* 332–345.

Whiting, J. B., Simmons, L. A., Havens, J. R., Smith, D. B., & Oka, M. (2009). Intergenerational transmission of violence: The influence of self-appraisals, mental disorders and substance abuse. *Journal of Family Violence, 24,* 639–648.

Wickrama, K. A. S., & O'Neal, C. W. (2013). Family of origin, race/ethnicity, and socioeconomic attainment: Genotype and intraindividual processes. *Journal of Marriage and Family, 75,* 75–90.

Widom, C. S. (1989). Does violence beget violence? A critical examination of the literature. *Psychological Bulletin, 106,* 3–28.

Widom, C. S., Czaja, S. J., & Dutton, M. A. (2008). Childhood victimization and lifetime revictimization. *Child Abuse and Neglect, 32*, 785–796.

Widom, C. S., & Morris, S. (1997). Accuracy of adult recollections of childhood victimization, Part 2: Childhood sexual abuse. *Psychological Assessment, 9*, 34–46.

Widom, C. S., Schuck, A. M., & White, H. R. (2006). An examination of pathways from childhood victimization to violence: The role of early aggression and problematic alcohol use. *Violence and Victims, 21*, 675–690.

Widom, C. S., & Shepard, R. L. (1996). Accuracy of adult recollections of childhood victimization: Part 1. Childhood physical abuse. *Psychological Assessment, 8*, 412–421.

Wildeman, C. (2012). Imprisonment and infant mortality. *Social Problems, 59*, 228–257.

Wildeman, C. (2014). Parental incarceration, child homelessness, and the invisible consequences of mass imprisonment. *Annals of the American Academy of Political and Social Science, 651*, 74-96.

Wildeman, C., Schnittker, J., & Turney, K. (2012). Despair by association? The mental health of mothers with children by recently incarcerated fathers. *American Sociological Review, 77*, 216–243.

Williams, J., & Nelson-Gardell, D. (2012). Predicting resilience in sexually abused adolescents. *Child Abuse and Neglect, 36*, 53–63.

Williams, L. M. (1994). Recall of childhood trauma: A prospective study of women's memories of child sexual abuse. *Journal of Consulting and Clinical Psychology, 62*, 1167–1176.

Williams, S. L., & Frieze, I. H. (2005). Patterns of violent relationships, psychological distress, and marital satisfaction in a national sample of men and women. *Sex Roles, 52*, 771–784.

Williams, S. T., Conger, K. J., & Blozis, S. A. (2007). The development of interpersonal aggression during adolescence: The importance of parents, siblings, and family economics. *Child Development, 78*, 1526–1542.

Willoughby, M. T., Mills-Koonce, W. R., Gottfredson, N. C., & Wagner, N. J. (2014). Measuring callous unemotional behaviors in early childhood: Factor structure and the prediction of stable aggression in middle childhood. *Journal of Psychopathology and Behavioral Assessment, 36*, 43–46.

Wilsnack, S. C., Wilsnack, R. W., Kristjanson, A. F., Vogeltanz-Holm, N. D., & Harris, T. R. (2004). Child sexual abuse and alcohol use among women: Setting the stage for risky sexual behavior. In L. J. Koenig, L. S. Doll, A. O'Leary, & W. Pequegnat (Eds.), *From child sexual abuse to adult sexual risk: Trauma, revictimization, and intervention* (pp. 181–200). Washington, DC: American Psychological Association.

Wise, L. A., Palmer, J. R., Rothman, E. F., & Rosenberg, L. (2009). Childhood abuse and early menarche: Findings from the Black Women's Health Study. *American Journal of Public Health, 99* (Suppl. 2), S460–S466.

Wiseman, H., Barber, J. P., Raz, A., Yam, I., Foltz, C., & Livne-Snir, S. (2002). Parental communication of Holocaust experiences and interpersonal patterns in offspring of Holocaust survivors. *International Journal of Behavioral Development, 26,* 371–381.

Woffordt, S., Mihalic, D. E., & Menard, S. (1994). Continuities in marital violence. *Journal of Family Violence,* 195–225.

Wohl, M. J. A., & Van Bavel, J. J. (2011). Is identifying with a historically victimized group good or bad for your health? Transgenerational post-traumatic stress and collective victimization. *European Journal of Social Psychology, 41,* 818–824.

Wolfe, D. A., Scott, K., Wekerle, C., & Pittman, A.-L. (2001). Child maltreatment: Risk of adjustment problems and dating violence in adolescence. *Journal of the American Academy of Child and Adolescent Psychiatry, 40,* 282–289.

Wolfe, D. A., Wekerle, C., Scott, K., Straatman, A.-L., & Grasley, C. (2004). Predicting abuse in adolescent dating relationships over 1 year: The role of child maltreatment and trauma. *Journal of Abnormal Psychology, 113,* 406–415.

Wolfe, D. A., Wekerle, C., Scott, K., Straatman, A.-L., & Reitzel-Jaffe, D. (2003). Dating violence prevention with at-risk youth: A controlled outcome evaluation. *Journal of Consulting and Clinical Psychology, 71,* 279–291.

Wolke, D., Woods, S., Bloomfield, L., & Karstadt, L. (2000). The association between direct and relational bullying and behavior problems among primary school children. *Journal of Child Psychology and Psychiatry, 41,* 989–1002.

Woodhouse, S. S., Dykas, M. J., & Cassidy, J. (2009). Perceptions of secure base provision within the family. *Attachment and Human Development, 11,* 47–67.

Woods, S., & White, E. (2005). The association between bullying behaviour, arousal levels, and behavior problems. *Journal of Adolescence, 28,* 381–395.

Worley, K. O., Walsh, S., & Lewis, K. (2004). An examination of parenting experiences in male perpetrators of domestic violence: A qualitative study. *Psychology and Psychotherapy, 77,* 35–54.

Wray, A. M., Hoyt, T., & Gerstle, M. (2013). Preliminary examination of a mutual intimate partner violence intervention among treatment-mandated couples. *Journal of Family Psychology, 27,* 664–670.

Wright, J., Friedrich, W., Cinq-Mars, C., Cyr, M., & McDuff, P. (2004). Self-destructive and delinquent behaviors of adolescent female victims of child sexual abuse: Rates and covariates in clinical and nonclinical samples. *Violence and Victims, 19,* 627–643.

Wright, J. C., Binney, V., & Smith, P. K. (1995). Security of attachment in 8–12-year-olds: A revised version of the Separation Anxiety test, its psychometric properties and clinical interpretation. *Child Psychology and Psychiatry and Allied Disciplines, 36,* 757–774.

Wright, J. P., Schnupp, R., Beaver, K. M., Delisi, M., & Vaughn, M. (2012). Genes, maternal negativity, and self-control: Evidence of a gene × environment interaction. *Youth Violence and Juvenile Justice, 10,* 245–260.

Wright, K. M., Foran, H. M., Wood, M. D., Eckford, R. D., & McGurk, D. (2012). Alcohol problems, aggression, and other externalizing behaviors after return from deployment: Understanding the role of combat exposure, internalizing symptoms, and social environment. *Journal of Clinical Psychology, 68,* 782–800.

Wright, M. O., Fopma-Loy, J., & Fischer, S. (2005). Multidimensional assessment of resilience in mothers who are child sexual abuse survivors. *Child Abuse and Neglect, 29,* 1173–1193.

Wright, M. O., Fopma-Loy, J., & Oberle, K. (2012). In their own words: The experience of mothering as a survivor of childhood sexual abuse. *Development and Psychopathology, 24,* 537–552.

Yang, B.-Z., Zhang, H., Ge, W., Weder, N., Douglas-Palumberi, H., Pereplet-chikova, F., et al. (2013). Child abuse and epigenetic mechanisms of disease risk. *American Journal of Preventive Medicine, 44,* 101–107.

Yates, T. M., & Wekerle, C. (2009). The long-term consequences of childhood emotional maltreatment on development: (Mal)adaptation in adolescence and young adulthood. *Child Abuse and Neglect, 33,* 19–21.

Yehuda, R., Bell, A., Bierer, L. M., & Schmeidler, J. (2008). Maternal, not paternal, PTSD is related to increased risk for PTSD in offspring of Holocaust survivors. *Journal of Psychiatric Research, 42,* 1104–1111.

Yehuda, R., & Bierer, L. M. (2009). The relevance of epigenetics to PTSD: Implications for the DSM-V. *Journal of Traumatic Stress, 22,* 427–434.

Yehuda, R., Flory, J. D., Southwick, S., & Charney, D. (2006). Developing an agenda for translational studies of resilience and vulnerability following trauma exposure. *Annals of New York Academy of Science, 1071,* 379–396.

Yehuda, R., Halligan, S. L., & Bierer, L. M. (2001). Relationship of parental trauma exposure and PTSD to PTSD, depressive and anxiety disorders in offspring. *Journal of Psychiatric Research, 35,* 261–270.

Yehuda, R., Halligan, S. L., & Grossman, R. (2001). Childhood trauma and risk for PTSD: Relationship to intergenerational effects of trauma, parental PTSD, and cortisol excretion. *Development and Psychopathology, 13,* 733–753.

Yehuda, R., Schmeidler, J., Giller Jr., E. L., Siever, L. J., & Binder-Brynes, K. (1998). Relationship between posttraumatic stress disorder characteristics of Holocaust survivors and their adult offspring. *American Journal of Psychiatry, 155,* 841–843.

Yehuda, R., Schmeidler, J., Wainberg, M., Binder-Brynes, K., & Duvdevani, T. (1998). Vulnerability to posttraumatic stress disorder in adult offspring of Holocaust survivors. *American Journal of Psychiatry, 155,* 1163–1171.

Yehuda, R., Teicher, M. H., Seckl, J. R., Grossman, R. A., Morris, A., & Biere, L. M. (2007). Parental posttraumatic stress disorder as a vulnerability factor for low cortisol trait in offspring of Holocaust survivors. *Archives of General Psychiatry, 64,* 1040–1048.

Young, M. D., Deardorff, J., Ozer, E., & Lahiff, M. (2011). Sexual abuse in childhood and adolescence and the risk of early pregnancy among women ages 18–22. *Journal of Adolescent Health, 49,* 287–293.

Young, M. H., Justice, J., & Erdberg, P. (2012). A comparison of rape and molest offenders in prison psychiatric treatment. *International Journal of Offender Therapy and Comparative Criminology, 56,* 1103–1123.

Yuan, C., Wang, Z., Inslicht, S. S., McCaslin, S. E., Metzler, T. J., Henn-Haase, C., et al. (2011). Protective factors for posttraumatic stress disorder symptoms in a prospective study of police officers. *Psychiatry Research, 188,* 45–50.

Zabin, L. S., Emerson, M. R., & Rowland, D. L. (2005). Childhood sexual abuse and early menarche: The direction of their relationship and its implications. *Journal of Adolescent Health, 36,* 393–400.

Zaccagnino, M., Cussino, M., Cook, R., Jacobvitz, D., & Veglia, F. (2011). Alternative attachment figures and their impact on the intergenerational transmission of attachment. *Psicologia Clinica dello Sviluppo, 15,* 669–691.

Zahs, A., Curtis, B. J., Saldschmidt, T. J., Brown, L. A. S., Gauthier, T. W., Choudhry, M. A., et al. (2012). Alcohol and epigenetic changes: Summary of the 2011 Alcohol and Immunology Research Interest Group (AIRIG) meeting. *Alcohol, 46,* 783–787.

Zanarini, M. C., Dubo, E. D., Lewis, R. E., & Williams, A. A. (1997). Childhood factors associated with the development of borderline personality disorder. In M. C. Zanarini (Ed.), *Role of sexual abuse in the etiology of borderline personality disorder* (pp. 29–44). Arlington, VA: American Psychiatric Association.

Zavala, E. (2013). Testing the link between child maltreatment and family violence among police officers. *Crime and Delinquency, 59,* 468–483.

Zayas, V., & Shoda, Y. (2007). Predicting preferences for dating partners from past experiences of psychological abuse: Identifying the psychological ingredients of situations. *Personality and Social Psychology Bulletin, 33,* 123–138.

Zeanah, C. H., & Benoit, D. (1995). Clinical applications of a parent perception interview in infant mental health. *Child and Adolescent Psychiatric Clinics of North America, 4,* 539–554.

Zeanah, C. H., Danis, B., Hirshberg, L., Benoit, D., Miller, D., & Heller, S. S.

(1999). Disorganized attachment associated with partner violence: A research note. *Infant Mental Health Journal, 20,* 77–86.

Zeanah, C. H., Scheeringa, M., Boris, N. W., Heller, S. S., Smyke, A. T., & Trapani, J. (2004). Reactive attachment disorder in maltreated toddlers. *Child Abuse and Neglect, 28,* 877–888.

Zimmermann, P., Mohr, C., & Spangler, G. (2009). Genetic and attachment influences on adolescents' regulation of autonomy and aggressiveness. *Journal of Child Psychology and Psychiatry, 50,* 1339–1347.

Zinzow, H., Seth, P., Jackson, J., Niehaus, A., & Fitzgerald, M. (2010). Abuse and parental characteristics, attributions of blame, and psychological adjustment in adult survivors of child sexual abuse. *Journal of Child Sexual Abuse, 19,* 79–98.

Ziv, Y., Oppenheim, D., & Sagi-Schwartz, A. (2004). Social information processing in middle childhood: Relations to infant-mother attachment. *Attachment and Human Development, 6,* 327–348.

Zoccolillo, M., Paquette, D., Azar, R., Cote, S., & Tremblay, R. (2004). Parenting as an important outcome of conduct disorder in girls. In M. Putallaz & K. L. Bierman (Eds.), *Aggression, antisocial behavior, and violence among girls* (pp. 242–261). New York: Guilford.

Index